Robert P. Cary
1918 ½ Orrington Street
Evanston, Illinois 60201

Multitask Windows NT

JOEL POWELL

①

Waite Group Press™
Corte Madera, California

Publisher • *Mitchell Waite*
Editorial Director • *Scott Calamar*
Managing Editor • *John Crudo*
Content Editor • *Harry Henderson*
Technical Reviewer • *Richard S. Wright, Jr.*
Production Director • *Julianne Ososke*
Design • *Cecile Kaufman*
Production • *Sestina Quarequio*
Illustrations • *Ben Long*
Cover Design • *Ted Mader*

© 1993 by The Waite Group, Inc.®
Published by Waite Group Press™, 200 Tamal Plaza, Corte Madera, CA 94925.

Waite Group Press™ is distributed to bookstores and book wholesalers by Publishers Group West, Box 8843, Emeryville, CA 94662, 1-800-788-3123 (in California 1-510-658-3453).

Printed in the United States of America
93 94 95 96 • 10 9 8 7 6 5 4 3 2 1

Library of Congress Cataloging-in-Publication Data
Powell, Joel.
    Multitask Windows NT / Joel Powell
        p.   cm.
    Includes index.
    ISBN 1-878739-57-3 : $34.95
    1. Operating systems (Computers) 2. Windows NT. 3. Multitasking (Computer science) I. Title.
QA76.063P68   1993
005.4'469–dc20
                                                                    93-28291
                                                                    CIP

DEDICATION

In Loving Memory of
William A. Pless

Joel Powell

ACKNOWLEDGMENTS

I would like to thank Mitch Waite for the inspiration and ideas that sent me scurrying to my office and into a flurry of activity, of which this book resulted. Thanks to Scott Calamar, who guided the project during its early stages, and John Crudo, who kept the project moving from start to finish. Thanks also to Julianne Ososke for managing the production issues.

Special thanks to Harry Henderson, who edited this book for content and clarity. His comments and suggestions are most appreciated. Also, I would like to thank Richard S. Wright, Jr., who edited this book for technical accuracy. Thanks also to the members of the MSWIN32 forum who fielded questions from time to time.

Finally, I would like to thank Lori for her understanding, help, and kindness throughout the project. I couldn't have done it without her.

ABOUT THE AUTHOR

Joel Powell is a technical writer, programmer, and educator. He currently writes technical documentation for commercial graphic imaging equipment. Joel is the author of *Falcon 3: The Complete Handbook,* another Waite Group Press book. He has also written several training documents for the United States Air Force on ground radar technology. He has provided training for over 3,000 students for the U.S.A.F., vocational schools, and private companies. Over 25 countries are represented by his former students. When he is not teaching or writing, he is usually in front of a personal computer. Joel is an avid C/C++ and Windows programmer.

Dear Reader:

What is a book? Is it perpetually fated to be inky words on a paper page? Or can a book simply be something that inspires—feeding your head with ideas and creativity regardless of the medium? The latter, I believe. That's why I'm always pushing our books to a higher plane; using new technology to reinvent the medium.

I wrote my first book in 1973, *Projects in Sights, Sounds, and Sensations.* I like to think of it as our first multimedia book. In the years since then, I've learned that people want to *experience* information, not just passively absorb it—they want interactive MTV in a book. With this in mind, I started my own publishing company and published *Master C,* a book/disk package that turned the PC into a C language instructor. Then we branched out to computer graphics with *Fractal Creations,* which included a color poster, 3-D glasses, and a totally rad fractal generator. Ever since, we've included disks and other goodies with most of our books. *Virtual Reality Creations* is bundled with 3-D Fresnel viewing goggles and *Walkthroughs & Flybys, CD* comes with a multimedia CD-ROM. We've made complex multimedia accessible for any PC user with *Ray Tracing Creations, Multimedia Creations, Making Movies on your PC, Image Lab,* and three books on Fractals.

The Waite Group continues to publish innovative multimedia books on cutting-edge topics, and of course the programming books that make up our heritage. Being a programmer myself, I appreciate clear guidance through a tricky OS, so our books come bundled with disks and CDs loaded with code, utilities, and custom controls.

Waite Group Press ™

By 1993, The Waite Group will have published 135 books. Our next step is to develop a new type of book, an interactive, multimedia experience involving the reader on many levels. With this new book, you'll be trained by a computer-based instructor with infinite patience, run a simulation to visualize the topic, play a game that shows you different aspects of the subject, interact with others on-line, and have instant access to a large database on the subject. For traditionalists, there will be a full-color, paper-based book.

In the meantime, they've wired the White House for hi-tech; the information super highway has been proposed; and computers, communication, entertainment, and information are becoming inseparable. To travel in this Digital Age you'll need guidebooks. The Waite Group offers such guidance for the most important software— your mind.

We hope you enjoy this book. For a color catalog, just fill out and send in the Satisfaction Report Card at the back of the book. You can reach me on CIS as 75146,3515, MCI mail as mwaite, and usenet as mitch@well.sf.ca.us.

Sincerely,

Mitchell Waite

Mitchell Waite
Publisher

INTRODUCTION

You probably have heard the old adage "time waits for no one." We can say the same thing about technology. It seems that, virtually every day, there is an introduction of a new computer hardware and software product. Programmers and engineers must keep abreast of new technology to create these new products and stay competitive in the marketplace.

Over four years ago, Microsoft had a vision to create a new operating system: Windows NT (New Technology). In the summer of 1993, this vision became reality. Windows NT provides a preemptive multitasking operating system with a Windows 3.1 look and feel. This gives potential developers the ability to create products that take advantage of the new features of NT, and a huge number of existing Windows 3.1 users targeted as an initial market.

With a new operating system, a programmer usually has to face another learning curve. For example, if you wrote programs in MS-DOS, writing your first Windows programs required a new approach—a learning curve. Fortunately, Microsoft did not "reinvent the wheel" when they designed Windows NT (from the user's or programmer's point of view). Instead they incorporated the look and feel of Windows 3.1 (easy on the user) and much of the existing Windows API (easier on the programmer).

The Win32 (32-bit Windows) API closely resembles its Windows 3.1 counterpart; however, there are obvious (and not so obvious) changes to it. For example, in some cases, the programmer does not have to be concerned that the new API takes advantage of a 32-bit data path. Many enhancements occur behind the scenes; the programmer doesn't have to worry about the details.

There are cases where the new Win32 API does affect the programmer. For example, message packing and memory addressing have changed. Other cases include extensions to the API to take advantage of the new features of the operating system (preemptive multitasking, new GDI calls, system security, and so on). That's where *Multitask Windows NT* comes in. This book is designed to help you make the transition from writing Windows 3.1 applications to writing 32-bit Windows applications.

WHAT IS A WIN32 APPLICATION?

Windows NT runs several types of programs—for example, MS-DOS, Windows 3.x, and OS/2 character-based applications. In addition, Windows NT runs *Win32 applications*. Writing Win32 programs gives you the ability to take full advantage of this new operating system. All of the example programs in this book (and on the disk) are Win32 applications.

WHO THIS BOOK IS FOR

This book is intended for programmers and engineers with a familiarity in Windows programming and the C programming language. However, you do not have to be a "Windows wizard" to follow the example programs in this book. Most chapters review how things were done in Windows 3.x and contrast them with Win32 techniques.

If you are new to multitasking operating systems, need to brush up on multitasking concepts, or would like to learn how to take advantage of the multitasking features in Windows NT, this book is for you.

Windows NT is an enormous topic. There are literally hundreds of new API functions. This book covers the *fundamental* changes to help bridge the gap between Windows 3.1 and Windows NT. However, some topics (such as network support) are very complex and would be better served in a book that specifically addresses the topic.

HOW THIS BOOK IS STRUCTURED

This book contains ten chapters. Each chapter covers a broad topic (such as file management). Most chapters start with a discussion that compares Window 3.x and Win32 techniques. This is followed by example Win32 applications that demonstrate the new features and API functions. Here is a summary of the chapters.

▵   *Chapter 1: From Windows to Windows NT An Overview* provides a broad overview of the differences between Windows 3.x and Windows NT. It also provides an overview of some of the new features in NT.

▵   *Chapter 2: Building Your First Application for Windows NT* contrasts a Windows 3.x and Win32 minimal application. You will build GENERIC, a minimal Win32 example application.

▵   *Chapter 3: Memory Management* compares memory management in Windows 3.x and Win32. Three example applications demonstrating heap, virtual, and shared memory APIs are also provided.

▵   *Chapter 4: File Management* compares file management and file systems in Windows 3.x and Windows NT. Example applications demonstrate file and directory management, and how to obtain file and drive information.

▵   *Chapter 5: Using GDI in Windows NT* discusses the extensions to the Window 3.x GDI. Example applications demonstrating new arc, pen, polyline, and Bezier APIs are included.

▵   *Chapter 6: Multitasking in Windows NT* compares non-preemptive and preemptive multitasking. Example applications demonstrate creating threads, thread competition, and creating a process. Differences between Windows 3.x and Windows NT DLLs are covered. There are also example programs demonstrating load-time and link-time DLLs.

▵   *Chapter 7: Synchronization of Threads and Processes* discusses the use of synchronization objects (such as events and semaphores) in multithreaded applications. Example applications demonstrating event, critical section, mutex, and semaphore objects are provided.

Chapter 8: Introduction to NT System Security introduces the topic of security, a feature that does not exist in Windows 3.x. Security identifiers (representing a user) and security descriptors (representing an object) are covered. An example application demonstrates a portion of NT security.

Chapter 9: Portability Issues in Windows NT covers portability concerns when running 32-bit applications under Windows NT or Win32s. Win32s is a extension of the Windows 3.1 API that allows 32-bit Windows applications to run under the Windows 3.x platform.

Chapter 10: Multithreaded MDI contrasts Windows 3.x and Win32 Multiple Document Interface (MDI) applications and provides examples of a single and multithreaded MDI application.

Appendix A: A Map to WINDOWS.H breaks down the WINDOWS.H files and the files it includes by reference.

Appendix B: Installing the Source Code provides installation instructions for the source code and executables on the provided disk.

Appendix C: C Run-Time Library Compatibility lists alphabetically C run-time library calls supported in Win32 applications.

THE SOURCE CODE DISK

The supplied source code disk contains the program files for all of the examples in this book. The disk contains a self-extracting archive that installs the example applications to subdirectories divided by chapter and example. Complete instructions for loading the files are given in *Appendix B: Installing the Source Code*. Executable files for each of the projects are also installed.

TIME TO GET STARTED!

Technology is a moving target. This book is designed to help Windows 3.x programmers make the transition to write 32-bit Windows applications for Windows NT. It also provides example applications that concentrate on the topic at hand. Its overall intent is to get you writing Win32 applications in a short time. Let's start with *Chapter 1: From Windows to Windows NT: An Overview.*

TABLE OF CONTENTS

CONTENTS

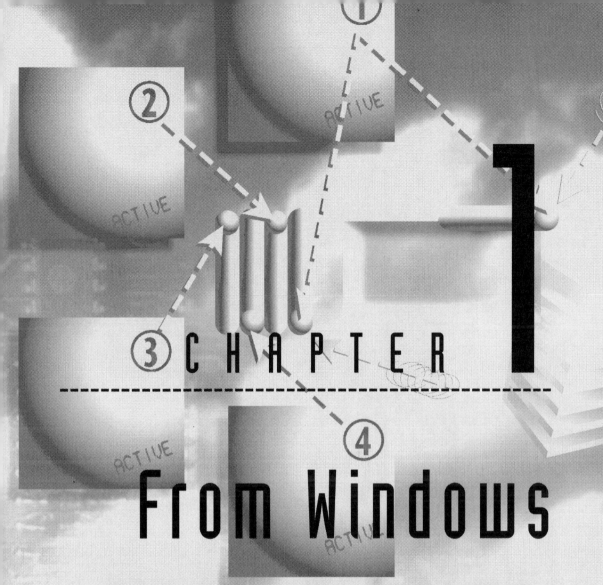

CHAPTER 1

From Windows to Windows NT: An Overview

From Windows to Windows NT: An Overview

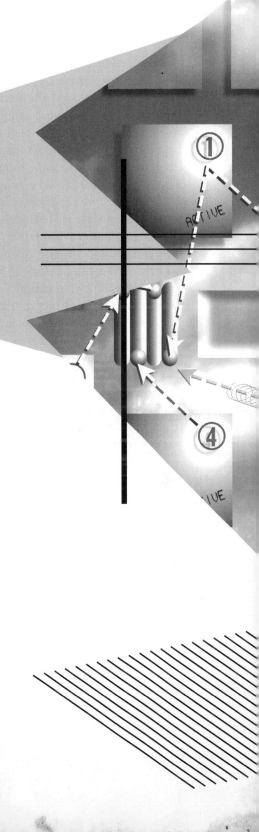

Operating systems, hardware, and software seem to have one thing in common: they are in a state of constant change. At times it appears to be impossible to keep up with the technological advancements. In the past few decades, manufacturers have introduced products at a breakneck pace. Some have the discipline and commitment to ensure their product is *backwardly compatible*. This means that the new product will run everything that the previous generations of products did. Other manufacturers seem to reinvent the wheel every time a new product hits the market.

By any standards MS-DOS was a tremendous success for Microsoft. But by the mid–1980s, innovative developers and increasingly demanding users were pushing to go beyond the text-based user interfaces of traditional DOS applications. Users also increasingly wanted to be able to run several programs at once (through multitasking, or at least task-switching). Microsoft had a huge investment in DOS compatibility to protect, and had to meet these emerging needs at the same time. Their answer was Microsoft Windows, the 3.1 version of which has become a mature and highly successful platform.

Windows provided very high DOS compatibility, while enabling developers to write a new generation of software that took advantage of a consistent graphical user interface (GUI), as well as superior memory management and a limited form of multitasking. But by building Windows on top of the foundation of DOS, Microsoft also had to accept some important technical limitations—for example, the limitations of the DOS file system and the need to use segmented memory addressing. Furthermore, Windows and DOS were essentially tied to one platform—machines based on the Intel 80x86 processors. Overcoming these technical limitations and gaining access to a wider market required that a new operating system be designed from the ground up.

In the fall of 1988, Microsoft extended their vision once again. They set out to design a new operating system: Windows NT. Over the course of four years, this vision became reality. Not only does Windows NT capture the current trends and needs of computer users around the world, but it also maintains a high degree of backward compatibility by running DOS and Windows 3.x applications. In addition, Windows NT also runs character-based OS/2 and LAN Manager applications.

Let's look at an overview of the topics we will be discussing in this chapter.

Before we get into the new features and capabilities of Windows NT, let's briefly compare this new operating system and previous versions of Windows. This will provide a solid foundation to aid in crossing the gap into the world of new technology.

CHAPTER OVERVIEW

Concepts Covered

◢ Review of Windows 3.x functionality

◢ Overview of Windows NT functionality

◢ Review of nonpreemptive multitasking

◢ Overview of preemptive multitasking

◢ Review of Windows 3.x (MS-DOS) segmented memory addressing

◢ Overview of Windows NT flat memory addressing

◢ Review of Windows 3.x file management

◢ Overview of Windows NT file management

◢ Overview of Windows NT security

◢ Overview of file mapping and pipes

◢ Overview of synchronization

◢ Overview of synchronization

WINDOWS 3.X—A LOOK BACK

If you were familiar with the programming of DOS applications, you may have had to adjust your thought processes when switching to the Windows world. DOS programmers had virtually complete control over the personal computer. You didn't have to worry about other programs (barring a few renegade TSRs) causing conflicts with your program. Whether your language of choice was C, BASIC, or assembly language, you had a very high level of control.

The introduction of multitasking environments, with Windows emerging as a leader, created major changes in program design. Programmers and their programs no longer had control of the entire computer. Windows uses a message-based operating system. Whenever an event occurs (mouse movement, key presses, and so on), Windows sends a message to the application, notifying it of the type of action that is taking place. Figure 1-1 overviews this process.

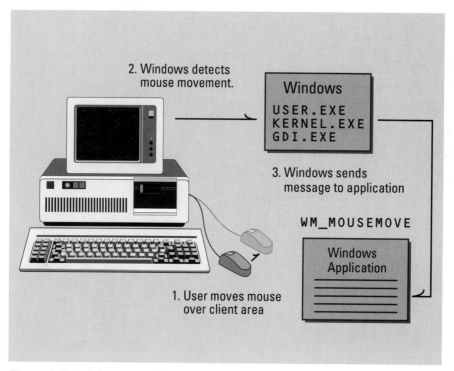

Figure 1-1 Windows sends a message

To the programmer this message-based concept required a different approach to program design. Each window processes (or passes back) messages from the operating system. You could implement code to process these messages. For example, if Windows sent a WM_DESTROY message, this meant that the window was about to be destroyed. You could intercept this message and perform an action—for instance, prompting the user, "Are you sure..." or cleaning up (freeing memory, saving files, and so on).

Windows programs also contain both code and resources. Resources (such as bitmaps, icons, dialogs, and menus) provide you with a quick start in application design. Windows provides a rich variety of graphical elements that are available to all applications.

Of course Microsoft did not design Windows to redefine programming techniques or to cause confusion to the programmer. The introduction of Windows provided an easy-to-use GUI that many computer users could learn quickly. Different programs, whether they be spreadsheets or word processors, would have the same look and feel. Once the user mastered one program, he or she would adapt to another program quickly.

The minor discomfort experienced by the new Windows programmer was far outweighed by the tasks for which Windows started to take responsibility. The DOS programmer had to spend hours making sure that an application would run correctly on a huge variety of systems, video cards, printers, and so on. Although Windows didn't take care of every detail in this area, it significantly reduced the burden on the programmer.

Windows was very helpful to users and programmers alike, and the time spent scaling the learning curve was well worth it. Now programmers are faced with yet another learning curve in designing applications for Windows NT. Microsoft didn't pull the rug out from under you, however. Although the NT environment does add new APIs and new concepts, the basic structure of a Windows NT program closely resembles that of a Windows 3.1 program—as you will see in the next chapter. The purpose of this book is to help you master the new tools and concepts of Win32 programming, and to that end we will concentrate on the *Win32 subsystem* of Windows NT.

THE WIN32 SUBSYSTEM

Windows NT runs several different types of applications (Windows 3.x, MS-DOS, OS/2 character based, and so on). Each of these applications runs under a particular subsystem. 32-bit Windows applications run under the Win32 subsystem.
The Win32 Software Development Kit includes the Win32 API. This API is a modification and an extension of the Windows 3.x API. Existing Windows 3.x APIs now have 32-bit equivalents.

WINDOWS NT VS. WINDOWS 3.X

Much of the new functionality of Windows NT is in the operating system itself; it doesn't require that the user or programmer know what is going on behind the scenes. But being aware of what is different can be very beneficial, especially to the programmer.

Don't let yourself get bogged down in the details that follow. Try to gain an overall understanding of the new operating system. Remember, it took a large team of programmers four years to create Windows NT. Fortunately most of the system is transparent to you, the developer.

NT—THE OPERATING SYSTEM

Windows 3.x is sometimes referred to as an operating system. While this is true to a degree, another layer exists under the Windows code. This layer is MS-DOS. Windows somewhat isolates the programmer from the low-level details of DOS, and this brings up one of the first major differences between Windows 3.x and NT.

Windows NT is a complete operating system. The diagram in Figure 1-2 shows the differences between 3.x and NT. Note the absence of DOS in the NT diagram. Although this book concentrates on 80386 and 80486 systems (hereinafter referred to as x86 systems), the NT system can also reside on multiprocessor systems such as MIPS.

Windows NT is still capable of running DOS programs, despite the absence of the MS-DOS operating system. It accomplishes this in another manner, known as subsystems. For example, if the user attempts to run a DOS program, NT uses a DOS subsystem to carry out the task. NT has the sole responsibility of running different applications (such as Win32, OS/2, and DOS). It is for this reason that you should not refer to your programs as "NT applications." Instead we are going to call the programs created in this book "applications for Windows NT," or to be even more accurate, "Win32 applications."

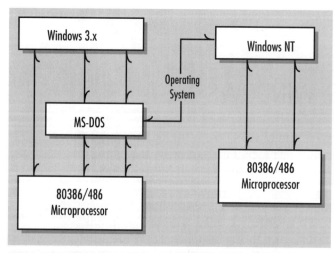

Figure 1-2 Windows 3.x and Windows NT design

MULTITASKING— NONPREEMPTIVE/PREEMPTIVE

Another key enhancement introduced in Windows NT is *preemptive multitasking*. Preemptive multitasking occurs when the operating system has the ability to interrupt a section of code and run a different section of code at prescribed intervals. Windows 3.x versions did not have this ability; they employed a less powerful method known as *nonpreemptive multitasking*. Figure 1-3 shows an overview of the Windows 3.x multitasking method.

Notice that Application 1 has received a message from Windows. While the window procedure for Application 1 is processing the message, all other application activity is halted. For example, if Application 1 received a WM_PAINT message from Windows, and the code intercepted the message (usually in a *switch* statement), no other applications would receive any

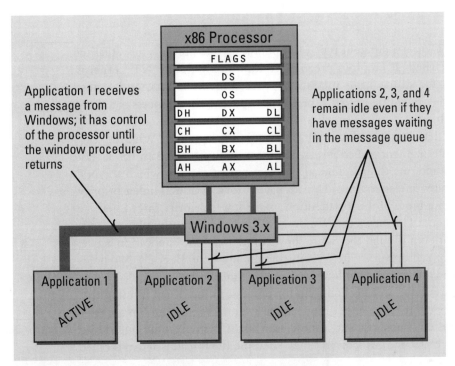

Figure 1-3 Windows 3.x—nonpreemptive multitasking

processor time. If the code in the WM_PAINT section of the window procedure was complex and lengthy, the rest of the applications would appear to screech to a halt.

The answer to this type of problem (in Windows 3.x) is to ensure that your code does its job swiftly and efficiently. You may have used the invalid rectangle to update only the portion of the screen that needs updating. This saves time and *returns control* to Windows in a timely manner. The key phrase in this topic is returns control. Grabbing and maintaining control of the Windows environment is considered poor programming practice.

Put another way, the overall efficiency and responsiveness of the Windows environment depends on the cooperation and "good citizenship" of each active application. This also means that the application developer cannot make many assumptions about how quickly or how often an application can gain access to processing time. This can be a problem for time-sensitive applications.

THE WINDOWS NT SOLUTION

Windows NT uses a different type of multitasking that prevents the situation we just discussed. It employs preemptive multitasking. The NT kernel is responsible for dispatching messages, processing interrupts, and—most importantly—scheduling. How it performs the scheduling process is a fairly complex subject.

For now, let's keep the discussion simple. Each program in Windows NT is broken into segments called *processes* and *threads.* Every program has at least one process and one thread. Threads are the unit of code to which the NT kernel allocates processor time. Threads have priority values. Higher priority threads receive more processor attention, while lower priority threads receive less time. Figure 1-4 shows the Windows NT scheme of multitasking.

Note that even though the figure shows more than one application active, the processor can only execute one instruction at a time. Basically NT holds a stopwatch and decides how long a particular thread can run.

The figure shows threads lining up for processor time. Keep in mind that more than one thread per application can be awaiting execution. On a single-processor system (such as a single-processor 80x86 system), only one thread can actually be running at a given time. The time the thread is active is called

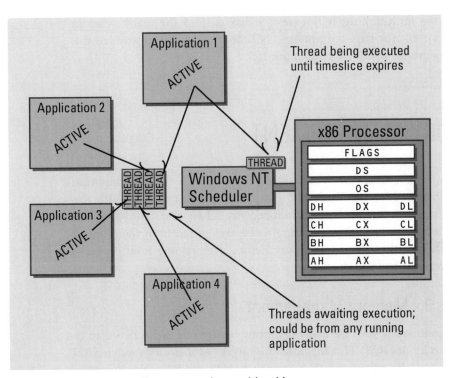

Figure 1-4 Windows NT—preemptive multitasking

a *timeslice*. At each clock interrupt, the NT scheduler must make a decision either to continue to execute the current thread, or to shelve it and replace it with another. Again this is based on priority. You can set the priority of the threads within a Win32 application. We will show an example of this in Chapter 6, Multitasking in Windows NT.

Compare the scenario in Windows 3.1 with the new functionality of Windows NT. If a program takes more than a timeslice to complete an action (it probably will), this does not stop the other applications from functioning. The NT scheduler will simply stop a thread and replace it with another —the original thread has been *preempted*. Eventually the original thread will find its way back to the processor to complete its action.

Admittedly this is a simplified overview of the preemptive multitasking process. In Chapter 6 we will take an in-depth look into the way Windows NT schedules and prioritizes thread execution. We will also create processes and threads in our own applications for the NT operating system.

Preemptive multitasking is not new, it has existed for many years in operating systems for large computers. NT does, however, introduce this powerful feature to Windows programming.

MEMORY MANAGEMENT

Another major milestone that Windows NT has reached is the reorganization of memory management. With NT Microsoft has done away with the segmented memory models and introduced *flat 32-bit addressing*. This is a much needed breakthrough and is sure to be welcomed by programmers. Before we define the new addressing schemes, let's review how previous Windows versions handled memory.

Windows 3.x Memory Management

Because Windows 3.x was essentially operating on top of MS-DOS, it had to play by the rules of DOS. This included the subject of memory models. You most likely recall the infamous 64K barrier that DOS and Windows programs adhered to. To break that barrier, we had to use different compiler memory models to manage larger amounts of memory. For example, the small memory model consisted of one 64K code segment and one 64K data segment. The medium memory model permitted multiple code segments and a single data segment. The remaining memory models were used primarily by DOS programs (although they were not completely off-limits to Windows programming).

One of the advantages of Windows is the feature of relocatable code and data. Windows usually had our permission to relocate our code and data based on the needs of the system. However, if we stepped into the realm of the compact or large memory models, we created a problem. Multiple data segment memory models require that we place the data in fixed segments. The Windows system, the applications, and the users suffer from the resulting loss of flexibility and efficiency.

Of course there were ways around having to use the compact or large model. You could allocate large expanses of memory dynamically or employ user-defined resource techniques. This worked adequately, but there must be a better way (and it's coming up soon!).

Another drawback of the segment-offset memory scheme is the use of keywords such as NEAR and FAR, and memory allocation functions such as

LocalAlloc() and GlobalAlloc(). Although it was completely necessary (and most of us adapted to it), it added frustration and time to many programming projects. The time for change has come!

NT and 32-Bit Addressing

One of the priorities in the design of Windows NT was the implementation of a flat 32-bit addressing scheme (flat meaning not segmented but linear). This is a giant plus for the programmer, the applications, and the operating system itself.

What are the results of such a scheme? One result is that each application in Windows NT sees a large expanse of virtual memory. In 16-bit Windows (and MS-DOS as well), we were limited to a segment of 216 bytes or 64K bytes. In 32-bit Windows, we now have access to 232 bytes or 4 gigabytes! Well, not quite. We must share this virtual memory with the NT operating system. Basically it is split down the middle, the lower 2 gigabytes for our applications, and the upper 2 gigabytes for the NT operating system. Figure 1-5 shows the layout of Windows NT virtual memory.

Note that the virtual addresses start at 0000000h and end at 7FFFFFFFh for the user virtual memory. This is memory that each application sees in the NT operating system. Windows NT also uses this space for some system threads as well. The bulk of the system threads are located in the upper 2

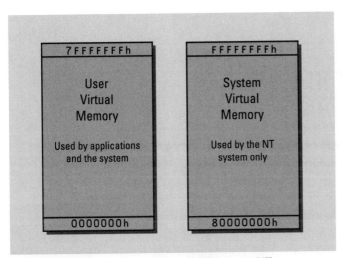

Figure 1-5 Virtual memory in the Windows NT operating system

gigabytes. Most of the details of memory management are transparent to the user and programmer, so we can ignore the details.

In reality, of course, physical memory covers a much smaller range of addresses than virtual memory. If you have eight megabytes of memory installed in your PC, the valid range of physical addresses would span from 000000h to 7FFFFFh. Some method must bridge this physical-virtual memory gap. The NT system, similar to Windows 3.x, swaps virtual memory in and out of physical memory as needed. The method of swapping is different in Windows NT, however, but the changes are essentially transparent to the user and programmer and should not cause concern at this time.

NT employs a new *virtual memory manager* (VMM) that takes care of the demands on physical vs. virtual memory. When a thread is to be executed by the processor, the VMM swaps the necessary code into physical memory (if it isn't already there). Whether or not the code gets swapped back out of physical memory depends on the demands of the system and other running applications.

Windows NT, like 3.x, uses a disk swap file to help in the management of memory. This file can be varied in size by the user in Windows NT Setup. Microsoft recommends a minimum swap file size of 20 megabytes. The swap file is always permanent in Windows NT; in Windows 3.x the user can specify if the swap file is permanent or temporary.

Although it requires a little effort to get familiar with the new memory addressing scheme, it is very beneficial in the long run. Chapter 3, Memory Management, provides more detailed information on managing memory in Windows NT.

FILE MANAGEMENT

Managing files in Windows NT requires new approaches and techniques for two reasons. We have already discussed the first reason: MS-DOS is no longer running under Windows; Windows NT *is* the operating system. Therefore Microsoft has introduced new services to manage files in applications for NT. The second reason a new approach is necessary is the possibility of multiple-file systems. The MS-DOS File Allocation Table (FAT) approach is just one of three possible file systems.

Gaining a good understanding of the new file management functions and file systems is essential for writing well-behaved applications. For example, you could write an application that takes advantage of the new NT file system if it exists on a user's system. The same application could also use the FAT file system if the user's system doesn't have an NT file system partition. Let's review the basics of how we handle files in Windows 3.x.

Windows 3.x File Management

Previous Windows versions run on 80x86 microprocessors only. When we needed to open a file in Windows 3.1, we used the _lopen() or OpenFile() function. These functions are based on code that is geared strictly for an MS-DOS (80x86) system. For Windows 3.1 compatibility, these functions and others still exist in Win32; but new functions are available to isolate the programmer from the underlying microprocessor architecture.

NT File Management

Prior versions of Windows were restricted to the MS-DOS file system, referred to as the FAT or File Allocation Table system. In order to create and manipulate files, we used standard C library calls to carry out the tasks. Since Windows NT is a complete operating system, and MS-DOS is no longer beneath us, several new methods and functions were created to handle files.

Another reason for these changes is to free the programmer from worrying about the structure of the actual file system or the system architecture. Making calls to a specific processor binds the application to one type or family of processors. Since one of Microsoft's goals was to have the NT operating system run on different platforms, the programmer should be isolated from making calls to a specific processor or file system.

NT supports three types of file structures: FAT, HPFS, and NTFS. The FAT file structure is necessary for backward compatibility with 16-bit Windows and DOS applications. Since the NT operating system will also run OS/2 applications, the requirement to support the High Performance File System (HPFS) came about. The New Technology File System (NTFS) is completely new and has all the features of HPFS plus a few new ones, such as 64-bit file addresses, file recoverability, large volume checking, and security attributes.

Figure 1-6 shows an example of an application creating a file on one of the hard drives in a system. Note that the Windows NT operating system isolates the application from the file system type; however, some features are only available on certain file systems. For example, you cannot create a file with security attributes on a FAT partition.

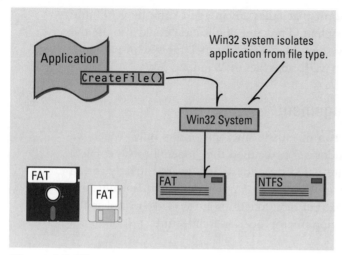

Figure 1-6 File systems on Windows NT

Another feature that is available in Windows NT is file sharing. More than one process can possess a handle to a specific file. Functions are also available for locking a file during a write operation. Once the operation is complete, the application can then unlock the file so that other applications (with the appropriate handle) can access and manipulate the same file.

The NT file system, and the resultant API expansion, are covered in Chapter 4, File Management.

NEW FEATURES OF WINDOWS NT

Many of the features of Windows NT are new and cannot be compared with previous versions of Windows. System security, file mapping, and synchronization are a few of these new features. Most of these introductions created an expansion in the API. Let's take a closer look at some of the new features before we write our first NT program.

System Security

Microsoft has designed Windows NT with system security in mind, so several security features are built into the operating system. The initial release of Windows NT conforms to conditions required by the United States government for level C2 security clearance. Plans exist to upgrade this security to B-level compliance in subsequent releases.

Windows NT has an object-oriented design. Each component (system resources, subsystems, and so on) is encapsulated. This design reaps two major benefits. The first benefit is extensibility. Having such an object-based or modular design makes future changes to the operating system easier to implement; changes in one area of the operating system are much less likely to cause problems in other areas.

The second benefit of this design is security. Each user of Windows NT must log on to the system. The user has a specific security profile that

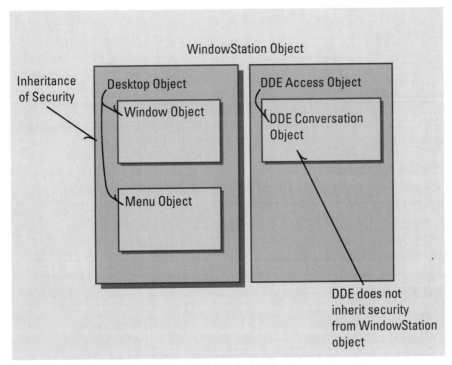

Figure 1-7 Windows NT system security on a single workstation

determines whether or not certain system resources are available. Figure 1-7 shows an overview of the NT security system on a single workstation.

The front-line security for the workstation is called the *WindowStation object*. This object represents a single user's keyboard/mouse/screen combination and contains all subsequent objects. The security of the WindowStation is inherited by a *Desktop object*. This object represents the user's desktop and contains two additional objects: the *Window* and *Menu objects*. These objects represent windows and menus respectively and inherit security from the Desktop object. Keep in mind that several Window and Menu objects can exist on a single desktop. Each inherits the security of the user's desktop.

The *DDE Access object* is contained by the WindowStation object, but it does not inherit the security of the window station. This permits DDE applications to exchange data without giving the user such access. This object establishes access to a DDE server; the security for this object is controlled by a DDE application. The *DDE Conversation object* inherits security from the DDE Access object. This object establishes a DDE conversation between a DDE server and DDE client.

Security Within Applications

Although the previous description illustrates how a single workstation handles security, it does not show the security features within an application. An example of application security can be shown by considering a multithreaded program. When an application creates threads, it can pass on certain security attributes. For example, if an application has opened a file before creating additional threads, the application can determine whether or not the new threads receive the open file handle.

Default security exists throughout the APIs whenever security comes into play. Taking advantage of these features enables you to create robust applications for the NT operating system. Chapter 8, Introduction to NT System Security, provides a more in-depth view of security and how you can employ security features in your programs.

File and I/O Specifics

Several new file and I/O features are specific to Windows NT, for example, *file mapping,* which provides an efficient way for two or more applications to share files, and *pipes,* which let two or more programs communicate with each other (also known as *interprocess communication*).

File Mapping

Mapping files creates the ability for more than one program to access the same file. When a file is mapped, programs view the file as part of their own virtual address space. This means that careful programming techniques are needed to avoid conflicts, such as two programs writing to the file at the same time. Figure 1-8 shows an example of file mapping.

Pipes

Pipes are not new to Windows NT. You may recall that pipes in MS-DOS let you redirect the input or output of data. For example, if you entered TYPE FILE | MORE at the DOS prompt, the output end of the TYPE command was redirected (by the pipe character "|") to the input end of the MORE program. This resulted in the MORE program displaying the contents of FILE a page at a time, displaying "__More__" at the bottom of the display, and pausing until the user pressed a key.

The basic concept of pipes (redirected I/O) applies to Windows NT; however, the features are much more powerful. New APIs let you create *anonymous* and *named* pipes. You use anonymous pipes to let two related processes communicate, while named pipes let unrelated processes communicate. Pipes are not covered in this book.

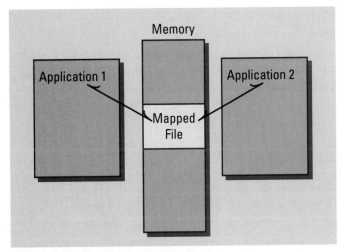

Figure 1-8 File mapping

Synchronization

As you have seen, Windows 3.x was strictly a message-based system. Windows (or another application) sent a message to an application procedure (such as WndProc or DialogProc). No other action could occur while the target application was processing the message. In this situation there is no need to synchronize any action; Windows simply had to wait until the target application returned control.

The Windows NT operating system uses preemptive multitasking, which can bring up some interesting (and perhaps undesirable) conditions. The discussion earlier in the chapter showed how an application can contain multiple threads. As long as the threads perform completely unrelated tasks, there is no problem; but in some situations threads may conflict with one another during execution.

Consider this simple example. If you create a program with two threads that access the same file, you must avoid the possibility of the threads manipulating the file at the same time. How can you avoid this? Win32 provides new APIs to create *synchronization objects*. Your threads can utilize these objects to control each other's execution.

Here is another example. If one thread relies on another for a specific action to occur, there must be a way for the second thread to notify the first that the action is complete. Once again, synchronization objects are used to achieve this. The first thread waits for the object to change to a specific state before it continues. The second thread is responsible for changing the state of the object, which in turn notifies the first thread that the action is complete. Figure 1-9 illustrates this example.

You will use different types of synchronization objects, depending on the specific situation. There are four types of objects. All are discussed in Chapter 7, Synchronization of Threads and Processes.

Network Support

Windows NT has built-in support for communicating with different types of networks. Win32 provides a new set of services to add network implementation without worrying about the specific type of network. This is much like the method in which prior versions of Windows lifted the burden of writing code to access a specific graphics adapter or printer. The new services let your application determine network configurations as well as other network information during execution. The network API functions are not covered in this book.

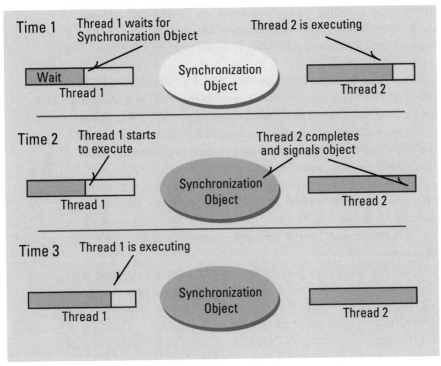

Figure 1-9 Synchronization of threads

- - - - - - - - -

SUMMARY

Microsoft clearly didn't reinvent the wheel when they set out to create Windows NT. Instead they created an operating system that gets the most out of today's more powerful personal computer, while maintaining compatibility with the past. This combination is sure to widen the path of success Microsoft has created.

Adapting to changes in computer technology is frustrating at times, but crucially important. Most likely that's why you're reading this book right now. You want to keep up with the new technology without taking too much of your valuable time. This book is designed to help you acquire the new techniques in a short span.

Fortunately programming for Windows NT closely resembles programming for previous versions of Windows. This is a big plus. With the basics of Windows programming under your belt, the step into Windows NT is a natural one.

The ways some programming tasks are performed in Windows NT have changed; most of them for the better. For starters, NT is a complete operating system. It is no longer a shell running on top of MS-DOS. It is also designed to run on multiple platforms. No longer is it limited to the Intel 80386/486 architecture. More platforms means more users; more users means more potential clients for your applications.

Perhaps the biggest change in Windows NT is the introduction of preemptive multitasking. You can run an application, then run another, even before the window of the first application appears. This could not be done in Windows 3.x. You had to wait for the first application to initialize and return control to Windows.

You can also take advantage of preemptive multitasking to fine-tune your applications, making them responsive to user input, while processing the mundane tasks in the background. We all know how annoying it is to click and wait for some time before we carry out the next action.

Other breakthroughs in Windows NT include full 32-bit addressing of memory, virtual memory, multiple file systems (including the new NTFS), security features, and built-in network support. This book addresses most of the new features of Windows NT and Win32 programming. Let's get started!

Building Your First Application for Windows NT

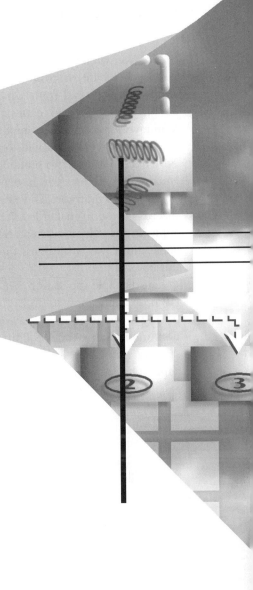

CHAPTER 2

Building Your First Application for Windows NT

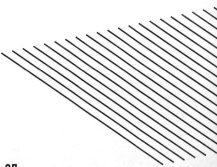

Our approach to learning Windows NT programming is modular. The purpose of this chapter is to create a generic Win32 application. We will analyze the differences between Win32 and previous Windows programs to bring out the areas that have changed. Then, with a good understanding of the new fundamentals, we will build and run the new application and observe the results.

First we will review a generic Windows 3.1 application. This will provide you with a base to compare the structure of Windows 3.x and Win32 applications. Recall from Chapter 1 that Win32 is a *subsystem* on which 32-bit Windows applications execute. If you haven't programmed in Windows for a while, this application also serves as a refresher.

After this review we will look at Microsoft's project management utility, NMAKE, as it relates to building Win32 applications. If you are familiar with Microsoft compilers, you have probably already used NMAKE. Similar to the Windows 3.x Software Development Kit (SDK), the Win32 SDK provides macros to use in makefiles. These macros make the job of building your applications much easier. Since this book concentrates on Win32 applications, we will discuss the macros as they relate to the applications in this book.

The example application, GENERIC, is a near minimum Windows 32-bit (Win32) application. GENERIC could have been reduced further (by not having a menu or icon resource), but this would result in a completely nonfunctioning window. This application provides a solid framework and starting point for developing further applications. After discussing the application source files, we will build and run GENERIC.

CHAPTER OVERVIEW

Concepts Covered

- ◢ Review of a generic Windows 3.x application
- ◢ Using NMAKE with the Win32 SDK
- ◢ Using NMAKE for applications in this book

- ◢ Overview of the differences in Win32 applications
- ◢ Generic 32-bit Windows application

Win32 Defines

- ◢ APIENTRY
- ◢ WINAPI

A REVIEW OF A GENERIC WINDOWS APPLICATION

Before we get into our first 32-bit application, let's review a minimal Windows 3.1 application. Doing so will help highlight the differences between the two applications and help make the transition easier. Listings 2-1 through 2-4 show the module definition, header, resource, and source files, respectively. If you are familiar with Windows programming, you may wish to skip to the next segment.

The module definition file is a requirement in Windows 3.x applications. It is optional in Win32 applications. A module definition file is required for Win32 Dynamic Link Libraries (DLLs) where it builds an import library. Win32 applications use the resulting import library to resolve imports and exports.

In Windows 3.x module definition files provide information to resolve external references and define certain characteristics of the executable file. For example, the file in Listing 2-1 provides the name (GENERICW), a description (a string of characters which the compiler embeds in the executable), and an EXETYPE (in this case Windows). It also defines the stub. If the user tries to start a Windows application from the DOS prompt, the stub program displays a message on the screen indicating that the application requires Microsoft Windows.

The module definition file also determines whether or not to preload the application's code or data, and whether or not the code or data is moveable in memory, discardable, and so on. The heapsize and stacksize entries specify the size of the program's heap and stack, respectively. The exports entry defines the functions that are made available to other applications. In Listing 2-1 WndProc( ) is an export; this is a callback window procedure. Windows itself calls this function to pass messages to the window procedure.

- - - - - -
Listing 2-1 Module definition file—Windows 3.x

```
NAME            GENERICW
DESCRIPTION     'Generic Windows 3.x Application'
EXETYPE         WINDOWS
STUB            'WINSTUB.EXE'
CODE            PRELOAD MOVEABLE DISCARDABLE
DATA            PRELOAD MOVEABLE MULTIPLE
HEAPSIZE        1024
STACKSIZE       5120
EXPORTS         WndProc
```

The header file, although not a requirement, helps organize the application, thus making it easier to maintain. Our header file in Listing 2-2 defines a single menu selection, a function prototype, and two global variables for the program instance and the main window handle. We will see that the header file for our minimal Win32 application is very similar.

- - - - - -
Listing 2-2 Header file—Windows 3.x

```
/* GENERICW.H--Header file for generic Windows 3.x application */

/* Menu defines */
#define IDM_EXECUTE     101

/* Function prototype */
long PASCAL WndProc (HWND, WORD, WORD, LONG);

/* Global variables */
HANDLE ghInst;
HANDLE ghWnd;
```

Resource files are basically the same for Windows 3.x and Win32. They contain definitions of resources (icons, bitmaps, menus, dialog boxes, and so on). In our minimal Windows 3.x application, we define an icon and a menu resource. The top-level menu in Listing 2-3 contains one item, a popup named *Example.* The popup has one selection, *Execute.* Other than the names of the resources (GenericwIcon and GenericwMenu), this file is the same as its Win32 counterpart.

Listing 2-3 Resource file—Windows 3.x

```
/* GENERICW.RC--Header file for generic Windows 3.x application */

#include "windows.h"
#include "genericw.h"

GenericwIcon ICON    genericw.ico

GenericwMenu MENU
    BEGIN
        POPUP "Example"
        BEGIN
            MENUITEM "Execute",  IDM_EXECUTE
        END
    END
```

The source file is where most of the Windows 3.x/Win32 differences occur. Review Listing 2-4 if you are a bit rusty in Windows programming.

Listing 2-4 Source file—Windows 3.x

```
/* GENERICW.C--generic program for Windows 3.x */

#include <windows.h>           /* include for Windows 3.x apps */
#include "genericw.h"           /* include for genericw.c */

int PASCAL WinMain (HANDLE hInstance, HANDLE hPrevInstance, LPSTR lpCmdLine, int nCmdShow)
{
   MSG  msg;
   WNDCLASS wndclass;

   ghInst = hInstance;                              /* Assign global instance handle */

   if (!hPrevInstance)
   {
      wndclass.style = CS_HREDRAW | CS_VREDRAW;      /* Fill in window class structure */
      wndclass.lpfnWndProc = (WNDPROC)WndProc;
      wndclass.cbClsExtra = 0;
      wndclass.cbWndExtra = 0;
      wndclass.hInstance = hInstance;
      wndclass.hIcon = LoadIcon (hInstance, "GenericwIcon");          /* Generic icon */
```

continued on next page

continued from previous page

```
        wndclass.hCursor = LoadCursor (NULL, IDC_ARROW);
        wndclass.hbrBackground = GetStockObject (WHITE_BRUSH);
        wndclass.lpszMenuName = "GenericwMenu";                    /* Generic menu */
        wndclass.lpszClassName = "GenericwClass";

        RegisterClass(&wndclass);
    }

    ghWnd = CreateWindow ("GenericwClass",        /* Create main window */
                          "Generic Application for Windows 3.x", /* Title bar text */
                          WS_OVERLAPPEDWINDOW,
                          CW_USEDEFAULT,
                          CW_USEDEFAULT,
                          CW_USEDEFAULT,
                          CW_USEDEFAULT,
                          NULL,
                          NULL,
                          hInstance,
                          NULL);

    ShowWindow(ghWnd, nCmdShow);                       /* Display window */

    while (GetMessage (&msg, NULL, 0, 0))              /* Message Loop */
    {
        TranslateMessage (&msg);
        DispatchMessage (&msg);
    }

    return (msg.wParam);                               /* Return exit code */
}

/* WndProc - Main Window Procedure for genericw.c */

LONG FAR PASCAL WndProc (HWND hwnd, WORD message, WORD wParam, LONG lParam)
{

    switch (message)                /* check message */
    {
        case WM_CREATE:             /* no initialization */
            return (0);

        case WM_COMMAND:
            switch (wParam)
            {
                case IDM_EXECUTE:   /* do-nothing menu choice */
                    return (0);

                default:
                    return (0);
            }

        case WM_DESTROY:            /* no cleanup necessary */
            PostQuitMessage (0);
```

```
        return (0);

    }
    return DefWindowProc (hwnd, message, wParam, lParam);
}
```

The Entry Point—WinMain()

Our application starts at WinMain(). This function is called by Windows and receives four parameters. The first parameter is a handle to the instance of the application. Recall that Windows can start more than one instance of an application. The second parameter is a handle to the previous instance, if one exists. If it is the first instance of the application, this handle is NULL. The third parameter is a pointer to a null-terminated string containing optional command-line arguments. The fourth parameter is an integer specifying how the main window is initially displayed (maximized, minimized, and so on).

Registering the Window Class

After assigning the program instance handle to a global variable *(ghInst),* we must register a window class. Notice that we use an *if* statement to see if a previous instance of the application is running. The window class only needs to be registered with the first instance. Subsequent instances will use the window class created by the first instance.

To register the window class, we must fill in a WNDCLASS structure. This structure's members define certain attributes of the window. For example, the *wndclass.lpfnWndProc* member points to our window procedure. We also define the window style, the associated icon, cursor, window background, and menu. The last member, *wndclass.lpszClassName,* gives the window class a name. We will use this name when creating the main window.

We finally register the window class with a call to RegisterClass(). The single argument to this function is the address of the filled WNDCLASS structure. Now that we have a registered window class, we can create the main window.

Creating the Window

We create the main window with a call to CreateWindow(). This function takes several parameters, the first of which is the name of the registered window class. Other entries include a string indicating the title bar text, window style, size, and initial position of the window. The return value of CreateWindow() is a handle to the window. In this case, we are assigning this value to the global variable *ghWnd.*

The CreateWindow() call does not immediately return. Windows first sends messages to our window procedure, WndProc(). One of these messages is WM_CREATE. Many applications trap this message to perform initialization specific to the window.

When the CreateWindow() call returns, we call ShowWindow(). The window is not visible until this point. ShowWindow() requires two parameters: a handle to the window and the *nCmdShow* integer.

The Message Loop

Now that we have created the main window, we enter a message loop. This loop obtains messages from Windows (stored in a queue), translates them, and dispatches them to the appropriate window procedure. In this case there is only one window procedure, WndProc().

The Window Procedure—WndProc()

WndProc() accepts four parameters. The first parameter is the window handle. The second parameter is a WORD containing a message. The third and fourth parameters, *wParam* and *lParam,* contain information specific to the message. *wParam* is a WORD and *lParam* is a LONG value. This is an area in which we will see a difference in Win32 applications.

Most Windows applications use a *switch* statement to determine the type of message being received. For example, when Windows sends a WM_CREATE message, we trap the message with the *case* statement. In our case we are simply returning 0 to Windows; however, we could have performed some initialization here. Likewise Windows sends the WM_DESTROY message when the main window is about to be destroyed. We trap this message and call PostQuitMessage(), which terminates the application.

Processing the Menu Selection

Our simple example application has only one menu selection. If the user selects *Execute* from the *Example* menu, Windows sends a WM_COMMAND message to our window procedure. In this case *wParam* contains the menu ID value. We use another *switch* statement to determine which menu selection has been made. We use a *case* statement to see if this message is IDM_EXECUTE. Again, we are not performing any action to respond to the menu selection in this example. We simply return 0 to Windows.

Before we get into the differences between the Windows 3.x generic application and a Win32 application, let's look at makefiles for the Win32 SDK.

NMAKE AND MAKEFILES

NMAKE is a project management utility that is provided by Microsoft in the Win32 SDK. Although the purpose of makefiles is virtually the same as Windows 3.x, Win32 makefiles are structured differently. How makefiles are used is a matter of personal preference; we will discuss the method in which makefiles are implemented for the example programs in this book.

Listing 2-5 shows a typical makefile for projects in this book. The only modifications (other than program names) are occasional changes to switch macros for multithreaded programs and dynamic link libraries (both are covered in Chapter 6, Multitasking in Windows NT).

Listing 2-5 An example makefile

```
# MAKEFILE for GENERIC (minimum application for Windows NT)

# NMAKE macros for Win32 apps
!include <ntwin32.mak>

# all pseudotarget
all: generic.exe

# Update the resource.
generic.res: generic.rc generic.h
    rc -r -fo generic.tmp generic.rc
    cvtres -$(CPU) generic.tmp -o generic.res
    del generic.tmp

# Update the object file.
generic.obj: generic.c generic.h
    $(cc) $(cflags) $(cvars) generic.c

# Update the executable file and add the resource file.
generic.exe: generic.obj generic.res
    $(link) $(guilflags) -IGNORE:505 -out:generic.exe generic.obj generic.res $(guilibs)
```

NTWIN32.MAK

The first (noncomment) line of the makefile includes the NTWIN32.MAK file. This file contains macros for most of the cryptic entries in the makefiles. You could open the NTWIN32.MAK file and cross-reference each entry in the file; for ease, however, we have provided a complete explanation for each entry in Table 2-1. Each entry in the table shows what the macro evaluates to, and the phase of the build in which it is used. Keep in mind that these macros are for 80x86 processors. The macros equate to other values on MIPS RISC systems.

Pseudotargets

Pseudotargets are used to build more than one application from a single makefile. The pseudotarget in makefile is *all:*. If you wanted to build multiple applications in addition to GENERIC.EXE, you could specify the .EXE or .DLL names on the same line.

   Although we are not using multiple applications in the GENERIC project, the all: pseudotarget is included for future use. We will use this technique in a DLL example program, MULTIDLL, in Chapter 6. The MULTIDLL project builds an executable and a dynamic link library from the same makefile.

Compiling Resources

The first work to get done in the build process is resource compiling. There are four lines to accomplish this task; these lines are referred to as a *description*

Macro	Evaluates to	Phase Used
$(CPU)	i386*	resource compile
$(cc)	cl386	compile
$(cdebug)	-Zi -Od	compile
$(cflags)	-c -W3 -G3 -D_X86_=1	compile
$(cvars)	-DWIN32	compile
$(link)	link32	link
$(ldebug)	-debug:full -debugtype:cv	link
$(guilflags)	-subsystem:windows	link
	-entry:WinMainCRTStartup	
$(guilibs)	GUI libraries (see Table 2-2)	link

*i386 is actually defined in the NT environment variables

Table 2-1 NTWIN32.MAK definitions for x86 processors

block. The first line of each description block is the dependency line. The *dependency line* for the resource compiler is

```
generic.res: generic.rc generic.h
```

The name to the left of the colon (generic.res) specifies the target file. The names to the right of the colon (generic.rc and generic.h) are dependent files. The time and date of the dependent files compared to the target file time and date determine whether or not the compile takes place.

For example, if the time and date of either dependent file is later than the time and date of the target, the build will take place. In other words if either of the dependents has been edited since the last compile, another compile must be performed to bring the target up to date. Of course, all of this requires that the system time and date are accurate.

The second line of the resource description block runs the resource compiler (RC). The -r switch is ignored in Win32. The presence of *-r* ensures compatibility with previous versions of makefiles. The *-fo* switch forces the resource compiler to use the name that immediately follows (in this case generic.tmp) as the output file. The last part of the resource compile line is the file that we will be compiling, in this case, GENERIC.RC.

The third line converts the temporary resource file to a 32-bit resource. This is a requirement for Win32 applications. The output file is a 32-bit resource module that we will link in the last portion of the makefile. The fourth line of the resource compile portion of the makefile deletes the temporary resource file which we created in the second line.

This completes the resource compile. The resources are now in linkable form in a file named GENERIC.RES.

Compiling the Source Code

The next resource block is responsible for compiling the source file. Once again, the first line of the block is the dependency line. The target file is GENERIC.OBJ. It is dependent on the source file (GENERIC.C) and the header file (GENERIC.H). If either of these files has been modified since the last compile, the remainder of the dependency block will execute and the source and header files will be recompiled. This block will also execute if the target file does not exist.

The next line is full of macros. Using Listing 2-5 and Table 2-1, we can evaluate this line. After evaluation the line becomes

```
cl386 -c -G3 -W3 -D_x86_=1 -DWIN32 generic.c
```

You will notice that NMAKE displays this line during compilation of GENERIC.C.

Let's break this line apart. The *-c* switch preserves source file comments—that is, the compiler includes the source file comments in the object file. The *-W3* switch sets the warning level of the compiler. This setting can range from *-W0* (does not display warnings) to *-W4* (displays even the simplest warnings). As an example, the –W3 switch will not check for ANSI keywords, but the *-W4* warning level will.

The *-G3* switch targets the 80386 microprocessor. This is the lowest common denominator for Win32 applications. The *-G4* switch could be used in its place, but the resultant application will only run on an 80486.

The *-D_x86_=1* switch indicates that the processor is an 80x86 processor. Recall that Windows NT runs on systems other than the 80x86. Since this book targets the 80x86, all makefiles contain this switch.

The last switch, *-DWIN32,* is also a define. It is actually two parts, *-D* and *WIN32.* This is necessary to resolve issues within WINDOWS.H and the files it includes. The Windows header files use conditional compilation techniques. For example, the header file may include (or exclude) a particular data type, depending on whether or not *WIN32* is defined.

The last entry on the compile line is the source file. In our case this is GENERIC.C. Note that the source filename is not case-sensitive. Now we have compiled resources and compiled source code. The last step the makefile performs is the link process.

Linking

The dependency line of the link description block indicates that GENERIC.EXE is the target. The object file and resource file are the dependents. Once again, take a look at Listing 2-5 and Table 2-1 to translate this macro–filled line. The line translates as:

```
link32 --subsystem:windows -entry:WinMainCRTStartup -IGNORE:505 -out:generic.exe
generic.obj generic.res $(guilibs)
```

The first switch, *-subsystem,* informs the linker of the target subsystem. All of the examples in this book target the Windows subsystem. Other subsystems available to Windows NT are POSIX, Console, and OS/2.

The *-entry:* switch specifies the entry point of the program; this is usually the first byte of the code section. In our examples the entry point is *WinMainCRTStartup,* which translates to *WinMain* in the actual source code. The *CRTStartup* portion refers to the C run-time libraries.

The *-IGNORE:505* switch suppresses the linker from displaying the "Module not extracted from..." error during the link process. The last switch, *-out:,* specifies the output file of the linker. This is an executable (as in our case), or a DLL.

| C.LIB | NTDLL.LIB | KERNEL32.LIB | COMMDLG.32LIB |
| USER32.LIB | GDI32.LIB | WINSPOOL.LIB | |

Table 2-2 Libraries in the $(GUILIBS) macro

With the switches out of the way, the remainder of the line contains the object file, the resource file, and the *$(guilibs)* macro. This macro expands into all library names necessary for Win32 GUI applications. These libraries are shown in Table 2-2.

That completes our look at makefiles for Win32 applications. The majority of the remaining projects use the same or very similar makefiles. Major differences will be explained as they come up. If you are using a compiler other than Microsoft's cl386, you can use these command-line parameters as a guide to create makefiles specific to your compiler.

MODULE DEFINITION FILES

Module definition files are optional for Win32 applications. You can still use a module definition file, but there are some differences in module definition files that exist in Win32. Let's take a look at the individual entry for Win32 DEF files.

Name

The Name entry indicates that the program is an executable file; it must be the first line in the definition file. For dynamic link libraries, the Name entry is replaced by Library. Only one of these two entries can occur in a DEF file.

If no name exists on the Name statement line, the linker assumes that the executable file uses the same name as the DEF file. For example, if we omitted the entry on the Name line in the above example, the linker would assume the executable file would be GENERIC.EXE. In this case, there is no difference.

Description

The Description entry is a text string that is inserted into the application's private data section. You can use either single or double quotation marks to surround the text string. If you have a need to include a quotation mark in the text string, use the opposite type of quotation mark to delimit the text string. For example, "Generic for 'The Waite Group'" would result in the text between the double quotes (including the single quotes) being inserted in the data section of the application.

Stub

Similar to Windows 3.x, the Stub entry is a file that will execute if an attempt is made to run the Win32 application from MS-DOS. Unlike the Windows 3.x stub, the Win32 stub displays, "This program cannot be run in DOS mode." when such an attempt is made.

You can replace WINSTUB.EXE with your own stub program; however, the default stub is sufficient for most applications.

Code

As we will describe in Chapter 3, Windows NT manages memory much differently from Windows 3.x. It is for this reason that the Code entry has changed. The new code memory protection attributes are Execute, Read, Write, and Shared. These attributes protect (or allow) other programs from accessing the code segment of your applications. The default attributes are Execute and Read.

Data

The Data entry has also undergone changes. The possible Data attributes are the same as those in the Code statement. The default memory protection attributes for Data are Read and Write.

Heapsize

The Heapsize entry in Win32 supports two arguments: *reserve* and *commit*. The arguments must be separated by a comma. The reserve argument is the amount of memory (in bytes) reserved for the application. Reserved means the application has been assigned a global block of memory addresses, but the memory is not ready for use. The commit argument is the amount of memory (in bytes) committed for the application. Committed means that the memory is ready for use.

The reserve and commit arguments are discussed in greater detail in Chapter 3, Memory Management. The defaults are 1 megabyte (0x100000h) for reserve, and 4K (0x1000h) for commit.

The heap is used for dynamic allocation of memory. The default values are sufficient for most programs in this book.

Stacksize

The Stacksize entry contains the same arguments as the Heapsize entry. The defaults for the *reserve* and *commit* arguments are also the same, 1 megabyte and 4K, respectively. The stack is used for automatic variables, function return addresses, and other temporary purposes.

Exports

The Exports entry is identical to those used in Windows 3.x module definitions. You can give the exported functions ordinal values or other names instead of the function name as it appears in the exporting program.

- -

A GENERIC START IN WIN32

We will start out with the minimum Windows 32-bit example application, GENERIC. GENERIC's basic purpose is to create a main window with a menu. We also add an icon resource to the program. The icon can be seen by adding the completed program to an existing group in the Program Manager or by minimizing the window. The icon also gives an indication of the chapter and example in which the program originated. For example, GENERIC is the first example of Chapter 2; therefore the icon will display "2.1" in its lower-left corner.

Examining GENERIC.C

Before we compile and link our first example program, let's take a close look at what is different between this code and Windows 3.x code. Some of the differences will be obvious, while others are quite subtle and difficult to notice. In either case we analyze these differences following the source code listing.

Listing 2-6 is the complete source file for GENERIC.C. Take a moment to examine the file before continuing with the text. See if you can find the obvious changes that 32-bit programming brought to the example. Then read the complete list of changes that follow the listing.

Listing 2-6 GENERIC.C

```c
/* generic.c      Minimum program for Windows NT */

#include <windows.h>            /* include for Windows NT apps */
#include "generic.h"            /* include for generic.c */

int APIENTRY WinMain (HANDLE hInstance, HANDLE hPrevInstance, LPSTR lpCmdLine, int nCmdShow)
{
    MSG   msg;
    WNDCLASS wndclass;

    UNREFERENCED_PARAMETER (lpCmdLine);             /* Prevent compiler warnings */
    UNREFERENCED_PARAMETER (hPrevInstance);

    ghInst = hInstance;                             /* Assign global instance handle */

    wndclass.style = CS_HREDRAW | CS_VREDRAW;       /* Fill in window class structure */
    wndclass.lpfnWndProc = (WNDPROC)WndProc;
    wndclass.cbClsExtra = 0;
    wndclass.cbWndExtra = 0;
    wndclass.hInstance = hInstance;
    wndclass.hIcon = LoadIcon (ghInst, "GenericIcon");
    wndclass.hCursor = LoadCursor (NULL, IDC_ARROW);
    wndclass.hbrBackground = GetStockObject (WHITE_BRUSH);
    wndclass.lpszMenuName = "GenericMenu";          /* Generic menu */
    wndclass.lpszClassName = "GenericClass";

    RegisterClass(&wndclass);

    ghWnd = CreateWindow ("GenericClass",           /* Create main window */
                          "Generic Application for Windows NT",   /* Title bar text */
                          WS_OVERLAPPEDWINDOW,
                          CW_USEDEFAULT,
                          CW_USEDEFAULT,
                          CW_USEDEFAULT,
                          CW_USEDEFAULT,
                          NULL,
                          NULL,
                          hInstance,
                          NULL);

    ShowWindow(ghWnd, nCmdShow);                    /* Display window */

    while (GetMessage (&msg, NULL, 0, 0))           /* Message Loop */
    {
        TranslateMessage (&msg);
```

```
        DispatchMessage (&msg);
    }

    return (msg.wParam);                        /* Return exit code */

}

/* WndProc - Main Window Procedure for generic.c */

LONG APIENTRY WndProc (HWND hWnd, UINT message, UINT wParam, LONG lParam)
{

    switch (message)
    {
      case WM_CREATE:                           /* No initialization */
          return (0);

      case WM_COMMAND:
          switch (LOWORD(wParam))               /* Extract LOWORD of wParam for Win32) */
          {
            case IDM_EXECUTE:                   /* Do-nothing menu choice */
                return (0);

            default:
                return (0);
          }

      case WM_DESTROY:                          /* No cleanup necessary */
          PostQuitMessage (0);
          return (0);

      default:
          return DefWindowProc (hWnd, message, wParam, lParam);
    }

    return (0L);
}
```

The APIENTRY Define

The first difference you may have noticed is in the function definitions for
WinMain() and WndProc(). Each contains the APIENTRY define, instead
of the PASCAL define used in Windows 3.x applications. The following
code fragments show the differences between the function prototypes.

```
/* Windows 32-bit WinMain definition */
int APIENTRY WinMain (HANDLE hInstance, HANDLE hPrevInstance, LPSTR lpCmdLine, int nCmdShow)

/* Windows 3.x WinMain definition */
int PASCAL WinMain (HANDLE hInstance, HANDLE hPrevInstance, LPSTR lpCmdLine, int nCmdShow)
```

Where is APIENTRY defined? Figure 2-1 shows how APIENTRY is defined in GENERIC.C. On the first line of our source code, we included the WINDOWS.H header file. WINDOWS.H itself includes WINDEF.H, another header file, which actually contains the definition of APIENTRY as type WINAPI. WINAPI is defined as type _stdcall, which establishes the calling convention of the function; this is much like PASCAL defining the calling convention in Windows 3.x applications. Calling conventions determine the order that arguments get pushed on the stack and also which function is responsible for cleaning up the stack (calling function or receiving function).

Even though we are still using the HANDLE type for *hInstance* and *hPrevInstance,* there has been a change in HANDLE. As you'll see later, there has also been a change in the string to which *lpCmdLine* points.

Differences in Handles

Most likely you have used handles extensively in your Windows 3.x programs. Handles are used for windows, menus, bitmaps, and many other objects. The handles were assigned by the Windows 3.x kernel; they are 16-bit values that refer to a specific object.

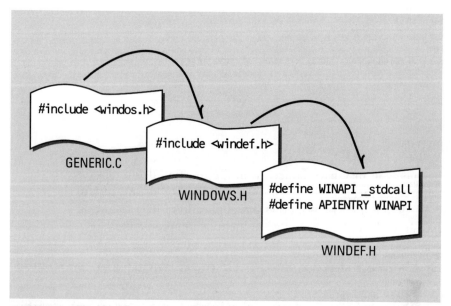

```
#include <windos.h>
```
GENERIC.C

```
#include <windef.h>
```
WINDOWS.H

```
#define WINAPI _stdcall
#define APIENTRY WINAPI
```
WINDEF.H

FIGURE 2-1 The definition of APIENTRY

Win32 applications use 32-bit handles. This doesn't present much difficulty to the programmer; most of the differences are transparent. New types of handles are available in Win32. You can use these handles for stricter type checking. For example, if you pass an HWND (handle to a window) to a function expecting an HDC (handle to a device context), the compiler will complain. This will only occur when using the STRICT option of compiling, however. If STRICT is defined, the compiler performs very strict type checking.

Differences in Instances and Previous Instances

Another important change to note is the usage of *hPrevInstance*. In Windows 3.x, we use the *hPrevInstance* handle to determine if a previous instance of the application is running. This is generally used for two purposes. The most common usage of *hPrevInstance* is to make a decision to register (or not to register) a window class. Using an *if* statement, a check is made to see if this is the first instance. If it is the first instance of the application, *hPrevInstance* returns NULL. The body of the *if* statement contains the code that fills the window class structure and registers the window class. In Win32 applications, we will register a window class for each instance. The reason we do this is that each Win32 application runs in its own private virtual address space, even if it is two instances of the same application.

Another use for *hPrevInstance* in Windows 3.x is to prevent the user from executing another instance of the application. The Control Panel and the Print Manager are programs that use *hPrevInstance* for this purpose. Instead of starting a new copy of the application, these programs simply shift the input focus back to the original instance of the program.

Applications written for Win32 can no longer use *hPrevInstance* for either of these purposes; *hPrevInstance* always returns a NULL value in Win32. Therefore, if your applications must know if a previous instance is running, other methods must be used. One method of finding the existence of a previous instance is the FindWindow function. Figure 2-2 illustrates these *hPrevInstance* differences.

Differences in lpCmdLine

In Windows 3.x the *lpCmdLine* parameter provides a long pointer to a string that contains the command-line parameters. In Win32 applications this is no longer true. The string now contains the entire command line. For example, say you start a program (NOTEPAD.EXE) with a command-line parameter (TESTFILE). In Windows 3.x, *lpCmdLine* points to a string

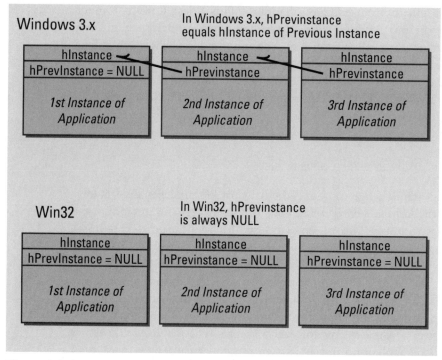

Figure 2-2 Windows 3.x/Win32 hPrevInstance differences

containing "TESTFILE." In Win32 *lpCmdLine* points to a string containing "NOTEPAD.EXE TESTFILE." Keep this in mind if you plan to use command-line parameters with your Win32 applications.

Differences in WndProc()

Take a close look at the function definition for WndProc(). There are some very important changes here. The following lines show the WndProc() function definition for GENERIC followed by a typical Windows 3.x WndProc():

```
/* WndProc--A window procedure for Win32 */
LONG APIENTRY WndProc (HWND hwnd, UINT message, UINT wParam, LONG lParam)

/* WndProc--A window procedure for Windows 3.x */
LONG FAR PASCAL WndProc (HWND hwnd, WORD message, WORD wParam, LONG lParam)
```

One of the changes is the replacement of FAR PASCAL with APIENTRY. This is for the same reason we discussed earlier in WinMain. The FAR keyword is dropped because of the new 32-bit addressing scheme. NEAR and FAR are now meaningless. The compiler will not choke on these keywords (they are defined as "nothing"—an empty define statement—in the header files), but it's good programming practice to start using APIENTRY.

The other noticeable change is the replacement of WORD with UINT for the *message* and *wParam* parameters. This is necessary because the *message* and *wParam* values are 32 bits in Win32. The WORD data type is defined as 16 bits in both Windows 3.x and Win32. On the other hand, the UINT data type is defined as 16 bits in Windows 3.x and 32 bits in Win32. Using UINT will result in the correct data type, regardless of the target system.

New Message Handling—wParam and lParam

The way a window procedure handles the WM_COMMAND message has also been affected by the changes in Win32. Figure 2-3 shows the differences

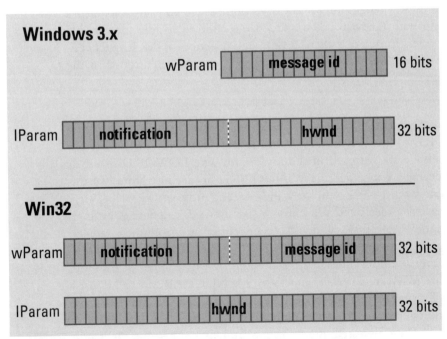

Figure 2-3 wParam and lParam packing for WM_COMMAND— Windows 3.x vs WIN32

in the packing of *wParam* and *lParam*. Notice that the *message id* uses the 16-bit *wParam* in Windows 3.x. This is the reason that WORD is sufficient in Windows 3.x programs. In Win32, however, *wParam* has been expanded to 32 bits. The *message id* is now in the lower 16 bits of a UINT data type.

Although *lParam* is still 32 bits (a LONG data type), it is still affected by the new message packing. The reason for the change is *hwnd* has been expanded to 32 bits. Recall that handles in Win32 are all 32 bits. In Windows 3.x the *hwnd* parameter shared *lParam* with the *notification code*. Now that *hwnd* takes up the entire *lParam,* the *notification code* was forced to move to the high WORD of *wParam*.

Let's take a quick review of how these parameters are used in the WM_COMMAND message. The WM_COMMAND message is sent by menu selections, controls, and keyboard accelerators. The *message id* is the message being sent from the control (IDM_DOSOMETHING for a menu). The *hwnd* parameter is the handle of the control; this value is NULL for menus and accelerators. The *notification code* is also used exclusively with controls; its value is 0 if the message is from a menu, or 1 if the message is from an accelerator.

How do these changes affect GENERIC.C? Since we have included a simple menu with GENERIC, we added the code to handle the possible menu selections. In our case there is only one selection, IDM_EXECUTE. The place where the message packing affects the code is illustrated in the following line:

```
switch (LOWORD(wParam))    /* Extract LOWORD of wParam for Win32 */
```

In the *switch* statement, we extract the low order word of *wParam* by using the LOWORD macro. We need to do this because *wParam* is now two words and the message ID is stored in the low word. The LOWORD macro is available because we included the WINDOWS.H header file. Note that this arrangement would work with a Windows 3.x program as well. Why? Because the low order word still exists in Windows 3.x. There is no high order word in 3.x, but that will not cause any complaints from the compiler, because we are not requesting it.

Many other window messages are affected by this change in packing. Examples are WM_ACTIVATE and WM_MENUCHAR, to name just a few. We will bring up the effects of these changes when the topics that use them are addressed. The changes in each window message are very similar to the example we just discussed; most changes are required because the handle in lParam is now 32 bits.

That completes our look into the changes that affect the GENERIC program. Let's take a look at the effects on the remaining files for GENERIC.

Examining GENERIC.H

The header file for the GENERIC program, shown in Listing 2-7, is GENERIC.H. Fundamentally there is nothing new here other than the use of the APIENTRY define for WndProc(). The listing is provided for completeness only. The header file contains menu defines (in this case one menu selection), a function prototype for WndProc(), and two global variables.

Although the two globals (*ghInst* and *ghWnd*) are assigned values in GENERIC.C, they are not used in the program. They are included to provide a complete template to help you when starting your own programming project. Most programs require handles to the main window and program instance.

------ -- --

Listing 2-7 GENERIC.H

```
/* generic.h -- Include file for generic.c and generic.rc */

/* Menu defines */
#define IDM_EXECUTE   101

/* Function prototype */
LONG APIENTRY WndProc (HWND, UINT, UINT, LONG);

/* Global variables */
HANDLE ghInst;
HANDLE ghWnd;
```

Examining GENERIC.RC

Listing 2-8 shows the resource file for the GENERIC program. Other than handles expanding to 32 bits, resource files in Win32 are virtually the same as those used in Windows 3.x.

This resource file includes WINDOWS.H and GENERIC.H. GENERIC.H resolves the references to the menu command, IDM_EXECUTE. We have provided the icon file (GENERIC.ICO) on disk. You can edit it or create your own using the resource tools of your choice.

Listing 2-8 GENERIC.RC

```
#include "windows.h"
#include "generic.h"

GenericIcon ICON generic.ico

GenericMenu MENU
    BEGIN
        POPUP "&Example"
        BEGIN
            MENUITEM "E&xecute",   IDM_EXECUTE
        END
    END
```

BUILDING GENERIC

Now it's time to build the GENERIC example program and give it a run! All example programs in this book use the Microsoft Project Management Utility (NMAKE) to automate the building process. In addition, all example programs in this book use a makefile, aptly named MAKEFILE, to pass to NMAKE.

Examining the MAKEFILE

Let's take a close look at MAKEFILE for the GENERIC project. Listing 2-9 shows the entire makefile. Although makefiles can contain more sections than those in the listing, the sections we will be dealing with are: compiling resources, compiling the source code, and linking.

Listing 2-9 MAKEFILE for GENERIC

```
# MAKEFILE for GENERIC (minimum application for Windows NT)

# NMAKE macros for Win32 apps
!include <ntwin32.mak>

# all pseudotarget
all: generic.exe

# Update the resource.
```

```
generic.res: generic.rc generic.h
    rc -r -fo generic.tmp generic.rc
    cvtres -$(CPU) generic.tmp -o generic.res
    del generic.tmp

# Update the object file.
generic.obj: generic.c generic.h
    $(cc) $(cflags) $(cvars) generic.c

# Update the executable file and add the resource file.
generic.exe: generic.obj generic.res
    $(link) $(guilflags) -IGNORE:505 -out:generic.exe generic.obj generic.res $(guilibs)
```

Using NMAKE

If you haven't loaded the source files from the supplied disk, do so now. Complete instructions for loading the files are listed in Appendix B.

Ensure your environment is properly set up before starting NMAKE. You can check this by double-clicking on the Control Panel icon in the Main group. Then double-click on the System icon. Examine the contents of the *User Environment Variables.* Four variables are necessary to use NMAKE. The following list shows the proper set of environment variables. Substitute *X:* with the drive letter that you installed Windows NT on. If you installed the SDK to a directory other than the default, substitute *mstools* with your directory.

USER ENVIRONMENT VARIABLES FOR WIN32 SDK

```
CPU = I386
INCLUDE = X:\MSTOOLS\H; X:\MSTOOLS\MFC\H;
LIB = X:\MSTOOLS\LIB; X:\MSTOOLS\MFC\LIB
PATH = X:\MSTOOLS\BIN
```

There are two methods of setting the user environment variables. For the first method, perform the following steps:

1. Open a Command Prompt window (located in the Main group).

2. Change to the *X:\MSTOOLS* directory; substitute *X:* with the drive letter that NT is installed on. Also substitute your directory for MSTOOLS if you chose an install directory other than the default.

3. Type SETENV X:\MSTOOLS and press (ENTER). Use the same substitution method as step 2. SETENV is a batch file that automatically sets the environment variables for you.

To use the second method, perform the following steps. You must be at the System window to complete these steps.

1. Type the variable (such as, CPU, Include) in the Variable edit control.

2. Type the value (such as, i386, X:\MSTOOLS...) in the Value edit control.

3. Click on the SET button (to the right of the edit controls).

4. Repeat steps 1 through 3 for all four environment variables.

Starting NMAKE

To execute NMAKE and build GENERIC.EXE, perform the following steps:

1. Open a Command Prompt window (if one isn't open already).

2. Change to the \CHAPTER2\2.1 directory. This is where the files for the GENERIC project reside.

3. Type NMAKE. NMAKE uses MAKEFILE as its input file if you do not specify a makefile on the command line.

That's it! You now should have several new files in the current directory. One of these files is GENERIC.EXE. Now let's run GENERIC.

RUNNING GENERIC

You can run GENERIC by typing GENERIC at the command line and pressing (ENTER). You should see a window comparable to the one shown in Figure 2-4. You can see the GENERIC icon by minimizing the application's window.

What Is Happening in GENERIC?

Now that we have our first Win32 application up and running, let's review what is going on inside of GENERIC.

The WinMain() function contains the code that fills the window class structure and registers the window class. The window class structure contains elements for the icon (GenericIcon) and the menu (GenericMenu). The

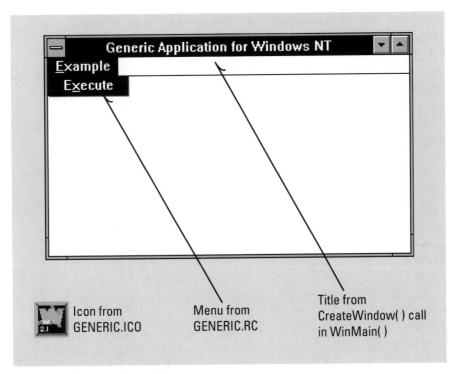

Figure 2-4 GENERIC in action

window is created with a call to CreateWindow() and displayed by a call to ShowWindow(). Finally the message loop is started.

The WndProc() function only processes one user message at this time: IDM_EXECUTE. It processes this message every time the user opens the *Example* menu, and clicks on *Execute*. In this minimum application, we simply return 0. We will add more menu options and start processing messages in the next example application.

That completes our coverage of the GENERIC project. If you have a grasp of what is going on in this example, you have a great start to the many example programs in this book.

SUMMARY

This chapter reviewed a minimal Windows 3.x program and introduced a minimal 32-bit Windows program. Using these two programs, you were able to compare and see some of the changes that were brought about in Win32 programming. We also looked at makefiles used with Microsoft's project management utility, NMAKE.

Windows 3.x applications usually consist of a module definition file, a header file, a resource file, and a source file. The module definition file defines characteristics of an executable file or dynamic link library, as well as resolving external references. The header file, although not mandatory, contains function prototypes, global variables, and define statements. They help keep your programs organized, especially in multiple file/module programs.

Resource files contain definitions of resources such as menus, dialog boxes, bitmaps, and icons. This file is compiled by a resource compiler. The source file contains the program itself. This file is compiled then linked with the resource file and several libraries.

In our minimal Windows 3.x example program, you saw how a window class was registered and the main window created in WinMain(). The window class contains a pointer to the main window procedure, in our case WndProc(). The WndProc() function is responsible for processing messages sent to the main window.

Our first Win32 application is very similar to the Windows 3.x application. The main differences are in the way previous instances are handled, the expansion of handles from 16 to 32 bits, and module definition files are optional. Windows 3.x applications can use the second parameter, *hPrevInstance,* of WinMain() to determine whether or not a previous instance of the same application is running. In Win32 *hPrevInstance* is always NULL because each instance runs in its own private address space.

The expansion of the size of a handle affects message packing in Win32. For example, *lParam* is consumed by the 32-bit handle. This resulted in moving the notification ID to *wParam*. In Windows 3.x *wParam* is a WORD containing the message ID. In Win32 *wParam* is a UINT (unsigned integer). An integer is 32 bits in Win32; the high word of *wParam* contains the notification ID and the lower word contains the *message id*. We used the LOWORD macro to extract the *message id* when processing the WM_COMMAND window message.

You also saw how to use makefiles in Win32. By including the NTWIN32.MAK file, you can use macros that aid in simplifying your makefiles. You can use the makefile for the GENERIC application (as well as the other files) as a template to start your own Win32 applications.

With the skeletal program structure changes out of the way, let's turn our attention to the way memory is handled in Win32 applications. The next chapter discusses how memory is managed in Windows NT and Win32 applications.

CHAPTER

3

Memory
Management

OK

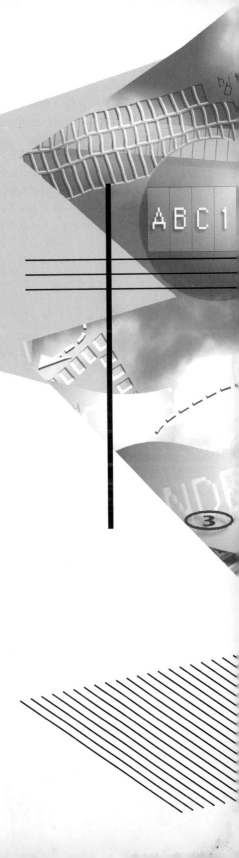

CHAPTER 3

Memory Management

Managing memory has changed significantly with the introduction of Windows NT. Most of the tasks involving memory are easier because of the introduction of 32-bit memory addressing (and the demise of the segment-offset memory schemes). On the other hand, the changes take a little getting used to. There are new API functions, new concepts, and a few new terms to learn while making the transition to 32-bit memory management. This chapter is designed to help you make the transition quickly.

This chapter starts with a comparison of Windows 3.x and Windows memory. You'll find that some Windows 3.x techniques can still be applied to Win32 applications (although the system handles the old techniques differently). We will also look at three example programs that demonstrate the new API functions. The last example is actually a set of two programs. These new functions provide you with control over heap memory, virtual memory, and shared memory.

Before we get into the details and differences of memory management, let's look at the topics that we will cover in this chapter.

CHAPTER OVERVIEW

Concepts Covered

◢ Addressing 32-bit memory

◢ Using the virtual memory manager (VMM)

◢ Managing heap memory

◢ Managing virtual memory

◢ file mapping (shared memory)

API Functions Covered

◢ VirtualAlloc()

◢ VirtualFree()

◢ VirtualProtect()

◢ VirtualQuery()

◢ HeapCreate()

◢ HeapDestroy()

◢ HeapAlloc()

◢ HeapFree()

◢ HeapSize()

◢ CreateFileMapping()

◢ OpenFileMapping()

◢ MapViewOfFile()

Data Types Covered

◢ MEMORY_BASIC_INFORMATION (structure)

Parameters Covered

◢ PAGE_NOACCESS

◢ PAGE_READWRITE

◢ PAGE_READONLY

◢ MEM_COMMIT

◢ MEM_DECOMMIT

◢ MEM_RELEASE

◢ FILE_MAP_READ

◢ FILE_MAP_WRITE

WINDOWS 3.X / WINDOWS NT MEMORY

Let's take a closer look at the new 32-bit memory scheme we discussed briefly in Chapter 1. Having a solid understanding of memory will help you make the right decisions in your projects. Nearly all applications need to allocate memory at run time (dynamic allocation). That's where this knowledge pays off.

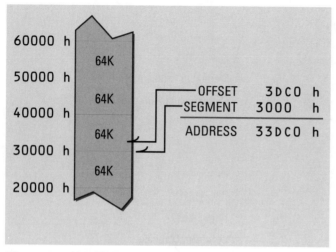

Figure 3-1 MS-DOS segmented memory

Windows 3.x and MS-DOS Memory

If you have been writing programs for IBM PCs and compatibles before you picked up this book, you undoubtedly have run into the segmented memory scheme. The early 16-bit microprocessor addressing forced this issue. Having only 16 bits to address memory resulted in a maximum range of 2^{16} bytes, or 65,536 bytes (64K). To access more than this amount, you had to use segments and offsets. Figure 3-1 shows the segment:offset scheme.

By combining a 16-bit segment value (shifted to the left 4 bits) with a 16-bit offset value, we ended up with a 20-bit value to address memory. These 20 bits covered a range of 2^{20} bytes, or 1,048,576 bytes (1M), which fit the early MS-DOS limit of 640K memory just fine.

In order to allocate and access memory using the above method, you must specify the segment and the offset. This created the need for compiler terms such as near and far, or local and global. The near and local terms referred to data within a specific segment, while the far and global terms referred to data outside a specific segment.

Compilers also had to deal with the need for multiple code and data segments in a program. This solution was the provision for various memory models. This lets us create programs that had code and/or data segments that were larger than one segment (64K). Most of the problems brought on by segmented memory were resolved by the compiler; however, some nasty, hard to track bugs came up anyway. This resulted in costly delays in many programming projects. In Windows NT, the segmented memory goes away!

Memory in Windows NT

Windows 3.x applications were forced into the segmented memory because Windows itself ran under MS-DOS. This is no longer true in Windows NT because Windows NT is the operating system. This introduces the 32-bit flat memory addressing scheme. The word flat means "not segmented." This new scheme results in memory that is easier to manage, as well as a huge span of addresses (232 bytes, or 4 gigabytes). The Windows NT kernel manages this memory with a virtual memory manager (VMM).

The Perspective of an Application in Windows NT

Each application in Windows NT sees a large range of memory addresses. This is shown in Figure 3-2. Note that even though the total 32-bit range of addresses is 4 gigabytes, only the lower 2 gigabytes is available to individual applications—still an enormous range compared to memory schemes of the past.

As the name implies, virtual memory is not real. It only represents values that a particular application sees. In order to see how the real memory is

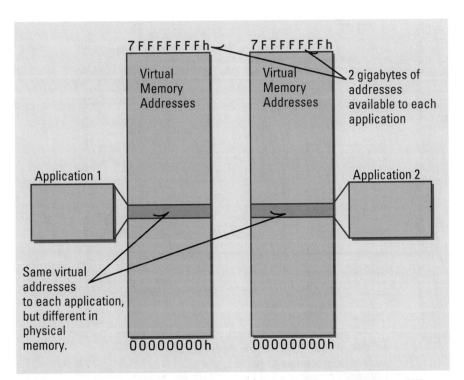

Figure 3-2 Virtual memory addresses for an application in Windows NT

addressed, we need to discuss the *virtual memory manager,* which is a part of the Windows NT kernel.

Virtual Memory and Physical Memory

The *virtual memory manager* is responsible for translating virtual memory addresses (which your application sees) to physical memory addresses (actual system RAM). Figure 3-3 shows this process. You, as the programmer, are isolated from this action. Your programs only need to handle virtual addresses; the NT kernel takes care of the rest.

Note that total memory storage is made up of two components: physical RAM installed and the system paging file. Another term for the system paging file is a *backing store.* The sum of these two storage values makes up the total amount of *physical storage.* For example, if you have 8 megabytes of RAM and a 20-megabyte system paging file, this results in a total storage of 28 megabytes.

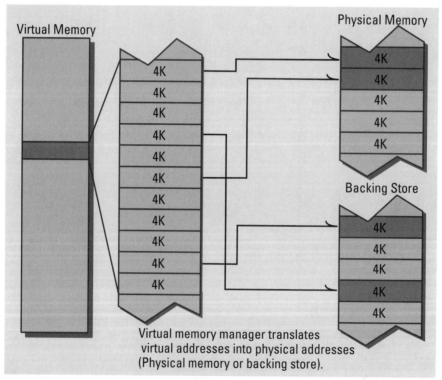

Figure 3-3 Windows NT virtual memory manager

ANATOMY OF VIRTUAL MEMORY

Virtual memory is broken up into 4K sections called pages. The virtual memory manager handles these pages by swapping them between physical memory and the backing store. The VMM has total control of where the pages reside in physical memory, as well as whether or not the page should be swapped out to the backing store. Figure 3-4 shows this action.

The VMM has some intelligence. Pages that have not been used recently are swapped to the backing store, while pages that are active remain in physical memory. The VMM maintains a table of all pages and makes its decision on a least recently used algorithm.

States of Virtual Memory Pages

Recall that each application has 2 gigabytes of virtual memory addresses to work with. This large range is broken up into 4K pages (over 500,000 of

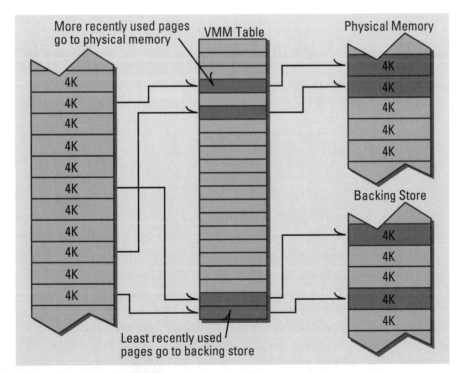

Figure 3-4 How the VMM controls storage

them). Each of these pages has a particular state at any given time. The three states are *free, reserved,* and *committed.*

Free Pages

A free page is a 4K segment that has not been reserved or committed. All pages are free when your application starts, except for those that are taken up by the application itself. A reserved page that is released becomes a free page.

Reserved Pages

A reserved page is a 4K segment that is allocated, but no physical storage exists yet. You can reserve several pages to allocate a block of contiguous memory addresses. You cannot read or write to a reserved page. Doing so will result in a *page fault.* You can handle page faults by using structured exception handlers in your code. An example of exception handling is covered in the MEMORY2 example later in this chapter. A committed page that is decommited becomes a reserved page.

Committed Pages

A committed page is a 4K segment that has physical storage allocated. Committed pages can have one of three types of access protection: no access, read only access, and read/write access. The committed page state is the only one of the three that allows reading and writing to the memory. This makes sense because it is also the only page for which physical storage exists.

THE HEAP

Each running application or DLL in Windows NT can create a heap to dynamically allocate memory. A heap is created by the system (based on the DEF file or defaults) for applications; however, DLLs must manage their own private heap. Nevertheless you can still create a heap in a Win32 application. The size of the heap is limited to the total storage (physical memory + backing store). The heap is private to the application that created it, that is, no other running application can access the heap data. Figure 3-5 shows the heap in action.

Note that the heap has an initial number of committed pages. If your application reaches the bounds of this initial value, additional pages are

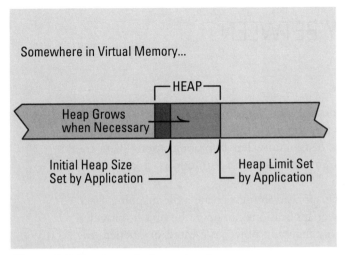

Somewhere in Virtual Memory...

Figure 3-5 The heap (private data)

automatically allocated by the operating system (up to the limit specified for the application). You do not have to commit additional pages within your code.

Table 3-1 shows the fundamental differences between virtual memory and heap memory management.

Note that you can still allocate heap memory by using the standard C library functions (malloc(), free(), and so on), the Global and Local functions from Windows 3.x (GlobalAlloc(), LocalAlloc()), or the new heap functions in the Win32 API (HeapAlloc). All new types of allocation are demonstrated in the examples that follow.

Memory Type	Functions	Page Control By	Contiguous?
Heap	Standard C Global/Local Heap	NT Kernel	No
Virtual	Virtual	Application	Yes

Table 3-1 Virtual memory and heap memory management differences

SHARED MEMORY BETWEEN APPLICATIONS

Two applications can share memory in Windows NT. The Win32 API provides a set of functions that accomplish this. The process is called file mapping, because the same set of functions lets two applications share the same file. Given the right parameters, the same functions create shared memory instead of a shared file.

To create shared memory, one application must create a file mapping *object*. The object is given a name. Other applications can open the object, provided they know the name. Once a file mapping object is created or opened, the applications can create, or *map,* a view to the file (or memory). At this point both applications can read or write to the file. Each application is using its own set of memory addresses, although the file exists in physical memory. Figure 3-6 shows how two applications share memory.

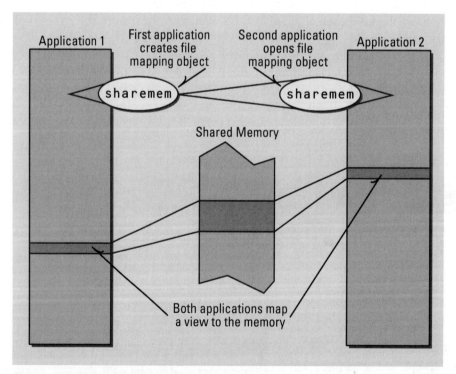

Figure 3-6 Memory sharing between applications

The last example program in this chapter demonstrates memory sharing between applications.

HEAP MANAGEMENT FUNCTIONS

Our first example program, MEMORY1, demonstrates the heap allocation functions that are introduced by the Win32 API. The program will create a heap, allocate memory from the heap, free allocated memory, test the size of heap allocations, and destroy the heap upon exit. Before we get into the program itself, let's take a close look at each of the new heap functions.

HeapCreate()

The HeapCreate() function creates a private heap of a specified size. The function requires three parameters for behavior, initial size, and maximum size. It also returns a handle to the heap. Listing 3-1 shows the syntax for the HeapCreate() function along with an example call.

Listing 3-1 HeapCreate() syntax and example call

```
/* HeapCreate() Syntax */
HANDLE HeapCreate (DWORD dwHeap, DWORD dwInitial, DWORD dwMaximum)

/* Example Call to HeapCreate */
HANDLE hHeap;

hHeap = HeapCreate (NULL, 0x1000, 0x4000);
```

Note that the HeapCreate() function returns a handle to the heap. Allocation requests are made using this handle. Table 3-2 shows a description of the three parameters in HeapCreate().

For our example call in Listing 3-1, the result would be an initial heap size of 0x1000h (4K) and a maximum heap size of 0X4000 (16K). The handle is assigned to *hHeap*, which will be used in the remaining heap management functions. The HeapCreate() function returns NULL if the system cannot create the heap. The first parameter, set to NULL, indicates that only one thread will access the heap at any given time. (Multithreaded programs are covered in Chapter 6, Multitasking in Windows NT.)

Now that the heap has been created, let's look at the other functions that rely on a valid handle.

Parameter	Description
dwHeap	Describes the behavior of the heap. There are only two possible values: NULL and HEAP_SERIALIZE. Use NULL for applications that only allow one thread to access the heap at a time. Use HEAP_SERIALIZE for applications that allow multiple threads to access the heap.
dwInitial	Sets the initial (committed) size of the heap in bytes. The size of the heap can grow beyond this initial size, up to the amount specified in dwMaximum.
dwMaximum	Sets the maximum size (in bytes) of the heap. If this value is set to NULL, the heap will be limited only by physical memory. Allocation requests will fail after the heap has reached this maximum.

Table 3-2 HeapCreate() parameters

The amount of heap available to your application will be slightly less than the exact amount requested. The NT operating system uses a portion of the heap to allocate heap support structures.

HeapAlloc()

The HeapAlloc() function allocates memory from the heap (similar to malloc() or GlobalAlloc()). The function requires two parameters: the handle to the heap and the size (in bytes) being requested. Listing 3-2 shows the syntax for the HeapAlloc() function and an example call.

Listing 3-2 HeapAlloc() syntax and example call

```
/* HeapAlloc() Syntax */
LPSTR HeapAlloc (HANDLE hHeap, DWORD  dwFlags, DWORD dwbytes);

/* Example Call to HeapAlloc */
LPSTR lpAlloc;

lpAlloc = HeapAlloc (hHeap, HEAP_ZERO_MEMORY 0x100);
```

This function returns a long pointer to a string that points to the first byte of the allocated heap memory. You can use this pointer to check the size of

Parameter	Description
hHeap	Handle of the heap returned by HeapAlloc().
dwFlags	Heap allocation control flags.
dwAlloc	The size of the allocation request in bytes.

Table 3-3 HeapAlloc() parameters

the allocation using HeapSize(), as well as free the allocation with HeapFree(). Table 3-3 shows the parameters for HeapAlloc.

Our example call in Listing 3-2 would result in a heap allocation request of 0x100h bytes, or 256 bytes. A pointer to the first byte in the allocation is assigned to *lpAlloc*. The return value of HeapAlloc() is NULL if the allocation fails.

HeapSize()

The HeapSize() function checks the actual size of a previous call to HeapAlloc(). The function requires two parameters: the handle to the heap and a pointer to the specific allocation. Listing 3-3 shows the syntax for the HeapSize() function and an example call.

Listing 3-3 HeapSize() syntax and example call

```
/* HeapSize() Syntax */
DWORD HeapSize (HANDLE hHeap, DWORD dwFlags, LPSTR lpMem);)

/* Example Call to HeapSize*/
DWORD      dwSize;

dwSize = HeapSize (hHeap, 0, lpAlloc);
```

This function returns a DWORD with the size of a specific allocation. You can use this pointer to check the size of the allocation. Table 3-4 shows the parameters for HeapSize.

Our example call in Listing 3-3 would check the size of the allocation pointed to by *lpAlloc*. If it exists the size of the allocation is assigned to *dwSize*. The return value of HeapSize() is NULL if the specific allocation does not exist.

Parameter	Description
hHeap	Handle of the heap returned by HeapSize().
dwFlags	Must be zero; reserved for future use.
lpMem	Pointer to a specific allocation returned by HeapAlloc().

Table 3-4 HeapSize() parameters

HeapFree()

The HeapFree() function frees memory allocated by HeapAlloc(), similar to free() or GlobalFree(). The function requires two parameters: the handle to the heap and a long pointer to the first byte of the allocation. Listing 3-4 shows the syntax for the HeapFree() function and an example call.

Listing 3-4 HeapFree() syntax and example call

```
/* HeapFree() Syntax */
BOOL HeapFree (HANDLE hHeap, DWORD dwFlags, LPSTR lpMem);

/* Example Call to HeapFree */
HeapFree (hHeap, 0, lpAlloc);
```

This function returns a Boolean value indicating success or failure. Table 3-5 shows the parameters for HeapFree().

Our example call in Listing 3-4 would result in the heap allocation pointed to by *lpAlloc* being released. You can use the Boolean return value to verify that the memory has been freed. The return value of HeapFree() is TRUE on success, and FALSE on failure.

HeapDestroy()

The HeapDestroy() function destroys the heap created by HeapCreate(). The function only requires one parameter: the handle to the heap. Listing 3-5 shows the syntax for the HeapDestroy() function and an example call.

Parameter	Description
hHeap	Handle of the heap returned by HeapFree().
dwFlags	Heap Freedom flags—must be 0 for now.
lpMem	Pointer to a specific allocation returned by HeapAlloc().

Table 3-5 HeapFree() parameters

Listing 3-5 HeapDestroy() syntax and example call

```
/* HeapDestroy() Syntax */
BOOL HeapDestroy (HANDLE hHeap)

/* Example Call to HeapDestroy */
HeapDestroy (hHeap);
```

This function returns a Boolean value indicating success or failure. The function requires a valid handle to a heap.

Our example call in Listing 3-5 would result in the heap identified by the handle *hHeap* being destroyed. Any allocations that have not been freed with HeapFree() are destroyed as well. You can use the Boolean return value to verify that the heap has been destroyed. The return value of HeapDestroy() is TRUE on success, and FALSE on failure.

The Heap Functions in Action

Figure 3-7 shows an example of the heap functions in action. Note that all subsequent functions to HeapCreate() require the handle to the heap. Once this handle is obtained, you can use the handle to allocate blocks of memory to the heap. The exact location of the allocation is determined by the operating system. Allocations are not necessarily contiguous.

Calls to HeapFree() do not have to be in any particular order. You can free any allocation at any time, provided you have a handle to the heap and a pointer to the specific allocation. When HeapDestroy() is called, any remaining allocations are destroyed in the process.

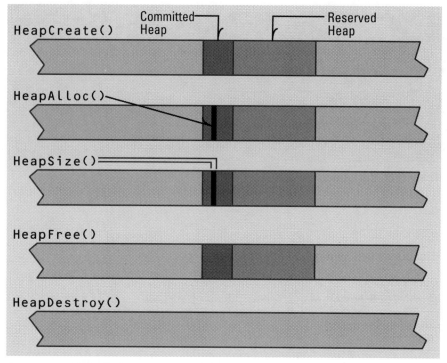

Figure 3-7 Heap functions in action

MEMORY1—HEAP DEMONSTRATION

Our first example program demonstrates each of the heap management functions. Review Listings 3-6, 3-7, and 3-8 before building MEMORY1. The calls to the heap functions are in boldface to highlight them. The source file will make much more sense if we take a look at the resource script and include files first.

MEMORY1.RC—Resource Script

The resource script for MEMORY1 is fairly straightforward. The icon used for this project is MEMORY1.ICO and is assigned the name *Memory1Icon*. The script for the menu follows and is assigned the name *Memory1Menu*.

The menu contains one popup named Heap Control. The submenu for this popup contains five MENUITEMs. There is a selection for each of the heap management functions. Note that all but the *Create Heap* selection are grayed initially. No other selections are valid until a heap is created.

Listing 3-6 MEMORY1.RC

```
#include "windows.h"
#include "memory1.h"

Memory1Icon ICON  memory1.ico

Memory1Menu MENU
    BEGIN
        POPUP "&Heap Control"
        BEGIN
            MENUITEM "&Create Heap",          IDM_CREATE_HEAP
            MENUITEM "&Allocate Heap Space",  IDM_HEAP_ALLOC, GRAYED
            MENUITEM "&Free Heap Space",      IDM_HEAP_FREE, GRAYED
            MENUITEM "Allocation &Status",    IDM_HEAP_SIZE, GRAYED
            MENUITEM "&Destroy Heap",         IDM_DESTROY_HEAP, GRAYED
        END
    END
```

MEMORY1.H—Header File

The header file contains the menu defines for the five menu options. It also contains the standard definition for the window procedure, WndProc().

Listing 3-7 MEMORY1.H

```
/* memory1.h -- Header file for memory1.c and memory1.rc */

/* Menu defines */
#define IDM_CREATE_HEAP     1
#define IDM_HEAP_ALLOC      2
#define IDM_HEAP_FREE       3
#define IDM_HEAP_SIZE       4
#define IDM_DESTROY_HEAP    5

/* Function prototype */
LONG APIENTRY WndProc (HWND, UINT, UINT, LONG);

/* Global Variables */
HANDLE      ghInst;
HANDLE      ghWnd;
```

MEMORY1.C—Source File

This is the complete listing of the MEMORY1 source file. The WinMain()
function is similar to the one used in Chapter 2's example program. The only
difference is the icon, menu, and window class names. The new activity in
this program is occurring in the WndProc() function. A complete description
of the program follows this listing.

Listing 3-8 MEMORY1.C

```
/* memory1.c      Heap Example for Win32 */

#include <windows.h>            /* include for Win32 apps */
#include "memory1.h"            /* include for memory1.c */

int APIENTRY WinMain (HANDLE hInstance, HANDLE hPrevInstance, LPSTR lpCmdLine, int nCmdShow)
{
    MSG  msg;
    WNDCLASS wndclass;

    UNREFERENCED_PARAMETER( lpCmdLine );                /* Prevent compiler warnings */
    UNREFERENCED_PARAMETER( hPrevInstance );

    ghInst = hInstance;                                 /* Global Instance Handle */

    wndclass.style = CS_HREDRAW | CS_VREDRAW;    /* Fill in window class structure */
    wndclass.lpfnWndProc = (WNDPROC)WndProc;
    wndclass.cbClsExtra = 0;
    wndclass.cbWndExtra = 0;
    wndclass.hInstance = ghInst;
    wndclass.hIcon = LoadIcon (ghInst, "Memory1Icon"); /* Memory1 Icon */
    wndclass.hCursor = LoadCursor (NULL, IDC_ARROW);
    wndclass.hbrBackground = GetStockObject (WHITE_BRUSH);
    wndclass.lpszMenuName = "Memory1Menu";              /* Memory1 menu */
    wndclass.lpszClassName = "Memory1Class";

    RegisterClass(&wndclass);

    ghWnd = CreateWindow ("Memory1Class",               /* Create main window */
              "Memory1--Demonstrating Heap Functions",  /* Title bar text */
              WS_OVERLAPPEDWINDOW,
              CW_USEDEFAULT,
              CW_USEDEFAULT,
              CW_USEDEFAULT,
              CW_USEDEFAULT,
              NULL,
              NULL,
              hInstance,
              NULL);
```

```
        ShowWindow(ghWnd, nCmdShow);                    /* Display window */

        while (GetMessage (&msg, NULL, 0, 0))           /* Message Loop */
        {
            TranslateMessage (&msg);
            DispatchMessage (&msg);
        }

        return (msg.wParam);                            /* Return exit code */

}

/* WndProc - Main Window Procedure for memory1.c */

LONG APIENTRY WndProc (HWND hWnd, UINT message, UINT wParam, LONG lParam)
{

HDC             hDC;
static HMENU    hMenu;                          /* Handle to menu */
static HANDLE   hHeap;                          /* Handle to heap */
static LPSTR    lpHeapPointer[10];              /* Array of heap allocation pointers */
char            cBuf[128];                      /* Buffer for output message */
int             iMenuEnable, iHeapAlloc;        /* Loop variables */
DWORD           dwHeapSize;

    switch (message)
    {

        case WM_CREATE:
            hMenu = GetMenu (hWnd);             /* Assign static handle to main menu */
            break;

        case WM_COMMAND:
            switch (LOWORD(wParam))             /* Extract LOWORD of wParam for Win32) */
            {
                case IDM_CREATE_HEAP:           /* Create 4K/64K heap and adjust menu */
                    hHeap = HeapCreate (0, 0x1000, 0x10000);
                    EnableMenuItem (hMenu,IDM_CREATE_HEAP, MF_BYCOMMAND | MF_GRAYED);
                    EnableMenuItem (hMenu,IDM_HEAP_ALLOC, MF_BYCOMMAND | MF_ENABLED);
                    EnableMenuItem (hMenu,IDM_DESTROY_HEAP, MF_BYCOMMAND | MF_ENABLED);
                    break;
                case IDM_HEAP_ALLOC:            /* Make 10 allocations to heap; adjust menu */
                    for (iHeapAlloc = 0; iHeapAlloc < 10; iHeapAlloc++)
                        lpHeapPointer[iHeapAlloc] = HeapAlloc (hHeap, HEAP_ZERO_MEMORY,
                                                     (DWORD) (iHeapAlloc * 100) + 100);
                    EnableMenuItem (hMenu,IDM_HEAP_ALLOC, MF_BYCOMMAND | MF_GRAYED);
                    EnableMenuItem (hMenu,IDM_HEAP_FREE, MF_BYCOMMAND | MF_ENABLED);
                    EnableMenuItem (hMenu,IDM_HEAP_SIZE, MF_BYCOMMAND | MF_ENABLED);
                    break;
                case IDM_HEAP_FREE:             /* Free 10 allocations to heap, adjust menu */
                    for (iHeapAlloc = 0; iHeapAlloc < 10; iHeapAlloc++)
                        HeapFree (hHeap, 0, lpHeapPointer [iHeapAlloc]);
```

continued on next page

continued from previous page

```
                    EnableMenuItem (hMenu,IDM_HEAP_FREE, MF_BYCOMMAND | MF_GRAYED);
                    EnableMenuItem (hMenu,IDM_HEAP_ALLOC, MF_BYCOMMAND | MF_ENABLED);
                    EnableMenuItem (hMenu,IDM_HEAP_SIZE, MF_BYCOMMAND | MF_GRAYED);
                    InvalidateRect (hWnd, NULL, TRUE);
                    break;
                case IDM_HEAP_SIZE:          /* Check size of 10 allocations */
                    for (iHeapAlloc = 0; iHeapAlloc < 10; iHeapAlloc++)
                    {
                        dwHeapSize = HeapSize (hHeap, 0, lpHeapPointer [iHeapAlloc]);
                        wsprintf (cBuf, "The heap request address is %lX and its size is %u bytes.",
                                  lpHeapPointer [iHeapAlloc], dwHeapSize);
                        hDC = GetDC (hWnd);
                        TextOut (hDC, 0, iHeapAlloc * 20, cBuf, lstrlen (cBuf));
                        ReleaseDC (hWnd, hDC);
                    }
                    break;
                case IDM_DESTROY_HEAP:        /* Destroy heap, adjust menu */
                    HeapDestroy (hHeap);
                   for (iMenuEnable = IDM_HEAP_ALLOC; iMenuEnable <= IDM_DESTROY_HEAP; iMenuEnable ++)
                        EnableMenuItem (hMenu,iMenuEnable, MF_BYCOMMAND | MF_GRAYED);
                    EnableMenuItem (hMenu,IDM_CREATE_HEAP, MF_BYCOMMAND | MF_ENABLED);
                    InvalidateRect (hWnd, NULL, TRUE);
                    break;
            }
            break;

        case WM_DESTROY:                      /* No cleanup necessary */
            PostQuitMessage (0);
            return (0);

        default:
            return DefWindowProc (hWnd, message, wParam, lParam);

    }

return (0L);
}
```

Initialization of MEMORY1

Several variables are declared at the top of WndProc(). Of particular interest are *hHeap, lpHeapPointer,* and *dwHeapSize.* The *hHeap* variable is declared as static and is used to store the handle provided by a call to HeapCreate(). We also declare an array of ten pointers of the LPSTR type. We call HeapAlloc() ten times during execution; the pointers track the ten allocations. We will use the *dwHeapSize* variable to store the return value from HeapSize().

When the main window is created, we obtain a handle to the main menu with a call to GetMenu(). The result is stored in the static handle *hMenu.* We use this handle in calls to EnableMenuItem() to enable or disable menu items based on menu selections. At first, the only selection that is enabled is *Create Heap*. Let's take a look at what happens when the user selects *Create Heap*.

The Heap Is Created

When the user chooses *Create Heap*, a WM_COMMAND message is sent to WndProc(). The LOWORD of *wParam* is extracted and used in a *switch* statement. The *message id* contains the menu selection IDM_CREATE_HEAP. The first line of the code that processes this message is

```
hHeap = HeapCreate (0, 0x1000, 0x10000);
```

In this program we create a heap with an initial size of 4K (0x1000h) and a maximum size of 64K (0x10000h). The first parameter is set to NULL, indicating that only one thread will access the heap at a time. The return value is assigned to the static variable *hHeap*. We now have a valid handle that we can use with the rest of the heap management functions. Technically we should have tested the return value to ensure a successful call to HeapCreate(). It is left out of this example for clarity. You should always test handles for validity before using them in other function calls.

The next three lines adjust the menu selections with calls to EnableMenuItem(). The first call disables (MF_GRAYED) the *Create Heap* selection. We don't want to allow the user to create a second heap (although this is possible). The remaining calls enable (MF_ENABLED) the *Allocate Heap Space* and *Destroy Heap* selections. We don't want to enable the other selections just yet, because we have not allocated any heap memory. Let's allocate some memory from the heap we just created.

Allocating Heap Space

The next section of code executes when the user selects *Allocate Heap Space* from the menu. This sends a *message id* of IDM_HEAP_ALLOC. We use an *if* statement to make ten calls to HeapAlloc(). We use the *iHeapAlloc* integer for the loop variable. The line that actually makes the call is:

```
lpHeapPointer[iHeapAlloc] = HeapAlloc (hHeap, HEAP_ZERO_MEMORY, (DWORD) (iHeapAlloc * 100) + 100);
```

The HeapAlloc() function is passed three parameters. The first, *hHeap*, is the handle of the heap returned from HeapCreate(). The second, HEAP_ZERO_MEMORY, is reserved for future use. The third value is the loop variable, multiplied by 100, plus 100. The first time through the *if* loop, *iHeapAlloc* is 0. The result of the equation is (0 times 100)+100, or 100. The result is cast to a DWORD, which HeapAlloc() expects. This results in the allocation of a 100-byte block of memory. The return value of HeapAlloc() is assigned to the pointer array. Recall that *lpHeapPointer* is an array of ten LPSTR.

This continues nine additional times. Each time, the amount of memory goes up by 100 and the array is indexed to the next pointer. We now have ten pointers to ten allocations.

The menu is adjusted once again. We no longer allow the user to allocate heap space. We do not want to write over the valid pointers stored in the array. We also enable the *Free Heap Space* and *Allocation Status* selections since we now have heap memory allocated. Let's look at the *Free Heap Space* selection.

Freeing Heap Space

If the user selects *Free Heap Space,* a loop similar to the allocation loop is used. Only this time, we are calling the HeapFree() function each time through the loop. The line that performs the freeing looks like this:

```
HeapFree (hHeap, 0, lpHeapPointer [iHeapAlloc]);
```

Each call to HeapFree() is passed three parameters. The first being the handle to the heap. The second parameter, 0, is reserved for future use. The third is a pointer from the array. The array is indexed using the loop variable *iHeapAlloc.* The heap allocations do not have to be freed in the order they were allocated. In this example, that is the case; however, it is not mandatory.

The menu is adjusted so the user can once again allocate heap space. The selections to free and test the heap size are disabled.

Checking the Size of the Allocations

The fourth menu selection, *Allocation Status,* contains the code that writes to the client area. The same loop is executed ten times, each time returning a value with the following line:

```
dwHeapSize = HeapSize (hHeap, 0, lpHeapPointer [iHeapAlloc]);
```

The HeapSize() function is called ten times. Each time, the function is passed three parameters: the heap handle, 0 (reserved for future use), and a pointer to a specific allocation. Again, the *iHeapAlloc* loop variable indexes through the array of pointers.

Also, for each iteration of the loop, a string is copied to a buffer. The string indicates the pointer *(lpHeapPointer[])* for the allocation and the size *(dwHeapSize)* of the allocation. Calls to TextOut() display the ten strings on the client area.

Destroying the Heap

The last menu *message id* to process is IDM_DESTROY_HEAP. The HeapDestroy() function is called with the handle to the heap as its only parameter. The bottom four menu items are disabled (grayed) using *iMenuEnable* loop variable. This returns the program to the state it was in upon initialization.

Building and Running MEMORY1

By now you should be familiar with building applications with NMAKE. Open a Command Prompt window and change to the \CHAPTER3\3.1 subdirectory. Type NMAKE and press (ENTER). The makefile is not different from the one we used in Chapter 2, except for the filenames.

Once the program is built, type MEMORY1 and press (ENTER). Try out the menu selections while reviewing the code in Listing 3-8. Figure 3-8 shows a typical output from MEMORY1 when *Allocation Status* is selected.

If you look closely at the addresses of the heap allocations, you may notice that there are more bytes between the allocations than the allocation itself. For example, the difference between the first allocation and the second is 128 bytes, even though only 100 bytes were allocated. The Windows NT operating system is responsible for allocating memory from the heap. You can see by this example that the heap is not contiguous.

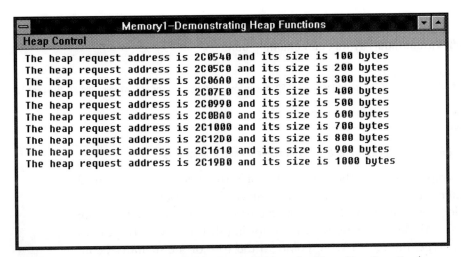

Figure 3-8 MEMORY1—Allocation Status (using the HeapSize function)

If your application needs a contiguous set of addresses, or you want more control over where specific data is stored, you should use the virtual memory management functions.

VIRTUAL MEMORY MANAGEMENT FUNCTIONS

The second example program in this chapter, MEMORY2, demonstrates the virtual memory management functions. The program creates a block of virtual memory addresses. With the menu we can: change the state (free, reserved, committed) of the memory, change the access level of the memory (no access, read only, read/write), and write to the memory if the right conditions exist. Let's look at the functions that control virtual memory management.

VirtualAlloc()

You can use the VirtualAlloc() function to reserve, or to reserve *and* commit a block of memory addresses. The function requires four parameters for starting address, size in bytes, type of allocation, and access protection. Listing 3-9 shows the syntax and an example call to VirtualAlloc().

Listing 3-9 VirtualAlloc() syntax and example call

```
/* VirtualAlloc() Syntax */
LPVOID VirtualAlloc (LPVOID lpvAddress, DWORD dwRegion, DWORD dwAllocationType, DWORD Protect);

/* Example Call to VirtualAlloc() */
CHAR *base;

base = VirtualAlloc (NULL, 0x1000, MEM_RESERVE, PAGE_NOACCESS);
```

This example call shows the return value of VirtualAlloc() being assigned to a pointer variable of the CHAR type. Since the function prototype of VirtualAlloc() is type LPVOID, any data type could have been used. We are choosing CHAR here because we will be storing that data type. Regardless of the data type, the return value points to the base of the memory being allocated.

The VirtualAlloc() function can be called more than once for the same block of memory. For example, you can call it a first time to reserve a block of addresses. Then you can call it again (using the base return from the first call) to commit the block to physical storage. Normally several pages are reserved, then individual pages are committed as they are required. Committing a large number of unnecessary pages can affect the performance of other applications.

VirtualAlloc() has a fairly complex parameter list. Table 3-6 shows a description of these parameters, and the possible values for each.

The example call in Listing 3-9 would result in a 4K (0x1000), or a one page region of addresses being reserved (MEM_RESERVE). The first parameter in the call is NULL, resulting in the operating system assigning the starting address. The last parameter is set to PAGE_NOACCESS, which is required for memory being reserved with VirtualAlloc(). Recall that reserved pages are not assigned physical memory, they are just a range of virtual *addresses.*

For the example in Listing 3-9, a subsequent call to VirtualAlloc() is required in order to commit the region to physical storage. Here is an example of such a call:

```
VirtualAlloc (base, 0x1000, MEM_COMMIT, PAGE_READWRITE);
```

Parameter	Description
lpvAddress	Desired starting address of the region. Setting this value to NULL results in the operating system choosing the starting address. If you specify an address, the address is adjusted to a page boundary. NULL is usually sufficient.
dwRegion	The size of the region in bytes. This value is rounded up to the next page boundary.
dwAllocationType	The type of allocation. Set to MEM_RESERVE to reserve the region. Set to MEM_COMMIT on a second call to commit the region. Set to MEM_RESERVE | MEM_COMMIT to commit the region in a single call.
dwProtect	The protection type of the region. Set to PAGE_NOACCESS if no access is allowed. Set to PAGE_READONLY to allow only reading from the region. Set to PAGE_READWRITE to allow reading and writing from the region. Must be set to PAGE_NOACCESS if dwAllocation type is MEM_RESERVE.

Table 3-6 VirtualAlloc() parameters

Now the base address returned in the first call is used as the *lpvAddress* parameter. The *dwRegion* parameter is still 0x1000 (4K), although you can commit a portion of the reserved region if desired. The *dwAllocation* parameter is set to MEM_COMMIT specifying that the memory is to be committed to physical storage. The *dwProtect* parameter is set to PAGE_READWRITE. This value could have been set to any of the three values listed in Table 3-6.

Now that we can reserve and commit a virtual memory region, let's see how we can remove it.

VirtualFree()

The VirtualFree() function can also be used in stages, as with the VirtualAlloc() function. This function requires three parameters: a pointer to the base of the region, the size of the region to be freed, and the type of free. It returns a Boolean value that you can test for success or failure of the function call; TRUE indicates success and FALSE indicates failure.

Listing 3-10 shows the syntax and two example calls to VirtualFree(). The first call decommits the region, while the second call releases the region.

Listing 3-10 VirtualFree() syntax and example calls

```
/* VirtualFree() Syntax */
BOOL VirtualFree (LPVOID lpvAddress, DWORD dwSize, DWORD dwFreeType);

/* Example Calls to VirtualFree() */

VirtualFree (base, 0, MEM_DECOMMIT); /* Decommits a region; base is still valid */

VirtualFree (base, 0, MEM_RELEASE);  /* Releases a region; base no longer valid */
```

The first example call simply *decommits* a region of virtual memory. This assumes that the region specified by *base* is already committed. The second example call releases the region; the second parameter must be 0 if the third parameter is MEM_RELEASE. The *base* region in the second call can be committed or reserved memory. The base pointer is invalid after the second example call. This is because the virtual memory page is now *free,* not reserved or committed.

Let's take a look at the parameters for the VirtualFree() function. Table 3-7 shows these parameters and their values.

The example call in Listing 3-9 allocated a 4K region. This amounts to a single page on x86 systems. Normally you will use the virtual memory

Parameter	Description
lpvAddress	Starting address of the region to be freed. This value is obtained as the return value of VirtualAlloc() or can be any valid address within the range of allocated pages.
dwSize	Size of region to be freed in bytes. This value is rounded up by the operating system to the next page boundary. This value must be 0 if dwFreeType is MEM_RELEASE.
dwFreeType	The type of free requested. Set this value to MEM_DECOMMIT to change the state from committed to reserved. Set the value to MEM_RELEASE to change the state from committed to released.

Table 3-7 VirtualFree() parameters

management functions with multiple pages of virtual memory. Figure 3-9 illustrates how you can use VirtualAlloc() and VirtualFree() on multiple pages of memory.

VirtualProtect()

The VirtualProtect() enables you to dynamically control the access protection value of a region of committed pages only. You cannot change the access protection of free or reserved pages. This function requires four parameters: the starting address of the region, the size of the region in bytes, the new access protection, and a pointer to store the old protection value. Listing 3-11 shows the syntax and example call for the VirtualProtect() function.

Listing 3-11 VirtualProtect() syntax and example call

```
/* VirtualProtect() Syntax */
BOOL VirtualProtect (LPVOID lpvAddress, DWORD dwRegion, DWORD dwNewProtect, PDWORD
pdwOldProtect);

/* Example Call to VirtualProtect() */
DWORD pdwOldProtect;

VirtualProtect (base, 0x1000, PAGE_READWRITE, &pdwOldProtect);
```

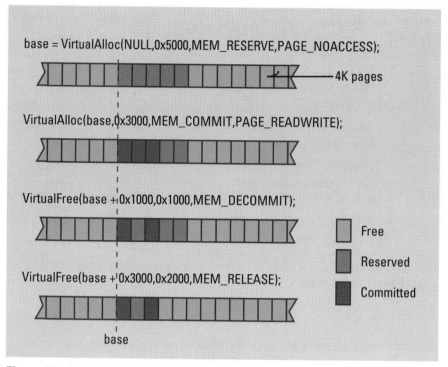

Figure 3-9 Using virtual functions with multiple pages

The base value and the entire range of pages must be committed for the function to successfully change the access protection. In the example shown in Listing 3-11, only one page exists. If the page is committed, the access protection is changed to PAGE_READWRITE and VirtualProtect() returns TRUE. If the page is free or reserved or if the address is invalid, there is no change in access and the function returns FALSE.

Table 3-8 shows the VirtualProtect() parameters and their possible values.

Like VirtualAlloc() and VirtualFree(), this function can specify more than one page. It is important to note that any committed page, or portion of a committed page, specified by the *lpvAddress* and *dwRegion* parameter combination, will result in all of the pages being affected by the access change. Figure 3-10 shows this effect.

Parameter	Description
lpvAddress	Starting address of the region to change access protection. This value is obtained as the return value of VirtualAlloc(), or can be any valid address within the range of allocated pages.
dwRegion	Size of region to change access protection, in bytes. If the region spans over a page boundary, both pages must be committed and access protection for both will change.
dwNewProtect	New access protection value. Can be PAGE_NOACCESS, PAGE_READONLY, or PAGE_READWRITE.
pdwOldProtect	Pointer to old access protection value. This parameter must point to a valid address.

Table 3-8 VirtualProtect() parameters

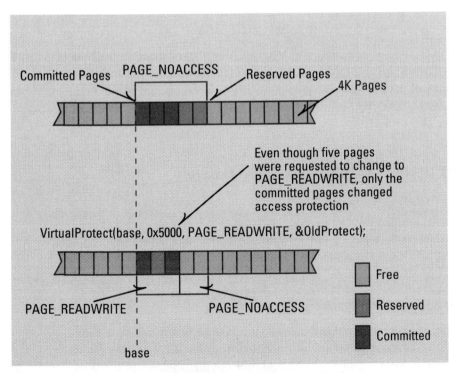

Figure 3-10 VirtualProtect() effects on multiple committed pages

VirtualQuery()

The VirtualQuery() function retrieves information about the page state and access protection values of allocated pages. The function will scan upward from the base address until it finds a page with a different state or access protection. For example, if you called VirtualQuery() to return the status of pages, and the first three pages each had a different access protection, the return value would indicate only the first page's information.

VirtualQuery() requires three parameters: the base address of the region, a pointer to a buffer that stores the information, and the length of the buffer in the second parameter. Listing 3-12 shows the syntax and an example call to VirtualQuery().

Listing 3-12 VirtualQuery() syntax and example call

```
/* VirtualQuery() Syntax */
DWORD VirtualQuery (LPVOID lpvAddress, PMEMORY_BASIC_INFORMATION lpBuffer, DWORD dwLength);

/* Example Call to VirtualQuery() */
MEMORY_BASIC_INFORMATION MemInfo;

VirtualQuery (base, &MemInfo, sizeof (MEMORY_BASIC_INFORMATION));
```

A new data type is required for VirtualQuery(), a structure named MEMORY_BASIC_INFORMATION. Before we look at the parameter to this function call, let's look at the details of this new structure. Listing 3-13 shows the MEMORY_BASIC_INFORMATION structure. This structure is defined in WINNT.H.

Listing 3-13 MEMORY_BASIC_INFORMATION structure

```
typedef struct _MEMORY_BASIC_INFORMATION {
    PVOID BaseAddress;          /* base address of region specified in VirtualQuery */
    PVOID AllocationBase;       /* allocation base of entire region */
    DWORD AllocationProtect;    /* original protection when allocated */
    DWORD RegionSize;           /* size of region with like attributes */
    DWORD State;                /* MEM_FREE, MEM_RESERVE, or MEM_COMMIT */
    DWORD Protect;              /* PAGE_NOACCESS, PAGE_READONLY, or PAGE_READWRITE */
    DWORD Type;                 /* only MEM_PRIVATE allowed */
} MEMORY_BASIC_INFORMATION, *PMEMORY_BASIC_INFORMATION;
```

Using the example call in Listing 3-12, the system fills in the structure, MemInfo. You can then access any of the structure elements. For example if MemInfo.State = MEM_FREE, this would indicate that the region contains free pages.

Let's now take a look at the three VirtualQuery() parameters and their possible values, now that you've seen the contents of MEMORY_BASIC_INFORMATION. Table 3-9 shows the parameters.

The next example program will shed some light on the usage of VirtualQuery() and other virtual memory management functions.

MEMORY2—VIRTUAL MEMORY DEMONSTRATION

This example demonstrates virtual memory management functions. The program allocates 4K of virtual memory. You can change the state and access protection of the region. You can also write a character to the region, provided the page is committed and has read/write access privileges. We will start by looking at Listings 3-14 and 3-15 the resource script and header file for the program.

MEMORY2.RC—Resource Script

As in MEMORY1.RC we have an icon and menu resource. The menu contains three popup entries: *Page State*, *Page Protection*, and *Write Test*. The first two popups enable us to change the state and access protection of the allocated page. The menu items are checked or unchecked by the program itself.

Parameter	Description
lpvAddress	Starting address of the region to query. This value is obtained as the return value of VirtualAlloc(), or can be any valid address within the range of allocated pages.
PMEMORY_BASIC_INFORMATION	Pointer to MEMORY_BASIC_INFORMATION structure.
dwLength	Length of buffer in second parameter; normally sizeof (MEMORY_BASIC_INFORMATION).

Table 3-9 VirtualQuery() parameters

Listing 3-14 MEMORY2.RC

```
#include "windows.h"
#include "memory2.h"


Memory2Icon ICON        memory2.ico

Memory2Menu MENU
   BEGIN
      POPUP "Page &State"
      BEGIN
         MENUITEM "&Free",        IDM_FREE
         MENUITEM "&Reserved",    IDM_RESERVE
         MENUITEM "&Committed",   IDM_COMMIT
      END
      POPUP "Page &Protection"
      BEGIN
         MENUITEM "&No Access",   IDM_NOACCESS
         MENUITEM "Read/&Write",  IDM_READWRITE
         MENUITEM "&Read Only"    IDM_READONLY
      END
      POPUP "&Write Test"
      BEGIN
         MENUITEM "&Write to Page", IDM_WRITETEST
      END
   END
```

MEMORY2.H—Header File

The header file for MEMORY2 contains defines for the seven menu selections. It also contains the function prototypes for WndProc() and MenuSet(). The MenuSet() function will set or reset the checkmarks on the menu selections. We add two new global variables: *base* and *MemInfo*. We will use the *base* variable to point to the base of the allocation. The *MemInfo* variable is used to store information from VirtualQuery().

Listing 3-15 MEMORY2.H

```
/* memory2.h -- Header file for memory2.c and memory2.rc */

/* Menu defines */
#define IDM_FREE        1
#define IDM_RESERVE     2
#define IDM_COMMIT      3
#define IDM_NOACCESS    4
#define IDM_READWRITE   5
#define IDM_READONLY    6
```

```
#define IDM_WRITETEST  7

/* Function prototype */
LONG APIENTRY WndProc (HWND, UINT, UINT, LONG);
VOID MenuSet (VOID);

/* Global variables */
HANDLE ghInst;
HANDLE ghWnd;
CHAR   *base;                         /* pointer to virtual memory base */
MEMORY_BASIC_INFORMATION MemInfo;     /* memory information status */
```

MEMORY2.C—Source File

Listing 3-16 is a partial listing of MEMORY2.C. WinMain() is omitted from the listing since nothing really changes there (aside from the new icon, menu, and title bar text). A description of the workings of MEMORY2 follows the listing. Both WndProc() and MenuSet() are shown in their entirety in Listing 3-16.

Listing 3-16 MEMORY2.C

```
/* memory2.c     Win32 Virtual Memory Allocation */

#include <windows.h>           /* include for Win32 apps */
#include "memory2.h"           /* include for memory2.c */

/* WndProc - Main Window Procedure for memory2.c */

LONG APIENTRY WndProc (HWND hWnd, UINT message, UINT wParam, LONG lParam)
{

DWORD OldProtect;      /* Variable to store old protection value in VirtualProtect */

   switch (message)
   {
      case WM_CREATE:  /* Allocate 4K virtual memory */
         base = VirtualAlloc (0, 0x1000, MEM_RESERVE, PAGE_NOACCESS);
         if (!base)                         /* Check for success */
            MessageBox (hWnd, "Error Allocating Virtual Memory", "ERROR", MB_OK);
         PostMessage (hWnd, WM_USER, 0, 0);        /* Delayed message for startup */
         return (0);

      case WM_USER:
         MenuSet();                          /* Set menu checks initial */
         return (0);

      case WM_COMMAND:
         switch (LOWORD(wParam))            /* Extract LOWORD of wParam for Win32 */
         {
```

continued on next page

87

continued from previous page

```
        VirtualQuery (base,       /* char pointer to base of virtual memory */
                      &MemInfo,   /* Address of memory information structure */
                      sizeof (MEMORY_BASIC_INFORMATION)); /* size of struct */

    case IDM_FREE:                /* Free virtual memory */
      switch (MemInfo.State)    /* Check current virtual memory status */
      {
        case MEM_COMMIT:
        case MEM_RESERVE:
          VirtualFree (base, 0, MEM_RELEASE); /* Release Virtual memory */
          break;
        default:
          return (0);
      }
      MenuSet();                  /* Update menu checks */
      return (0);
    case IDM_RESERVE:             /* Reserve virtual memory */
      switch (MemInfo.State)    /* Current virtual memory status */
      {
        case MEM_RESERVE:                         /* Already reserved */
          return (0);
        case MEM_COMMIT:                          /* Commit --> Reserve */
          VirtualFree (base, 0, MEM_DECOMMIT);
          break;
        case MEM_FREE:                            /* Commit --> Free */
          VirtualAlloc (0, 0x1000, MEM_RESERVE, PAGE_NOACCESS);
          break;
        default:
          break;
      }
      MenuSet();                                  /* Update menu checks */
      return (0);
    case IDM_COMMIT:              /* Commit virtual memory */
      switch (MemInfo.State)    /* Current virtual memory status */
      {
        case MEM_COMMIT:        /* Already committed */
          return (0);
        case MEM_RESERVE:                         /* Reserve --> Commit */
          VirtualAlloc (base, 0x1000, MEM_COMMIT, PAGE_READWRITE);
          break;
        case MEM_FREE:                            /* Reserve --> Free */
          base = VirtualAlloc (0, 0x1000, MEM_RESERVE | MEM_COMMIT, PAGE_READWRITE);
          break;
        default:
          break;
      }
      MenuSet();                                  /* Update menu checks */
      return (0);
    case IDM_NOACCESS:           /* No access allowed */
      if (MemInfo.State != MEM_COMMIT)            /* Must be committed */
      {
        MessageBox (hWnd, "You must commit the page first", "Error", MB_OK);
```

```
              return (0);
              }
          VirtualProtect(base,              /* Base of virtual memory */
                      0x1000,              /* 4K page size */
                      PAGE_NOACCESS,       /* No access */
                      &OldProtect);        /* Address to store old prot value */
          MenuSet();                        /* Update menu checks */
          return (0);
       case IDM_READWRITE:          /* Read/write access allowed */
          if (MemInfo.State != MEM_COMMIT)          /* Must be committed */
              {
              MessageBox (hWnd, "You must commit the page first", "Error", MB_OK);
              return (0);
              }
          VirtualProtect(base, 0x1000, PAGE_READWRITE, &OldProtect);
          MenuSet();                          /* Update menu checks */
          return (0);
       case IDM_READONLY:          /* Read/write access allowed */
          if (MemInfo.State != MEM_COMMIT)          /* Must be committed */
              {
              MessageBox (hWnd, "You must commit the page first", "Error", MB_OK);
              return (0);
              }
          VirtualProtect(base, 0x1000, PAGE_READONLY, &OldProtect);
          MenuSet();                     /* Read only access allowed */
          return (0);
       case IDM_WRITETEST:          /* Attempt to write to virtual memory */
          try                      /* try-except exception handling */
          {
              base [50] = 'W';      /* Write to 51st byte of page */
          MessageBox (hWnd, "'W' successfully written to byte 51 of Virtual Memory",
                      "Success!!!", MB_OK);
          }
          except (EXCEPTION_EXECUTE_HANDLER) /* exception testing */
          {
          MessageBox (hWnd, "The page must be committed and have read/write access",
                      "Write Error", MB_OK);
          }
          return (0);
       default:
          return (0);

       }

    case WM_DESTROY:                  /* No cleanup necessary */
       PostQuitMessage (0);
       return (0);

    }
 return DefWindowProc (hWnd, message, wParam, lParam);
}
```

continued on next page

continued from previous page

```
/* MenuSet-- updates checked menu items using VirtualQuery() */
VOID MenuSet (VOID)
{

HMENU hMenu;
INT    iMenu;

   hMenu = GetMenu (ghWnd);      /* Get handle to main menu */

   for (iMenu = IDM_FREE; iMenu <= IDM_READONLY; iMenu++)    /* Uncheck all */
      CheckMenuItem (hMenu, iMenu, MF_BYCOMMAND | MF_UNCHECKED);

   VirtualQuery (base, &MemInfo, sizeof (MEMORY_BASIC_INFORMATION));

   switch (MemInfo.State)        /* State information test */
   {
      case MEM_FREE:             /* Page is free */
         CheckMenuItem (hMenu, IDM_FREE, MF_BYCOMMAND | MF_CHECKED);
         break;
      case MEM_RESERVE:          /* Page is reserved */
         CheckMenuItem (hMenu, IDM_RESERVE, MF_BYCOMMAND | MF_CHECKED);
         break;
      case MEM_COMMIT:           /* Page is committed */
         CheckMenuItem (hMenu, IDM_COMMIT, MF_BYCOMMAND | MF_CHECKED);
         break;
   }

   switch (MemInfo.Protect)      /* Protect information test */
   {
      case PAGE_NOACCESS:        /* No access to page */
         CheckMenuItem (hMenu, IDM_NOACCESS, MF_BYCOMMAND | MF_CHECKED);
         break;
      case PAGE_READWRITE:       /* Read/Write access to page */
         CheckMenuItem (hMenu, IDM_READWRITE, MF_BYCOMMAND | MF_CHECKED);
         break;
      case PAGE_READONLY:        /* Read only access to page */
         CheckMenuItem (hMenu, IDM_READONLY, MF_BYCOMMAND | MF_CHECKED);
         break;
   }
}
```

There is a lot going on in this example program, but don't let it overwhelm you. We'll break the program apart to analyze what is happening in each section. After you have broken each section down, it will be much easier to see what's going on. Let's start with initialization.

Initialization of MEMORY2—WM_CREATE and WM_USER

In processing the WM_CREATE message, we make a call to VirtualAlloc(). We allocate a 4K (0x1000h) page and assign the return value to *base*. Recall that *base* is defined in MEMORY2.H. Our initial allocation is a reserved page (MEM_RESERVE). The access protection level, PAGE_NOACCESS, is required for reserved pages.

We then test the value of *base*. If the allocation fails, we display a message box indicating the failure. You could also add code to exit the program if the failure occurs; in our case we'll keep the program running.

The next step is to send a WM_USER message to our own window procedure, which delays the call to MenuSet() so the WM_CREATE message can complete. This returns control to Windows and ultimately WinMain(), where the main window is displayed with a call to ShowWindow(). We do not want to adjust the menu before the main window exists!

Once the window is built, our window procedure processes the WM_USER message. We simply make a call to MenuSet() and return. Let's see what goes on in MenuSet().

MenuSet()

The purpose of MenuSet() is to update the checkmarks of the first two popup menus. The first thing we do in MenuSet() is get a handle to the main menu, using the global window handle *(ghWnd)*. We then use a *for* loop to uncheck each of the six menu items.

The next step is to make a call to VirtualQuery() using the global variables *base* and *MemInfo*. Note that we use the *address of MemInfo* since VirtualQuery is expecting a pointer. This fills our MEMORY_BASIC_INFORMATION structure.

We use MemInfo in two *switch* statements to determine the menu items that need a checkmark. For example, the first *switch* statement uses *MemInfo.State*. If the result is MEM_FREE (a free page), the IDM_FREE menu item is checked using CheckMenuItem(). The first time through this function, *MemInfo.State* will be MEM_RESERVE.

The second *switch* statement performs a similar operation, only this time on *MemInfo.Protect*. The first time through the function, *MemInfo.Protect* will be PAGE_NOACCESS.

We will call this function any time a change is made to the state or access protection of the allocated page.

IDM_FREE Menu Selection

If the user selects *Free* from the *Page State* popup, the kernel sends a WM_COMMAND message to the window procedure. Each time we process a WM_COMMAND message, we call VirtualQuery() to obtain the current virtual memory information. We use this information for all menu selections. The *message id* is IDM_FREE. This indicates that we must free the page and update the menu.

If the current state of the virtual memory (pointed to by the base) is MEM_RESERVE or MEM_COMMIT, we free the page with VirtualFree() and break out of the *switch*. Note that MEM_RELEASE is passed to VirtualFree() to indicate that the page must be freed. MenuSet() is called to update the menu.

If the page is already free, *default* is processed in the *switch* statement. This simply returns without updating the menu since no change is necessary.

IDM_RESERVE Menu Selection

If the user selects *Reserve* from the *Page State* popup, the *message id* IDM_RESERVE is sent. This indicates that the page must be reserved.

We use a *switch* statement to determine the current state of the page. If the page is already reserved, we simply return 0. You could display a message to the user indicating that the memory is already reserved. If the current page state is MEM_COMMIT, we call VirtualFree() with MEM_DECOMMIT as its third parameter. This changes the state of the page from committed to reserved. If the current state of the page is free, we call VirtualAlloc() to reserve a page. This call is identical to the one in WM_CREATE. Note that we must assign the return of VirtualAlloc() to *base* in this instance. If the page was free, the value of *base* would be invalid. We now have a reserved page with a valid *base* pointer.

The menu checkmarks are updated with a call to MenuSet().

IDM_COMMIT Menu Selection

If the user selects *Commit* from the *Page State* popup, the *message id* would be IDM_COMMIT. We must commit the page.

If the page is already committed, we return 0. If the page is reserved, we make a call to VirtualAlloc, this time using *base* as the first parameter. The third parameter is set to MEM_COMMIT, and the fourth to PAGE_READWRITE. We could have used any of the three access protection values with a committed page.

If the page is free, we need to make a call that will both reserve *and* commit the page. This is done by using MEM_RESERVE | MEM_COMMIT as the third parameter. Using the *or* symbol combines the two parameter values. The result is a committed page. Again, PAGE_READWRITE is the access protection value of choice. The page was free before this call, so we assign the pointer value to *base*. We now have a committed page with a valid *base* pointer.

Changing Access Protection

The code that changes the access protection value of the page is virtually the same for each of the three possibilities (IDM_NOACCESS, IDM_READWRITE, and IDM_READONLY). First we fill the *MemInfo* structure. We test *MemInfo.State* to determine if the page is committed. A page *must* be committed to change the protection value.

If the page is not committed, we display a message box indicating the problem. If the page is committed, we call VirtualProtect(). The first parameter is the *base,* which will be valid if the page is committed. The second parameter is 0x1000; this indicates that size of memory is 4K. Keep in mind that if you change the protection on *any portion* of the page, the *entire* page is affected. You cannot change protection on a portion of a page. The third parameter is the desired access protection: PAGE_NOACCESS, PAGE_READONLY, or PAGE_READWRITE.

After the access protection value is changed, we call MenuSet() to update the menu checkmarks.

IDM_WRITETEST—Structured Exception Handling

The last portion of this program tests to see if we can write to the allocated virtual memory. We use a technique called *structured exception handling.* Look closely at this portion of the code. We are using a *try-except* block to attempt a write to the 51st byte of the memory. This is a feature provided by the Microsoft compiler; consult your compiler's documentation for specific methods of exception handling. You may need to modify this code to reflect your compiler's method. An alternative method is to check to make sure the page is committed and has read/write access. You can do this using the VirtualQuery() function.

We use the *try* block to attempt to write to *base[50]* (an arbitrary decision). If this is successful, we display a success message box. If the attempt fails (usually due to the page not being committed, or no read/write access), the system generates the EXCEPTION_EXECUTE_HANDLER parameter. Using the *except* block, we can display a message indicating the failure.

It is important to note that there are other reasons that cause exceptions. Using structured exception handling allows your applications to recover from exceptions, or at least exit gracefully. Not handling the exception will result in the system displaying a message box that indicates a failure. The contents of this box are cryptic and of no use to the user. It is better to trap the failure and provide a more descriptive message to the user or provide an alternate routine.

That covers the ins and outs of MEMORY2. Let's build it and give it a try!

Building and Running MEMORY2

Open a command prompt window and change to the \CHAPTER3\3.2 subdirectory. Type NMAKE and press (ENTER). The files are compiled and linked. Type MEMORY2 and press (ENTER).

Try out each of the menu selections. After some experimentation you should come to the following conclusions:

- You cannot change the access protection unless the page is committed.

- You cannot write successfully unless the page is committed and has read/write access privileges.

- A reserved page does not have an access protection value (no menu item is checked in the *Page Protection* popup).

Figure 3-11 shows the message box that appears when the exception handling reaches the except block.

Continue to experiment with MEMORY2 and examine the code until you gain an understanding of the virtual memory management functions. Using this knowledge you should be able to create programs that manage a larger span of memory.

MEMORY SHARING FUNCTIONS (FILE MAPPING)

The last example program in this chapter demonstrates memory sharing between applications. So far all of the memory allocation has been visible to the creating program only. Both HeapAlloc() and VirtualAlloc() allocate memory that is *private* to the calling application.

We are using a technique called file mapping in this example. You can use these functions to share open files between applications. You can also use these same functions to create shared memory between applications. For that reason this example will consist of two complete programs. The first will

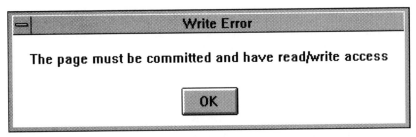

Figure 3-11 MessageBox from MEMORY2—exception handling message

create the *shared memory* object, and the second will open the object created by the first.

Before we get into the program, let's look at the functions that make this possible.

CreateFileMapping()

This is the function that we will use in the first program (MEMORY3). CreateFileMapping() creates a file mapping object. Despite its name, it is not restricted to files; you can also use this function to create shared memory. That is our goal in this example. The function requires six parameters, all of which we will discuss shortly. Listing 3-17 shows the syntax and an example call to CreateFileMapping().

Listing 3-17 CreateFileMapping() syntax and example call

```
/* CreateFileMapping() Syntax */
HANDLE CreateFileMapping (HANDLE hFile,
                    LPSECURITY_ATTRIBUTES lpSA,
                    DWORD dwProtect,
                    DWORD dwMaxSizeHigh,
                    DWORD dwMaxSizeLow,
                    LPSTR lpszMapName);

/* Example Call to CreateFileMapping() */
HANDLE hMapObj;

hMapObj = CreateFileMapping ((HANDLE) OxFFFFFFFF),
                    NULL,
                    PAGE_READWRITE,
                    0,
                    0x1000,
                    "shared_memory");
```

Note that this function returns a handle to a file mapping object, in this case *hMapObj*. The function only creates the file mapping object; your application cannot view the file until you call MapViewOfFile(). This function will require the handle returned by CreateFileMapping().

This function has a fairly lengthy parameter list. Table 3-10 breaks down these parameters and their possible values.

Note that in our example call in Listing 3-17, we use 0xFFFFFFFF as the file handle. This indicates that the object is to be used for shared memory rather than a file. The security attributes parameter is set to NULL. We will not use security attributes until Chapter 8. The *dwProtect* value in the example call is set to PAGE_READWRITE. We are using this value because our example program will perform read and write operations.

You can specify a huge maximum file size for a mapping object (up to 64 bits in length). Normally the high order parameter is set to 0. In our example call, *dwMaxSizeHigh* is set to 0 and *dwMaxSizeLow* is set to 0x1000h, this creates a 4K area of shared memory.

The last parameter in the example call is "shared_memory." This gives the object a name that other applications can use to open the file mapping object. MEMORY3 will create a file mapping object using this name.

We still do not have a *view* to the file that will allow our program to access the shared memory object. To accomplish this we use the MapViewOfFile()

Parameter	Description
hFile	Handle to a file (returned by CreateFile()). File handles are discussed in Chapter 4, File Management. If this parameter is set to 0xFFFFFFFF, the function creates a mapping object to shared memory.
lpSA	Pointer to a SECURITY_ATTRIBUTES structure. Refer to Chapter 8, NT System Security, for more information.
dwProtect	Protection value for mapping object: PAGE_READONLY or PAGE_READWRITE.
dwMaxSizeHigh	High 32 bits of maximum size of object.
dwMaxSizeLow	Low 32 bits of maximum size of object.
lpszMapName	Pointer to NULL terminated string to name the object.

Table 3-10 CreateFileMapping() parameters

function. Before we look at MapViewOfFile(), let's look at the function that the second example program will use.

OpenFileMapping()

The second example program in this set, MEMORY4, will use the OpenFileMapping() function to obtain a handle to the mapping object created by the first program MEMORY3. This function requires three parameters: the desired access mode of the object, an inherit flag, and a pointer to the name of the object to be opened. Listing 3-18 shows the syntax and an example call to OpenFileMapping().

Listing 3-18 OpenFileMapping() syntax and example call

```
/* OpenFileMapping() Syntax */
HANDLE OpenFileMapping (DWORD dwDesiredAccess, BOOL bInheritHandle, LPSTR lpName);

/* Example Call to OpenFileMapping() */
HANDLE hMapObj;

hMapObj = OpenFileMapping (FILE_MAP_WRITE, FALSE, "shared_memory");
```

This function also returns a handle to a file mapping object. The major difference in this function is that it requires a named object, "shared_memory," that has been created by another process (in this case our first program, MEMORY3).

Let's look at the OpenFileMapping() parameters and their possible values in Table 3-11.

The example call in Listing 3-18 uses FILE_MAP_WRITE as the desired access parameter. This is necessary in order for MEMORY4 to write to the mapped memory. The second parameter is set to FALSE. This indicates that another process (created by this application) cannot inherit the handle to the object. The last parameter is set to "shared_memory." This matches the name used by the first program, MEMORY3.

Now that both example applications have a handle to the file mapping object, the next step is for both to obtain a view of the file.

MapViewOfFile()

This function is used by both MEMORY3 and MEMORY4. We use this function to obtain the starting address to the shared memory. Up until this point, we do not know where the shared memory is located. This function

Parameter	Description
dwDesiredAccess	The desired access to the object: FILE_MAP_READ or FILE_MAP_WRITE or both. Windows NT checks the security descriptor of the original object for permission. Refer to Chapter 8 for more information on security descriptors.
bInheritHandle	Determines if the object handle can be inherited if a new process is started. Chapter 6 covers process creation.
lpName	Points to a NULL terminated string of the name of the desired object.

Table 3-11 OpenFileMapping() parameters

requires five parameters: the object handle (from CreateFileMapping() or OpenFileMapping()), the desired access mode, the high 32 bits of offset, the low 32 bits of offset, and the number of bytes to map.

Listing 3-19 shows the syntax and an example call to MapViewOfFile().

Listing 3-19 MapViewOfFile() syntax and example call

```
/* MapViewOfFile() Syntax */
LPVOID MapViewOfFile (HANDLE hMapObject,
                      DWORD dwAccess,
                      DWORD dwOffsetHigh,
                      DWORD dwOffsetLow,
                      DWORD dwMap);

/* Example Call to MapViewOfFile() */
char *cMappedView;

cMappedView = MapViewOfFile (FILE_MAP_READ | FILE_MAP_WRITE, 0, 0, 0);
```

The return value is the starting address of the file, or in our case, shared memory. We also use the *or* symbol to combine the desired access; both programs in this example will read and write to the shared memory area. The third and fourth parameters are set to 0. This indicates no offset to the file. The last parameter indicates the number of bytes to map. This parameter is set to 0, which results in the entire area specified by the object being mapped.

Let's look at the parameters for MapViewOfFile() and their possible values. Table 3-12 provides this information.

Parameter	Description
hMapObject	The file mapping object (from CreateFileMapping() or OpenFileMapping()).
dwAccess	The desired access to the object: FILE_MAP_READ or FILE_MAP_WRITE or both. The object must be created with write access in order for the mapped view to obtain write privileges.
dwOffsetHigh	High 32-bit offset into the file (or memory) where mapping is to begin.
dwOffsetLow	Low 32-bit offset into the file (or memory) where mapping is to begin. Must be 0 or on a 64K boundary.
dwMap	Number of bytes to map. Using 0 results in the entire file (or memory region) being mapped.

Table 3-12 MapViewOfFile() parameters

This completes the overview of the functions used to create shared memory between applications. Now let's see the functions in action.

MEMORY3/4—SHARED MEMORY DEMONSTRATION

The demonstration consists of two applications. The first application, MEMORY3, creates a file mapping object for shared memory. The second application, MEMORY4, opens the object created by MEMORY3. After mapping a view to the shared memory, both applications can read and write to shared memory. The read is shown by displaying data on the client area of the respective applications.

We will list and describe the files for MEMORY3. MEMORY4 is nearly the same code; the differences between the programs are given after the source file listing for MEMORY3. You may want to print out the files for MEMORY4 and compare them with the following listings. They are located in the \CHAPTER3\3.3 subdirectory on the supplied disk. Both applications are in the same subdirectory so we can use one makefile to compile and link both applications.

MEMORY3.RC—Resource Script

The resource script is shown in Listing 3-20. We have three items on the main menu: *Create, Map View,* and *Data.* Data is a popup menu consisting of *Send* and *Receive.* The *Map View* selection is initially grayed, since we do not want to map a view until the mapping object has been created.

The only difference in the MEMORY4 resource script is the *Create* menu item which is replaced by *Open.*

Listing 3-20 MEMORY3.RC

```
#include "windows.h"
#include "memory3.h"


Memory3Icon ICON        memory3.ico

Memory3Menu MENU
    BEGIN
    MENUITEM "&Create",         IDM_CREATE_FM
    MENUITEM "&Map View",       IDM_MAP_FV, GRAYED
    POPUP "&Data"
        BEGIN
        MENUITEM "&Send",       IDM_DATA_SEND
        MENUITEM "&Receive",    IDM_DATA_RECV
        END
    END
```

MEMORY3.H—Header File

The header file for MEMORY3 is straightforward. It contains the defines for the menu selections and the function prototype for WndProc(). Listing 3-21 shows this header file.

Listing 3-21 MEMORY3.H

```
/* memory3.h -- Header file for memory3.c and memory3.rc */

/* Menu defines */
#define IDM_CREATE_FM   1
#define IDM_MAP_FV      2
```

```
#define IDM_DATA_SEND   3
#define IDM_DATA_RECV   4

/* Function prototype */
LONG APIENTRY WndProc (HWND, UINT, UINT, LONG);

/* Global variables */
HANDLE ghInst;
HANDLE ghWnd;
```

MEMORY3.C—Source File

Since the WinMain() function is typical, it is omitted from the source file listing. WndProc() for MEMORY3.C is shown in its entirety in Listing 3-22. Examine the source file, then proceed to the description that follows the listing.

Listing 3-22 MEMORY3.C

```
/* memory3.c      Shared memory--creating process */

#include <windows.h>           /* include for Windows NT apps */
#include "memory3.h"           /* include for memory3.c */

/* WndProc - Main Window Procedure for memory3.c */

LONG APIENTRY WndProc (HWND hWnd, UINT message, UINT wParam, LONG lParam)
{
static char    *cMappedView;    /* Pointer to mapped view */
static HANDLE  hMapObj;         /* Handle to mapping object */
static HMENU   hMenu;           /* Handle to main menu */
                                /* Message to send */
char           cSendMessage[] = "This data was sent to mapped memory by Memory 3";
char           cRecvBuffer[60]; /* Buffer for receiving data */
HDC            hDC;


    switch (message)
    {
      case WM_CREATE:
        hMenu = GetMenu (hWnd);                        /* static hMenu */
        EnableMenuItem (hMenu, 2, MF_BYPOSITION | MF_GRAYED); /* disable popup */
        return (0);

      case WM_COMMAND:
        switch (LOWORD(wParam))             /* Extract LOWORD of wParam for Win32) */
        {
          case IDM_CREATE_FM:               /* Create file mapping object */
            hMapObj = CreateFileMapping ((HANDLE) 0xFFFFFFFF, /* paging file */
```

continued on next page

continued from previous page

```
                                    NULL,                 /* No security inheritance */
                                    PAGE_READWRITE,       /* Access level of object */
                                    0,                    /* HIWORD of size (0) */
                                    0x1000,               /* LOWORD of size (4k) */
                                    "shared_memory");     /* object name to create */
                EnableMenuItem (hMenu, IDM_CREATE_FM, MF_BYCOMMAND | MF_GRAYED); /* No 2nd create */
                EnableMenuItem (hMenu, IDM_MAP_FV, MF_BYCOMMAND | MF_ENABLED);   /* Can map now */
                    DrawMenuBar (hWnd);           /* Update menu bar */
                    return (0);
                case IDM_MAP_FV:                  /* Map view of paging file */
                  cMappedView = (char *) MapViewOfFile (hMapObj, /* Handle to mapping object */
                            FILE_MAP_READ | FILE_MAP_WRITE, /* Access to mapped view */
                            0,                              /* Use all 4K—no offset */
                            0,
                            0);
                EnableMenuItem (hMenu, IDM_MAP_FV, MF_BYCOMMAND | MF_GRAYED); /* No 2nd map */
                EnableMenuItem (hMenu, 2, MF_BYPOSITION | MF_ENABLED);        /* Can send/recv now */
                    DrawMenuBar (hWnd);           /* Update menu bar */
                    return (0);
                case IDM_DATA_SEND:               /* Write data to paging file */
                    lstrcpy (cMappedView, cSendMessage);     /* copy message to */
                    return (0);
                case IDM_DATA_RECV:               /* Read data from paging file */
                    lstrcpy (cRecvBuffer, cMappedView + 100); /* copy message from */
                    hDC = GetDC (hWnd);
                    TextOut (hDC, 0, 0, cRecvBuffer, lstrlen(cRecvBuffer)); /* display result */
                    ReleaseDC (hWnd, hDC);
                    return (0);
                default:
                    return (0);
            }

        case WM_DESTROY:                          /* No cleanup necessary */
            PostQuitMessage (0);
            return (0);

        default:
            return DefWindowProc (hWnd, message, wParam, lParam);
    }

    return (0L);
}
```

WM_CREATE

We obtain a handle to the menu while processing this message. The handle is used to enable or disable menu options. The next step is to disable the *Data* menu popup. It must be performed in this manner since there is no way to gray a popup in the resource script. We don't want to send or receive data until the file mapping object is created and we have a view of the file.

IDM_CREATE_FM (IDM_OPEN_FM in MEMORY4)

This message is sent when you select *Create* from the *Main* menu. We call CreateFileMapping() to create an object. The object handle is assigned to *hMapObj*. The first parameter is 0xFFFFFFFF, indicating that we are creating shared memory. The second parameter, NULL, indicates no security inheritance. The third parameter specifies read/write access for the object. The fourth and fifth parameters specify a size of 0x1000h, or a 4K block of memory. The last parameter is the name of the object, "shared_memory."

We then adjust the menu with two calls to EnableMenuItem(). The *Create* selection is disabled to prevent another call. The *Map View* selection is enabled since this is the next logical step. We call DrawMenuBar() to redraw the *Main* menu, reflecting the changes.

MEMORY4 performs similar actions, except it calls OpenFileMapping() in place of CreateFileMapping().

IDM_MAP_FV

This message is sent when you select *Map View*. We call MapViewOfFile() and assign the return value to *cMappedView* (pointer to CHAR). This points to the starting address of the shared memory area. The call to MapViewOfFile() requested read and write privileges. This will work because we created the object with the same privileges. Once again, we update the menu. The only valid selection left is *Data*.

The IDM_MAP_FV code in MEMORY4 is identical.

IDM_DATA_SEND

Now that the mapping object has been created and a view is mapped, we can send (write) data to memory. We do so using lstrcpy(). We copy a string, *cSendMessage,* to the shared memory, *cMappedView. cSendMessage* indicates which application the string came from. In MEMORY4, we perform the same action, only we offset the copy by 100 bytes (cMappedView +100) so that the programs do not write over each other's data.

IDM_DATA_RECV

We can receive the string by reading the memory area where the other application wrote. For example, MEMORY3 uses lstrcpy() to copy *cMappedView + 100* into a buffer, *cRecvBuffer.* MEMORY4 does the same, only it looks at the starting address of the mapped view, or *cMappedView.*

We then write the contents of the receive buffers to the respective client areas. MEMORY3 displays the message written by MEMORY4 and vice versa. We can see that the mapped memory is working.

Building and Running MEMORY3 and MEMORY4

Open a Command Prompt window, change to the \CHAPTER3\3.3 subdirectory, and type NMAKE. We have provided a single makefile that compiles and links both MEMORY3 and MEMORY4. You must start both applications to see the effects. Perform the following steps to try out the programs:

1. Type START MEMORY3 and press (ENTER). Typing START starts the first application and doesn't tie up the Command Prompt window.

2. Click on the Command Prompt window and type START MEMORY4.

3. Minimize all windows except for the two applications. Resize the application so they don't overlap.

4. Select Create from MEMORY3 and Open from MEMORY4. The file mapping objects are created.

5. Select Map View on both MEMORY3 and MEMORY4. Both applications now have a view of the shared memory.

6. Open the Data menu of each application and select Send. Both applications write to the shared memory.

7. Finally open the Data menu of each application and select Receive. The results should appear similar to Figure 3-12. Each application has read the other's message from shared memory.

This completes the example of shared memory using file mapping. How you manage memory is completely up to you. It's nice to have the flexibility but remember that some care is necessary when managing the shared space.

SUMMARY

This chapter covered a lot of ground. You can see that there is a learning curve involved when it comes to managing memory in Windows NT, but

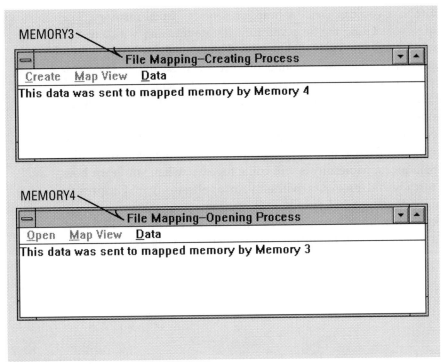

Figure 3-12 Output of MEMORY3 and MEMORY4—evidence of shared memory

we have helped you learn it a step at a time. In the long run, it is worthwhile to master the techniques introduced in this chapter. Microsoft was careful not to make obsolete every memory management function from the past. You can still use many of the old functions (malloc, GlobalAlloc, and so on) without trouble. However, when it comes to managing large amounts of data dynamically, the new Win32 API functions provide the most efficient way of doing so.

The most significant change in memory management is the introduction of the 32-bit flat addressing scheme. You no longer have to worry about near and far, segments and offsets. Each application has a large number of virtual addresses to work with. You don't have to worry about the physical location of your data; the NT kernel and virtual memory manager take care of that. Windows NT can move your data without affecting your addresses. The virtual memory addresses remain constant, as far as your applications are concerned.

For private data you can create a heap, or allocate virtual memory. The choice is up to you. Using the heap you can allocate memory with any data type or size; it is only limited by the physical storage space. Using virtual memory you can reserve large amounts of virtual address space. Then you can commit a page at a time, as your applications needs increase. You can also use virtual memory without regard to data type; however, you must manage it within your application.

Finally you saw how to create shared memory between applications using file mapping. This feature will come into play again when you share files between applications. More pieces will come together when you learn how to create threads and processes within your applications in Chapter 6, Multitasking in Windows NT.

Let's take a break from memory and shift our focus to files. The next chapter introduces the new file management functions in the Win32 API.

CHAPTER 4

File Management

File

Management

In previous versions of Windows, only a few API functions for managing files existed. Since Windows 3.x runs on MS-DOS, most of the file-related functions are actually MS-DOS file functions, not Windows APIs. This works fine because the target on which the functions operate is always the same operating system. In Windows 3.x we only have to worry about one type of file system and processor.

Windows NT is much more flexible when it comes to file management. Out of the gate, NT supports three file systems: File Allocation Table system (FAT), High-Performance File System (HPFS), and New Technology File System. The FAT, which is the traditional MS-DOS file system, is fairly straightforward, and as a Windows programmer, you are probably familiar with its operation. The additional file systems, however, are quite different from the FAT system. For example, HPFS supports extended filenames and larger file sizes. NTFS has the capabilities of HPFS plus even more (for example, security of files and directories).

Another major change in NT is the total absence of DOS. Now that Windows NT is a complete operating system, it requires new API functions to handle files. Most of the old functions still work, but the actual code generated by them is quite different. The new API functions work regardless of the type of file system or processor. Whether you are accessing the FAT system on an 80386 system, or NTFS on a MIPS 9000, you use the same set of functions to manage files.

In this chapter we will introduce you to several of these new APIs. The possibilities for using these functions are many—to cover every example would fill a book twice this size. We can, however, examine the new APIs and build a solid understanding of them. Using this knowledge you will be able to overcome the challenges that may crop up in your programming projects. Let's take a look at the topics for this chapter.

CHAPTER OVERVIEW

Concepts Covered

- Creating files
- Opening files
- Reading files
- Deleting files
- Using the file pointer
- Creating directories
- Removing directories
- Copying files
- Moving files
- Finding files
- Obtaining file information
- Getting and setting file attributes
- Obtaining drive information

Win32 API Functions Covered

- CreateFile()
- ReadFile()
- WriteFile()
- DeleteFile()
- SetFilePointer()
- SetEndOfFile()
- CloseHandle()
- FlushFileBuffers()
- FindFirstFile()
- FindNextFile()
- FindClose()
- GetDiskFree Space()
- GetLogicalDrives()
- MoveFile()
- CopyFile()
- GetCurrentDirectory()
- CreateDirectory()
- RemoveDirectory()
- GetFileInformationByHandle()
- GetFileSize()
- GetFileAttributes()
- SetFileAttributes()
- GetDriveType()
- GetLogicalDriveStrings()
- GetVolumeInformation()

Data Types Covered

- WIN32_FIND_DATA (structure)
- BY_HANDLE_FILE_INFORMATION

Parameters Covered

- GENERIC_READ
- GENERIC_WRITE
- FILE_SHARE_READ
- FILE_SHARE_WRITE
- FILE_BEGIN
- FILE_CURRENT
- FILE_END
- FILE_ATTRIBUTE_ARCHIVE
- FILE_ATTRIBUTE_HIDDEN
- FILE_ATTRIBUTE_NORMAL
- FILE_ATTRIBUTE_READONLY
- FILE_ATTRIBUTE_SYSTEM
- FILE_ATTRIBUTE_DIRECTORY

WINDOWS 3.X/WINDOWS NT FILE MANAGEMENT

Before we get into the new functions, let's look at the differences that caused the expansion of file-related facilities in the Win32 API. Understanding these differences will help you decide which functions to use as a replacement for Windows 3.x APIs and DOS functions.

Windows 3.x and DOS Files

Since Windows 3.x is really an MS-DOS program, it must adhere to the DOS file functions. You are most likely familiar with functions like OpenFile(), _lopen(), and _lwrite(). To open a file, you called OpenFile(), which filled a structure called OFSTRUCT. The structure provided information such as the full path and filename. The only problem is that the size of the buffer in the OFSTRUCT structure is 128 bytes. This is fine for the MS-DOS FAT file system, but not adequate for HPFS or NTFS. Figure 4-1 shows an overview of a Windows 3.x application opening a file.

Another feature lacking from these file management functions is security. Security did not exist in Windows 3.x, so there was no need to handle it. Although these functions will still compile and run under Win32, they are

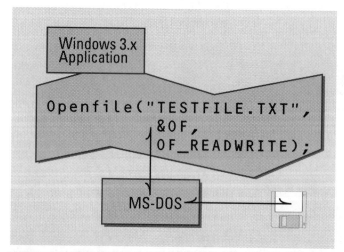

Figure 4-1 Opening a file in Windows 3.x

lacking when it comes to handling the new features of Windows NT. Let's look at the new features that NT accomodates with the Win32 API.

Windows NT Files

There are three major differences when managing files in Windows NT: processor type, file system, and file security. Fortunately the designers of NT have eliminated most of the programmer's concern in these areas. Windows NT can run on different types of processors, and you can manipulate files without worrying about what type of processor is involved. Figure 4-2 shows an example of how Windows NT accomplishes this.

The figure also shows that the NT kernel handles the file system type for you. You can create and manipulate a file on any of the supported file systems without any special code. Your applications must, however, be well designed to take advantage of certain features of file systems. For example, if you want to give the user the ability to use long filenames, you must ensure that the target drive supports them. You should also allow the alternative of reverting

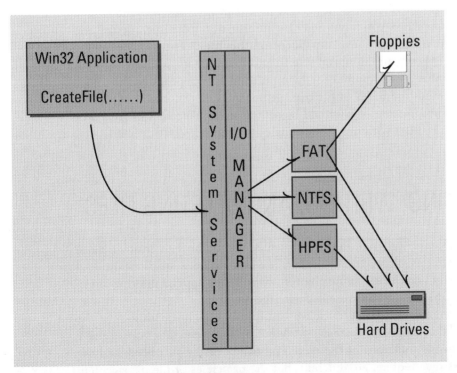

Figure 4-2 Overview of NT file management

back to the FAT system, indicating to the user that he or she must use an 8.3-character filename. You can, of course, require the user to have a specific file system, but doing so limits the potential audience of your program.

The only file system that allows security in filenames is NTFS. All of the example applications in this chapter use NULL for security attributes. Examples of security are given in Chapter 8, Introduction to Windows NT System Security. Let's take a look at the file functions in more depth and create some sample applications to demonstrate their usage.

FILE MANAGEMENT FUNCTIONS IN THE WIN32 API

We will demonstrate the new file management functions in four example programs. The first program will show you how to create a file, open a file, use the file pointer, and delete a file. The second program shows you how to create and remove directories, search for files, copy files, and move files. The third program shows you how to get file information (filename, filesize, and so on) and manipulate the attributes of the files. The final example demonstrates how you can obtain system information with your applications.

The number of techniques for manipulating files appears endless. This chapter provides the basics of file management. Using this basic knowledge, and a little imagination, you should be able to manipulate files in your own programs. Let's start with our first example application.

CREATING, WRITING, AND DELETING FILES

The first example program in this chapter shows you how to create a file in Win32. After we have created a file, we will write a small amount of information to it. Using the file pointer, we will then append information to the end of the file. Finally we will delete the file.

To accomplish these objectives, we will first take an in-depth look at the functions that perform these tasks. Most of the new functions behave similarly to file functions of the past. The names of the functions, and the parameters they require, are different, but the principles of file management remain the same.

Creating a File in Win32

The Win32 API provides a new function for creating files, appropriately named CreateFile(). This function is a replacement for the OpenFile() or _lcreat() functions. You may recall that the OpenFile() function performed multiple tasks. For example, you could create, open, or delete a file using OpenFile(). CreateFile() is similar in those respects, but it is even more versatile. In addition to the capabilities of OpenFile(), CreateFile() can also specify security attributes and flags for file behavior. Example types of behavior are *random access* and *sequential scan*. These flags assist the operating system in determining optimum disk caching.

The examples in this chapter will concentrate on the basics (opening, writing, and closing files). The security attributes of files and other security issues are discussed in Chapter 8. Let's look at this function in detail.

Using CreateFile()

Like the memory management functions, the parameter list for CreateFile() is fairly long. Listing 4-1 shows the proper syntax and an example call to create a new file. Note that the function returns a file handle that can be used in subsequent API calls.

Listing 4-1 CreateFile() syntax and example call

```
/* CreateFile() Syntax */
HANDLE CreateFile (LPCTSTR lpszFilename,        /* filename */
                   DWORD dwAccess,              /* read/write access */
                   DWORD dwShare,               /* share? */
                   LPSECURITY_ATTRIBUTES lpsa,  /* security attributes */
                   DWORD dwCreate,              /* how to create */
                   DWORD dwAttrAndFlags,        /* attributes and flags */
                   HANDLE hTemplateFile);       /* template file */

/* Example Call to CreateFile() */
HANDLE hFile;

hFile = CreateFile ("TESTFILE.TXT",             /* filename */
             GENERIC_READ | GENERIC_WRITE,      /* allow read and write */
             0,                                 /* no sharing */
             NULL,                              /* no security */
             CREATE_NEW,                        /* create a new file */
             FILE_ATTRIBUTE_NORMAL,             /* normal file attributes */
             NULL);                             /* no template file */
```

The example call in the listing opens a file named TESTFILE.TXT, with read and write access. It also specifies to create a new file and use normal file attributes. The rest of the parameters are set to 0 or NULL, indicating that they are not used in the call. Let's break down the individual parameters to a CreateFile() call and examine the possibilities. Table 4-1 shows the CreateFile() parameters.

Note that the *dwCreate* parameter contains several possible values. Therefore we have separated this into Table 4-2. This table describes the values, and their results, depending on whether the file pointed to by *lpszFilename* exists.

Even though the combination of parameters are numerous, the CreateFile() function is actually quite easy to use in your applications. Always start by using basic parameters, and build on them once you've got your program working. In our first example program, FILE1, we make some simple calls to CreateFile().

Parameter	Description
lpszFileName	Long pointer to null-terminated filename. Filename must be valid for type of file system.
dwAccess	Access level of file. Set to GENERIC_READ or GENERIC_WRITE or a combination.
dwShare	Specifies if the file can be shared. Set to 0 (no sharing), FILE_SHARE_READ, or FILE_SHARE_WRITE.
lpsa	Long pointer to security attributes structure (see Chapter 8).
dwCreate	Creation type. Refer to Table 4-2 for possible parameters.
dwAttrAndFlags	File attributes. Set to FILE_ATTRIBUTE_NORMAL (no attributes) or any combination of FILE_ATTRIBUTE_ARCHIVE, FILE_ATTRIBUTE_READONLY, FILE_ATTRIBUTE_HIDDEN, or FILE_ATTRIBUTE_SYSTEM.
hTemplateFile	Handle to template file containing file and security attributes. These attributes override all other attributes.

Table 4-1 CreateFile() parameters

dwCreate	If File Exists	If File Does Not Exist
CREATE_NEW	Fails	Creates file
CREATE_ALWAYS	Overwrites existing	Creates file
OPEN_EXISTING	Opens file	Fails
OPEN_ALWAYS	Opens file	Creates new file
TRUNCATE_EXISTING*	Opens/truncates	Fails

* *dwAccess* must be GENERIC_WRITE or GENERIC_READ | GENERIC_WRITE for this parameter.

Table 4-2 dwCreate parameters for CreateFile()

The Return Value of CreateFile()

As you can see in the example call in Listing 4-1, the CreateFile() function returns a handle to the file. If the function fails the return value is INVALID_FILE_HANDLE.

Reading Data from a File

The ReadFile() function uses the file handle returned by CreateFile() to read data from the file. This function requires five parameters: the file handle, a pointer to a buffer to store the data, the number of bytes to read, a pointer to a DWORD to indicate how many bytes were read, and an optional pointer to an OVERLAPPED structure. More information on overlapped I/O is given following the description of ReadFile(). Listing 4-2 shows the syntax and an example call to ReadFile().

Listing 4-2 ReadFile() syntax and example call

```
/* ReadFile() Syntax */
BOOL ReadFile (HANDLE hFile,              /* handle to file */
               LPVOID lpBuffer,           /* long pointer to buffer */
               DWORD dwNumBytesToRead,    /* number of bytes to read */
               LPDWORD dwNumBytesRead,    /* number of bytes read */
```

continued on next page

continued from previous page

```
                    LPOVERLAPPED lpOverlapped);  /* overlapped I/O structure */

/* Example Call to ReadFile() */
DWORD dwNumBytesRead;
char  lpBuffer[1000];

ReadFile (hFile,               /* valid file handle */
          lpBuffer,            /* pointer to buffer */
          1000,                /* number of bytes to read */
          &dwNumBytesRead,     /* pointer to DWORD to store number of bytes read */
          NULL);               /* no overlapped I/O
```

In this example call, we use a valid handle to a file, *hFile,* to read data. We use a 1000-byte buffer, *lpBuffer,* to store the data. We specify that we want to read 1000 bytes from the file in the third parameter. A pointer to a DWORD is passed to ReadFile() as the fourth parameter. The fifth parameter is not used.

When this function returns, the actual number of bytes read is available in variable *dwNumBytesRead.* For example, if the number of actual bytes read were less than the amount requested, say 540, then *dwNumBytesRead* would contain 540. This would result if the end of the file was reached.

The file pointer is adjusted to the end of a call to ReadFile(). Figure 4-3 shows an overview of ReadFile() with repeated calls.

The return value of ReadFile() is a Boolean value. You can (and should) test this value to verify that the function was successful. As with most functions, a TRUE return value indicates success, while FALSE indicates failure.

USING GETLASTERROR() TO GET EXTENDED ERROR INFORMATION

Most of the Win32 functions that return a Boolean value will store extended information about the error if the function fails. You can call GetLastError() to get this extended value. GetLastError() returns a DWORD. A table of error codes in numerical order is available in the Win32 SDK manuals. Make sure the function has failed (by testing the return value) before calling GetLastError(), otherwise you will obtain an error code from a previous failure. Here is an example:

```
bTest = ReadFile (hFile, lpBuffer, 1000, &dwNumBytesRead, NULL);if (!bTest)
   dwError = GetLastError();  /* dwError now contains the error code
                                 indicating the type of failure */
```

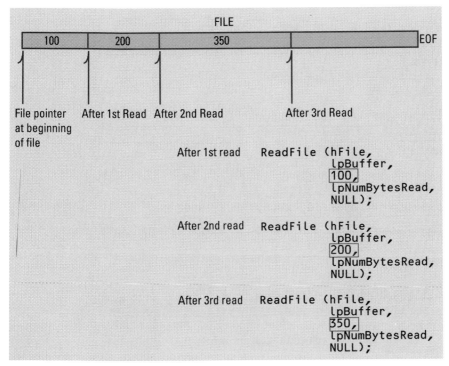

Figure 4-3 ReadFile() operation

About Overlapped I/O

Overlapped or asynchronous I/O is an advanced topic. By using overlapped I/O, you can allow your program to continue while the I/O operation is in progress. To use overlapped I/O, you must fill in an OVERLAPPED structure, and pass a pointer to the structure in the ReadFile() call, in addition, the file *must* have been created with a FILE_FLAG_OVERLAPPED flag. Since this topic is beyond the scope of this book, we will pass NULL in place of the structure pointer. This means that our programs will wait for the I/O operation to finish before continuing.

Manipulating the File Pointer

Although the file pointer is updated to the end of each block of data read, there are times when you want to randomly access data within the file. You can use the SetFilePointer() function to accomplish this task. This function

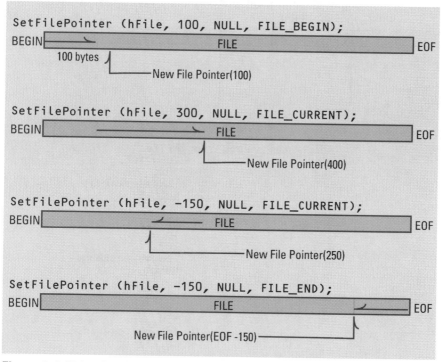

Figure 4-4 Using SetFilePointer()

requires four parameters: a valid file handle, a LONG value with the number of bytes to move the file pointer, a pointer to a LONG value (if you want to move more than $2^{32}-2$ bytes), and a DWORD indicating the *move method*. Here are three example calls to SetFilePointer():

```
SetFilePointer (hFile, 100, NULL, FILE_BEGIN);
SetFilePointer (hFile, -50, NULL, FILE_CURRENT);
SetFilePointer (hFile, -90, NULL, FILE_END);
```

The first example call moves the file pointer 100 bytes from the beginning of the file. The second example moves the pointer back 50 bytes from the current pointer position. The last example moves the pointer back 90 bytes from the end of the file.

Most files are well under the $2^{32}-2$ byte limit, therefore, the third parameter is usually set to NULL. Note that the second parameter is a *signed* LONG to move the pointer forward and backward. There are two cases where the second parameter is handled as unsigned LONG. One case is if the move method is FILE_BEGIN (we have to move forward). The second case is if the third parameter is given. Figure 4-4 illustrates the use of SetFilePointer().

The programmer is responsible for keeping track of the data within a file. You must be familiar with the contents of the file if you randomly access data. For example, if you have a file of records, each 200 bytes in length, you would probably want to move the pointer in 200-byte increments.

Now we can open a file, read its contents, and position the file pointer. The next step is to attempt to write data to the file.

Writing Data to a File

The WriteFile() function is very similar to the ReadFile() function as far as parameters go. The notable difference is the direction in which the data moves. In order to write to a file successfully, the file must have been opened with write access. In other words the second parameter to CreateFile() must be GENERIC_WRITE. Listing 4-3 shows the proper syntax and example call to WriteFile().

Listing 4-3 WriteFile() syntax and example call

```
/* WriteFile() Syntax */
BOOL WriteFile (HANDLE hFile,            /* handle to file */
               CONST VOID *lpBuffer,     /* long pointer to buffer */
               DWORD dwNumBytesToWrite,  /* number of bytes to write */
               LPDWORD dwNumBytesWritten, /* number of bytes written */
               LPOVERLAPPED lpOverlapped); /* overlapped I/O structure */

/* Example Call to WriteFile() */
DWORD dwNumBytesWritten;
char  lpBuffer["This is some test data to write to a file"];

WriteFile (hFile,                /* valid file handle */
           lpBuffer,             /* pointer to buffer containing data to be written*/
           lstrlen (lpBuffer)    /* number of bytes to write */
           &dwNumBytesWritten,   /* pointer to DWORD to store number of bytes written */
           NULL);                /* no overlapped I/O
```

Note that the WriteFile() function, like most file functions, requires a valid handle to a file. In this example call, we are writing a short string to the file. The second parameter is the pointer to the buffer. The third parameter is the number of bytes to write. In this case we are using the lstrlen() function to determine the length of the buffer. As with ReadFile(), we pass a pointer to a DWORD as the fourth parameter. The WriteFile() function will place the actual number of bytes written in this variable. Figure 4-5 shows an example call to WriteFile().

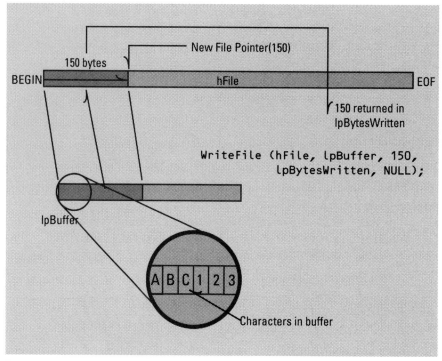

Figure 4-5 Using WriteFile()

The WriteFile() function returns a Boolean value to indicate if the function succeeds or fails. In case of a FALSE (failure) return value, you can call GetLastError() to obtain extended error information.

A DIFFERENCE BETWEEN WIN32 AND MS-DOS WRITES

WriteFile() has one characteristic that is different from the corresponding MS-DOS file functions. If you write a NULL *(dwNumBytesToWrite == 0)* to the file, it does not truncate or extend the file in any way. To truncate a file at a specific position, you should instead use the SetEndOfFile() function.

Truncating a File with SetEndOfFile()

In order to truncate a file using the Win32 API, you must position the file pointer, then make a call to SetEndOfFile(). This function only requires one parameter, the file handle. Assume we have a file open, with write access.

The file is 26 bytes and contains the consecutive capital letters of the alphabet. Using this example, we execute the following:

```
SetFilePointer (hFile, 10, NULL, FILE_BEGIN);  /* position file pointer */
SetEndOfFile (hFile);                           /* truncate file */
```

This code results in the file being truncated to 10 bytes. The file now contains only the first 10 bytes of the alphabet. The rest of the file is destroyed. Now let's assume we have the original file back and we'll look at another example usage of SetEndFile():

```
SetFilePointer (hFile, 36, NULL, FILE_BEGIN);       /* position file pointer past EOF */
SetEndOfFile (hFile);                               /* extend file 10 bytes file */
```

In this code we set the file pointer 10 bytes past the end of the file. A subsequent call to SetEndOfFile() results in the file being extended 10 bytes. The file now contains the alphabet (26 characters) plus 10 undetermined (garbage) bytes.

Flushing Data from File Buffers to Disk

Similar to MS-DOS, Windows NT maintains file buffers. You can read and write file data several times without the physical disk file getting updated. You can force the file update with the FlushFileBuffers() function. This call requires a valid handle to a file.

There are a few circumstances when a call to this function is necessary. If you have critical data that must be updated immediately, you may want to use FlushFileBuffers() to force the file update in case of system or power failure. Another example is if you have a file open for extended periods of time without closing the file handle. In this case you may want to flush the buffers to disk from time to time. Otherwise the data will be lost.

This function is not without its drawbacks, however. Flushing data to disk takes time, especially if the volume of data is significant.

Closing the File Handle

Once you have finished using the file handle, you should close it by calling CloseHandle(). This call requires a valid handle as its only parameter. Closing a file handle flushes data to disk and invalidates the file handle. If it is necessary to use the handle again, you should call CreateFile() to obtain another valid file handle.

Handles are used for other purposes in Win32. We will use handles for multitasking in Chapter 6 and for synchronization in Chapter 7. You can also close these other types of handles using the same CloseHandle() function.

Deleting a File

Deleting a file is easy in Win32 applications. The Win32 API provides the DeleteFile() function to delete a file. The function requires one parameter, a null-terminated string indicating the file to be deleted. If the file is not in the current directory, the parameter must also contain the full pathname as well as the filename. Here are two example calls to DeleteFile(). The first assumes the file is in the current directory, the second assumes the file is in a directory outside the current directory.

```
DeleteFile ("FILETEST.TXT");        /* Deletes file in current directory */
DeleteFile ("C:\DATA\FILETEST.TXT") /* Deletes file outside current directory */
```

PUTTING THE WIN32 FILE FUNCTIONS TO WORK

Our next step is to use some of these file functions in an application. The first example application is FILE1. The files for this project are located in the \CHAPTER4\4.1 subdirectory. Since the WinMain() function is typical, we will only show the WndProc() function in the text.

The FILE1 application has four menu selections: *Create, Read, Append,* and *Delete.* The *Create* selection demonstrates how to create and write data to a file using CreateFile() and WriteFile(). The *Read* selection shows how to open a file for read access and reading data from the file. The *Append* selection shows how to open a file with read/write access, position the file pointer, and write additional data to the file. The *Delete* selection shows how to delete a file.

Take a close look at the files for FILE1, shown in Listings 4-4 through 4-6. The header file, resource script, and the WndProc() function of FILE1.C are provided. Calls to the new Win32 API file functions are in boldface. A complete description of this example application follows the listing.

Listing 4-4 FILE1.RC—resource script

```
#include "windows.h"
#include "file1.h"


File1Icon ICON   file1.ico


File1Menu MENU
```

```
    BEGIN
        MENUITEM "&Create",   IDM_CREATE
        MENUITEM "&Read",            IDM_READ
        MENUITEM "&Append",   IDM_APPEND
        MENUITEM "&Delete",   IDM_DELETE
    END
```

Listing 4-5 FILE1.H—header file

```c
/* file1.h -- Include file for file1.c and file1.rc */

/* Menu defines */
#define IDM_CREATE  1
#define IDM_READ    2
#define IDM_APPEND  3
#define IDM_DELETE  4

/* Function prototype */
LONG APIENTRY WndProc (HWND, UINT, UINT, LONG);

/* Global variables */
HANDLE ghInst;
HANDLE ghWnd;
```

Listing 4-6 FILE1.C—Source File—WndProc()

```c
/* file1.c    Demonstrating Win32 File Management Functions */

#include <windows.h>            /* include for Win32 apps */
#include "file1.h"              /* include for file1.c */

/* WndProc - Main Window Procedure for file1.c */

LONG APIENTRY WndProc (HWND hWnd, UINT message, UINT wParam, LONG lParam)
{
HANDLE hFile;
char   cWriteData[]="This is data from WriteFile";
char   cAppendData[]="--and Appended using SetFilePointer and WriteFile";
char   cReadData[1024];                  /* Buffer for ReadFile() */
HDC    hDC;
DWORD  dwNumBytes;                        /* Used for read and write */
int    i;

    switch (message)
    {
      case WM_CREATE:                      /* No initialization */
          return (0);

      case WM_COMMAND:
```

continued on next page

continued from previous page

```
            switch (LOWORD(wParam))              /* Extract LOWORD of wParam for Win32) */
            {
                case IDM_CREATE:              /* Create a file--FILETEST.TXT */
                    hFile = CreateFile ("FILETEST.TXT",
                                        GENERIC_READ | GENERIC_WRITE,
                                        0,
                                        NULL,
                                        CREATE_NEW,
                                        FILE_ATTRIBUTE_NORMAL,
                                        NULL);
                    /* Write data to file */
                    WriteFile (hFile, cWriteData, lstrlen (cWriteData), &dwNumBytes, NULL);
                    CloseHandle (hFile);      /* Close file handle */
                    return (0);

                case IDM_READ:               /* Open file for reading */
                    hFile = CreateFile ("FILETEST.TXT",
                                        GENERIC_READ,
                                        0,
                                        NULL,
                                        OPEN_EXISTING,
                                        0,
                                        NULL);
                    /* Check to see if file exists */
                    if(hFile == INVALID_HANDLE_VALUE)
                    {
                      MessageBox (hWnd, "TESTFILE.TXT does not exist", "CreateFile() Failed", MB_OK);
                      return (0);
                    }
                    /* Read data from file into buffer */
                    ReadFile (hFile, cReadData, 1000, &dwNumBytes, NULL);
                    hDC = GetDC (hWnd);
                    /* Display buffer on client area */
                    TextOut (hDC, 0, 0, cReadData, lstrlen (cReadData));
                    ReleaseDC (hWnd, hDC);
                    CloseHandle (hFile);      /* Close file handle */
                    return (0);

                case IDM_APPEND:             /* Open file with read/write access */
                    hFile = CreateFile ("FILETEST.TXT",
                                        GENERIC_READ | GENERIC_WRITE,
                                        0,
                                        NULL,
                                        OPEN_EXISTING,
                                        0,
                                        NULL);
                    /* Check to see if file exists */
                    if(hFile == INVALID_HANDLE_VALUE)
                    {
                      MessageBox (hWnd, "TESTFILE.TXT does not exist", "CreateFile() Failed", MB_OK);
                      return (0);
                    }
                    /* Position file pointer at end of file */
```

```
            SetFilePointer (hFile, 0, NULL, FILE_END);
            /* Write data to file */
            WriteFile (hFile, cAppendData, lstrlen (cAppendData), &dwNumBytes, NULL);
            CloseHandle (hFile);          /* Close file handle */
            return (0);

        case IDM_DELETE:                      /* Delete FILETEST.TXT */
            DeleteFile ("FILETEST.TXT");
            for (i = 0; i < 1000; i++)    /* Clear buffer */
                cReadData[i] = 0;
            InvalidateRect (hWnd, NULL, TRUE); /* Erase client area */
            return (0);

        default:
            return (0);
    }

case WM_DESTROY:                      /* No cleanup necessary */
    PostQuitMessage (0);
    return (0);

default:
    return DefWindowProc (hWnd, message, wParam, lParam);
    }

return (0L);
}
```

Creating a File in FILE1

When the user selects *Create* from the *Main* menu, a WM_COMMAND message is sent to WndProc(). The LOWORD of *wParam* is IDM_CREATE. The first step in processing this message is to create a file named FILETEST.TXT. This is accomplished by calling CreateFile() with seven parameters. The first parameter is a null-terminated string containing the filename. The second parameter, GENERIC_READ | GENERIC_WRITE, specifies the access level of the file; in this case read and write access are requested. The third parameter is 0, indicating the file cannot be shared. The fourth parameter is NULL, meaning no security attributes are used. The fifth parameter, CREATE_NEW, indicates that we want to create a new file. The sixth parameter, FILE_ATTRIBUTE_NORMAL, indicates that the file must be created with normal attributes.

The last parameter is also NULL, indicating that no attribute template file exists.

The return value of CreateFile() is a valid handle is assigned to *hFile*. We can use this handle in a call to WriteFile() to write some data to FILETEST.TXT.

Writing Data to FILETEST.TXT

The next step in the processing of IDM_CREATE is to write some data to the newly created file. A call to WriteFile() performs this task. The first parameter is the handle obtained with CreateFile(). For the second parameter, we use a pointer to a buffer, *cWriteData,* to supply the data to write. The buffer is defined at the top of WndProc() and contains the string "This is data from WriteFile".

The third parameter to WriteFile() must be the length (in bytes) of the data to write. In this case we use *lstrlen()* to obtain the length of the string. Recall that *lstrlen()* does not include the terminating NULL character. Therefore only the characters from the string are actually written to the file.

The fourth parameter in WriteFile() is an address of a DWORD, *&dwNumBytes.* The WriteFile() function will place the actual number of bytes written in the address of *dwNumBytes.* Although we do not check this value in the example program, you may want to check it in your programs to make sure that WriteFile() has written all of the bytes successfully.

We set the last parameter of WriteFile() to NULL. This indicates that we are not using overlapped I/O. This means that we must wait for the I/O operation to complete before the next program line executes.

We are done with the file handle, so we call CloseHandle() to close the file. The file handle, *hFile,* is invalid after this line executes.

Reading Data from FILETEST.TXT

Now that FILETEST.TXT exists, we can read the data back from the file using ReadFile(). The IDM_READ segment of the *switch* statement executes when the user selects Read from the main menu. In order to call ReadFile(), we must have a valid file handle. So, we make another call to CreateFile(), this time to open the file. Since we are only going to read from the file, the desired access parameter is set to GENERIC_READ.

Another difference in the CreateFile() parameters is the fifth parameter, OPEN_EXISTING. Recall from Table 4-2, the OPEN_EXISTING parameter results in the file being opened, *if it exists.* If the file does not exist, CreateFile() returns INVALID_FILE_HANDLE. Since the user may select *Read* before the file exists, we must test the handle to make sure it is valid. If the handle is invalid, we display a message box indicating the failure and return immediately.

Assuming the file does exist, the next step is to make a call to ReadFile(). The first parameter to ReadFile() is the valid file handle. The second parameter, *cReadData,* is a pointer to a buffer to store the data. Note that we chose an arbitrary buffer size of 1,024 bytes when we defined *cReadData*. This is more than enough space to store the small amount of data in this example program.

The third parameter in ReadFile() is the number of bytes to read from the file. Again an arbitrary number of 1,000 is chosen, but the actual number of bytes read from the file is 27. Why? Because that is the total length of the file. Attempting to read more bytes than the file contains does not produce an error. The fourth parameter is an address of a DWORD, *&dwNumBytes*. ReadFile() places the actual number of bytes read in this variable.

The last parameter is set to NULL, indicating that we are not using overlapped I/O. At this point we have read 27 bytes into the buffer *cReadData*.

Now we display the data read from FILETEST.TXT in the upper-left corner of the client area. This is done using calls that are virtually identical to Windows 3.x applications. We get a handle to a device context, use TextOut() to display the data, then release the device context handle. The only difference between Win32 and Windows 3.x in this code is that *hDC* is 32 bits instead of 16 bits.

The last step in processing IDM_READ is closing the file handle. We use CloseHandle() to do so, and return.

Appending Data to FILETEST.TXT

Now we can create a file, write data to a file, and read data from a file. Let's open the file again and add some data to it. This section of code executes when the user selects *Append* from the main menu (IDM_APPEND). In order to write to the file, we must get a valid file handle. This CreateFile() call is almost identical to that in the IDM_READ section of the code. The only change is the *desired access* parameter. We use GENERIC_READ | GENERIC_WRITE for desired access, since we will write to the file. GENERIC_READ enables us to move the file pointer and GENERIC_WRITE enables us to write to the file.

As in the IDM_READ code, we test the validity of *hFile* to ensure the file exists before continuing. We don't want to attempt to append data to a file that does not exist. Once we know the file does exist, we move the file pointer to the end of the file using SetFilePointer(). This function is called with the valid file pointer as its first parameter. The other parameters to note are the second (*distance to move,* 0) and fourth (*move method,* FILE_END). This combination places the file pointer at the end of the file.

With the file pointer at the end of the file, we make another call to WriteFile(). This time we use the *cAppendData* buffer. This buffer contains the string "--and Appended using SetFilePointer and WriteFile". This results in the string (minus the NULL character) being appended onto the original file data. Once again, we close the file handle and return.

Deleting FILETEST.TXT

Now that we are done with FILETEST.TXT, we can delete it using DeleteFile(). Note that in Windows 3.x, you would make another call to OpenFile() to delete a file. In Win32 you should use DeleteFile(). There is no way to delete a file with another call to CreateFile(). CreateFile() can only create and open files. The code that deletes this file executes when the user selects *Delete* from the menu.

The DeleteFile() function is simple enough to use. The only required parameter is a null-terminated string containing the filename. The file must be in the current directory. Since our program didn't change the current directory, the DeleteFile() function will succeed. If you wish to delete a file in a different directory, you can supply a null-terminated string containing the full path and filename. We'll discuss changing directories in our next example application.

After deleting FILETEST.TXT, we fill *cReadData* with zeroes. This is done to ensure the old data is destroyed if you choose to create another FILETEST.TXT and display the data. You may have noticed that the *cReadData* buffer was also cleared in WM_CREATE. Finally we call InvalidateRect() to clear the client area. This creates the visual effect that the data was destroyed.

BUILDING AND USING FILE1

The FILE1 project is located in the \CHAPTER4\4.1 subdirectory. Open a command window and change to this directory. Type NMAKE and press (ENTER). The program will compile and link. You do not have to specify a makefile because MAKEFILE exists in the same directory. Either use the Command Prompt window to start the program, or add the FILE1 program to an existing group in the Program Manager. If you start FILE1 from the Command Prompt, type START FILE1 and press (ENTER). This will start the application and return control to the Command Prompt.

Look over the code in Listing 4-6 while performing the following steps:

1. Select the *Create* option from the main menu. This creates FILETEST.TXT.

2. Open a Command Prompt window, change to the \CHAPTER4\4.1 directory. Display the contents of the directory by typing DIR and pressing (ENTER). You should see the new file with a file size of 27 bytes.

3. Select the *Read* option. FILE1 reads the contents of FILETEST.TXT and displays them in the upper-left corner of the client area.

4. Select the *Append* option. FILE1 opens the file positions the file pointer at the end of the file and writes to FILETEST.TXT again.

5. Get another directory listing from the Command Prompt window. The file size should be 76 bytes.

6. Select the *Read* option again. The client area now shows the new contents of FILETEST.TXT. Figure 4-6 shows the output at this stage.

7. Select the *Delete* option. This deletes FILETEST.TXT and clears the client area.

8. Check the directory contents again. FILETEST.TXT should be gone.

This concludes the FILE1 example. This example application demonstrated several of the Win32 API file management functions. Using the knowledge gained in this program you are now able to:

✦ create a new file

✦ open an existing file

✦ write data to a file

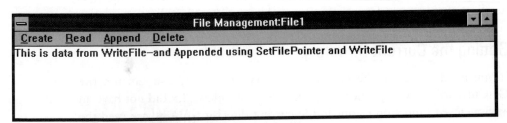

Figure 4-6 FILE1 output after append and read

- read data from a file

- position the file pointer

- append data to a file

- test the file handle to see if it's valid

- close a file handle

- delete a file

With this basic knowledge you can accomplish several tasks in Win32 file management. Some of your applications, however, may need to copy files, move files, and change directories while the program is running. These are the main topics of our next example application, FILE2. Before we get to the application, let's look at the Win32 API functions that help us carry out these tasks.

DIRECTORIES, SEARCHING, COPYING, AND MOVING

Many applications require the ability to access multiple directories at run time. They may also have the need to search for a specific file or a group of files. Once the files are located, there could be a requirement to move or copy files. The second example application in this chapter, FILE2, addresses all of these needs.

In addition to the FILE2 program files (resource file, header file, and source file), the \CHAPTER4\4.2 directory also contains six short text files. We will use these files to demonstrate several of the additions to the Win32 API. FILE2 creates two directories under the \CHAPTER4\4.2 directory. It also searches, copies, and moves files from one directory to another. Let's look at the new functions that let us perform these tasks within our Win32 applications.

Getting the Current Directory

If you need to obtain the current directory in Win32, you can use the GetCurrentDirectory() function to retrieve it. Windows 3.x did not have an equivalent API function to obtain the current directory. Instead we used the getcwd() function to retrieve it. Both Borland and Microsoft compilers have getcwd() in their run-time libraries. Since MS-DOS has been eliminated, the designers of Windows NT provide this new function as a replacement to retrieve the current directory.

GetCurrentDirectory() requires two parameters. The first is a DWORD indicating the length of the buffer in which the directory name is stored. The second parameter is a pointer to the same buffer. Listing 4-7 shows the syntax and an example call to GetCurrentDirectory().

‒ ‒ ‒ ‒ ‒ ‒ ‒

Listing 4-7 GetCurrentDirectory() syntax and example call

```
/* GetCurrentDirectory() Syntax */
DWORD GetCurrentDirectory (DWORD dwCurDir,        /* size of directory buffer */
                           LPTSTR lpszCurDir);    /* address of buffer in which to store
                                                     the directory */

/* GetCurrentDirectory() Example Call */
DWORD dwCurDir = MAX_PATH;                         /* length of buffer */
char  lpszCurDir[MAX_PATH];                        /* buffer to store directory */

   GetCurrentDirectory (dwCurDir, lpszCurDir);     /* get current directory */
```

Note that we are using the MAX_PATH define to set the buffer length. MAX_PATH is defined in WINDEF.H as 260. WINDEF.H is included automatically when we include WINDOWS.H. As long as the path doesn't exceed 260 bytes (including the NULL terminator), the function places the current directory in the buffer. The true purpose of MAX_PATH in Windows NT is to define the maximum *filename* length. Recall that the NTFS and HPFS file systems allow long filenames. Directory pathnames can exceed 260 bytes easily; however, for our example purposes, the 260-byte length is sufficient.

Although it is not shown in the above example, GetCurrentDirectory() returns a DWORD indicating the number of bytes placed in the buffer (not including the NULL terminator). If the function fails, the return value is 0. If the buffer is not large enough, the return value indicates the space needed by the buffer (again, not including the NULL terminator). Normally you will use dynamic allocation in your programs to create the buffers. If the buffer is not large enough, you can allocate additional space on the fly using the return value of GetCurrentDirectory().

Creating a Directory

When we needed to create a directory in Windows 3.x, we used the mkdir() function. This is also a part of the C run-time libraries. The Win32 API replacement for mkdir() is CreateDirectory(). This new function requires two parameters: a pointer to a string containing the pathname of the new directory, and an optional pointer to a security attributes structure. Since we won't be covering security until Chapter 8, we will use NULL as the second parameter in this chapter. Listing 4-8 shows the syntax and two example calls to CreateDirectory().

Listing 4-8 CreateDirectory() syntax and example call

```
/* CreateDirectory() Syntax */
BOOL CreateDirectory (LPTSTR lpszNewDir,              /* pointer to string for new directory */
                   LPSECURITY_ATTRIBUTES lpsa); /* pointer to optional security attr */

/* CreateDirectory() Example Calls */
   CreateDirectory ("C:\\NEWDIR", NULL);    /* create directory named NEWDIR on drive C: */

   CreateDirectory ("NEWDIR", NULL);       /* create directory under current directory */
```

Note that the second example doesn't supply the full pathname as its first parameter. This would simply create a directory under the current directory. This is the same effect as typing MD NEWDIR at the Command Prompt. The double backslash in the first call prevents the backslash from being interpreted as an escape character.

CreateDirectory() returns a Boolean value; TRUE on success and FALSE on failure. You can follow up a failed call with GetLastError() to obtain extended error information.

Removing a Directory

The RemoveDirectory() function is the replacement for the rmdir() function from the run-time library. This function requires one parameter: a pointer to a null-terminated string indicating the directory to be removed. Listing 4-9 shows the syntax and an example call to RemoveDirectory().

Listing 4-9 RemoveDirectory() syntax and example call

```
/* RemoveDirectory() Syntax */
BOOL RemoveDirectory (LPTSTR lpszDir); /* pointer to directory name to delete */

/* RemoveDirectory() Example Call */

   RemoveDirectory ("C:\\NEWDIR");  /* removes directory NEWDIR on drive C: */
```

RemoveDirectory() also returns a Boolean value, which you can test for success or failure. Three common failures for this function are: the specified directory does not exist, the directory is not empty, or your program does not have access to the directory. Not having *access* is the result of security attributes (if used) or of another application using the directory.

Searching for Files

To find files in Windows 3.x, we used the findfirst() and findnext() functions. The replacement functions in Win32 are similar in operation, but the parameters are quite different. These new Win32 functions are FindFirstFile() and FindNextFile().

Using FindFirstFile()

FindFirstFile() finds the first occurrence of a file specified by the first parameter to the function. This function requires two parameters, the first being a pointer to a null-terminated string indicating the path and filename to find. The second parameter is a pointer to a WIN32_FIND_DATA structure. This structure is filled in by FindFirstFile(), provided the function is successful. The filename specified in the first parameter can contain wildcard characters (such as. *.TMP, FILE?.TXT). Listing 4-10 shows the syntax and two example calls to FindFirstFile().

Listing 4-10 FindFirstFile() syntax and example calls

```
/* FindFirstFile() Syntax */
HANDLE FindFirstFile (LPTSTR lpszSearchFile,          /* pointer to name of file to search for */
                      LPWIN32_FIND_DATA lpFindData); /* pointer to find data structure */

/* FindFirstFile() Example Calls */
WIN32_FIND_DATA   FindData;
HANDLE            hSearch;

    /* finds first file in WINNT directory with an EXE extension */
    hSearch = FindFirstFile ("C:\\WINNT\\*.EXE", &FindData);

    /* finds first file in the current directory that matches the FILE?.TXT wildcard */
    hSearch = FindFirstFile ("FILE?.TXT", &FindData);
```

Notice that this function returns a *search handle*. This handle is used in the next function we will be covering, FindNextFile(). If this FindFirstFile() function fails, the return value is INVALID_HANDLE_VALUE. If the function succeeds, *hSearch* contains a valid handle and the *FindData* structure is filled with the appropriate information. Listing 4-11 shows the WIN32_FIND_DATA data structure.

Listing 4-11 WIN32_FIND_DATA structure

```
typedef struct _WIN32_FIND_DATA {
    DWORD dwFileAttributes;
    FILETIME ftCreationTime;
    FILETIME ftLastAccessTime;
    FILETIME ftLastWriteTime;
    DWORD nFileSizeHigh;
    DWORD nFileSizeLow;
    DWORD dwReserved0;
    DWORD dwReserved1;
    CHAR    cFileName[ MAX_PATH ];
    CHAR    cAlternateFileName[ 14 ];
} WIN32_FIND_DATA;
```

This structure contains just about all the information you will ever need about a file—the file attributes, creation time, last access time, last write time, file size, and two types of filenames. The *cFileName* member is a null-terminated string containing the filename found. The *cAlternateFileName* member is used if you are switching between the FAT and NTFS systems. For example, since NTFS supports extended filenames, a filename could exceed the 8.3 format used on FAT partitions. This structure lets you obtain a name for either type of system; *cFileName* for NTFS and *cAlternateFileName* for FAT.

In the following application examples, we use the *cFileName* member, since all our filenames in this book adhere to the 8.3 format. In this case *cAlternateFileName* contains the identical data.

Using FindNextFile()

Once we have a valid search handle (returned by FindFirstFile()), we can continue our search for additional files that match the same criteria. FindNextFile() requires two parameters: a valid search handle, and a pointer to a WIN32_FIND_DATA structure. The function returns a Boolean value that indicates if the find is successful. Listing 4-12 shows the syntax and an example call to FindNextFile().

Listing 4-12 FindNextFile() syntax and example call

```
/* FindNextFile() Syntax */
BOOL FindNextFile (HANDLE hFindFile,          /* search handle from FindFirstFile() */
```

```
                LPWIN32_FIND_DATA lpFindData);   /* pointer to find data structure */

/* FindNextFile() Example Call */
BOOL             bNotDone = TRUE;
WIN32_FIND_DATA FindData;

   while (bNotDone)                              /* continue until FindNextFile() fails */
   {
      [do something with the results]
      bNotDone = FindNextFile (hSearch, &FindData); /* find another file */
   }
```
[other program lines]

Note that we do something with the results *before* calling FindNextFile(). Otherwise we would not do anything to the first file found. This function searches for additional files that match the criteria set in the original call to FindFirstFile(). As long as the function finds another file that matches the criteria, the *FindData* structure is filled and the function returns TRUE. When no more files match the criteria, FindNextFile() returns FALSE and we drop out of the *while* loop. Note that we can do anything we want with the results during the loop (such as open, delete, copy files). We find the next file after performing on the previous file. This way, when FindNextFile() fails, we do not perform any other action. It is for this reason that you will normally place FindNextFile() at the bottom of the loop.

Figure 4-7 shows an overview of FindFirstFile() and FindNextFile() in action.

FindClose()—Closing the Search Handle

FindClose() is a very easy function to use. It's also an easy function to forget. It is very important to close a file search handle when you are finished with a search. Failing to close the search handle can result in hard-to-find bugs. For example, if you attempt to remove a directory, and a search handle is open on the directory, the attempt will fail. It appears to the system as if another program (called a *process* in Windows NT) has control of the directory.

The FindClose() function requires one parameter, a valid file search handle. It is important to remember the following steps when searching for files:

1. Call FindFirstFile() to start the search (file search handle created).

2. Repetitively call FindNextFile() if necessary (using the valid handle).

3. Close file handle with FindClose().

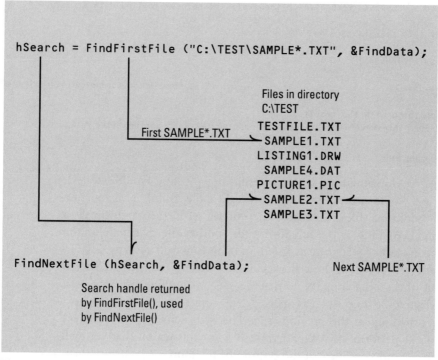

Figure 4-7 FindFirstFile() and FindNextFile() in action

Copying Files

Copying files is a multistep process in Windows 3.x. There is no single function in the Windows 3.x API (or the C run-time library) to copy a file. Fortunately, in Win32, copying files is a one-step process. This is accomplished by calling the CopyFile() function.

CopyFile() requires three parameters. The first parameter is a pointer to a null-terminated string indicating the file to be copied. The second parameter is a null-terminated string containing the destination filename. The last parameter is a Boolean variable. This parameter specifies whether the function should fail if the destination file already exists. If this parameter is TRUE, CopyFile() fails if the destination file exists. If the third parameter is FALSE, the destination file is overwritten. Listing 4-13 shows the syntax and some example calls to CopyFile().

▬ ▬ ▬ ▬ ▬ ▬
Listing 4-13 CopyFile() syntax and example calls

```
/* CopyFile() Syntax */
BOOL CopyFile (LPTSTR lpszSource,    /* pointer to existing filename */
               LPTSTR lpszDest,      /* pointer to filename to copy to */
               BOOL   bFileExists);  /* fail if file exists? */


/* CopyFile() Example Calls */

   /* Copies file TESTFILE.TXT to TESTFILE.BAK if TESTFILE.BAK does not exist */
   CopyFile ("TESTFILE.TXT", "TESTFILE.BAK", TRUE);

   /* Copies TESTFILE.TXT (in DIR1 directory) to TESTFILE.TXT (in DIR2 directory)
      overwrites destination if it exists */
   CopyFile ("C:\\DIR1\\TESTFILE.TXT", "C:\\DIR2\\TESTFILE.TXT", FALSE);

   /* This always fails you cannot copy a file onto itself, even if third parameter is FALSE */
   CopyFile ("TESTFILE.TXT", "TESTFILE.TXT", FALSE);
```

The first example assumes the files are in the current directory. The function fails if TESTFILE.BAK exists, because the third parameter is TRUE. The second example demonstrates that you can specify full pathnames in the call. This will copy over TESTFILE.TXT in C:\DIR2 if it already exists, because the third parameter is FALSE. The last example will never work, because, in MS–DOS, you cannot copy a file onto itself. The third parameter doesn't matter in this case.

The CopyFile() function returns a Boolean value that can be tested for success or failure. Common failures of CopyFile include:

◁ Source file does not exist.

◁ Destination file exists, and third parameter to CopyFile() is set to TRUE.

◁ Pathname in source or destination is bad.

◁ Attempting to copy a file onto itself.

There are other possibilities for CopyFile() failure (disk full, hardware problem, and so on). Most of the problems you will run into, however, are the four cases listed above.

Moving Files

Like copying files, moving files in Windows 3.x is also a multistep process. The Win32 API provides a function to move files easily. MoveFile() takes an existing file, copies it to a new location, and deletes the original. If the pathname of the source and destination file are the same, MoveFile() simply renames the file. This function requires two parameters: a pointer to a null-terminated string indicating the file to be moved, and a pointer to a second null-terminated string indicating the new location (or filename). Listing 4-14 shows the syntax and some example calls to MoveFile().

Listing 4-14 MoveFile() syntax and example calls

```
/* MoveFile() Syntax */
BOOL MoveFile (LPTSTR lpszSource,     /* pointer to existing filename */
               LPTSTR lpszNewName);   /* pointer to new filename */

/* MoveFile() Example Calls */

    /* Renames TESTFILE.001 to TESTFILE.002 (current directory) */
    MoveFile ("TESTFILE.001", "TESTFILE.002");

    /* Moves file, TESTFILE.001, from C:\DIR1 to C:\DIR2 */
    MoveFile ("C:\DIR1\TESTFILE.001", "C:\\DIR2\\TESTFILE.001");

    /* Moves file, TESTFILE.001 from C:\DIR1 to C:\DIR2 and renames to TESTFILE.002 */
    MoveFile ("C:\DIR1\TESTFILE.001", "C:\\DIR2\\TESTFILE.002");
```

The first example call simply *renames* the file. Since the strings don't contain pathnames, the current directory is assumed. The second example call *moves* a file from one directory to another. The original file is deleted. The last example *moves* and *renames* the file. Again, the original file is deleted.

The MoveFile() function returns a Boolean value. This function always fails (returns FALSE) if the destination file exists. MoveFile() also fails if either pathname does not exist.

FILE2—DIRECTORY AND FILE EXAMPLES

Now that you have a basic understanding of these new Win32 API functions, let's look at an example program that puts them to the test. Our second example, FILE2, demonstrates a number of topics. These topics are

 getting the current directory

 creating new directories

- searching for files
- copying files
- moving files
- removing directories

The FILE2 application creates two directories under the current directory. After the directories are successfully created, we search for and copy six files into one of the new directories. Then we start a new search in the new directory. This results in three of the files matching the search criteria. We move the three files into the second directory. Finally we clean up by deleting all of the new files and removing the directories. This restores the directory status to the same state it was when the program began.

Let's take a look at the program files for FILE2. The WinMain() function is typical, and is therefore omitted from the listing. You can browse FILE2.C in its entirety by loading it into a text editor or printing it out. The files for this project are located in the \CHAPTER4\4.2 subdirectory. In addition to the program files, this directory contains six sample files that the FILE1 program uses to demonstrate searching, copying, and moving files. Listings 4-15 through 4-17 show the resource, header, and partial source file for FILE2. A complete description of the program follows the listings.

Note that the only menu item that is enabled in the resource script is *Create Directory*. We will enable the other menu items within the program.

Listing 4-15 FILE2.RC—resource script

```
#include "windows.h"
#include "file2.h"

File2Icon ICON  file2.ico

File2Menu MENU
    BEGIN
        MENUITEM "&Create Directory",    IDM_CREATE_DIR
        MENUITEM "Copy &Files",          IDM_COPY, GRAYED
        MENUITEM "&Move Files",          IDM_MOVE, GRAYED
        MENUITEM "&Delete Files",        IDM_DELETE, GRAYED
        MENUITEM "&Remove Directory",    IDM_REMOVE_DIR, GRAYED
    END
```

The header file contains a new function prototype for UpdateMenu(). This function enables and disables menu items.

Listing 4-16 FILE2.H—header file

```
/* file2.h -- Include file for file2.c and file2.rc */

/* Menu defines */
#define IDM_CREATE_DIR    1
#define IDM_COPY          2
#define IDM_MOVE          3
#define IDM_DELETE        4
#define IDM_REMOVE_DIR    5


/* Function prototype */
LONG APIENTRY WndProc (HWND, UINT, UINT, LONG);
VOID UpdateMenu (WORD wMenuID);


/* Global variables */
HANDLE ghInst;
HANDLE ghWnd;
```

Listing 4-17 FILE2.C—source file (partial)

```
/* file2.c       Demonstrating Win32 File Management Functions */

#include <windows.h>              /* include for Win32 apps */
#include "file2.h"                /* include for file2.c */


/* WndProc - Main Window Procedure for file2.c */

LONG APIENTRY WndProc (HWND hWnd, UINT message, UINT wParam, LONG lParam)
{
DWORD           dwCurDir = MAX_PATH;   /* length of directory buffer */
HANDLE          hSearch;               /* file search handle */
                                       /* static buffers for directory paths */
static char     lpszCurDir[MAX_PATH], lpszNewDir1[MAX_PATH], lpszNewDir2[MAX_PATH];
                                       /* buffers for search, copy, delete, and move paths */
char            lpszSearchPath[MAX_PATH], lpszCopyPath[MAX_PATH];
char            lpszDelPath[MAX_PATH], lpszMovePath[MAX_PATH];
BOOL            bNotDone = TRUE;        /* boolean for searches */
WIN32_FIND_DATA FindData;

   switch (message)
   {
      case WM_CREATE:                    /* get current directory on startup */
         GetCurrentDirectory (dwCurDir, lpszCurDir);
         return (0);

      case WM_COMMAND:
```

```
switch (LOWORD(wParam))            /* Extract LOWORD of wParam for Win32 */
{
    case IDM_CREATE_DIR:           /* create two directories under current */
        lstrcpy (lpszNewDir1, lpszCurDir);
        lstrcat (lpszNewDir1, "\\CREATE1");
        CreateDirectory (lpszNewDir1, NULL);
        lstrcpy (lpszNewDir2, lpszCurDir);
        lstrcat (lpszNewDir2, "\\CREATE2");
        CreateDirectory (lpszNewDir2, NULL);
        UpdateMenu (IDM_CREATE_DIR); /* update menu */
        return (0);

    case IDM_COPY:                 /* copy SAMPLE*.* to \CREATE1 */
        lstrcpy (lpszSearchPath, lpszCurDir);
        lstrcat (lpszSearchPath, "\\SAMPLE*.*");
        hSearch = FindFirstFile (lpszSearchPath, &FindData);  /* find first file */
        while (bNotDone)           /* search loop */
        {
            lstrcpy (lpszCopyPath, lpszNewDir1);
            lstrcat (lpszCopyPath, "\\");
            lstrcat (lpszCopyPath, FindData.cFileName);
            CopyFile (FindData.cFileName, lpszCopyPath, FALSE);/* copy file */
            bNotDone = FindNextFile (hSearch, &FindData);      /* find next file */
        }
        FindClose (hSearch);        /* close search handle */
        UpdateMenu (IDM_COPY);      /* update menu */
        return (0);

    case IDM_MOVE:                 /* move *.DAT to \CREATE2 */
        lstrcpy (lpszSearchPath, lpszNewDir1);
        lstrcat (lpszSearchPath, "\\*.DAT");
        hSearch = FindFirstFile (lpszSearchPath, &FindData);  /* find first file */
        while (bNotDone)
        {
            lstrcpy (lpszCopyPath, lpszNewDir1);
            lstrcat (lpszCopyPath, "\\");
            lstrcat (lpszCopyPath, FindData.cFileName);        /* source file */
            lstrcpy (lpszMovePath, lpszNewDir2);
            lstrcat (lpszMovePath, "\\");
            lstrcat (lpszMovePath, FindData.cFileName);        /* destination file */
            MoveFile (lpszCopyPath, lpszMovePath);             /* move file */
            bNotDone = FindNextFile (hSearch, &FindData);      /* find next file */
        }
        FindClose (hSearch);        /* close search handle */
        UpdateMenu (IDM_MOVE);      /* update menu */
        return (0);

    case IDM_DELETE:               /* delete files in \CREATE1 and \CREATE2 */
        lstrcpy (lpszSearchPath, lpszNewDir1);
        lstrcat (lpszSearchPath, "\\SAMPLE*.*");
        hSearch = FindFirstFile (lpszSearchPath, &FindData);   /* find first file */
        while (bNotDone)                                       /* \CREATE1 search */
        {
```

continued on next page

continued from previous page

```
                    lstrcpy (lpszDelPath, lpszNewDir1);
                    lstrcat (lpszDelPath, "\\");
                    lstrcat (lpszDelPath, FindData.cFileName);
                    DeleteFile (lpszDelPath);  /* delete file */
                    bNotDone = FindNextFile (hSearch, &FindData);       /* find next file */
                }
                FindClose (hSearch);      /* close handle */
                lstrcpy (lpszSearchPath, lpszNewDir2);                 /* \CREATE2 search */
                lstrcat (lpszSearchPath, "\\SAMPLE*.*");
                hSearch = FindFirstFile (lpszSearchPath, &FindData);   /* find first file */
                bNotDone = TRUE;                                       /* reset bNotDone */
                while (bNotDone)
                 {
                    lstrcpy (lpszDelPath, lpszNewDir2);
                    lstrcat (lpszDelPath, "\\");
                    lstrcat (lpszDelPath, FindData.cFileName);
                    DeleteFile (lpszDelPath);                          /* delete file */
                    bNotDone = FindNextFile (hSearch, &FindData);      /* find next file */
                }
                FindClose (hSearch);           /* close search handle */
                UpdateMenu (IDM_DELETE);  /* update menu */
                return (0);

            case IDM_REMOVE_DIR:                  /* remove directories */
                RemoveDirectory (lpszNewDir1); /* remove \CREATE1 */
                RemoveDirectory (lpszNewDir2); /* remove \CREATE2 */
                UpdateMenu (IDM_REMOVE_DIR);   /* update menu */
                return (0);

            default:
                return (0);
        }

    case WM_DESTROY:                       /* No cleanup necessary */
        PostQuitMessage (0);
        return (0);

    default:
        return DefWindowProc (hWnd, message, wParam, lParam);
    }

    return (0L);
}


/* UpdateMenu -- This function cycles the menu selections. It is called
   with the menu ID from WndProc()*/

VOID UpdateMenu (WORD wMenuID)
{
HANDLE hMenu;

    hMenu = GetMenu (ghWnd);               /* get handle to main menu */

    EnableMenuItem (hMenu, wMenuID++, MF_BYCOMMAND | MF_GRAYED);  /* gray current selection */
```

```
    if (wMenuID > IDM_REMOVE_DIR) wMenuID = IDM_CREATE_DIR;    /* cycle back to start? */
    EnableMenuItem (hMenu, wMenuID, MF_BYCOMMAND | MF_ENABLED); /* and enable the next */
    DrawMenuBar (ghWnd);                                        /* redraw menu bar */

}
```

Some Background Information about FILE2

FILE2 operates on six files that you don't see in the listings. These are small text files named SAMPLE1.TXT, SAMPLE2.TXT, SAMPLE3.TXT, SAMPLE1.DAT, SAMPLE2.DAT, and SAMPLE3.DAT. Note that these files use three distinct filenames with two different extensions. These files are in the \CHAPTER4\4.2 directory along with the program files.

The UpdateMenu() Function

The FILE2 program has five menu selections: *Create Directory, Copy Files, Move Files, Delete Files,* and *Remove Directory*. Since each consecutive menu selection relies on the previous one, we added the UpdateMenu() function to enable and disable selections. Recall that the only selection enabled at start up is *Create Directory*.

The function takes one parameter, a WORD containing the *menu id (wMenuID)*. When the user selects a menu item, the code in WndProc() processes the message and calls UpdateMenu(), along with the current *menu id*. UpdateMenu() disables the current selection and enables the next selection.

The only sticky part is when the selection is *Remove Directory*, or IDM_REMOVE_DIR, we cannot increment the *wMenuID* past the end of the selections. So we included an *if* statement to check for this event and set the *wMenuID* back to the first selection.

Buffers, Buffers, and More Buffers

If you looked at the top of WndProc(), you may have noticed several static and automatic buffers. We created all of these buffers to make the example application easier to understand. Admittedly this program could be rewritten to maximize efficiency; it is much more important, however, to understand how the file and directory functions are working. Some of the buffers could have been used in different sections of the program. Even better, we could have dynamically allocated the buffers at run time. But this would involve too many allocations and cloud the issue at hand: files and directories.

Three of the buffers are defined as static: *lpszCurDir* (for the current directory), *lpszNewDir1* (for the \CREATE1 directory), and *lpszNewDir2* (for this \CREATE2 directory). These buffers are used throughout

145

WndProc(), and must retain the pathnames of the three directories. Let's analyze this example.

Getting the Current Directory

The first thing FILE2 does (during the processing of WM_CREATE) is get the current working directory. This is the directory from which FILE2 is executed. The call to GetCurrentDirectory() uses *dwCurDir* (length of buffer) and *lpszCurDir* (the buffer itself). At this point the current directory is stored in *lpszCurDir.*

Creating the New Directories

When the user selects *Create Directory*, we must process the IDM_CREATE_DIR message by creating two new directories. Let's look at the first new directory. We copy the current directory name into *lpszNewDir1* with lstrcpy(). We then tack on the new directory (\\CREATE1) to *lpszNewDir1* with lstrcat(). Now we have a complete path to the new directory. We call CreateDirectory() with *lpszNewDir1* as its first parameter (the second parameter is NULL: no security attributes). If you didn't move your disk files after installing them, you now have the following path: \CHAPTER4\4.2\CREATE1.

The same procedure is repeated to create a second directory (\CREATE2). We now have two new subdirectories under the current directory. We call UpdateMenu() to cycle to the next menu selection.

Searching and Copying Files

The next menu selection is *Copy Files,* or IDM_COPY as it's known to WndProc(). We copy the current directory into a buffer named *lpszSearchPath.* We will use this buffer to search for our sample files. We tack on the search criteria with lstrcat(). The *lpszSearchPath* now contains ...\4.2\SAMPLE*.*.

Now we call FindFirstFile() using *lpszSearchPath* and a pointer to a WIN32_FIND_DATA structure (FindData). The function returns a valid search handle, which we store in *hSearch.* We have now reached the *while* loop.

The first step in the *while* loop is to build the destination of our file. We copy the first new directory into *lpszCopyPath,* append a backslash, and append the first filename. This is done using the *FindData* structure element *cFileName.* We can copy the file using CopyFile(), with the filename as the first parameter and the new filename as the second parameter. This new filename is the new directory path plus the original filename. The first file that matches the SAMPLE*.* criteria has been copied to the new directory.

The last step in the *while* loop is a call to FindNextFile(). All this function requires is the search handle and a pointer to the structure. If the function finds another file, *bNotDone* is TRUE and the *while* loop executes again. At this point, FindNextFile() will return TRUE because all six sample files match the criteria. After the sixth file is copied, the FindNextFile() function returns FALSE, *bNotDone* is set to FALSE, and the *while* loop is done. All six files have been copied to the new directory.

Now that we have finished searching, we close the file search handle with FindClose(). Another call to UpdateMenu() advances the menu to the next selection.

Moving Files

The next menu option is *Move Files*. The code in the IDM_MOVE section of WndProc() handles the moving of files in our sample program. As with the copy functions, we first search for some files. This time, however, we will search the \CREATE1 directory *(lpszNewDir1)* for files with the extension DAT.

The other difference in this section of code is in the *while* loop. Instead of moving files from the current directory, we move them from the \CREATE1 directory into the \CREATE2 directory. To accomplish this we build two paths. One path, *lpszCopyPath,* is the source (\CREATE1 plus the filename), and the other, *lpszMovePath,* is the destination (\CREATE2 plus the filename). Instead of copying the files, we call MoveFile() instead. This loop executes three times, because three of the sample data files have the DAT extension.

After the MoveFile() has moved the three files, the *while* loop ends and we close the file search handle. We now have three files in \CREATE1 and three files in \CREATE2. A call to UpdateMenu() cycles the menu to the fourth selection, which will delete the files.

Cleaning Up the Files

Before we can remove the two directories, we must search both directories and delete the files we moved or copied into them. We use the search criteria SAMPLE*.* since this matches all of the files, but we have to search each directory individually. The first portion of code searches the \CREATE1 directory, while the second portion searches \CREATE2.

Each file that is found by the two searches is deleted using DeleteFile(). After both searches have been completed, the two directories are empty and, as a result, can be removed by the next menu selection.

Notice that we reset the *bNotDone* variable to TRUE before starting the next search. Otherwise the second *while* loop would fail on the first pass. We did not have to reset this variable in the other sections since it is always set to TRUE when it is defined at the top of WndProc(). This is the only section of code that performs *two* searches before returning to Win32. A call to UpdateMenu() sets the last menu selection.

Removing the Directories

The last step in this program occurs when the user selects *Remove Directory*. Since both of our new directory paths are still in tact in static buffers, we simply call RemoveDirectory() for each path. We call UpdateMenu(), which cycles the menu back to the first selection. We are now back to the original state of our application.

BUILDING AND USING FILE2

You may have noticed that FILE2 never provided any output to the client area. There are two ways to observe the effects of FILE2, the File Manager or a Command Prompt window. We will use the Command Prompt method in our demonstration. Before we get to this demo, you need to compile and link FILE2. Open a Command Prompt window and change to the \CHAPTER4\4.2 directory. Type NMAKE and press (ENTER).

You may want to review the source code in Listing 4–17 while performing the following steps:

1. Start FILE2 by typing START FILE2 and pressing (ENTER) at the Command Prompt.

2. Size the FILE2 window vertically so you can see both the Command Prompt window and the FILE2 window.

3. Use the Command Prompt window to get a directory listing. You should see the files for the FILE2 program, the sample files, and no subdirectories.

4.   Select *Create* from the FILE2 main menu, then get another directory from the Command Prompt window. You should see two new directory entries: CREATE1 and CREATE2.

5.   Select *Copy Files*. Go back to the Command Prompt window, change to the CREATE1 directory by typing CD CREATE1, and press (ENTER). Get a directory listing. The six files have been copied to the new directory.

6.   Select *Move Files*. Get another directory listing of CREATE1; three of the files are gone, only the TXT files remain in CREATE1. Change to the CREATE2 directory by typing CD ..\CREATE2 and press (ENTER). Get a directory listing. Here are the files that were moved. Figure 4-8 shows the program at this point.

7.   Select *Delete Files*. Get a directory listing of CREATE2. All files have been deleted. You can also check the contents of the CREATE1 directory.

8.   Before selecting *Remove Directory*, make sure you have changed the Command Prompt window out of the CREATE1 or CREATE2 directory (CD ..). With that done, select the last menu option. Get

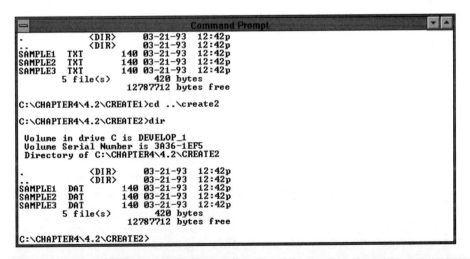

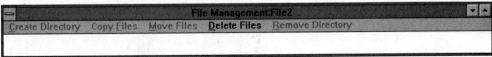

Figure 4-8 FILE2 after Move Files

a directory listing of \CHAPTER4\4.2; CREATE1 and CREATE2 have been removed.

If you did not change the Command Prompt window out of one of the new directories, the directory cannot be removed. Why? Because the Command Prompt window has access to the directory. You cannot remove a directory when another process has access to it. This will not have the same effect if you are using the File Manager. The File Manager displays the contents of the disk to the client area, then releases control of the subdirectory. If you try to access the directories after deleting them, the File Manager indicates the directory no longer exists.

This completes the FILE2 example application. Now, in addition to creating, reading/writing, and manipulating individual files, you also have the ability to:

 create and remove directories

 copy and move files

 search for files

 get file information by searching

Although we can get file information by searching, there are faster, more efficient ways to get file information. There is only one catch. We must know the filename in advance. The next section of this chapter deals with this issue.

GETTING FILE INFORMATION DIRECTLY

We have already seen that we can find just about everything we want to know about a file by searching. However, when we already have a filename, we can find specific information faster. We can get and set attributes of a specific file, find the file size, and find a host of file information using a valid file handle.

The third example program in this chapter, FILE3, demonstrates the Win32 API functions that obtain file information. Also, we will get and set file attributes for a sample file. Let's take a close look at the new functions that we will use in FILE3.

Getting File Information by Handle

We can get detailed file information on any open file by using its handle. The Win32 API function that lets us accomplish this has a lengthy, yet descriptive name: GetFileInformationByHandle(). This function requires two parameters, the first being the open file handle. The second parameter is a pointer to a structure of BY_HANDLE_FILE_INFORMATION type. A call to this function fills the structure with data about the file. Here is an example call, assuming that a file is opened, and its handle is *hFile.*

```
HANDLE                     hFile;
BY_HANDLE_FILE_INFORMATION    FileInfo;

    GetFileInformationByHandle (hFile, &FileInfo);  /* fill the FileInfo struct with info */
```

Now let's take a look at the typedef of the structure with the huge name. Listing 4-18 shows the BY_HANDLE_FILE_INFORMATION structure. Note the similarity between this structure and the WIN32_FIND_DATA structure we used in the last example program. The major difference is the lack of the filenames at the bottom of the structure. This makes sense; since we opened the file (and obtained the file handle) we *should* know its name already.

Listing 4-18 BY_HANDLE_FILE_INFORMATION structure

```
typedef struct _BY_HANDLE_FILE_INFORMATION {
    DWORD dwFileAttributes;      /* file attributes */
    FILETIME ftCreationTime;     /* creation time, 0 if file system does not support */
    FILETIME ftLastAccessTime;   /* last access, 0 if file system does not support */
    FILETIME ftLastWriteTime;    /* last write, works for all file systems */
    DWORD dwVolumeSerialNumber;  /* volume/serial of drive containing file */
    DWORD nFileSizeHigh;         /* high 32-bits of filesize */
    DWORD nFileSizeLow;          /* low 32-bits of filesize */
    DWORD nNumberOfLinks;        /* number of links to the file (NTFS only) */
    DWORD nFileIndexHigh;        /* high 32-bits of file unique ID */
    DWORD nFileIndexLow;         /* low 32-bits of file unique ID */
} BY_HANDLE_FILE_INFORMATION;
```

New members to this structure are *dwVolumSerialNumber, nNumberOfLinks, nFileIndexHigh,* and *nFileIndexLow.* The first of these members is a DWORD indicating the volume/serial of the media containing the file. This member, combined with the last two members, forms a unique ID to the file. The *nNumberOfLinks* member is for the NT file system only. It indicates the current number of links to the file. File links are beyond the scope of this book.

In our example application, we will demonstrate accessing the file attributes using a file handle.

Getting the Size of a File

The GetFileSize() function retrieves the size of a file in bytes. The function requires two parameters: a valid file handle and an optional pointer to a DWORD. The pointer to a DWORD is needed if the file size exceeds $2^{32}-2$ bytes (nearly 4 gigabytes). It's safe to say that most of our files will stay under this modest limit. But if the technology advances to that point, Win32 and Windows NT are ready for it! Listing 4-19 shows the syntax and an example call to GetFileSize().

— — — — — —

Listing 4-19 GetFileSize() syntax and example call

```
/* GetFileSize() Syntax */
DWORD GetFileSize (HANDLE hFile,              /* handle to file */
                   LPDWORD lpdwFileSizeHigh);  /* high 32 bits of file size */

/* GetFileSize() Example Call */
DWORD  dwFileSize;

   dwFileSize = GetFileSize ("SAMPLE.TXT", NULL); /* get size of SAMPLE.TXT */
```

The GetFileSize() function returns a DWORD indicating the size of the file in bytes. We will use this function in our next example application.

Getting File Attributes

If you need to determine the attributes of a file from within your application, the Win32 API provides a function to do just that: GetFileAttributes(). This function requires a pointer to a null-terminated string indicating the filename. If the string contains only the filename, the file is assumed to be in the current directory. You can also use a string with the entire path and filename to get attributes of files outside the current directory. Listing 4-20 shows the syntax and two example calls to GetFileAttributes().

— — — — — —

Listing 4-20 GetFileAttributes() syntax and example calls

```
/* GetFileAttributes() Syntax */
DWORD GetFileAttributes (LPTSTR lpszFilename); /* pointer to filename */
```

```
/* GetFileAttributes() Example Calls */
DWORD dwAttributes;

    dwAttributes = GetFileAttributes ("SAMPLE.TXT");  /* retrieves attributes of SAMPLE.TXT */
    dwAttributes = GetFileAttributes ("C:\DOS\EMM386.EXE"); /* accessing another directory */
```

The DWORD that GetFileAttributes() returns contains the attributes in bit form. Figure 4-9 shows the individual bits and the attributes they represent.

Each of the attributes is defined in WINNT.H. This header file is automatically included if you include WINDOWS.H. Table 4-3 shows the file attributes and their defined hexadecimal values.

Masking an Attribute

To check to see if a file has a particular attribute, you can mask the attributes returned by GetFileAttributes() with the attribute define. We do this by using

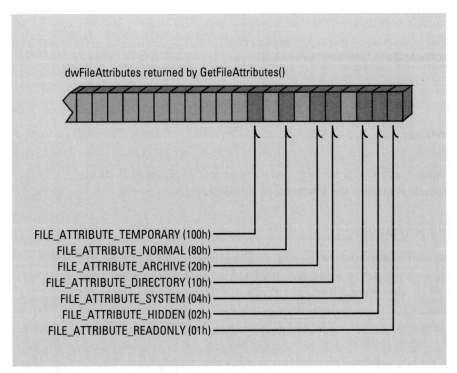

Figure 4-9 DWORD containing file attributes

Attribute	Defined as
FILE_ATTRIBUTE_READONLY	0x00000001
FILE_ATTRIBUTE_HIDDEN	0x00000002
FILE_ATTRIBUTE_SYSTEM	0x00000004
FILE_ATTRIBUTE_DIRECTORY	0x00000010
FILE_ATTRIBUTE_ARCHIVE	0x00000020
FILE_ATTRIBUTE_NORMAL	0x00000080

Table 4-3 Attribute definitions from WINNT.H

the *bitwise and* (&) to mask out the desired archive bit. Here is an example of masking to see if a *read only* attribute exists:

```
DWORD dwAttributes;

   dwAttributes = GetFileAttributes ("SAMPLE.TXT");
   if (dwAttributes & FILE_ATTRIBUTE_READONLY)
   {
      [yes it's readonly!]
   }
   else
   {
      [no, it's not readonly]
   }
```

If the specified attribute is set, the *if* statement is TRUE (non-0). If the specified attribute is not set, the *if* statement is FALSE (0).

Setting File Attributes

You can also set file attributes using the SetFileAttributes() function. This function requires a pointer to a null-terminated string specifying the filename and a DWORD with the attribute bits. Listing 4-21 shows the syntax for SetFileAttributes() and an example that gets a file's existing attributes and adds the archive bit.

▬ ▬ ▬ ▬ ▬ ▬

Listing 4-21 SetFileAttributes() syntax and example call

```
/* SetFileAttributes() Syntax */
BOOL SetFileAttributes (LPTSTR lpszFilename,       /* pointer to filename */
                        DWORD  dwFileAttributes);  /* file attributes to set */


/* SetFileAttributes() Example Call */
DWORD dwAttributes;

    dwAttributes = GetFileAttributes ("SAMPLE.TXT");        /* get current attributes */
    dwAttributes = dwAttributes | FILE_ATTRIBUTE_ARCHIVE;   /* bitwise OR the new attribute */
    SetFileAttributes ("SAMPLE.TXT", dwAttributes);         /* set new attributes */
```

This time we use the *bitwise or* (|) to combine the existing attributes with the new attribute. If the bit is already set, the attributes remain the same.

THE LONELY NORMAL ATTRIBUTE

If you set the FILE_ATTRIBUTE_NORMAL attribute (80h), all other bits (Archive, Read Only, etc.) are reset automatically in the call to SetFileAttributes(). The only exception is the FILE_ATTRIBUTE_DIRECTORY bit. But for files the normal bit always stands alone; no other bit can be set at the same time. Likewise, if a file has a normal attribute, setting any other attribute resets the normal attribute.

▬ ▬

FILE3—FILE INFORMATION AND ATTRIBUTES

This example application demonstrates the new Win32 API functions for file information and file attributes. This application has three selections on the menu bar: *File Information, File Size,* and *Attributes.* The *Attributes* menu is a popup containing five selections for specific attributes. We'll use checkmarks to indicate the current status of our sample file, SAMPLE.TXT.

The *File Information* selection calls on the GetFileInformationByHandle() function. The *File Size* selection uses GetFileSize(). The *Attributes* menu uses GetFileAttributes() and SetFileAttributes() to manipulate the sample file's attributes.

Listings 4-22 through 4-24 show the files for the FILE3 project. As with most examples, WinMain() is omitted from the source listing. The complete source is available in the \CHAPTER4\4.3 subdirectory.

Listing 4-22 FILE3.RC—resource script

```
#include "windows.h"
#include "file3.h"

File3Icon ICON    file3.ico

File3Menu MENU
   BEGIN
      MENUITEM "&File Information",   IDM_FILE_INFO
      MENUITEM "File &Size",         IDM_FILE_SIZE
      POPUP    "&Attributes"
         BEGIN
         MENUITEM "&Normal",         IDM_NORMAL
         MENUITEM "&Archive",        IDM_ARCHIVE
         MENUITEM "&Read Only",      IDM_READONLY
         MENUITEM "&Hidden",         IDM_HIDDEN
         MENUITEM "&System",         IDM_SYSTEM
      END
   END
```

Listing 4-23 FILE3.H—header file

```
/* file3.h -- Include file for file3.c and file3.rc */

/* Menu defines */
#define IDM_FILE_INFO   1
#define IDM_FILE_SIZE   2
#define IDM_NORMAL      3
#define IDM_ARCHIVE     4
#define IDM_READONLY    5
#define IDM_HIDDEN      6
#define IDM_SYSTEM      7

/* Function prototype */
LONG APIENTRY WndProc (HWND, UINT, UINT, LONG);
VOID ChangeAttribute (DWORD dwAttribChange);
VOID MenuSet(VOID);

/* Global variables */
HANDLE ghInst;
HANDLE ghWnd;
char   lpFileName[] = "SAMPLE.TXT";
```

Listing 4-24 FILE3.C—source file (partial)

```c
/* file3.c      Demonstrating Win32 File Management Functions */

#include <windows.h>            /* include for Win32 apps */
#include "file3.h"              /* include for file3.c */

/* WndProc - Main Window Procedure for file3.c */

LONG APIENTRY WndProc (HWND hWnd, UINT message, UINT wParam, LONG lParam)
{
static HANDLE             hFile;            /* file handle */
BY_HANDLE_FILE_INFORMATION FileInfo;        /* struct for file information */
static char               lpBuffer[80];     /* buffer for output */
PAINTSTRUCT               ps;
DWORD                     dwFileSize;       /* DWORD to store filesize */

   switch (message)
   {
      case WM_CREATE:                        /* open sample file on startup */
         hFile = CreateFile (lpFileName,
                             GENERIC_READ,
                             0,
                             NULL,
                             OPEN_EXISTING,
                             0,
                             NULL);
         PostMessage (hWnd, WM_USER, 0, 0);  /* delay menu update */
         return (0);

      case WM_USER:                          /* called after main window is created */
         MenuSet();                          /* set checkmarks with current attributes */
         return (0);

      case WM_PAINT:                         /* display information on client area */
         BeginPaint (hWnd, &ps);
         TextOut (ps.hdc, 0, 0, lpBuffer, lstrlen (lpBuffer));
         EndPaint (hWnd, &ps);
         return (0);

      case WM_COMMAND:
         switch (LOWORD(wParam))             /* Extract LOWORD of wParam for Win32 */
         {
            case IDM_FILE_INFO:              /* get file information using file handle */
               GetFileInformationByHandle (hFile, &FileInfo);
               wsprintf (lpBuffer, "%s attributes are %08lXh", lpFileName,
                         FileInfo.dwFileAttributes);
               InvalidateRect (hWnd, NULL, TRUE); /* force WM_PAINT */
               return (0);

            case IDM_FILE_SIZE:                /* get file size */
```

continued on next page

```
            dwFileSize = GetFileSize (hFile, NULL);
            wsprintf (lpBuffer, "%s size is %u bytes", lpFileName, dwFileSize);
            InvalidateRect (hWnd, NULL, TRUE); /* force WM_PAINT */
            return (0);

        case IDM_NORMAL:                    /* change attributes to normal */
            ChangeAttribute (FILE_ATTRIBUTE_NORMAL);
            return (0);

        case IDM_ARCHIVE:                   /* set or reset archive bit */
            ChangeAttribute (FILE_ATTRIBUTE_ARCHIVE);
            return (0);

        case IDM_READONLY:                  /* set or reset readonly bit */
            ChangeAttribute (FILE_ATTRIBUTE_READONLY);
            return (0);

        case IDM_HIDDEN:                    /* set or reset hidden bit */
            ChangeAttribute (FILE_ATTRIBUTE_HIDDEN);
            return (0);

        case IDM_SYSTEM:                    /* set or reset system bit */
            ChangeAttribute (FILE_ATTRIBUTE_SYSTEM);
            return (0);

        default:
            return (0);
        }

    case WM_DESTROY:                        /* No cleanup necessary */
        PostQuitMessage (0);
        return (0);

    default:
        return DefWindowProc (hWnd, message, wParam, lParam);
    }

    return (0L);
}

/* ChangeAttribute() receives one parameter, a DWORD indicating the attribute to change */
VOID ChangeAttribute (DWORD dwAttribChange)
{
DWORD dwAttributes;    /* DWORD stores current attributes */

    if (dwAttribChange == FILE_ATTRIBUTE_NORMAL)  /* if choice is normal, set immediately */
    {
        SetFileAttributes (lpFileName, FILE_ATTRIBUTE_NORMAL);
        MenuSet ();
        return;
    }
    dwAttributes = GetFileAttributes (lpFileName);      /* get current attributes */
```

```
   dwAttributes ^= dwAttribChange;                    /* XOR attribute to set/reset */
   if (dwAttributes == 0)                             /* are all bits gone? */
      dwAttributes == FILE_ATTRIBUTE_NORMAL;          /* if so, attributes must be normal */
   SetFileAttributes (lpFileName, dwAttributes);      /* set attributes of file */
   MenuSet ();                                        /* update the checkmarks */
}

/* MenuSet() updates the attribute checkmarks on the Attributes popup menu */
VOID MenuSet(VOID)
{
DWORD dwAttributes;      /* DWORD stores current attributes */
HMENU hMenu;
int   i;

   hMenu = GetMenu (ghWnd);                            /* get handle to menu */
   dwAttributes = GetFileAttributes (lpFileName);      /* get current attributes of file */

   for (i = IDM_NORMAL; i<=IDM_SYSTEM; i++)            /* uncheck all attribute menuitems */
      CheckMenuItem (hMenu, i, MF_BYCOMMAND |MF_UNCHECKED);

   if (dwAttributes & FILE_ATTRIBUTE_NORMAL)          /* if attributes are normal,
                                                              check Normal and return */
   {
      CheckMenuItem (hMenu, IDM_NORMAL, MF_BYCOMMAND | MF_CHECKED);
      return;
   }

   if (dwAttributes & FILE_ATTRIBUTE_ARCHIVE)         /* if archive bit set, check Archive */
      CheckMenuItem (hMenu, IDM_ARCHIVE, MF_BYCOMMAND | MF_CHECKED);
   if (dwAttributes & FILE_ATTRIBUTE_READONLY)        /* if readonly bit set, check Read Only */
      CheckMenuItem (hMenu, IDM_READONLY, MF_BYCOMMAND | MF_CHECKED);
   if (dwAttributes & FILE_ATTRIBUTE_HIDDEN)          /* if hidden bit set, check Hidden */
      CheckMenuItem (hMenu, IDM_HIDDEN, MF_BYCOMMAND | MF_CHECKED);
   if (dwAttributes & FILE_ATTRIBUTE_SYSTEM)          /* if system bit set, check System */
      CheckMenuItem (hMenu, IDM_SYSTEM, MF_BYCOMMAND | MF_CHECKED);
}
```

Background on FILE3

Before we get into the code for FILE3, let's look at some background information. FILE3 uses a sample ASCII text file, SAMPLE.TXT. This file is provided on your source code disk. The sample filename is stored in a global variable, *lpFileName*. This is defined in FILE3.H.

This program has two functions in addition to WinMain() and WndProc(). The first function, ChangeAttribute(), is called by WndProc(). The function is passed the file attribute to change. The second function, MenuSet(), is called by WndProc() and ChangeAttribute(). It uses GetFileAttributes() to update the menu checkmarks on the *Attribute* popup menu. We'll see how in a moment.

FILE3 Initialization

During WM_CREATE we open the sample data file using CreateFile(). The return value is assigned to *hFile,* a static HANDLE. We then use PostMessage() to send a WM_USER message to ourselves. This ensures that the main window is created before setting the checkmarks on the *Attribute* popup.

When we receive the WM_USER message, we call MenuSet() to update the checkmarks. FILE3 is now initialized. We have a valid static file handle and the menu is initialized.

Getting File Information by Handle in FILE3

The first menu selection, *File Information,* sends the IDM_FILE_INFO *menu id* to WndProc(). We pass GetFileInformationByHandle() the static file handle and the address to *FileInfo.* We defined *FileInfo* as a structure BY_FILE_HANDLE_INFORMATION at the top of WndProc(). The structure is filled by the GetFileInformationByHandle() call.

The next step is to display some file information on the client area of FILE3. This is done by calling wsprintf() and placing the data in *lpBuffer.* We end up formatting a string that indicates the current attributes of SAMPLE.TXT. Note that the attribute DWORD is formatted using %08lXh. The attribute is obtained using the structure member *dwFileAttributes.* This results in an eight digit long value, in hex, with leading padded zeroes.

A call to InvalidateRect() forces a WM_PAINT message. WM_PAINT displays the contents of the buffer with a call to TextOut(). The actual value that we display varies depending on the attributes of SAMPLE.TXT.

Getting the File Size in FILE3

The next menu selection sends an IDM_FILE_SIZE *menu id.* We call GetFileSize() with the file handle as the first argument, storing the result in *dwFileSize.* We format another string, placing the results in *lpBuffer.* A call to InvalidateRect() results in another WM_PAINT, and the buffer is displayed in the client area.

Note that the second parameter to GetFileSize() is NULL. This parameter is only needed on file sizes greater that $2^{32}-2$ bytes (nearly a 4 gigabyte file), which we would have had trouble fitting on your source code disk.

Getting and Setting Attributes

The *Attribute* menu contains five selections that reflect the common attribute types. Let's look at two examples. The first example is *Normal*. The only line of code in WndProc() for this selection calls ChangeAttribute(). In this case the parameter is FILE_ATTRIBUTE_NORMAL.

ChangeAttribute() receives the parameter as *dwAttribChange*. The first *if* statement in ChangeAttribute() checks to see if the *dwAttributeChange* is the normal attribute; in this case it is. We make a direct call to SetFileAttributes(). The parameters are: a pointer to the string containing the filename, and *dwAttributeChange* (normal attribute). We then update the menu checkmarks, and immediately return.

Why the quick exit? If the file attributes are normal, no other attribute bit can be set. By setting the attribute to FILE_ATTRIBUTE_NORMAL, all other attribute bits are automatically reset.

Now for the next scenario: the archive attribute. Since this bit can be set or reset, it requires a little more testing and manipulating. The ChangeAttribute() function receives the FILE_ATTRIBUTE_ARCHIVE value; again this is stored in *dwAttribChange*. Since the selection is not normal, the first *if* statement fails. We must now get the current attributes of the file with GetFileAttributes(). Recall that this function requires a pointer to the filename. We store the current attributes in *dwAttributes*.

We invert the archive bit using a *bitwise* XOR (^) operator on *dwAttributes* and *dwAttribChange*. We place the results of the XOR in *dwAttributes*. Therefore, if the bit was set, we reset it, and vice versa.

Now we must test to see if no attributes are set. If *dwAttributes* == 0, the file must be normal. Since a normal attribute has a value of 80h (not 0), we must assign this value to *dwAttribute*. Calling SetFileAttributes() with 0 as the parameter causes the function to fail; zero is not a valid attribute in Win32.

A call to MenuSet() updates the *Attribute* menu checkmarks. Let's take a look at this function.

Updating the Attribute Checkmarks

The only section of code we haven't looked at is the MenuSet() function. This function first gets a handle to the main menu and gets the attributes of SAMPLE.TXT with *dwAttributes*. A *for* loop follows; this loop unchecks the menu items in the *Attribute* popup.

The next check is an *if* statement. If the attributes are normal, we check the Normal menu selection and return immediately. There is no reason to check further, since the normal attribute always stands by itself.

If the file has attributes other than normal, it may be a combination of the other attribute. Therefore we check each possible attribute and check the appropriate menu items.

BUILDING AND USING FILE3

Let's give FILE3 a try. Open a Command Prompt window and change to the \CHAPTER4\4.3 directory. Type NMAKE and press (ENTER). After the files are compiled and linked, perform the following steps. Cross-reference the running program with the source code in Listing 4-24.

1. Start the FILE3 program by typing FILE3 at the Command Prompt.

2. Select *File Information* from the menu. This option displays the DWORD indicating the current attributes. Right now this should be 00000020h. Table 4-3 indicates the archive attribute is 20 hex. This value was obtained using the file handle and the GetFileInformationByHandle() function.

3. Select *File Size.* The program displays a string indicating the file size is 1,054 bytes. This value was obtained using the file handle and the GetFileSize() function. The file actually contains several lines of data indicating what the file is used for: the FILE3 example program.

4. Select *Attributes.* The *Archive* selection should have a checkmark by it.

5. Select *Read Only.* The *Attribute* menu closes. Open it up again; now both *Archive* and Read Only have checkmarks. The attributes were changed in ChangeAttributes() using GetFileAttributes() and SetFileAttributes. Figure 4-10 shows the FILE3 *Attribute* menu at this point.

6. Open the *Attribute* menu again and select Normal. Another check of the attribute menu indicates that the Normal selection is checked, while all others are unchecked.

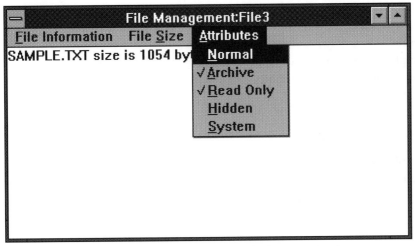

Figure 4-10 FILE3 Attribute menu—SAMPLE.TXT with Archive and Read Only attributes

7. Continue to experiment by changing attributes of the sample file, checking the File Information menu each time. You can see the value reflecting the attribute, or combined attributes.

The FILE3 program demonstrated

◢ getting file information by handle

◢ getting the file size by handle

◢ getting and setting file attributes

You can modify FILE3 to experiment obtaining other values by file handle. Modify the IDM_FILE_INFO handling code and use other structure members in place of *FileInfo.dwFileAttributes*.

WIN32 SYSTEM INFORMATION FUNCTIONS

Now let's look at our last topic for this chapter. Sometimes it is necessary to obtain system hardware information from within your applications. Win32 provides several functions that allow you to do this. You can get drive information such as type of file system, supported filenames, free space, and volume label. There is more than one way to find the number of logical disk drives installed in a system, and you can find out the drive type of each (fixed, floppy, removable).

The last example program in this chapter, FILE4, demonstrates the use of some of the system information functions. Let's look at the functions and their use before getting into FILE4.

Getting Volume Information

You can get volume information for any drive in a system using GetVolumeInformation(). This function requires eight parameters. Listing 4-25 shows the syntax and an example call to GetVolumeInformation().

Listing 4-25 GetVolumeInformation() syntax and example call

```
/* GetVolumeInformation() Syntax */

BOOL GetVolumeLabel (LPTSTR  lpRootPath,         /* root directory path of drive (ex. "C:\") */
                     LPTSTR  lpVolumeName,        /* pointer to buffer for volume name */
                     DWORD   dwVolBufferSize,     /* size of volume name buffer */
                     LPDWORD lpVolumeSerial,      /* pointer to DWORD to store volume serial */
                     LPDWORD lpMaxCompLength,     /* pointer to DWORD to store max filename */
                     LPDWORD lpFileSystemFlags,   /* pointer to DWORD for file system flags */
                     LPTSTR  lpFileSysName,       /* pointer to buffer for file system name */
                     DWORD   dwFileSysBufferSize); /* size of file system name buffer */

/* GetVolumeInformation() Example Call */
DWORD   dwVolBufferSize = 10, dwFileSysBufferSize = 10, dwVolumeSerial, dwMaxCompLength;
char    lpVolumeName [10], lpFIleSysName [10];

    GetVolumeLabel ("C:\",              /* check drive C: */
                    lpVolumeName,        /* buffer to store volume name */
                    dwVolBufferSize,     /* size of buffer is 10 bytes */
                    &dwVolumeSerial,     /* address to store volume/serial */
                    &dwMaxCompLength,    /* address to store max filename length */
                    NULL,                /* don't store file system flags */
                    lpFileSysName,       /* buffer to store file system name */
                    dwFileSystBufferSize); /* size of file system name buffer */
```

This function requires several parameters; most of them store results from the function. The above example checks drive C:\ (first parameter). Note that the root directory is specified, any other directory causes the function to fail. If NULL is specified in place of a drive string, the current drive is checked.

We pass two 10-byte buffers to store the volume name and file system name (second and seventh parameter). We pass two DWORDs indicating the lengths of these buffers (third and eighth parameter). We pass two addresses of DWORDs used to store the volume/serial and the maximum filename length for the system (fourth and fifth parameters).

The sixth parameter is not specified in the example call. If the parameter is specified (another pointer to a DWORD), a value is returned indicating the *file system flags*. The possible flags are: FS_CASE_IS_PRESERVED (upper/lowercase is preserved in filenames and directories), FS_CASE_SENSITIVE (filenames and directories are case sensitive), and FS_UNICODE_STORED_ON_DISK (indicates that the drive supports UNICODE. (UNICODE is a huge extension of ASCII, including most foreign language characters.)

This function returns a Boolean value indicating success or failure. Like most functions, you can call GetLastError() for extended error information, in the case of failure.

In FILE4 we will use the results of GetVolumeInformation() to display the information to the user.

Finding Disk Capacity and Free Space

The GetDiskFreeSpace() obtains total drive capacity and free space for any logical drive in the system. The function requires five parameters. Only one parameter, the first, is specified in the call. The rest of the parameters are filled by the function itself. Listing 4-26 shows the syntax and an example call to GetDiskFreeSpace().

Listing 4-26 GetDiskFreeSpace() syntax and example call

```
/* GetDiskFreeSpace() Syntax */

BOOL GetDiskFreeSpace (LPTSTR  lpRootPath,          /* root directory path of drive */
                       LPDWORD lpSectorsPerCluster, /* sectors per cluster */
                       LPDWORD lpBytesPerSector,    /* bytes per sector */
                       LPDWORD lpFreeClusters,      /* total free clusters */
                       LPDWORD lpClusters);         /* total clusters on drive */

/* GetDiskFreeSpace() Example Call */
DWORD   dwSectorsPerCluster, dwBytesPerSector, dwFreeClusters, dwClusters;

   GetDiskFreeSpace ("C:\",
                     &dwSectorsPerCluster,
                     &dwBytesPerSector,
                     &dwFreeClusters,
                     &dwClusters);
```

This example call checks drive C:. The results are stored in the second through fifth parameter. You can find the total free space on the drive by multiplying the second, third, and fourth parameters. Here is an example:

```
dwFreeSpace = dwSectorsPerCluster * dwBytesPerSector * dwFreeClusters;
```

By replacing the *dwFreeClusters* with *dwClusters,* you can obtain the total available drive space. The GetDriveFreeSpace() function returns a success/failure Boolean.

Getting Logical Drives Using a Bitmask

The GetLogicalDrives() function returns a DWORD that represents the logical drives available on the system. The function requires no parameters. The least significant bit of the DWORD represents drive A, the next higher bit is B, and so on. Figure 4-11 shows the details of the return value. You can shift and/or mask the DWORD to see if a particular drive exists. Here is an example call to Get LogicalDrives():

```
dwLogicalDrives = GetLogicalDrives();
```

We will use a shift and mask example for GetLogicalDrives() in the next example application. We can test for each drive installed on your system.

Getting Logical Drive Strings

GetLogicalDriveStrings() provides another method of determining the available drives in a system. Instead of a bitmask, the function supplies an

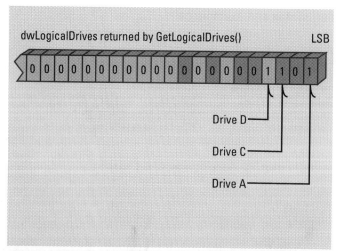

Figure 4-11 DWORD returned from GetLogicalDrives()

array of null-terminated strings for each drive. This function requires two parameters: the first is a DWORD specifying the size of the buffer, the second is a pointer to the buffer to store the drive strings. Listing 4-27 shows the syntax and an example call to GetLogicalDriveStrings().

Listing 4-27 GetLogicalDriveStrings() syntax and example call

```
/* GetLogicalDriveStrings() Syntax */
DWORD GetLogicalDriveStrings (DWORD dwBuffer,      /* Length of drive string buffer */
                             LPTSTR lpszBuffer);  /* address of buffer to store strings */

/* GetLogicalDriveStrings() Example Call */
DWORD dwBuffer = 105;      /* room for 26 drives, 4 bytes each, and final NULL */
char  lpszBuffer [105]    /* buffer to store drive strings */

    GetLogicalDriveStrings (dwBuffer, lpszBuffer);
```

This example call passes a 105-byte buffer and a DWORD indicating the size of the buffer. Each drive string takes up 4 bytes in the buffer: one each for the drive letter, a colon, a backslash, and a NULL terminator. The buffer also needs space for a final NULL. This function returns a DWORD indicating the length of the drive strings (if successful) or the length need to store the drive strings (if it fails). You can compare the return value to the initial buffer size to determine whether or not the function failed. This signifies the end of the string. Figure 4-12 shows an example buffer after a call to GetLogicalDriveStrings() for a system with drives A, C, and D.

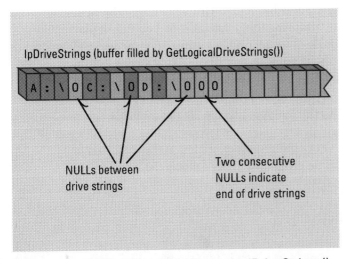

Figure 4-12 Buffer after call to GetLogicalDriveStrings()

Determining Drive Type

Once you know the logical drive letters in a system, you may need to find out what type of drive a particular device is (removable, fixed, CD-ROM, and so on). The Win32 API function GetDriveType() performs this action. This function requires one parameter, a null-terminated string indicating the root path of the drive to check. It returns a UINT indicating the type of drive. Listing 4-28 shows the syntax and an example call to GetDriveType().

Listing 4-28 GetDriveType() syntax and example call

```
/* GetDriveType() Syntax */
UINT GetDriveType (LPTSTR plszRootPathname); /* pointer to root path */

/* GetDriveType() Example Call */
UINT uDriveType;

   uDriveType = GetDriveType ("C:\");
   if (uDriveType == DRIVE_FIXED)
     [ yes C:\ is a fixed drive! ]
```

In FILE4 we will use the drive strings collected with GetLogicalDriveStrings() to make calls to GetDriveType(). This way we can find the available drives and types at the same time. Let's take a look at FILE4.

FILE4—Getting System Information

FILE4 is an example application that demonstrates the Win32 API system information functions. The application has four menu selections. The first, *Volume Info,* uses the GetVolumeInformation() function to get and display information on the current drive. The second selection, *Free Space,* uses GetDiskFreeSpace() to display the amount of disk space. The *Drives* selection uses the GetLogicalDrives() function and displays the drives available on the system. Finally the *Drive Types* selection uses a combination of GetLogicalDriveStrings() and GetDriveType() to display the available drives and their respective types.

Listings 4-29 through 4-31 show the resource, header, and partial source file for FILE4. A description of the program activity follows the listings.

Listing 4-29 FILE4.RC—resource script

```
#include "windows.h"
#include "file4.h"
```

```
File4Icon ICON    file4.ico

File4Menu MENU
    BEGIN
        MENUITEM "&Volume Info",    IDM_VOL_INFO
        MENUITEM "&Free Space",     IDM_DISK_SPACE
        MENUITEM "&Drives",         IDM_DRIVES
        MENUITEM "Drive &Types",    IDM_DRIVE_TYPE
    END
```

Listing 4-30 FILE4.H—header file

```c
/* file4.h -- Include file for file4.c and file4.rc */

/* Menu defines */
#define IDM_VOL_INFO    1
#define IDM_DISK_SPACE  2
#define IDM_DRIVES      3
#define IDM_DRIVE_TYPE  4

/* Function prototype */
LONG APIENTRY WndProc (HWND, UINT, UINT, LONG);

/* Global variables */
HANDLE ghInst;
HANDLE ghWnd;
```

Listing 4-31 FILE4.C—source file (partial)

```c
/* file4.c     Demonstrating Win32 System Functions */

#include <windows.h>            /* include for Win32 apps */
#include "file4.h"              /* include for file4.c */

/* WndProc - Main Window Procedure for file4.c */

LONG APIENTRY WndProc (HWND hWnd, UINT message, UINT wParam, LONG lParam)
{
static char     lpBuffer[6][60];
char            lpVolumeName[10], lpFileSysName[10];
char            lpDrives[66];
static char     lpDriveBuf[105];
char            *lpDriveStrings;
DWORD           dwVolumeSerial, dwMaxCompLength;
DWORD           dwSectorsPerCluster, dwBytesPerSector, dwFreeClusters, dwClusters;
DWORD           dwFreeSpace, dwTotalSpace, dwDrives, dwSizeBuf = 105;
int             i, iNumDrives = 0;
static          iLines = 0;
PAINTSTRUCT     ps;
```

continued on next page

continued from previous page

```
    switch (message)
    {
        case WM_CREATE:                      /* No initialization */
            return (0);

        case WM_PAINT:                       /* display contents of buffers */
            BeginPaint (hWnd, &ps);
            for (i = 0; i < iLines; i++)
                TextOut (ps.hdc, 0, i * 20, lpBuffer[i], lstrlen (lpBuffer[i]));
            EndPaint (hWnd, &ps);
            return (0);

        case WM_COMMAND:
            switch (LOWORD(wParam))          /* Extract LOWORD of wParam for Win32 */
            {
                case IDM_VOL_INFO:           /* get volume info for current drive */
                    GetVolumeInformation (NULL,         /* current drive */
                                          lpVolumeName,     /* volume name buffer */
                                          10,               /* volume name buffer size */
                                          &dwVolumeSerial,  /* address to store vol/ser */
                                          &dwMaxCompLength,  /* address to store max filename */
                                          NULL,             /* no file system flags */
                                          lpFileSysName,    /* buffer for file system name */
                                          10);              /* size of file sysname buffer */
                    /* fill buffers for WM_PAINT */
                    wsprintf (lpBuffer[0], "The volume name is %s", lpVolumeName);
                    wsprintf (lpBuffer[1], "The volume serial is %lX", dwVolumeSerial);
                    wsprintf (lpBuffer[2], "The maximum component length is %lu", dwMaxCompLength);
                    wsprintf (lpBuffer[3], "The file system for this drive is %s", lpFileSysName);
                    iLines = 4;                          /* set number of lines in buffer */
                    InvalidateRect (hWnd, NULL, TRUE);   /* force WM_PAINT */
                    return (0);

                case IDM_DISK_SPACE:                     /* get disk space */
                    GetDiskFreeSpace (NULL,              /* current drive */
                                      &dwSectorsPerCluster,
                                      &dwBytesPerSector,
                                      &dwFreeClusters,
                                      &dwClusters);
                    /* calculate total space */
                    dwTotalSpace = dwClusters * dwSectorsPerCluster * dwBytesPerSector;
                    /* calculate free space */
                    dwFreeSpace = dwFreeClusters * dwSectorsPerCluster * dwBytesPerSector;
                    /* fill buffers for WM_PAINT */
                    wsprintf (lpBuffer[0], "%lu sector(s) per cluster", dwSectorsPerCluster);
                    wsprintf (lpBuffer[1], "%lu bytes per sector", dwBytesPerSector);
                    wsprintf (lpBuffer[2], "%lu free clusters", dwFreeClusters);
                    wsprintf (lpBuffer[3], "%lu total clusters", dwClusters);
                    wsprintf (lpBuffer[4], "%lu bytes free", dwFreeSpace);
                    wsprintf (lpBuffer[5], "%lu bytes total", dwTotalSpace);
                    iLines = 6;                          /* set number of lines in buffer */
                    InvalidateRect (hWnd, NULL, TRUE);   /* force WM_PAINT */
```

```
        return (0);

case IDM_DRIVES:                                    /* get drives by bitmasking */
    dwDrives = GetLogicalDrives();
    for (i = 0; i < 32; i++)                        /* cycle through 32 bits */
    {
        if (dwDrives & 1)                           /* is bit set */
        {
          lpDrives[iNumDrives] = (char) i + 65;  /* copy ASCII uppercase to buffer */
          lpDrives[iNumDrives + 1] = ' ';          /* copy a space to buffer */
          iNumDrives += 2;                          /* increment buffer index */
        }
        dwDrives >>= 1;                             /* shift right drive DWORD */
    }
    lpDrives[iNumDrives] = (char) NULL;            /* append NULL at end of buffer */
    wsprintf (lpBuffer[0], "Logical drives: %s", lpDrives); /* format output */
    iLines = 1;                                     /* set number of lines */
    InvalidateRect (hWnd, NULL, TRUE);        /* force WM_PAINT */
    return (0);

case IDM_DRIVE_TYPE:           /* get drives by strings and get drive type */
    iLines = 0;                                     /* reset number of lines */
    GetLogicalDriveStrings (dwSizeBuf, lpDriveBuf); /* get drive strings */
    lpDriveStrings = lpDriveBuf;                    /* initialize pointer */
    for (i = 0; i < 6; i++, lpDriveStrings += 4) /* loop through six drives */
    {                                               /* and increment pointer 4 bytes */
        if (*(lpDriveStrings) == 0) break;         /* if end of drives, break */
        lstrcpy (lpBuffer[i], lpDriveStrings);     /* copy string into buffer */
        switch (GetDriveType (lpDriveStrings))     /* get drive type */
        {                                           /* and append appropriate string */
            case (DRIVE_REMOVABLE):
                lstrcat (lpBuffer[i], " is a removable drive");
                break;
            case (DRIVE_FIXED):
                lstrcat (lpBuffer[i], " is a fixed drive");
                break;
            case (DRIVE_REMOTE):
                lstrcat (lpBuffer[i], " is a network drive");
                break;
            case (DRIVE_CDROM):
                lstrcat (lpBuffer[i], " is a CD ROM drive");
                break;
            default:
                lstrcat (lpBuffer[i], " is unidentified");
        }
        iLines++;                                       /* increment number of lines */
    }
    InvalidateRect (hWnd, NULL, TRUE);             /* force WM_PAINT */
    return (0);

default:
```

continued on next page

continued from previous page

```
                    return (0);
        }

    case WM_DESTROY:                                    /* No cleanup necessary */
    ·    PostQuitMessage (0);
        return (0);

    default:
        return DefWindowProc (hWnd, message, wParam, lParam);
    }

    return (0L);
}
```

Background for FILE4.C

FILE4 uses an array of six strings *(lpBuffer)* to output data to the client area. The number of strings used in each area of the program varies. For example, the IDM_DRIVES selection only uses one string, while the IDM_DISK_SPACE uses all three. A static int, *iLines,* is set to the number of lines to write to the client area.

The WM_PAINT processing calls TextOut() for each line of *lpBuffer.* Each line is spaced 20 pixels apart, vertically.

Getting Volume Information in FILE4

The *Volume Info* menu selection executes the code in IDM_VOL_INFO. The first thing we do is call GetVolumeInformation(). Note that the first parameter to this function is NULL. This results in obtaining information for the current drive, whatever that may be on your system. We obtain information for volume name *(lpVolumeName),* volume/serial *(dwVolumeSerial),* maximum filename length *(dwMaxCompLength),* and file system name *(lpFileSysName).*

This information is formatted by wsprintf() and placed into the first four buffers in *lpBuffer.* The lines indicator, *iLines,* is set to four to let WM_PAINT know how many lines are coming. We call InvalidateRect() to force a WM_PAINT message. The paint message displays the resultant strings on the client area.

Getting Disk Space in FILE4

When you select the *Free Space* menu option, the IDM_DISK_SPACE code is executed. We call GetDiskFreeSpace() to fill the four DWORDs (last four parameters). The first parameter is set to NULL, again specifying the current drive.

The next two lines calculate the total and free disk space respectively. This is accomplished by multiplying *dwSectorsPerCluster* and *dwBytesPerSector* by the appropriate value *(dwFreeClusters* for free space and *dwClusters* for total space).

This time we fill all six buffers in the *lpBuffer* array. All six strings are formatted using wsprintf(), using the format *%lu* (unsigned longs) for the values. We set *iLines* to six and InvalidateRect() is called to kick off WM_PAINT. Once again, the information is displayed on the client area.

Getting Drives with Bitmasking in FILE4

The next menu selection, Drives, calls the IDM_DRIVES portion of FILE4.C. We call GetLogicalDrives() and place the result in *dwDrives*. A *for* loop is initiated to cycle through the possible drives. The loop executes 32 times, since *dwDrives* has 32 bits.

Inside the *for* loop is an *if* statement. This statement *bitwise ands (&)* *dwDrives* and a 1. This masks to see if the least significant bit is set. Since most computers have an A drive, the *if* statement is true on the first pass. We use a buffer, *lpDrives,* to store our results, and an index, *iNumDrives,* to keep our place in the buffer.

Since the *if* statement is true, we cast the loop variable (*i*) plus 65 to type *char.* This results in an ASCII 'A' the first time through the loop (*i* is 0). We then write a space to the next byte in the buffer (*iNumDrives* + 1) to separate the drive letters. We increment the buffer index by two, which completes the *if* body.

Now we shift *dwDrives* to the right one bit. This places the next drive in the least significant position. This ends the first pass through the *for* loop. This process continues 32 times. Each time the *if* statement passes, the appropriate drive letter, plus a space, is added to the buffer.

When the loop is completed, we tack on a NULL character to the end of the buffer. We now have a null-terminated string with the system drive letters. We format the string along with "Logical Drives:" and place the results in the first line of *lpBuffer.*

The line indicator, *iLines,* is set to one since the string will fit on one line. We call InvalidateRect() and the results end up on the client area as a result of the code in WM_PAINT.

Getting Logical Drive Strings and Drive Types in FILE4

The last menu selection in FILE4 is *Drive Types.* The code in IDM_DRIVE_TYPE handles this selection. We call GetLogicalDriveStrings(), which places the resultant strings in *lpDriveBuf.* A pointer, *lpDriveStrings,* was declared at the top of WndProc(). We initialize this pointer by assigning it the starting address of the drive strings.

The next step is to cycle through the first six possibilities of logical drives. Since each drive will take a line in the buffer, we are limiting it to six drives. Let's follow the code through the *for* loop once to get a drive type.

The *for* loop, in addition to incrementing the loop variable, also increments the drive string pointer *(lpDriveStrings)* by four. Remember, each drive name is four bytes apart. The first line in the loop checks the contents of the buffer, to which *lpDriveStrings* points. If this is NULL, it indicates the end of the drives, and breaks out of the *for* loop.

Since we know we must have at least one drive, let's continue. The next line copies the first drive string into the first output buffer. We now reach a *switch* statement. The *switch* statement uses the results of a call to GetDriveType*(lpDriveStrings)* as its argument. Four cases are given in the body of the *switch*. Let's assume (with some confidence) that the first drive is a floppy. The result from the GetDriveType() is DRIVE_REMOVABLE (first case). We concatenate " is a removable drive" to the end of the drive string (in *lpBuffer*). We now have the first string which contains "A:\ is a removable drive."

We increment *iLines* after the *switch* and go through the *for* loop again. This process continues until there are no more drives, or the *for* loop ends. At this point we call InvalidateRect() and start the painting. We display a line for each drive (up to six) on the client area.

That concludes the theory behind FILE4; let's take a look at the application in action.

BUILDING AND USING FILE4

Let's build FILE4 and demonstrate the Win32 system functions. Open a Command Prompt window and change to the \CHAPTER4\4.4 directory. Type NMAKE and press (ENTER). After the files are compiled and linked, perform the following steps. Cross-reference the running program with the source code in Listing 4-31.

1.   Start the FILE4 program by typing FILE4 at the Command Prompt.

2.   Select *Volume Info* from the menu. The FILE4 program displays the results of the call to GetVolumeInfo(). You should see your volume

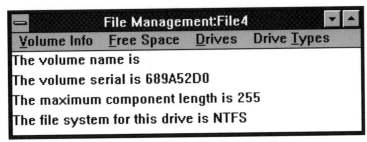

Figure 4-13 Volume Info—results from GetVolumeInfo()

name, volume/serial (eight digits), maximum filename length, and file system name. Figure 4-13 shows a sample output for the *Volume Info* menu selection.

3. Select *Free Space*. FILE4 displays the results of the call to GetDiskFreeSpace() function along with our calculated values for free and total disk space. Figure 4-14 shows a sample output for the *Free Space* menu selection.

4. Select *Drives*. A simple string is displayed with a letter for each drive on your system. Remember that our code did the work here; the actual drives are stored in a DWORD. This was the return value of GetLogicalDrives(). Figure 4-15 shows a sample output for the *Volume Info* menu selection.

5. Select *Drive Types*. Up to the first six drives are displayed on the client area, along with the drive type. These results are from calls to

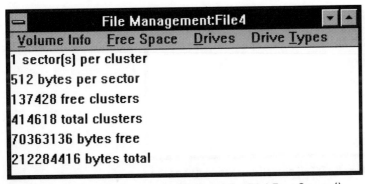

Figure 4-14 Free Space—results from GetDiskFreeSpace()

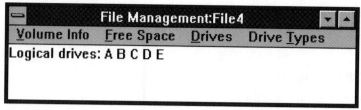

Figure 4-15 Drives—results for GetLogicalDrives()

GetLogicalDriveStrings() (for the drive root paths) and GetDriveTypes() for the types. Figure 4-16 shows a sample output for the Drive Types menu selection.

This concludes the last example in file system management. If you combine this information with a little imagination, you should be able to identify and manage the drives on any system running Windows NT.

SUMMARY

File management has undergone significant changes with the advent of Windows NT. Perhaps the largest change is caused by the disappearance of MS-DOS and the introduction of NT—the complete GUI operating system. Other changes, like supporting multiple file systems, affect the programmer as well.

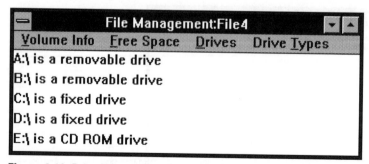

Figure 4-16 Drive Types—result of GetLogicalDriveStrings() and GetDriveType()

Since MS-DOS is not running behind the scenes, many changes and additions were designed into the Win32 API. In Windows 3.x most of file management was performed using C run-time library calls, not typical API calls. The C run-time library file functions were built around the x86 processor and the FAT file system. Now that Windows NT targets multiple processors and multiple file systems, changes are necessary for developers. You can use most of the old library functions; however, the Win32 API functions are more descriptive, efficient, and they have built-in support for three file systems (FAT, NTFS, and HPFS).

You were exposed to many of these new API functions in this chapter. We demonstrated how to create, open, delete, and manipulate files. We then turned to directory management —creating directories, and copying/moving files to and from directories. We saw how to get file information in a variety of ways. We also discussed and demonstrated getting and changing file attributes. Finally we looked at obtaining information about a system, getting disk drive, space information, and identifying types of disk drives.

Although file management is necessary, it usually goes on behind the scenes. Let's now turn our attention to the forefront, the display, and return to the graphics device interface. The next chapter addresses the new Win32 concepts in GDI.

Using GDI in Windows NT

CHAPTER 5

Using GDI in Windows NT

The Windows graphics device interface (GDI) module provides an interface to isolate the programmer from different types of display hardware. The GDI module is a DLL file with an .EXE extension in Windows 3.x, and a DLL in Windows NT. It calls device driver (.DRV) files for many different displays, printers, and plotters. If you have experience using the GDI in previous versions of Windows, starting to work with the new GDI functionality in Windows NT should be no problem. You are still able to call most of the Windows 3.x functions without altering any of your existing code; however, there are some subtle (and not so subtle) changes to be aware of as you make the transition. This chapter is designed to help you make the transition from Windows 3.x GDI to Win32 GDI with relative ease.

This chapter covers two segments of the GDI. The first of these segments concentrates on the existing calls and how they are affected by the move to NT. Some of these changes will be transparent to you, the programmer. On the other hand, some of the changes may affect your applications depending on how deep you delved into the pre-NT GDI.

After we cover the modifications to the existing GDI we'll take a look at some of the new offerings for GDI. The drawing functions have been expanded, adding support for widelines, additional polyline support, and new functions to handle Bezier curves. We also include two additional sample applications to demonstrate these new functions.

Covering the GDI is a huge task. Not every new enhancement or extension is covered in this chapter. Rather, we set out to explore the basic changes. Armed with a solid understanding of these changes, you will have the ability to get deeper into the Win32 GDI without running into unfamiliar terms or topics. The entire set of GDI features can be found in the Microsoft Win32 SDK manuals.

Before we look at the details of the Win32 GDI additions, let's look at an overview of the topics discussed in this chapter.

CHAPTER OVERVIEW

Concepts Covered

- Existing GDI function differences
- Using a dialog box in Win32
- Using wideline functions
- Using new arc functions
- Creating pens
- Using new polyline functions
- Using line joins
- Creating a path bracket
- Using Bezier functions

Win32 API Functions Covered

- ArcTo()
- AngleArc()
- ExtCreatePen()
- SetMiterLimit()
- GetMiterLimit()
- BeginPath()
- EndPath()
- CloseFigure()
- StrokePath()
- PolyLineTo()
- PolyPolyline()
- PolyBezier()
- PolyBezierTo()
- PolyDraw()
- FillPath()
- StrokeAndFillPath()
- PathToRegion()
- WidenPath()
- FlattenPath()
- GetPath()

Parameters Covered

- PS_GEOMETRIC
- PS_COSMETIC
- PS_ALTERNATE
- PS_SOLID
- PS_DASH
- PS_DOT
- PS_DASHDOT
- PS_DASHDOTDOT
- PS_NULL
- PS_USERSTYLE
- PS_INSIDEFRAME
- PS_ENDCAP_ROUND
- PS_ENDCAP_SQUARE
- PS_ENDCAP_FLAT
- PS_JOIN_BEVEL
- PS_JOIN_MITER
- PS_JOIN_ROUND
- PT_MOVETO
- PT_LINETO
- PT_BEZIERTO
- PT_CLOSEFIGURE

CHANGES TO THE EXISTING GDI API

Although most of the changes to the existing API are generally transparent to the programmer, it is helpful to be aware of the changes—especially if you use the GDI extensively in your programs. We have already seen how the widening of the data path to 32 bits affected memory and file management; the wider path affects the GDI as well.

Effects of 32 Bits on GDI Function Calls

Virtually all of the GDI API calls (and Windows API calls in general) have been affected by widening the path of data from 16 to 32 bits. Some existing functions can be used as is, while others require some attention. The GDI functions have been affected in three areas: handles, coordinates, and pointers.

GDI Handles—From 16 to 32 Bits

As with all handles in Win32, GDI handles have grown to a 32-bit width. Since most applications simply refer to a handle by a declared name, it doesn't really affect much in our programs. Consider the following code comparison:

```
/* ...in Windows 3.x */
HDC   hDC;                    /* 16-bit handle to a device context */
hDC = GetDC (hWnd);          /* GetDC returns a 16-bit value to a device context */
/* ...in Win32 */
HDC hDC;                      /* 32-bit handle to a device context */
hDC = GetDC (hWnd);          /* GetDC returns a 32-bit value to a device context */
```

As you can see, the only difference in the Windows 3.x and Win32 code is in the comments; the actual code is identical. If you examine the actual values using a debugger, you will see that the handle has grown to 32 bits in the latter example. Fortunately we do not treat a handle to a device context as a numeric value. We simply refer to it as *hDC*. If we call *GetDC()*, it automatically returns the appropriate value for the handle regardless of the compiler type (16- or 32-bit).

Graphics Coordinates—From 16 to 32 Bits

Handles are not the only area affected by the expansion to 32 bits; coordinates are affected as well. The following excerpt from WINDEF.H shows a new definition of the POINT structure:

```
typedef struct tagPOINT
{
    LONG  x;
    LONG  y;
} POINT;
```

The key difference here is the data type for the *x* and *y* members of the POINT structure; they have been changed to LONG. In Windows 3.x, *x* and *y* were declared as an *int* data type (in WINDOWS.H of Windows 3.x). If you include WINDOWS.H in Win32 applications, WINDEF.H is also included.

You can continue to use the POINT structure freely. Just be aware that the size of the coordinate space has grown significantly. Even the most graphics intensive programs won't reach the new LONG barrier.

Pointers in GDI Functions—From 16 to 32 Bits

GDI functions that pass pointers in Win32 now use 32-bit pointers. Again, this should not cause a problem in your programs. You can still use the *near* and *far* keywords, even though they don't mean anything in Win32. This is because of the 32-bit flat memory space in Win32.

GDI Functions that Have Changed in the Win32 API

Some of the GDI API functions have changed in the transition to 32-bit Windows, and may need to be modified in your existing programs. We are not covering these functions in depth. We're just showing the effects of the differences and how they might affect your programs. A Windows 3.x and Windows NT example call is given for each function so you can see precisely what has changed.

AddFontResource()—RemoveFontResource()

The AddFontResource() function has been split into two functions: AddFontResource() and AddFontModule(). The purpose of the function in

Windows 3.x was to load a file containing a *font resource* into the system, or to load a *font module* into the system. Loading a font resource required a pointer to a null-terminated string containing a filename for font resources, or a handle to a font module. Here are two example calls for AddFontResource() in Windows 3.x:

```
/* Windows 3.x AddFontResource() Example Call */

    AddFontResource ((LPSTR) "oldengl.fon");                /* load a font by filename */

    hFont = FindResource (hInst, "oldengl.fon", RT_FONT);   /* getting a handle to the font */
    AddFontResource (hFont);                                /* load the font by handle */
```

The first example call is still valid in Win32; however, you can no longer use AddFontResource() to load a font by module. Instead, you must call AddFontModule(). Here is an example of the new call:

```
/* Win32 AddFontModule() Example Call */

    hFont = FindResource (hInst, "oldengl.fon", RT_FONT);   /* getting a handle to the font */
    AddFontModule (hFont);                                  /* load the font by handle */
```

The RemoveFontResource() function has been split into two functions in the same way as AddFontResource(). If you add a font module using AddFontModule(), you should remove it by calling RemoveFontModule() before your application terminates.

CreatDIBPatternBrush()—.Changed to CreatDIBPatternBrushPt()

The purpose of this function is to create a pattern brush from a device-independent bitmap (DIB). The DIB is stored in a global memory block; therefore the first parameter to the function is a GLOBALHANDLE type. The function returns a handle to the new brush. Let's look at an example call to the CreatDIBPatternBrush in Windows 3.x.

```
/* Windows 3.x CreatDIBPatternBrush() Example Call */

    hDIBrush = CreatDIBPatternBrush (hDIB, DIB_RGB_COLORS);  /* creates a DIB brush based on
                                                                DIB identified by hDIB */
```

For Win32 Microsoft strongly recommends that you replace this function with a new call: CreatDIBPatternBrushPt(). The purpose of the function has not changed; however, the first parameter is now a pointer to a packed DIB. Recall that a *packed* DIB is a combination of a BITMAPINFO structure followed by an array of bytes that make up the bitmap itself. Here is an example call to CreatDIBPatternBrushPt():

```
/* Win32 CreatDIBPatternBrushPt() Example Call */

    /* Creates a DIB brush based on a packed DIB pointed to by &PackedDIB */
    hDIBrush = CreateDIBPatternBrushPt (&PackedDIB, DIB_RGB_COLOR);
```

In this example we are assuming that the packed DIB is somewhere in memory, and is identified by *PackedDIB*. We pass the address of the DIB to the function. Loading a packed DIB into memory is accomplished with LoadResource() (the same way it was done in Windows 3.x).

Enumeration Function Callbacks

Enumeration functions (EnumFonts, EnumObjects) use callback procedures. These procedures should be declared *CALLBACK,* not *FAR PASCAL.* Recall that all enumeration functions, even those used outside the GDI kernel, require an application-defined callback procedure. All callback procedures in Win32 are declared the *CALLBACK* type.

The Win32 header files take care of most of the types for you. For example, even if you declare a callback function as FAR PASCAL, the Win32 header files will translate it for you. It is good practice, however, to begin using the new keywords for Win32. We'll see more examples of keyword usage in Chapter 9, Portability Issues in Windows NT.

Other GDI Functions Changed in the Win32 API

A few other GDI functions are affected in the Win32 API. For example, metafile functions (CreateMetaFile, GetMetaFile, and so on) are affected by the widening of the data path (16 to 32 bits). Most of these changes should not affect your existing code. Just be aware that you are no longer limited to 16-bit values.

There are also several new additions to the metafile function family. For each metafile function in Windows 3.x, there is an enhanced equivalent in Win32. For example, CreateMetaFile() can be used in both Windows 3.x and Win32. However, Win32 provides a new function, CreateEnhMetaFile(). The *enhanced* metafiles are separate and distinct from Windows 3.x metafiles. Windows 3.x metafiles contain a group of variable-length structures that store an image in a device-independent format. Enhanced metafiles contain a header, a table of handles to GDI objects, a palette, and an array of metafile records. Enhanced metafiles are out of the scope of this book.

One Last Note About Device-Independent Bitmaps (DIB)

Since the original introduction of Windows, several methods of storing bitmaps have been established. The Win32 API is geared toward the DIB format. It is for this reason that you should use this format instead of the older choices. Although most of the older calls, such as CreateBitmap(), are still supported at this time, you should direct your code toward the DIB format for the future.

Calls Deleted in the Win32 GDI

Three calls no longer exist in the Win32 GDI. The first, GetDCOrg(), was used in Windows 3.x to realign a brush if the device context was moved. The Win32 GDI performs *automatic brush tracking,* so it is no longer necessary to align the brush from within your applications.

The other two calls that have been deleted are GetEnvironment() and SetEnvironment(). Both of these calls were used in device driver development. The calls have been removed from the application development API only. Writing device drivers requires the Win32 DDK (Device Driver Kit).

Summary of GDI Changes

You can adapt to most of these changes without altering your existing code. You can rewrite some code to take advantage of the 32-bit coordinates; however, the 16-bit values are still sufficient for most applications. The overall design of the Win32 API prepares us for the future. Now is the time to begin to get used to the new programming model.

The rest of this chapter describes and demonstrates some of the new API functions in GDI. A few new line and curve drawing functions, as well as wideline support, have been added. Let's take a look at these additions.

NEW ADDITIONS TO THE WIN32 API FOR GDI

There are several new drawing functions in the Win32 API. We will take a look at the usage of these functions in two example programs: GDI1 and GDI2. This first program shows two new arc drawing functions, a new way to create a pen, and new support for *widelines*. Widelines affect the appearance of lines drawn on the device context. Another subject, *paths,* is briefly introduced in GDI1. We also create a simple dialog box for the first time in the book.

The second program, GDI2, extends the discussion on paths. It also covers several additional drawing functions. We demonstrate the use of three new polyline functions and two *Bezier* functions. Beziers (pronounced *bez-e-ay*) are complex curves. Let's start by taking a look at the topics for the first example program.

ARCS, PENS, AND WIDELINE SUPPORT

Our first example program in this chapter, GDI1, demonstrates the use of two new arc drawing functions: ArcTo(), and AngleArc(). These functions expand the current arc functions that exist in the Windows 3.x API. We will also see some examples of widelines; this is accomplished by a new pen creation function: ExtCreatePen(). This function is similar to the existing CreatePen() function.

We will look at *paths* as they relate to the Win32 GDI. Paths are a new subject and did not exist in the Windows 3.x API. A path consists of a graphic object (or objects) that you can outline with a graphics pen and fill with a brush. They make it easier to draw and fill complex shapes. Let's take a look at these new functions in more detail.

New Arc Functions in Win32

There are two additions to the existing arc functions. AngleArc() draws a line segment and an arc. ArcTo() draws an elliptical arc. Currently only one true arc function exists: Arc(). ArcTo() is identical to Arc() except the current position is updated in the device context. Let's take a look at ArcTo().

Using ArcTo()

If you have already used the Arc() function in your programs, adapting to ArcTo() should be no problem. Like Arc(), ArcTo() takes nine parameters: a handle to a device context, four coordinates for a bounding rectangle, two coordinates for the start angle, and two coordinates for the end angle. Listing 5-1 shows the proper syntax and an example call for ArcTo().

Listing 5-1 ArcTo() syntax and example call

```
/* ArcTo() Syntax */
BOOL ArcTo (HDC hDC,            /* handle to a device context */
            int nLeftRect,      /* x-coordinate of upper-left corner of bounding rectangle */
            int nTopRect,       /* y-coordinate of upper-left corner of bounding rectangle */
            int nRightRect,     /* x-coordinate of lower-right corner of bounding rectangle */
            int nBottomRect,    /* y-coordinate of lower-right corner of bounding rectangle */
            int xStartAngle,    /* x-coordinate of radial for arc start angle */
            int yStartAngle,    /* y-coordinate of radial for arc start angle */
            int xEndAngle,      /* x-coordinate of radial for arc end angle */
            int yEndAngle);     /* y-coordinate of radial for arc end angle */

/* ArcTo() Example Call */
HDC hDC;

    hDC = GetDC (hWnd);                                 /* get handle to device context */
    ArcTo (hDC, 30, 30, 130, 100, 40, 15, 45, 115);    /* draw the arc */
```

The return value of ArcTo() is Boolean; however, we are not testing the value in our example call. The return value is TRUE if the function is successful and FALSE if it fails. Figure 5-1 shows a diagram that represents the sample call in Listing 5-1.

Note that the bounding rectangle is defined by the second through the fifth parameters. We have shown the rectangle here to clarify how the arc is created. The sixth and seventh parameters define the radial for the starting point of the angle. By drawing a line from the center of the bounding rectangle through this point, we can see the start angle of the arc. We use the same procedure to show the end angle using the last two parameters in the ArcTo() call.

A line is drawn from the current device context position to the starting point of the arc. We chose an arbitrary current position (100,10) for the example in the figure. Also notice that the current position is updated to reflect the ending point of the arc. These features differ from the Arc() function. The Arc() function does not use the current position as a starting point, nor does it update or affect the position in any way.

Like the Arc() function, ArcTo() always draws the arc counterclockwise. The arc is drawn using the currently selected pen and is not filled.

Using AngleArc()

The AngleArc() function draws a circular arc from a given starting point, radius, and sweep angle. AngleArc() requires six parameters: a handle to a device context, two coordinates specifying the center of the circle, the radius of the circle, the starting angle of the arc, and the amount in degrees to

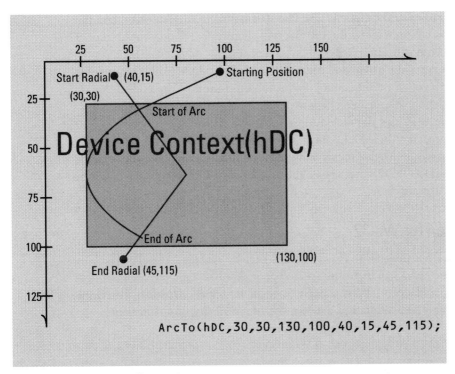

Figure 5-1 The ArcTo() function

sweep. Listing 5-2 shows the proper syntax and an example call for AngleArc().

Listing 5-2 AngleArc() syntax and example call

```
/* AngleArc() Syntax */
BOOL AngleArc (HDC hDC,          /* handle to a device context */
               int x,            /* x-coordinate of center of circle */
               int y,            /* y-coordinate of center of circle */
               DWORD dwRadius,   /* radius of circle */
               FLOAT StartAngle, /* starting angle of arc */
               FLOAT SweepAngle, /* number of degrees to sweep from start angle */

/* AngleArc() Example Call */
HDC hDC;

   hDC = GetDC (hWnd);
   AngleArc (hDC, 50, 50, 25, 10, 190);
```

Like most GDI drawing functions, AngleArc() returns TRUE if successful and FALSE if it fails. This example draws an arc with its center at x=50, y=50. The radius of the circle is 25. The starting angle is 10 degrees, and the angle sweeps counterclockwise 190 degrees. Figure 5-2 shows the results of the example call in Listing 5-2.

Like the ArcTo() function, AngleArc() draws a line from the current position in the device context and updates that position to the end of the arc upon completion. Again, we chose an arbitrary starting point in Figure 5-2. Also, the arc is always drawn counterclockwise. If the sweep angle is 360 degrees or greater, AngleArc() draws a complete circle.

An arc drawn by AngleArc() may appear elliptical if a mapping mode, such as MM_ANISOTROPIC, is set by the application. Otherwise the function draws a circular arc.

A New Pen for Win32

In Windows 3.x programs, you created a pen by calling CreatePen(). This function returned a handle to the created pen. You had a choice of line styles, line width, and color. Win32 introduces a new pen creation function: ExtCreatePen(). This function extends the functionality of CreatePen().

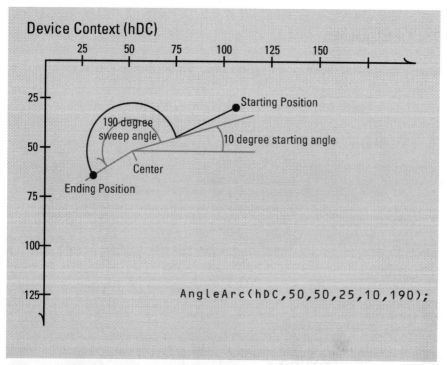

Figure 5-2 The AngleArc() function

Using ExtCreatePen()

This new pen creation function takes five parameters: pen style, width, a pointer to a LOGBRUSH structure indicating the attributes of the pen, and two optional parameters for a custom style pen. Listing 5-3 shows the proper syntax and an example call for ExtCreatePen().

Listing 5-3 ExtCreatePen() syntax and example call

```
/* ExtCreatePen() Syntax */
HPEN ExtCreatePen (DWORD dwPenStyle,      /* style of pen */
                   DWORD dwWidth,         /* the width of the pen */
                   LPLOGBRUSH lplb,       /* pointer to structure for brush attributes */
                   DWORD dwStyleCount,    /* optional length of array in next parameter */
                   LPDWORD lpStyle);      /* optional array of custom style bits */

/* ExtCreatePen() Example Call */
HPEN hPen;
HDC  hDC;
LOGBRUSH logbrush;

   hDC = GetDC (hWnd);                    /* get a handle to a device context */
   logbrush.lbStyle = BS_SOLID;           /* fill the logbrush structure */
   logbrush.lbColor = RGB (255, 0, 0);
   logbrush.lbHatch = (LONG) NULL;
   hPen = ExtCreatePen (PS_GEOMETRIC | PS_SOLID | PS_ENDCAP_FLAT | PS_JOIN_MITER, /* pen style */
                 5,                                                /* pen width */
                 &logbrush,                               /* pointer to LOGBRUSH structure */
                 0,                                       /* no custom line style */
                 NULL);
   SelectObject (hDC, hPen);              /* select pen into device context */
   [draw something]                       /* draw things using the new pen */
   DeleteObject (hPen);                   /* delete the pen */
```

ExtCreatePen() is very flexible and has many possible combinations of parameters. Let's discuss each parameter in turn to see the effects on the resultant pen.

Choosing a Pen Style with ExtCreatePen()

The first parameter of ExtCreatePen() defines the pen *style*. The style determines whether the pen is solid or broken, how the *endcaps* look, and how individual lines should be *joined*. Endcaps and joins are part of the new wideline support in the Win32 GDI.

Let's start by looking at the many pen styles. Table 5-1 shows the possible values for the first parameter of ExtCreatePen().

The values in Table 5-1 can be combined using a *bitwise or* (|) operator. In order to combine the values properly, we must determine how the values are grouped. Recall that the first parameter is a DWORD. Figure 5-3 shows how this DWORD is constructed. It also shows the grouping of the possible values from Table 5-1.

The possible values of the pen style are grouped into four categories: pen *type,* pen *style, endcap,* and *line joins,* and only one value may be used from each category; therefore you only have to combine a maximum of four values to define a pen. Let's go one step further and look at the effects of these four groups on a pen.

Value	Description
PS_GEOMETRIC	The line is measured in *world units* and is associated with a logical brush (see third parameter—LOGBRUSH).
PS_COSMETIC	The line is measured in *device units*. Supports line width of one.
PS_ALTERNATE	Pen draws every other pixel. Only effective with PS_COSMETIC.
PS_SOLID	Pen draws solid lines.
PS_DASH	Pen draws dashed lines.
PS_DOT	Pen draws dotted lines.
PS_DASHDOT	Pen draws alternating dash and dot.
PS_DASHDOTDOT	Pen draws alternating dash and two dots.
PS_NULL	Pen is invisible.
PS_USERSTYLE	Pen uses custom styling bits (see fourth and fifth parameters of ExtCreatePen).
PS_INSIDEFRAME	Solid pen—pen is drawn within a bounding rectangle if the GDI function uses one, even when wide line widths are defined.
PS_ENDCAP_ROUND	Endcaps of lines are rounded.
PS_ENDCAP_SQUARE	Endcaps of lines are square.
PS_ENDCAP_FLAT	Endcaps of lines are flat.
PS_JOIN_BEVEL	Joined lines are beveled (angled).
PS_JOIN_MITER	Joined lines are mitered (squared).
PS_JOIN_ROUND	Joined lines are rounded.

Table 5-1 Pen style values—first parameter of ExtCreatePen()

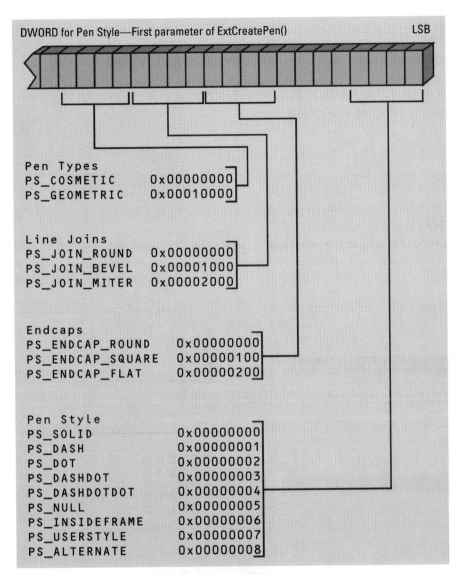

Figure 5-3 Anatomy of the Pen Style DWORD

Line Type

There are two possible line types: *geometric* and *cosmetic*. The geometric line type is measured in world units. If the line width (second parameter of ExtCreatePen()) is greater than 1, a logical brush is used to define the appearance of the line. Don't confuse the *appearance* with line style. For example, you could create a pen with a line *width* of 10 and a dotted line *style*. The logical brush affects the appearance of each dot. If the brush were hatched, each dot in the line would have a hatched appearance.

The cosmetic line type is much simpler. The width of a cosmetic line should be set to one. Cosmetic lines are measured in device units. The logical brush only affects the color of a cosmetic line.

Line Style

You can select one of nine possible line styles when creating a pen with ExtCreatePen(). Seven of these styles are identical to those used in the CreatePen() function. Two additional line styles are available to ExtCreatePen(): PS_ALTERNATE and PS_USERSTYLE.

PS_ALTERNATE only applies to cosmetic line types. This line style sets every other pixel when a line is drawn. PS_USERSTYLE indicates that the

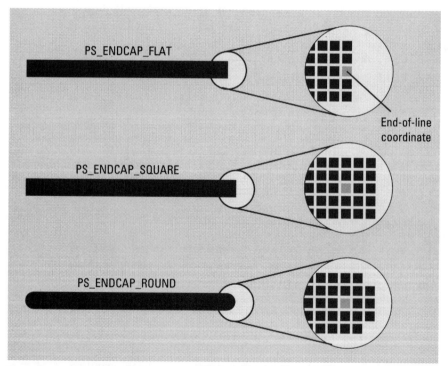

Figure 5-4 Endcaps—round, square, and flat

ExtCreatePen() function will use the fourth and fifth parameters to define a custom line style. We'll take a look at how to create a custom line style shortly.

Endcaps

The endcap determines how the ends of a line are drawn. Endcaps did not exist in Windows 3.x. Some application developers, especially those who created drawing and illustration packages, created their own endcaps. The Win32 GDI provides built-in support for endcaps.

Figure 5-4 shows examples of the three endcap types with a line width of 5. At first glance the PS_ENDCAP_SQUARE and PS_ENDCAP_FLAT appear to have the same effects. On close examination the flat endcap chops the line off at the exact end-of-line coordinate, while the square endcap squares the line off based on the line width. Note how the endcap extends beyond the end-of-line coordinate in the PS_ENDCAP_SQUARE example. The round endcaps have the same effect as square endcaps; they extend beyond the end-of-line coordinate. If the line width is thin (1 or 2), the endcaps have no effect.

Line Joins

Three types of line joins are another addition to the Win32 GDI: round, beveled, and mitered. In Windows 3.x all lines were mitered (squared off). Now you can specify how two lines are joined by combining one of the three line joins in the first parameter of ExtCreatePen() function. Figure 5-5 shows the effects of line joins. Again, the end-of-line coordinate is shown. The line width is 10 in this example to show the full effect of the round and beveled (angled) joins.

Getting and Setting the Miter Limit—GetMiterLimit() and SetMiterLimit()

Miter joins are limited by a default setting of 10. The *miter length* is the distance between the inside corner of the join to the outside corner of the join. The ratio of the miter length to current line width is compared against the miter limit. If the results of this ratio exceeds the miter limit, the system automatically bevels the join.

For example, the line joins at the top of Figure 5-6 form a right triangle; the adjacent angle is the line width and the hypotenuse is the miter length. This ratio works out to 1.414. Since the default miter limit is 10, the join is

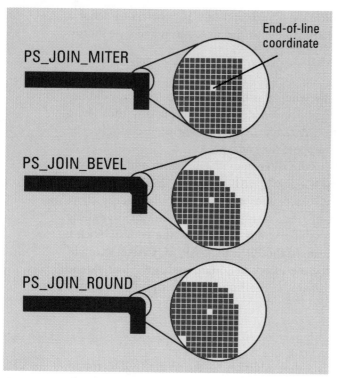

Figure 5-5 Line joins—round, beveled, and mitered

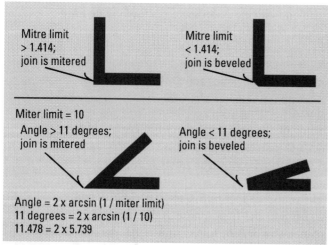

Figure 5-6 Miter limits

mitered. If you set the miter limit below 1.414, the join would become beveled, even if the pen called for a mitered join.

The bottom half of Figure 5-6 shows that with a decreasing angle, the miter ratio increases. If the join is less than 11°, the miter ratio exceeds 10 and the join is mitered. To find a miter limit given an angle, use the following formula:

Miter Limit = 1 / sin (angle / 2)

To find the angle below which the join will become beveled, use the following formula:

Angle = 2 x (arcsin (1 / Miter Limit))

You can increase or decrease the miter limit by calling SetMiterLimit(). The function returns a Boolean value indicating success or failure. Listing 5-4 shows the proper syntax and an example call to SetMiterLimit().

Listing 5-4 SetMiterLimit() syntax and example call

```
/* SetMiterLimit() Syntax */
BOOL SetMiterLimit (HDC hDC,              /* handle to a device context */
                    FLOAT NewLimit,       /* new miter limit */
                    PFLOAT OldLimit);     /* pointer to float to store old miter limit */

/* SetMiterLimit() Example Call */
HDC    hDC;
FLOAT OldLimit;

    SetMiterLimit (hDC, 5.5, &OldLimit); /* Sets miter limit to 5.5 and stores old value in OldLimit */
```

You can also get the current miter limit by calling GetMiterLimit(). You must pass a pointer to a float variable. This function places the current miter limit setting in the float variable's address. Listing 5-5 shows the syntax and an example call to GetMiterLimit().

Listing 5-5 GetMiterLimit() syntax and example call

```
/* GetMiterLimit() Syntax */
BOOL GetMiterLimit (HDC hDC,                 / * handle to a device context */
                    PFLOAT CurrentLimit); /* address to store miter limit */
```

continued on next page

continued from previous page

```
/* GetMiterLimit() Example Call */
HDC     hDC;
FLOAT CurrentLimit;


  GetMiterLimit (hDC, &CurrentLimit); /* Gets current miter limit and stores value in CurrentLimit */
```

Introduction to Path Brackets

A graphics *path* is a collection of GDI calls. Another new introduction to the Win32 GDI is *path brackets*. A path bracket is a collection of GDI calls bracketed by a BeginPath() and EndPath() function call. One path per device context can be open at a time. The only parameter required for path functions is a valid handle to a device context. Listing 5-6 shows the syntax and an example call for four path functions: BeginPath(), EndPath(), CloseFigure(), and StrokePath().

Listing 5-6 Path Function syntax and example calls

```
/* Syntax for BeginPath(), EndPath(), CloseFigure(), and StrokePath() */
BOOL BeginPath (HDC hDC);
BOOL EndPath (HDC hDC);
BOOL CloseFigure (HDC hDC);
BOOL StrokePath (HDC hDC);


/* Example Call Sequence for BeginPath(), EndPath(), CloseFigure(), and StrokePath() */
HDC hDC;

    hDC = GetDC (hWnd);      /* get handle to device context */
    BeginPath (hDC);         /* open a new path bracket */
       [calls to GDI functions (Arc(), Polyline(), LineTo(), etc.)]
    CloseFigure (hDC);       /* close open figure */
    EndPath (hDC);           /* close path bracket and select into DC */
    StrokePath (hDC);        /* render the path using the current pen */
```

The path bracket is opened with a call to BeginPath(). Then you can make calls to GDI drawing functions. If a figure is open, CloseFigure() connects the last point (current position) to the first point. For example, if you used LineTo to draw three sides of a square, call CloseFigure() would draw the fourth side, completing the figure.

Calling EndPath() closes the path bracket and selects it into the device context, but it does not display the figure on the device context. This requires a call to StrokePath(), which renders the path using the current pen.

StrokePath() requires a closed path, so calling this function before EndPath() has no effect.

We will see these functions in action in our first example program, GDI1. Later in this chapter, we will see some of the other uses of GDI paths.

DEMONSTRATING THE NEW ARC AND PEN FUNCTIONS

Our first example program in this chapter puts the new arc and pen functions to work. The application is titled GDI1, and you can find the program files in the \CHAPTER5\5.1 subdirectory.

Although the WinMain() function is not shown in the following listings, we have modified the function slightly. When we fill the window class structure the background brush line has changed. Here is the line from previous example programs and the new line:

```
/* the background brush line has changed from this line... */
wndclass.hbrBackground = GetStockObject (WHITE_BRUSH);

/* to this line */
wndclass.hbrBackground = GetStockObject (LTGRAY_BRUSH); /* brush for GDI programs */
```

Changing the background brush isn't mandatory for programs that use the GDI functions. It just presents a more appealing display for these applications.

What Does GDI1 Do?

This example application has two popup menus: *Figures* and *Pen Attributes*. The *Figures* selection has four options: *Lines*, *Square*, *AngleArc*, and *ArcTo*. Only the last two of these selections demonstrate the new arc functions. The other selections help demonstrate the effects of ExtCreatePen(). The *Pen Attributes* selection has five options: *Type*, *Style*, *End Cap*, *Join*, and *Line Width*. These selections let you try various combinations of pen styles.

Listings 5-7 through 5-9 make up the GDI1 application. The WinMain() function is not listed, although the complete listing of GDI1.C is available on your sample code disk. The calls to new functions are in boldface.

Additions to the Resource Script

In addition to the icon and menu resource, GDI.RC also contains a dialog resource. *GDI1Dlg* contains the information that makes up the AngleArc() dialog box. This resource enables the user to enter a start angle, sweep angle, and radius for the arc. It also contains two button controls to draw or cancel the arc.

Listing 5-7 GDI1.RC—resource script

```
#include "windows.h"
#include "GDI1.h"


GDI1Icon ICON  GDI1.ico

GDI1Menu MENU
BEGIN
    POPUP "&Figures"
    BEGIN
        MENUITEM "&Lines",       IDM_LINES
        MENUITEM "&Square",      IDM_SQUARE
        MENUITEM "&AngleArc",    IDM_ANGLEARC
        MENUITEM "Arc&To",       IDM_ARCTO
    END
    POPUP "&Pen Attributes"
    BEGIN
        POPUP "&Type"
        BEGIN
            MENUITEM "&Geometric",   IDM_GEOMET
            MENUITEM "&Cosmetic",    IDM_COSMET, CHECKED
        END
        POPUP "&Style"
        BEGIN
            MENUITEM "&Solid",       IDM_SOLID, CHECKED
            MENUITEM "&Dash",        IDM_DASH
            MENUITEM "Do&t",         IDM_DOT
            MENUITEM "D&ashDot",     IDM_DASHDOT
        END
        POPUP "&End Cap"
        BEGIN
            MENUITEM "&Round",       IDM_ROUNDEND, CHECKED
            MENUITEM "&Square",      IDM_SQUAREEND
            MENUITEM "&Flat",        IDM_FLATEND
        END
        POPUP "&Join"
```

```
        BEGIN
            MENUITEM "&Bevel",        IDM_BEVEL
            MENUITEM "&Miter",        IDM_MITER
            MENUITEM "&Round",        IDM_ROUND, CHECKED
        END
        POPUP "Line Width"
        BEGIN
            MENUITEM "&Fine",         IDM_1PIXEL, CHECKED
            MENUITEM "&Medium",       IDM_5PIXEL
            MENUITEM "&Thick",        IDM_10PIXEL
        END
    END
END

GDI1Dlg DIALOG 6, 18, 160, 59
LANGUAGE LANG_NEUTRAL, SUBLANG_NEUTRAL
STYLE DS_MODALFRAME | WS_POPUP | WS_VISIBLE | WS_CAPTION | WS_SYSMENU
CAPTION "AngleArc()"
FONT 8, "MS Sans Serif"
BEGIN
    CONTROL         "Start Angle", -1, "Static", SS_RIGHT | WS_GROUP, 12, 9,
                    52, 17
    CONTROL         "Sweep Angle", -1, "Static", SS_RIGHT | WS_GROUP, 12, 26,
                    52, 17
    CONTROL         "Radius", -1, "Static", SS_RIGHT | WS_GROUP, 12, 42, 52,
                    17
    CONTROL         "", DLI_START_ANGLE, "Edit", ES_AUTOHSCROLL | WS_BORDER |
                    WS_TABSTOP, 69, 7, 25, 12
    CONTROL         "", DLI_SWEEP_ANGLE, "Edit", ES_AUTOHSCROLL | WS_BORDER |
                    WS_TABSTOP, 69, 24, 25, 12
    CONTROL         "", DLI_RADIUS, "Edit", ES_AUTOHSCROLL | WS_BORDER |
                    WS_TABSTOP, 69, 41, 25, 12
    CONTROL         "Draw", IDOK, "Button", WS_TABSTOP, 109, 9, 40,
                    14
    CONTROL         "Cancel", IDCANCEL, "Button", WS_TABSTOP, 109, 33, 40,
                    14
END
```

Additions to the Header File

GDI1.H has a few additions as well. We have added two function prototypes:
one for the dialog procedure (DlgProc()), and one for the menu checkmark
function (MenuSet()). Three global UINT values specify the default values
for AngleArc(). For example, the default AngleArc() call uses a start angle of
0, a sweep angle of 90, and a radius of 40.

Listing 5-8 GDI1.H—header file

```
/* gdi1.h -- Include file for gdi1.c and gdi1.rc */

/* Menu defines */
#define IDM_LINES       1
#define IDM_SQUARE      2
#define IDM_ANGLEARC    3
#define IDM_ARCTO       4
#define IDM_GEOMET      5
#define IDM_COSMET      6
#define IDM_SOLID       7
#define IDM_DASH        8
#define IDM_DOT         9
#define IDM_DASHDOT     10
#define IDM_ROUNDEND    11
#define IDM_SQUAREEND   12
#define IDM_FLATEND     13
#define IDM_BEVEL       14
#define IDM_MITER       15
#define IDM_ROUND       16
#define IDM_1PIXEL      17
#define IDM_5PIXEL      18
#define IDM_10PIXEL     19


/* Object to draw defines */

#define DRAW_LINES      1
#define DRAW_SQUARE     2
#define DRAW_ARC        3
#define DRAW_ARCTO      4



/* Dialog defines */

#define IDOK            1
#define IDCANCEL        2
#define DLI_START_ANGLE 101
#define DLI_SWEEP_ANGLE 102
#define DLI_RADIUS      103

/* Function prototype */
LONG APIENTRY WndProc (HWND, UINT, UINT, LONG);
VOID MenuSet (DWORD dwPenStyle, DWORD dwPenWidth);
BOOL CALLBACK DlgProc (HWND hWnd, UINT message, WPARAM wParam, LPARAM lParam);

/* Global variables */
HANDLE ghInst;
HANDLE ghWnd;
UINT    gnStartAngle = 0, gnSweepAngle = 90, gnRadius = 40;
```

About the Source File

The source file for GDI1 is fairly large for an example application, but most of the code is literally window dressing. Most of the code handles the many menu selections, menu checkmarks, and the dialog procedure. This extra code is not without its benefits, however. It makes the program easier to use and has many possibilities of pen selections.

Listing 5-9 GDI1.C—source file

```
/* gdi1.c     Using GDI functions in Windows NT */

#include <windows.h>            /* include for Windows NT apps */
#include "gdi1.h"               /* include for gdi1.c */

/* WndProc - Main Window Procedure for gdi1.c */

LONG APIENTRY WndProc (HWND hWnd, UINT message, UINT wParam, LONG lParam)
{
HPEN            hPen;
PAINTSTRUCT     ps;
static LOGBRUSH lBrush;
static DWORD    dwPenStyle = 0;  /* set initial pen style DWORD to 0 */
static DWORD    dwPenWidth = 1;  /* set initial pen width to 1 */
static int      nDraw = 0;

    switch (message)
    {
        case WM_CREATE:          /* No initialization */
            return (0);

        case WM_PAINT:                          /* paint depending on nDraw */
            BeginPaint (hWnd, &ps);
            lBrush.lbStyle = BS_SOLID;          /* fill logical brush structure */
            lBrush.lbColor = RGB (0,0,0);       /* solid, black, and no hatch */
            lBrush.lbHatch = (LONG) NULL;
            hPen = ExtCreatePen (dwPenStyle,    /* create pen based on dwStyle */
                                 dwPenWidth,    /* dwPenWidth and logical brush */
                                 &lBrush,
                                 0,             /* no custom styling */
                                 NULL);
            SelectObject (ps.hdc, hPen);        /* select pen into DC */

            if (nDraw == DRAW_LINES)            /* draw two horizontal lines */
            {
                MoveToEx (ps.hdc, 50, 50, NULL);   /* move to coordinate 50,50 */
                LineTo (ps.hdc, 150, 50);          /* draw first line */
                MoveToEx (ps.hdc, 50, 150, NULL);  /* move to coordinate 50, 150 */
                LineTo (ps.hdc, 150, 150);         /* draw second line */
```

continued on next page

continued from previous page

```
          }
          if (nDraw == DRAW_SQUARE)              /* draw square */
          {
             BeginPath (ps.hdc);                  /* open path bracket */
             MoveToEx (ps.hdc, 50, 50, NULL);    /* move to corodiate 50,50 */
             LineTo (ps.hdc, 150, 50);           /* draw top of square */
             LineTo (ps.hdc, 150, 150);          /* draw right side of square */
             LineTo (ps.hdc, 50, 150);           /* draw bottom of square */
             CloseFigure (ps.hdc);               /* closing figure draws left side of square */
             EndPath (ps.hdc);                   /* close path bracket */
             StrokePath (ps.hdc);                /* draw the square */
          }
          if (nDraw == DRAW_ARC)                 /* draw an arc */
          {
             BeginPath (ps.hdc);                  /* open path bracket */
             MoveToEx (ps.hdc, 100, 100, NULL);  /* move to coordinate 100,100 */
             /* draw arc based on globals filled by DlgProc */
           AngleArc (ps.hdc, 100, 100, gnRadius, (FLOAT) gnStartAngle, (FLOAT) gnSweepAngle);
             CloseFigure (ps.hdc);               /* close figure completes the arc */
             EndPath (ps.hdc);                   /* close the path bracket */
             StrokePath (ps.hdc);                /* draw the arc */
          }
          if (nDraw == DRAW_ARCTO)               /* draw arc using ArcTo() and show rectangle */
          {
             Rectangle (ps.hdc, 30, 30, 130, 100); /* draw bounding rectangle */
             MoveToEx (ps.hdc, 40, 15, NULL);      /* draw lines indicating radials */
             LineTo (ps.hdc, 80, 65);
             MoveToEx (ps.hdc, 45,115, NULL);
             LineTo (ps.hdc, 80, 65);
             /* draw the arc inside the bounding rectangle */
             ArcTo (ps.hdc, 30, 30, 130, 100, 40, 15, 45, 115);
          }
          DeleteObject (hPen);                   /* delete pen */
          EndPaint (hWnd, &ps);
          break;

     case WM_COMMAND:
        switch (LOWORD(wParam)) /* Extract LOWORD of wParam for Win32) */
        {
           case IDM_LINES:                       /* user selected Lines */
              nDraw = DRAW_LINES;                /* set nDraw to DRAW_LINES */
              break;
           case IDM_SQUARE:                      /* user selected Square */
              nDraw = DRAW_SQUARE;               /* set nDraw to DRAW_SQUARE */
              break;
           case IDM_ANGLEARC:
              /* start dialog box--if dialog returns true, set nDraw to DRAW_ARCTO */
              if (DialogBox (ghInst, (LPCTSTR) "GDI1Dlg", hWnd, (DLGPROC) DlgProc))
                 nDraw = DRAW_ARC;
              break;
           case IDM_ARCTO:                       /* user selected ArcTo */
              nDraw = DRAW_ARCTO;                /* set nDraw to ArcTo */
```

```
        break;
    case IDM_GEOMET:                    /* pen type settings */
        dwPenStyle &= 0xFFF0FFFF;       /* mask out pen type */
        dwPenStyle |= PS_GEOMETRIC;     /* set to geometric */
        MenuSet (dwPenStyle, 0);        /* update checkmarks */
        break;
    case IDM_COSMET:
        dwPenStyle &= 0xFFF0FFFF;       /* mask out pen type */
        dwPenStyle |= PS_COSMETIC;      /* set to cosmetic */
        MenuSet (dwPenStyle, 0);        /* update checkmarks */
        break;
    case IDM_SOLID:                     /* pen style settings */
        dwPenStyle &= 0xFFFFFFF0;       /* mask out pen style */
        dwPenStyle |= PS_SOLID;         /* set to solid */
        MenuSet (dwPenStyle, 0);        /* update checkmarks */
        break;
    case IDM_DASH:
        dwPenStyle &= 0xFFFFFFF0;       /* mask out pen style */
        dwPenStyle |= PS_DASH;          /* set to dashed */
        MenuSet (dwPenStyle, 0);        /* update checkmarks */
        break;
    case IDM_DOT:
        dwPenStyle &= 0xFFFFFFF0;       /* mask out pen style */
        dwPenStyle |= PS_DOT;           /* set to dotted */
        MenuSet (dwPenStyle, 0);        /* update checkmarks */
        break;
    case IDM_DASHDOT:
        dwPenStyle &= 0xFFFFFFF0;       /* mask out pen style */
        dwPenStyle |= PS_DASHDOT;       /* set to dashdot */
        MenuSet (dwPenStyle, 0);        /* update checkmarks */
        break;
    case IDM_ROUNDEND:                  /* endcap settings */
        dwPenStyle &= 0xFFFFF0FF;       /* mask out endcaps */
        dwPenStyle |= PS_ENDCAP_ROUND;  /* set to round */
        MenuSet (dwPenStyle, 0);        /* update checkmarks */
        break;
    case IDM_SQUAREEND:
        dwPenStyle &= 0xFFFFF0FF;       /* mask out endcaps */
        dwPenStyle |= PS_ENDCAP_SQUARE;/* set to square */
        MenuSet (dwPenStyle, 0);        /* update checkmarks */
        break;
    case IDM_FLATEND:
        dwPenStyle &= 0xFFFFF0FF;       /* mask out endcaps */
        dwPenStyle |= PS_ENDCAP_FLAT;   /* set to flat */
        MenuSet (dwPenStyle, 0);        /* update checkmarks */
        break;
    case IDM_BEVEL:                     /* join settings */
        dwPenStyle &= 0xFFFF0FFF;       /* mask out joins */
        dwPenStyle |= PS_JOIN_BEVEL;    /* set to bevel */
        MenuSet (dwPenStyle, 0);        /* update checkmarks */
        break;
    case IDM_MITER:
```

continued on next page

continued from previous page

```
                    dwPenStyle &= 0xFFFF0FFF;        /* mask out joins */
                    dwPenStyle |= PS_JOIN_MITER;     /* set to miter */
                    MenuSet (dwPenStyle, 0);         /* update checkmarks */
                    break;
                case IDM_ROUND:
                    dwPenStyle &= 0xFFFF0FFF;        /* mask out joins */
                    dwPenStyle |= PS_JOIN_ROUND;     /* set to round */
                    MenuSet (dwPenStyle, 0);         /* update checkmarks */
                    break;
                case IDM_1PIXEL:                     /* pen width settings */
                    dwPenWidth = 1;                  /* set width to 1 */
                    MenuSet (0xF, dwPenWidth);       /* update checkmarks */
                    break;
                case IDM_5PIXEL:
                    dwPenWidth = 5;                  /* set width to 5 */
                    MenuSet (0xF, dwPenWidth);       /* update checkmarks */
                    break;
                case IDM_10PIXEL:
                    dwPenWidth = 10;                 /* set width to 10 */
                    MenuSet (0XF, dwPenWidth);       /* update checkmarks */
                    break;
                default:
                    return (0);
            }
            InvalidateRect (hWnd, NULL, TRUE);    /* force WM_PAINT */
            return (0);

        case WM_DESTROY:                             /* No cleanup necessary */
            PostQuitMessage (0);
            return (0);

        default:
            return DefWindowProc (hWnd, message, wParam, lParam);
    }

    return (0L);
}


/* MenuSet() updates checkmarks on the Pen Attributes popup menu */
VOID MenuSet (DWORD dwPenStyle, DWORD dwPenWidth)
{
int    i;
HMENU hMenu;

    hMenu = GetMenu (ghWnd);    /* get handle to menu */


    if (dwPenStyle != 0xF)        /* do pen style checkmarks need updating */
    {
        for (i = IDM_GEOMET; i <= IDM_ROUND; i++)  /* uncheck all pen style menuitems */
            CheckMenuItem (hMenu, i, MF_BYCOMMAND | MF_UNCHECKED);
```

```
        if (dwPenStyle & PS_GEOMETRIC)              /* is it geometric? */
            CheckMenuItem (hMenu, IDM_GEOMET, MF_BYCOMMAND | MF_CHECKED);
        else                                        /* then it must be cosmetic */
            CheckMenuItem (hMenu, IDM_COSMET, MF_BYCOMMAND | MF_CHECKED);


        if ((dwPenStyle & PS_DASHDOT) == PS_DASHDOT)/* is it a dashdot? */
            CheckMenuItem (hMenu, IDM_DASHDOT, MF_BYCOMMAND | MF_CHECKED);
        else if (dwPenStyle & PS_DASH)              /* is it a dash? */
            CheckMenuItem (hMenu, IDM_DASH, MF_BYCOMMAND | MF_CHECKED);
        else if (dwPenStyle & PS_DOT)               /* is it a dot? */
            CheckMenuItem (hMenu, IDM_DOT, MF_BYCOMMAND | MF_CHECKED);
        else                                        /* then it must be solid */
            CheckMenuItem (hMenu, IDM_SOLID, MF_BYCOMMAND | MF_CHECKED);


        if (dwPenStyle & PS_ENDCAP_SQUARE)          /* is it square? */
            CheckMenuItem (hMenu, IDM_SQUAREEND, MF_BYCOMMAND | MF_CHECKED);
        else if (dwPenStyle & PS_ENDCAP_FLAT)       /* is it flat? */
            CheckMenuItem (hMenu, IDM_FLATEND, MF_BYCOMMAND | MF_CHECKED);
        else                                        /* then it must be round */
            CheckMenuItem (hMenu, IDM_ROUNDEND, MF_BYCOMMAND | MF_CHECKED);


        if (dwPenStyle & PS_JOIN_BEVEL)             /* is it bevel? */
            CheckMenuItem (hMenu, IDM_BEVEL, MF_BYCOMMAND | MF_CHECKED);
        else if (dwPenStyle & PS_JOIN_MITER)        /* is it miter? */
            CheckMenuItem (hMenu, IDM_MITER, MF_BYCOMMAND | MF_CHECKED);
        else                                        /* then it must be round */
            CheckMenuItem (hMenu, IDM_ROUND, MF_BYCOMMAND | MF_CHECKED);
    }

    if (dwPenWidth != 0)        /* do pen width checkmarks need updating? */
    {
        for (i = IDM_1PIXEL; i <= IDM_10PIXEL; i++)/* uncheck all pen width menuitems */
            CheckMenuItem (hMenu, i, MF_BYCOMMAND | MF_UNCHECKED);

        if (dwPenWidth == 1)                        /* is it 1? */
            CheckMenuItem (hMenu, IDM_1PIXEL, MF_BYCOMMAND | MF_CHECKED);
        if (dwPenWidth == 5)                        /* is it 5? */
            CheckMenuItem (hMenu, IDM_5PIXEL, MF_BYCOMMAND | MF_CHECKED);
        if (dwPenWidth == 10)                       /* is it 10? */
            CheckMenuItem (hMenu, IDM_10PIXEL, MF_BYCOMMAND | MF_CHECKED);
    }
}

/* DlgProc() is a dialog box procedure that gets input from the user for AngleArc() */
BOOL CALLBACK DlgProc (HWND hDlg, UINT message, WPARAM wParam, LPARAM lParam)
{
    switch (message)
    {
        case WM_INITDIALOG:                         /* initialize dialog using current settings */
            SetDlgItemInt (hDlg, DLI_START_ANGLE, gnStartAngle, FALSE);
            SetDlgItemInt (hDlg, DLI_SWEEP_ANGLE, gnSweepAngle, FALSE);
```

continued on next page

continued from previous page

```
            SetDlgItemInt (hDlg, DLI_RADIUS, gnRadius, FALSE);
            return (TRUE);

        case WM_COMMAND:
            switch (LOWORD(wParam))
            {
                case IDOK:                          /* if Draw is selected, update settings */
                {
                    gnStartAngle = GetDlgItemInt (hDlg, DLI_START_ANGLE, NULL, FALSE);
                    gnSweepAngle = GetDlgItemInt (hDlg, DLI_SWEEP_ANGLE, NULL, FALSE);
                    gnRadius = GetDlgItemInt (hDlg, DLI_RADIUS, NULL, FALSE);
                    EndDialog (hDlg, TRUE);          /* pass TRUE back to caller */
                    break;
                }
                case IDCANCEL:                      /* cancel the arc */
                    EndDialog (hDlg, FALSE);         /* pass FALSE back to caller */
                    break;
            }
        return (TRUE);
    }
    return (FALSE);
}
```

The Mechanics of GDI1

Before we take a look at the new function calls in GDI1, let's look at the overall mechanics that make this application tick. We can break the program down into four segments: initialization, user selections, updating the menu, and the AngleArc() dialog procedure.

Initialization of GDI1

Most of the initialization of GDI1 occurs in the resource file. GDI1.RC defines the menu selections for the application. In addition, it specifies which options are checked initially in the *Pen Attributes* popup to serve as defaults. Five menu items are checked:

- *Cosmetic*—in the *Type* submenu
- *Solid*—in the *Style* submenu
- *Round*—in the *End Cap* submenu
- *Round*—in the *Join* submenu
- *Fine*—in the *Line Width* submenu

We set these default values at the top of WndProc(). Two static variables are initialized: *dwPenStyle* is set to 0, and *dwPenWidth* is set to 1. By referring back to Figure 5-3, you can see that the attributes in the pen style DWORD that are 0 match those with checkmarks. The static *dwPenWidth* is initialized to 1, which is associated with the *Fine* selection.

Another static variable, *nDraw,* is an integer WM_PAINT uses to determine which figure to draw (lines, square, and so on). *nDraw* is initially set to 0 so the first WM_PAINT message doesn't draw anything.

User Selections—Figures Menu

With the exception of the dialog box, user selections are processed in the WM_COMMAND section of WndProc(). The first four cases in the WM_COMMAND *switch* statement represent the *Figures* menu selections. If the user selects one of the figures, *nDraw* is set to the value that corresponds to the selection.

For example, if the user selects *Square* from the Figures menu, the case is IDM_SQUARE. In this instance, *nDraw* is set to DRAW_SQUARE. A break statement drops us out of the *switch.* Just below the end of the switch braces, we make a call to InvalidateRect(). This forces a WM_PAINT message. The WM_PAINT code uses nDraw (which in this example is DRAW_SQUARE) to draw the appropriate figure.

The only exception to this processing is IDM_ANGLEARC. This selection uses the dialog box, which we will discuss shortly.

User Selections—Pen Attributes Menu

The *Pen Attributes* menu and its submenus cause the remaining cases. These selections are broken down into *dwPenStyle* and *dwPenWidth* changes. Let's look at an example of modifying *dwPenStyle* first.

If the user selects *Flat* from the *End Caps* submenu, an IDM_FLATEND message is generated. Recall that the initial setting of *End Caps* is *Round.* The first step is to reset the bits in *dwPenStyle* that are associated with end caps. Referring back to Figure 5-3, you can see that *dwPenStyle* is divided into four bit sections. Since we are dealing with end caps at this time, this would be bit 8 through bit 11, or the ninth through the twelfth bit. We mask off these bits by performing a *bitwise and* (&) on *dwPenStyle* and 0xFFFFF0FF. This resets the appropriate bits without affecting any other bits in *dwPenStyle.* The result of the *bitwise and* is stored back in *dwPenStyle.*

The next step is to use a *bitwise or* (|) to set the new end cap. In this case we *or* PS_ENDCAP_FLAT into *dwPenStyle.* This sets the appropriate bit in *dwPenStyle.* We then make a call to MenuSet(), our application defined function that updates the checkmarks in the *Pen Attributes* submenus. We'll cover the MenuSet() function in a moment. For now, notice that we are passing *dwPenAttributes* in the first parameter, and 0 in the second parameter.

Changing *dwPenWidth* is much easier. This change is caused by the user selecting *Line Width* from the *Pen Attributes* menu. The three possible selections from the Line Width submenu are *Fine, Medium,* and *Thick.* These three selections translate into IDM_1PIXEL, IDM_5PIXEL, and IDM_10PIXEL, respectively. Let's assume the user selects *Medium.*

The code that processes IDM_5PIXEL sets *dwPenWidth* to 5. This is our arbitrary choice for a medium line. We then call MenuSet() once again. The only difference here is that the first parameter is 0xF and the second parameter is *dwPenWidth.* Let's look at how MenuSet() processes the *dwPenStyle* and *dwPenWidth* changes.

Updating the Menu Checkmarks—MenuSet()

The MenuSet() function receives two parameters; one represents *dwPenStyle* and the other *dwPenWidth.* We'll continue our example menu selections by seeing how they are processed in MenuSet().

When *dwPenStyle* was modified to change the end caps to flat, we called MenuSet() with *dwPenStyle* as the first parameter, and 0 as the second parameter. The first step in MenuSet() is to obtain a handle to the main menu with GetMenu(). The next step is to see if *dwPenStyle* is 0xF. Why 0xF? If we are changing the line width, there is no reason to update the menu checkmarks affected by *dwPenStyle.* We couldn't use 0 because it is a valid *dwPenStyle* (it's even the default!). We chose 0xF because it reflects a nonexistent possibility of *dwPenStyle.*

In this example *dwPenStyle* is not 0xF, so we are processing the body of the *if* statement. We uncheck all the menu items associated with *dwPenStyle* using a *for* loop. This is done by cycling through the selections starting with IDM_GEOMET and continuing through IDM_ROUND. Each pass through the loop we call CheckMenuItem() with the appropriate parameters.

The remaining four segments of code check the appropriate menu items. This is done by testing the value of *dwPenStyle* against the pen style values (such as PS_ENDCAP_FLAT). Again, a *bitwise and* (&) operator performs the comparison. If the bit is set, the appropriate menu item is checked with CheckMenuItem().

There are two tricky parts to this portion of the application. Notice how the last *else* statement in each of the four segments corresponds to the default values. We do this because we cannot test for 0 using the *bitwise and* operator. Doing so would always equate to 0 and the test would fail. So we test for all other possibilities first, then check the last item if all others fail. For example, in the third segment, we test for PS_ENDCAP_SQUARE. If that fails we test for PS_ENDCAP_FLAT. If that fails we assume the end cap must be round.

The other tricky situation is at the top of the second segment, where we test for PS_DASHDOT. Since PS_DASHDOT sets two bits, it would also pass if only one of the bits were set (PS_DASH or PS_DOT). So we compare the results of the *bitwise and* with PS_DASHDOT to see if it really is this value.

Once we have updated the checkmarks for *dwPenStyle,* we reach the next major *if* statement. We check to see if *dwPenWidth* is 0. Remember, this is not the actual pen width, it is the second parameter passed to MenuSet(). If the value passed is 0, we can assume that the *dwPenStyle* variable in WndProc() has not changed.

In WndProc() the cases that change the *dwPenStyle* parameter call MenuSet() with the first parameter set to 0xF. This skips the first *if* statement in MenuSet() since no changes have been made to *dwPenStyle*. The second major *if* statement is executed, however, since *dwPenWidth* now contains a valid width. We reset the checkmarks in the *Line Width* submenu, check the appropriate line width selection, and return.

The Dialog Procedure in Win32

This is our first dialog procedure in an example application. You may have noticed already that calling a dialog procedure is easier in Win32 than in Windows 3.x. First, we do not have a module definition file specifying that DlgProc() is an export. Furthermore, we do not have to create an *instance thunk* using MakeProcInstance() as we did in Windows 3.x. Why? To answer that question, let's quickly review why we needed the instance thunk in the first place.

Both Windows 3.x and the Windows NT move our code and data around in memory. In Windows 3.x we needed to get the address of the code for the dialog box before calling it. After all, Windows 3.x might have moved it. Windows NT moves our code around too, but we use virtual memory addresses for code and data. The virtual memory manager keeps track of where the code actually is in physical memory. We don't have to worry about the specific location.

We start the dialog box if the user selects *AngleArc* from the *Figures* menu. The call is in WndProc(), in the WM_COMMAND body, and in the IDM_ANGLEARC case. The call to the dialog box resembles a Windows 3.x call, with the exception of the last parameter. Here is code that shows the contrast of Windows 3.x and Win32:

```
/* Windows 3.x Call to DialogBox */

    DialogBox (ghInst, "GDI1Dlg", hWnd, lpfnDlgProc) /* last parameter obtained from
                                                         MakeProcInstance() */

/* Win32 Call to DialogBox */

    DialogBox (ghInst, (LPCTSTR) "GDI1Dlg", hWnd, (DLGPROC) DlgProc); /* Last parameter is
                                                                         actual name of func */
```

Notice that we cast the second parameter to LPCTSTR (long pointer to a character string). Also, we cast the fourth parameter to DLGPROC, indicating that the parameter points to a dialog procedure. Notice that we use the actual procedure name rather than an address returned from MakeProcInstance().

In GDI1.C, we are testing the return value to see if it's TRUE or FALSE. To see where this value comes from, we must examine the dialog procedure.

The Dialog Procedure—DlgProc()

The last function in GDI1.C is the dialog procedure. Notice that it is declared as BOOL CALLBACK; in Windows 3.x this would have been BOOL FAR PASCAL. The latter would still work, but it is good practice to start using CALLBACK for all dialog procedures. For now, the Windows NT header files take care of fixing up FAR PASCAL.

The remainder of the dialog procedure is identical to the format of Windows 3.x. In our case we process the WM_INITDIALOG message by setting the three edit controls: one each for start angle, sweep angle, and radius. The values DLI_START_ANGLE, DLI_SWEEP_ANGLE, and DLI_RADIUS are defined in GDI1.H. Since the edit controls contain integers, we set the values with SetDlgItemInt().

The only other operations our dialog procedure performs is to modify the globals and end the dialog, or just end the dialog. If the user selects Draw, it equates to ID_OK (defined in GDI1.H and equated in GDI1.RC). We update the globals (*gnStartAngle, gnSweepAngle,* and *gnRadius*) and end the dialog box with TRUE. If the user selects *Cancel,* we end the dialog box with FALSE without changing any values.

When we start the dialog box in WndProc(), we test this return value. If the dialog box returns TRUE (user selected *Draw*), we set *nDraw* to DRAW_ANGLEARC. If the dialog box returns FALSE, we simply break without setting *nDraw.*

The New Functions in GDI1

In the *Figures* menu, the user can select one of four simple figures: *Lines, Square, AngleArc,* and *ArcTo.* Let's look at the selections one at a time and see how the new GDI functions work.

Lines

Although the first selection does not use any of the new GDI functions, we will use it after we build GDI1 to demonstrate some of the effects of ExtCreatePen(). When the user selects *Lines* from the *Figures* menu, the action sends a WM_COMMAND message to WndProc. The menu message is IDM_LINES. We simply set *nDraw* to DRAW_LINES and break out of the *switch.* At the bottom of the *switch* body, we call InvalidateRect() which forces a WM_PAINT message.

The start of the WM_PAINT process contains the typical BeginPaint() function which fills a PAINTSTRUCT structure. The next three lines fill a LOGBRUSH structure that we'll use to create the pen. The first member, *lbStyle,* is set to BS_SOLID indicating a solid brush. Remember, this doesn't mean that this style determines whether or not the *line* is solid, dotted, or dashed; it defines the brush style. This could be hatched, for example. The *lbColor* member is set to RGB (0,0,0), which indicates the color is black. The *lbHatch* member is set to NULL, since we are not using a hatched brush. We cast the NULL to a LONG value because the LOGBRUSH *lpHatch* member is expecting a LONG.

The next step creates the pen using the new function ExtCreatePen(). The first parameter is *dwPenStyle,* a DWORD specifying the attributes of the pen. The second parameter is *dwPenWidth,* a DWORD specifying the width of the pen. In our application this could be 1, 5, or 10. The third parameter is a pointer to our brush structure, *lBrush.* The fourth and fifth parameters are set to 0 and NULL, respectively. This indicates that there is no custom line style.

Now that the pen is created, we select it into the device context with SelectObject(). We use *ps.hdc* for the device context handle and *hPen* for the pen handle. All of the steps so far are performed before we check the figure type.

Since *nDraw* is set to DRAW_LINES, the first *if* statement is true. We call MoveToEx() to set the current position to coordinate 50,50. The MoveToEx() function is identical to Windows 3.x's MoveTo(), except it has an additional parameter that can store the previous current position. This would require a pointer to a POINT structure. In our case we are not tracking the old position; therefore we set this parameter to NULL.

We follow this with a call to LineTo(). This draws a horizontal line spanning from coordinate 50,50 to 149,50. Recall that the last coordinate is not included as part of the line. We then move the current position to the 50, 150 coordinate and draw another line. This completes the *if* body for DRAW_LINES.

Since *nDraw* equals DRAW_LINES, the next three *if* statements are FALSE. We call DeleteObject() to delete the pen and EndPaint() to end the WM_PAINT processing.

Square

The next menu selection in the *Figures* menu is *Square*. This menu message is IDM_SQUARE, which sets *nDraw* to DRAW_SQUARE. InvalidateRect() causes a WM_PAINT message to be sent to WndProc().

We create the pen and select it into the device context. Since *nDraw* is set to DRAW_SQUARE, the second *if* statement is true. This time we call BeginPath() to open a path bracket in the device context. We call MoveToEx() to move the current position to 50,50. Then we define the top, right, and bottom of the square with three calls to LineTo(). A call to CloseFigure() draws the left side of the square, closing the figure.

The next line closes the path bracket with EndPath(). We then call StrokePath() which draws the square on the device context. Note that the square does not appear until we call this function.

At the bottom of the WM_PAINT case, we delete the pen, end the painting process, and break out of the *switch* statement.

AngleArc

The third *Figures* selection is *AngleArc*. This selection generates an IDM_ANGLEARC menu message. Before we set *nDraw*, we start the dialog box procedure, DlgProc(). This procedure gets input from the user that sets three global variables: *nStartAngle, nSweepAngle,* and *nRadius.* If the user closes the dialog box with the Draw (ID_OK) selection, the dialog box returns TRUE and *nDraw* is set to DRAW_ARC. If the user selects Cancel (ID_CANCEL), the dialog box returns FALSE and *nDraw* is not changed.

We're assuming that the dialog box is closed with *Draw*. We set *nDraw* to DRAW_ARC, break out of the *switch,* and call InvalidateRect(). The WM_PAINT message is processed with the code common to all figures in our example: BeginPaint(), fill the LOGBRUSH structure, create the pen, and select it into the device context.

The third *if* statement is TRUE in this case. We open a path bracket with BeginPath(). We move the current position to coordinate 100,100. You do not have to adjust the current position to call AngleArc(). We are doing so in this case to draw a pie-shaped figure.

We call AngleArc() with the six required parameters. The first is *ps.hdc,* the handle to the device context. The second and third parameters are the center of the arc. The remaining parameters define the arc itself: *nRadius, nStartAngle,* and *nSweepAngle.* Note that we cast the last two parameters to FLOAT. The AngleArc() function expects FLOAT values for the angles, even though our application is using integers for these values.

We then close the figure, end the path bracket, and stroke the path. Using the default global settings this does the following:

- moves the current position to 100,100
- draws a line to the right 40 pixels (default radius and 0°)
- sweeps angle counterclockwise 90° (twelve o'clock)
- draws a line back to 100,100 (CloseFigure())

ArcTo

The last *Figures* menu selection demonstrates a call to ArcTo(). The ArcTo selection results in an IDM_ARCTO menu message. This sets *nDraw* to DRAW_ARCTO and breaks out of the *switch* where we call InvalidateRect().

We perform the common tasks (BeginPaint(), fill the LOGBRUSH struct, create the pen, and so on), then proceed to the last *if* statement in WM_PAINT. In this example, we draw additional figures to help illustrate the ArcTo() function call. For example, we draw the bounding rectangle first by calling Rectangle(). Then we draw two lines that show the starting and ending radials of the arc. These lines are drawn from the center of the bounding rectangle to the radial points.

Finally we call ArcTo() with nine parameters. The first parameter is the handle to the device context. The second through fifth parameters specify the bounding rectangle which correspond to the rectangle we've already drawn. The last four parameters specify the starting and ending radial points. These points correspond to the two lines we've drawn.

The result is an elliptical arc and a line segment. The line segment starts at 80,65 and extends to the starting point of the arc. Note that this could be from any position on the device context. It just happens to be the last position in our example (result of the last call to LineTo). The arc sweeps until in intercepts the ending radial.

We delete the pen with DeleteObject( ), end the paint with EndPaint( ), and break out of the *switch.* A considerable amount of code is executed in this example. Let's build the application and view the results of the new pen and arc functions.

BUILDING AND USING GDI1

The GDI1 project is located in the \CHAPTER5\5.1 subdirectory, including MAKEFILE. Open a Command Prompt window and change to this directory. Type NMAKE and press (ENTER). The GDI1 application compiles and links. Either use the Command Prompt window to start the program, or add the GDI1 program to an existing group in the Program Manager.

Review the code in Listings 5-7 through 5-9 while performing the following steps:

1. Start with the *Figures* menu. Select each of the four options and observe the results. For *AngleArc,* click on *Draw* to close the dialog box without changing the default values. Figure 5-7 shows each of the figures.

2. Select *Lines* from the *Figures* menu. Select *Pen Attributes, Type,* then *Cosmetic.* Now try the various line styles by selecting *Pen Attributes, Style,* and each of the line styles (Solid, Dash, and so on). This is changing the *dwPenStyle* variable and redrawing the figure. Figure 5-8 shows these line styles.

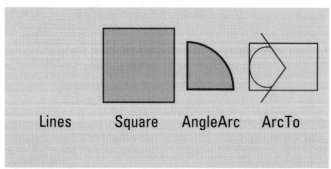

Lines   Square   AngleArc   ArcTo

Figure 5-7 Figures in GDI1—Lines, Square, AngleArc, and ArcTo

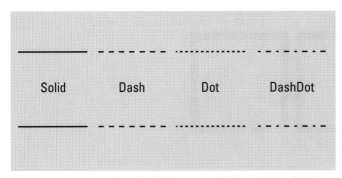

Figure 5-8 Line styles in GDI1—modifying dwPenStyle

3.   With *Geometric* still selected (it should have a checkmark next to it), change the *Line Width* to *Thick*. Then try each of the *End Cap* settings. Note the subtle difference between *Flat* and *Square*. Recall that *Flat* stops the line at the exact end coordinate, while *Square* extends the end cap based on line width. Figure 5-9 shows the end caps.

4.   To see the effects of line joins we need a complete figure. Choose *Square* from the *Figures* menu. Ensure the line type is set to *Geometric* and line width is *Thick*. Try each of the *Join* types. Figure 5-10 shows the three join styles using the *Square* figure.

5.   Now try the *AngleArc* selection from the *Figures* menu. Enter various starting angles, sweep angles, and radii. If the sweep angle is greater than 360°, the arc is swept multiple times. Figure 5-11 shows some example *AngleArcs* selections and the values that

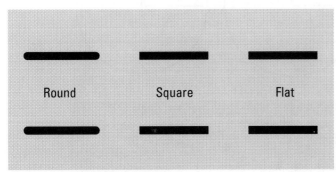

Figure 5-9 End caps in GDI1

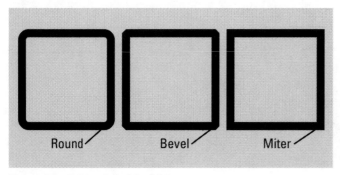

Figure 5-10 Line joins in GDI1

generated them. We used *Cosmetic, Solid, Square, Bevel,* and *Thin* pen attributes for the examples shown in the figure.

6. Try the *ArcTo* selection from the *Figures* menu. Remember, we also drew the bounding rectangle and two lines specifying the start and end radial. Note that the arc is swept from start radial to the end radial. Figure 5-12 shows the *ArcTo* selection.

7. Continue to experiment with the various figures and pen styles. Figure 5-13 shows several examples and the settings used to generate them.

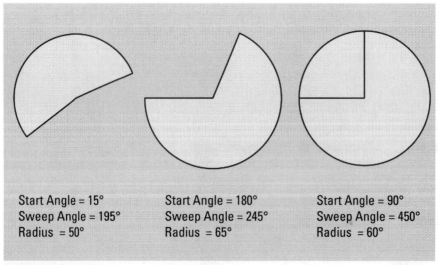

Start Angle = 15°
Sweep Angle = 195°
Radius = 50°

Start Angle = 180°
Sweep Angle = 245°
Radius = 65°

Start Angle = 90°
Sweep Angle = 450°
Radius = 60°

Figure 5-11 Various AngleArcs in GDI1

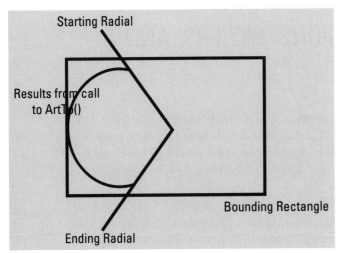

Figure 5-12 The ArcTo section

This concludes the GDI1 example application. You have seen the new arc functions, a new way to create a pen, and the basics of GDI paths. Let's continue with another GDI example program, GDI2. This application will expand upon the subject of paths, as well as introduce new polyline and Bezier API functions.

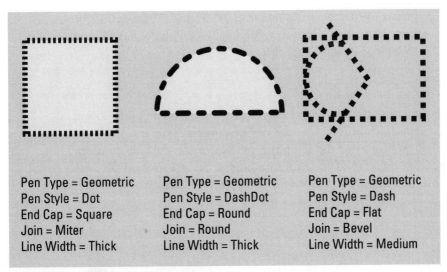

Figure 5-13 Examples from GDI1

POLYLINE EXTENSIONS, BEZIERS, AND MORE PATHS

If you are familiar with the Windows 3.x GDI functions, you may have used the polyline functions. Polyline(), Polygon(), and PolyPolygon() made up the polyline functions in the old API collection. The Win32 API extends the polyline functions with three new additions: PolylineTo(), PolyPolyline(), and PolyDraw().

The Win32 API also introduces new functions to draw complex curves called *Bezier curves*. If you have used advanced PC drawing applications or CAD systems, you may have used Bezier curves (sometimes referred to as *b-splines*).

The next example application will demonstrate these new functions. We will also expand on GDI path brackets in this example. For example, we can fill a complex figure using additional path functions. Before we get into the actual application, let's take a look at the new polyline, Bezier, and path functions.

Additions to Polyline Functions

In Windows 3.x the purpose of the Polyline() function was to draw lines with multiple segments. The points on the multisegment line were defined by an array of points on the device context. The Win32 API extends the Polyline() function with three additions: PolylineTo(), PolyPolyline(), and PolyDraw(). Let's look at PolylineTo() first.

Using PolylineTo()

Basically the only difference between PolylineTo() and Polyline() is how it affects the current position stored in the device context. Polyline() did not use the current position, nor did it update or change the current position. PolyLineTo(), like most GDI functions ending in the preposition *To*, uses the current position as the first point of the first line segment. It also updates the current position to the last point of the last line segment.

To see the effects of PolylineTo(), and compare it to its predecessor Polyline(), let's look at a sample call and the results. Listing 5-10 shows the syntax and an example call to PolyLineTo(). Figure 5-14 shows a comparison of the Polyline() and PolylineTo() functions given the same array of points. We are making an arbitrary assumption that the current position in the device context is coordinate 0,0.

Listing 5-10 PolylineTo() syntax and example call

```
/* PolylineTo Syntax */
BOOL PolylineTo (HDC hDC,          /* handle to device context */
                 LPPOINT lppt,     /* points to an array of POINT structures */
                 DWORD count);     /* specfies the number of points in the array */

/* PolyLineTo() Example Call */
HDC   hDC;
POINT pPoints[] = {30, 30, 30, 100, 50, 50, 75, 25};
DWORD dwPolyPts = 4;

   hDC = GetDC (hWnd);                              /* get handle to device context */
   PolylineTo (hDC, pPoints, dwPolyPts);           /* draw polyline using PolylineTo */
```

You can see by the comparison in Figure 5-14 that the PolylineTo() function uses the current position as the first point of the polyline. It also updates the current position to the last point in the polyline, in this case 75, 25. The PolyLine() function, however, neither uses nor updates the current position in the device context. PolyLineTo() always draws a number of line segments equal to the number of points in the array, while PolyLine() draws one less segment than the number of points in the array. Let's look at another polyline function that draws multiple polylines.

Using PolyPolyline()

This function is also similar to PolyLine(). Although PolyPolyline() does not use or update the current position, it draws multiple, disjointed polylines in one function call. To accomplish this action, the function requires another parameter. Listing 5-11 shows the syntax and an example call to PolyPolyline(). Figure 5-15 shows the results of the sample call in the listing.

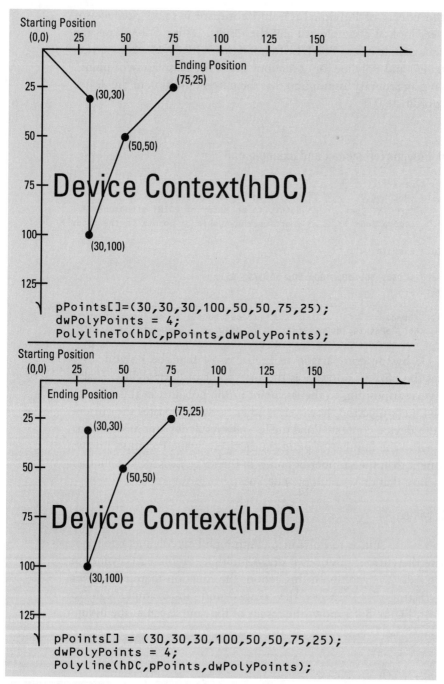

```
pPoints[]=(30,30,30,100,50,50,75,25);
dwPolyPoints = 4;
PolyLineTo(hDC,pPoints,dwPolyPoints);
```

```
pPoints[] = (30,30,30,100,50,50,75,25);
dwPolyPoints = 4;
Polyline(hDC,pPoints,dwPolyPoints);
```

Figure 5-14 PolyLine() and PolyLineTo() comparison

Listing 5-11 PolyPolyline() syntax and example call

```
/* PolyPolyline() Syntax */
BOOL PolyPolyline (HDC hDC,              /* handle to device context */
                   LPPOINT lppt,          /* pointer to array of points */
                   LPDWORD lpdwPolyPoints, /* pointer to array of DWORDS */
                   DWORD    dwCount);      /* total polylines */

/* PolyPolyline() Example Call */
HDC    hDC;
POINT pPoints[] = {25, 25, 25, 50, 50, 75, 50, 50, 50, 25, 75, 75, 50, 100, 100, 100};
DWORD pdwPolyPoints[] = {3, 3, 2};
DWORD dwCount = 3;

   hDC = GetDC (hWnd);
   PolyPolyline (hDC, pPoints, pdwPolyPoints, dwCount);
```

The first parameter to PolyPolyline() is a handle to the device context. Note that this function uses two arrays. The second parameter, *pPoints,* is the address of the first array. This array contains all points for all polylines. The third parameter, *pdwPolyPoints,* is the address of the second array. This is an array of DWORDs that specify the number of points in each polyline.

The last parameter, *dwCount,* indicates the total number of polylines. It is important that this parameter does not specify more polylines than the arrays can supply. For example, if the example call set *dwCount* to 4, the function would continue to read past the end of the *pPoints* and *pdwPolyPoint* arrays.

Bezier Functions in Win32

Bezier curves (also known as Bezier splines or b–splines) are complex line segments that can make up virtually any shape. Each Bezier spline consists of four points given in sequence. The first and last point define the end points. The second and third point are control points. Control points determine the shape of the curve. Figure 5-16 shows several examples of Bezier splines. The figure also shows the effects of control points on the spline.

Example 1 shows the control points directly on the start and end points. This results in a straight line similar to one drawn by LineTo(). Example 2 shows the control points away from the end points; however, they are still on a line between the end points. The line is still straight in this case.

In Example 3 we move Control Point 1 to the right of the line and Control Point 2 to the left of the line. Note how the line is attracted to the control points. Example 4 moves Control Point 1 closer to the end point and

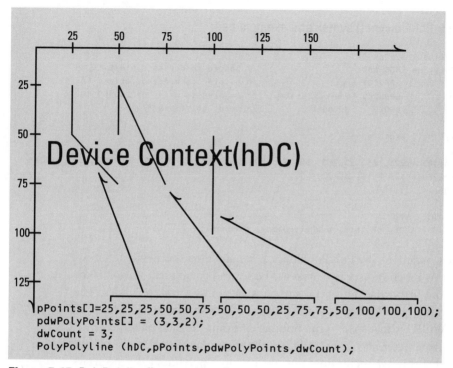

Figure 5-15 PolyPolyline() example call

Control Point 2 closer to the start point. Not only is the line pulled toward the control points, it is also pulled toward the opposite end point.

Example 5 shows the effect of moving the control points to the same side of the line segment. This results in a line segment that resembles a curve. In Example 6, we move the control points toward the opposite ends, and to one side of the line segment. This makes the line segment appear as two connected curves.

Using Bezier splines you can create virtually any shape for a single line segment. Your only limitation for control points is the coordinate space of the device context. Some commercial computer drawing applications support Bezier splines. These programs usually let the user move the start, end, and control points around on the drawing surface, then they draw the line based on these points.

There are two specific Bezier drawing functions in the Win32 GDI, and there is also another polyline function. We didn't cover this polyline function

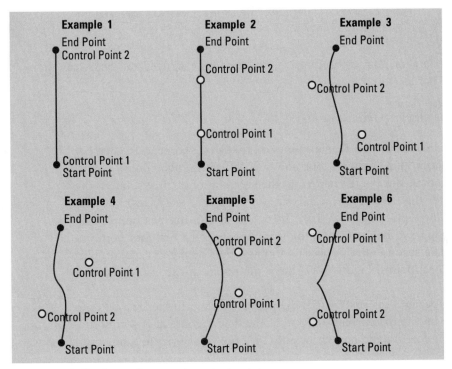

Figure 5-16 Bezier splines and control points

earlier because it also permits the use of Bezier splines. Let's look at the Bezier-specific functions first.

Using PolyBezier()

The PolyBezier() function draws one or more Bezier splines. The function requires three parameters: a handle to the device context, an address to an array of points, and a DWORD that indicates the total number of points. Listing 5-12 shows the proper syntax and an example call for PolyBezier().

Listing 5-12 PolyBezier() syntax and example call

```
/* PolyBezier() Syntax */
BOOL PolyBezier (HDC hDC,        /* handle to device context */
                 LPPOINT lppt,   /* pointer to array of points */
```

continued on next page

continued from previous page

```
                    DWORD dwPoints);   /* number of points in second parameter */

/* PolyBezier() Example Call */
HDC    hDC;
POINT pPoints[] = {50, 10, 30, 30, 70, 70, 50, 100, 80, 120, 120, 120, 150, 100};
DWORD dwPoints = 7;

   hDC = GetDC (hWnd);
   PolyBezier (hDC, pPoints, dwPoints);
```

This function draws two Bezier splines on the device context. Remember that each Bezier spline requires four points: a start point, two control points, and an end point. But PolyBezier() uses the endpoint of the first spline as the start point for the next. This means that the number in *dwPoints* must be a multiple of three plus one (4, 7, 10, 13, 16, and so on). In our example call, we are drawing two Bezier curves; the first curve uses the first four points in the array. The second curve uses the ending point of the first curve, plus three additional points. Figure 5-17 shows the results of the example call in Listing 5-12.

The PolyBezier() call strictly uses the points specified in the array; it does not use nor update the current position in the device context. If you need a function that does use the current position, try the PolyBezierTo() function.

Using PolyBezierTo()

The PolyBezierTo() function is similar to the PolyBezier(), but it uses the current position as the first point and updates the current position with the last point. This function also requires three parameters: a handle to a device context, an address to an array of points, and a DWORD specifying the total points. Listing 5-13 shows the syntax and an example call to PolyBezierTo().

- - - - - -

Listing 5-13 PolyBezierTo() syntax and example call

```
/* PolyBezierTo() Syntax */
BOOL PolyBezierTo (HDC hDC,          /* handle to device context */
                   LPPOINT lppt,     /* address of array of points */
                   DWORD dwCount);  /* number of points in second parameter */

/* PolyBezierTo() Example Call */
HDC    hDC;
POINT pPoints[] = {30, 40, 70, 70, 50, 100, 80, 120, 120, 120, 100, 100};
DWORD dwPoints = 6;

   hDC = GetDC (hWnd);
```

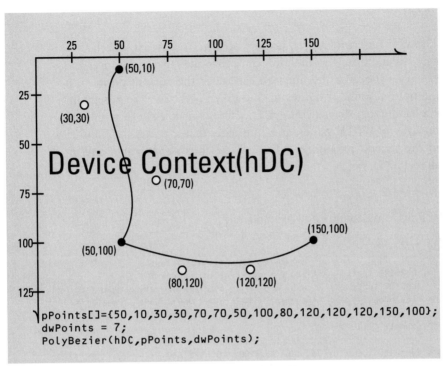

Figure 5-17 Results from PolyBezier() example call

```
MoveToEx (hDC, 50, 10, NULL);
PolyBezierTo (hDC, pPoints, dwPoints);
```

This function draws the exact same Bezier splines as the PolyBezier() example call. There are two differences, however. The first difference is PolyBezierTo() uses the current position as the first point of the first spline. We forced this issue by moving the current position to coordinate 50,10 with a call to MoveToEx(). The second difference is the current position is updated by PolyBezierTo(); in this case the position ends up being 150,100.

As with PolyBezier(), PolyBezierTo() uses the last point of a spline as the first point of each subsequent spline. Since PolyBezierTo() uses the current position as its first point, the number of points in the array should always be divisible by three (3, 6, 9, and so on).

What if you want to draw Bezier splines, polylines, and move the current position in one function call? PolyDraw() is the answer. Let's look at this new function.

Using PolyDraw()

The PolyDraw() function draws a set of line segments similar to PolyPolyline(). In addition, this function can move the current position and draw Bezier curves. Because the function can move the current position, it can draw multiple, disjointed figures in one call. PolyDraw() requires four parameters: a handle to a device context, an address to an array of points, an address to an array of BYTE values, and an integer that specifies the number of points in the second parameter. Listing 5-14 shows the syntax and an example call to PolyDraw().

Listing 5-14 PolyDraw() syntax and example call

```
/* PolyDraw() Syntax */
BOOL PolyDraw (HDC hDC,           /* handle to device context */
               LPPOINT lppt,      /* address of array of points */
               LPBYTE lpbTypes,   /* address of array of BYTES indicating types (see Table 5-2) */
               int nCount);       /* number of points in the second parameter */

/* PolyDraw() Example Call */
HDC    hDC;
POINT  pPoints [] = {10, 10, 10, 75, 50, 32, 100, 10, 125, 30, 125, 70, 100, 100};
BYTE   bTypes [] = {PT_MOVETO, PT_LINETO, PT_LINETO | PT_CLOSEFIGURE, PT_MOVETO,
                    PT_BEZIERTO, PT_BEZIERTO, PT_BEZIERTO | PT_CLOSEFIGURE};
int    nCount = 7;

    hDC = GetDC (hWnd);
    PolyDraw (hDC, pPoints, bTypes, nCount); /* draw disjoint figures */
```

The elements of the *bTypes* array require some additional description. Table 5-2 shows the possible array values for the third parameter of PolyDraw().

Now that you've seen the possible array values, let's look at the effect of the example call. Figure 5-18 shows the results of the PolyDraw() example.

The first figure (a triangle) drawn by PolyDraw() uses the first three points in the *pPoints* array, and the first three BYTES in the *bTypes* array. The first point (10,10), is a PT_MOVETO type. This is equivalent to a *MoveToEx (hDC, 10, 10, NULL);* call. The next point (10,75), is a PT_LINETO type. This is the equivalent of a LineTo (hDC, 10, 75); call. The third point (50,32), combines the PT_LINETO and PT_CLOSEFIGURE using a *bitwise or* operator. As a result a line is drawn to the point (PT_LINETO) *and* a line is drawn to the last PT_MOVETO (caused by PT_CLOSEFIGURE).

Array Value	Description
PT_MOVETO	Moves the current position to this point. Starts a new figure.
PT_LINETO	Draws a line from current position to this point.
PT_BEZIERTO	Specifies that this point is a part of a Bezier spline. Always use in groups of three (Control Point 1, Control Point 2, and end point).
PT_CLOSEFIGURE	Combine with PT_LINETO or PT_BEZIERTO to close figure. A line is drawn from

Table 5-2 BYTE array values for PolyDraw()'s third parameter

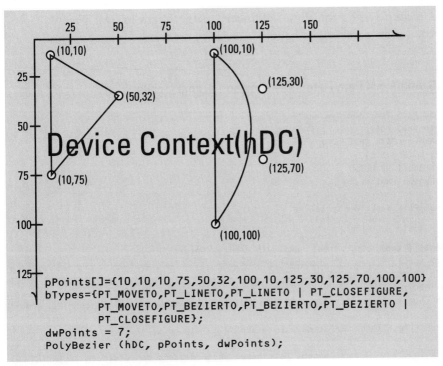

```
pPoints[]={10,10,10,75,50,32,100,10,125,30,125,70,100,100}
bTypes={PT_MOVETO,PT_LINETO,PT_LINETO | PT_CLOSEFIGURE,
        PT_MOVETO,PT_BEZIERTO,PT_BEZIERTO,PT_BEZIERTO |
        PT_CLOSEFIGURE};
dwPoints = 7;
PolyBezier (hDC, pPoints, dwPoints);
```

Figure 5-18 PolyDraw() example results

The second, disjoint figure (a Bezier spline closed with a straight line) uses the last four points of the array. The fourth point (100,10) is a PT_MOVETO. This starts a disjoint figure. The next three points (all PT_BEZIERTOs) define the two control points and the end point for the Bezier spline. In addition to being a Bezier spline type, the last point type also is PT_CLOSEFIGURE. This results in a line being drawn from the end point of the spline to the last PT_MOVETO (100,10).

The PolyDraw() function updates the current position to the last point in the array if the last point type is not PT_CLOSEFIGURE. If the last point is PT_CLOSEFIGURE, the current position is updated to the last PT_MOVETO. The latter situation reflects our example call. The current position ends up being 100,10.

More Path Functions in Win32 GDI

Our last example program, GDI1, demonstrated the use of three path functions: BeginPath(), EndPath(), and StrokePath(). There are other path functions that you can use in the Win32 GDI. Listing 5-15 shows the syntax and example calls for these additional path functions. All path functions require one parameter, a handle to a device context.

Listing 5-15 Additional Path Function syntax and example calls

```
/* Additional Path Function Syntax */
BOOL FillPath (HDC hDC);
BOOL StrokeAndFillPath (HDC hDC);
BOOL WidenPath (HDC hDC);
BOOL FlattenPath (HDC hDC);
BOOL PathToRegion (HDC hDC);

/* Additional Path Function Syntax */
HDC hDC;

    hDC = GetDC (hWnd);       /* get handle to device context */
    BeginPath (hDC);          /* open path bracket */
        [calls to GDI drawing functions]
    EndPath (hDC);            /* close path bracket and select into DC */
    FillPath (hDC);           /* fill the path with the current brush and polygon-fill mode */
        [or]
    StrokeAndFillPath (hDC); /* strokes path and fills figure(s) */
        [or]
    WidenPath (hDC);          /* widens path based on geometeric pen width */
        [or]
```

```
WidenPath (hDC);          /* widens path based on geometeric pen width */
   [or]
FlattenPath (hDC);        /* flattens curves in path to a series of lines—see GetPath() later
                             in this section */

   [or]
PathToRegion (hDC);       /* converts the path to a region */
```

Each of these additional path functions requires additional explanation. For example, one function destroys the path and discards it from the device context. Let's look at the functions individually.

Using FillPath()

The FillPath() function closes any open figure and fills it with the current brush. It also uses the current polygon-filling mode. Creating a brush and setting the polygon-filling mode are identical to Windows 3.x. The path is discarded from the device context after this call.

This function simply fills the figure; it does not use the current pen to outline the figure. If you need to fill and outline a figure with the current pen, use StrokeAndFillPath().

Using StrokeAndFillPath()

This function is identical to the FillPath() function, except it outlines the figure with the current pen. The filled region will not overlap the stroke region. This has the effect of filling the figure(s) first, then drawing the line around it. This effect is more obvious with wide pens.

Using WidenPath()

This function redefines the path area based on the current pen. WidenPath() works with geometric pens or pens created with CreatePen() that have a width greater than one. If you call this function with a cosmetic pen or a pen with a width of one, the function returns FALSE. Calling GetLastError() in this case returns ERROR_CAN_NOT_COMPLETE.

Consider this example. You open a path bracket and draw a square measuring 10 pixels wide and 10 pixels high. You also create a geometric pen with width of 5. You close the path bracket and call WidenPath(). The path area now spans 12 pixels by 12 pixels. The reason this expansion occurs is the line width of 5 overlaps the square by 2 pixels. The wide line also overlaps the inside of the square by 2 pixels; however, this has no effect on the WidenPath() call.

WidenPath() also converts Bezier splines to line segments that approximate the curves. This has little effect visually.

Using FlattenPath()

This function has one purpose: to convert curves into line segments. For example, if the path contains Bezier curves, this function converts them into line segments that render the curve. You can use GetPath() to retrieve the line segments from the device context. We'll cover GetPath() in a moment.

Using PathToRegion()

If you used the Windows 3.x GDI, you may have created regions in a device context. Examples of Window 3.x region functions are CreatePolygonRegion(), CreateEllipticRgn(), and CreateRectRgn(). A region defines an area on a device that creates boundaries for painting. You can also use a region for hit testing with PtInRegion().

The PathToRegion() function converts the current path bracket to a region. After doing so the current path is discarded from the device context.

Using GetPath()

GetPath() retrieves the individual coordinates of the current closed path. The coordinates can be end points or control points of lines. The GetPath() function requires four parameters: a handle to the device context containing the path, a pointer to a POINT array (to store the vertices), a pointer to an array of BYTE (to store the vertex types), and an *int* (to store the number of points). Listing 5-16 shows the syntax and an example call to GetPath().

Listing 5-16 GetPath() syntax and example call

```
/* GetPath() Syntax */
int GetPath (HDC hDC,          /* handle to device context */
             LPPOINT lpPts,    /* address of point buffer to store vertices */
             LPBYTE  lpTypes,  /* address of BYTE buffer to store vertex types */
             int     nSize);   /* int to store count of points */

/* GetPath() Example Call */
POINT pPts [50];
BYTE  bTypes [50];
int   nSize

   [other GDI and path calls];
```

```
GetPath (hDC, pPts, bTypes nSize);
```

```
[use PolyDraw() with results of GetPath() call];
```

The GetPath() function fills the buffers with the vertices and vertex types based on the GDI calls in the current closed path bracket. GetPath() returns the number of points enumerated. You can use the POINT and BYTE buffers (along with nSize) as arguments to a call to PolyDraw().

DEMONSTRATING THE NEW POLYLINES AND BEZIERS

The last example program in this chapter demonstrates the new polyline and Bezier functions. The application is titled GDI2 and you can find the program files in the \CHAPTER5\5.2 subdirectory.

The WinMain() function is not shown in the following listings. We have used the LTGRAY_BRUSH for the background of the window; this is the same method we used in GDI1.

What Does GDI2 Do?

This example application has two popup menus: *Polylines* and *Beziers*. The *Polylines* selection has three options: *PolylineTo*, *PolyPolyline*, and *PolyDraw*. These selections demonstrate the new polyline functions. They also demonstrate the effects of the additional path functions. The *Beziers* selection has two options: *PolyBezier*, and *PolyBezierTo*. These selections let you see the effects of Bezier splines in action. PolyBezierTo also uses path functions.

Listings 5-17 through 5-19 make up the GDI2 application. The WinMain() function is not listed, although the complete listing of GDI2.C is available on your sample code disk. The calls to new functions are in boldface.

Listing 5-17 GDI2.RC—resource script

```
#include "windows.h"
#include "gdi2.h"
```

continued on next page

continued from previous page

```
GDI2Icon ICON  gdi2.ico

GDI2Menu MENU
BEGIN
   POPUP "&Polylines"
   BEGIN
      MENUITEM "Polyline&To",    IDM_POLYTO
      MENUITEM "Poly&Polyline",  IDM_POLYPOLY
      MENUITEM "Poly&Draw",      IDM_POLYDRAW
   END
   POPUP "&Beziers"
   BEGIN
      MENUITEM "Poly&Bezier",    IDM_POLYBEZ
      MENUITEM "PolyBezier&To",  IDM_POLYBEZTO
   END
END
```

Changes in the Header File

The header file for GDI2 contains five defines that determine the *object to draw*. We'll set the static variable *DrawItem* in WndProc() to one of these values. We also added five function prototypes. These functions demonstrate the new functions in GDI2.C.

Listing 5-18 GDI2.H—header file

```
/* gdi2.h -- Include file for gdi2.c and gdi2.rc */

/* Menu defines */
#define IDM_POLYTO    1
#define IDM_POLYPOLY  2
#define IDM_POLYDRAW  3
#define IDM_POLYBEZ   4
#define IDM_POLYBEZTO 5


/* Object to draw defines */
#define DRAW_POLYTO    1
#define DRAW_POLYPOLY  2
#define DRAW_POLYDRAW  3
#define DRAW_POLYBEZ   4
#define DRAW_POLYBEZTO 5


/* Function prototype */
LONG APIENTRY WndProc (HWND, UINT, UINT, LONG);
void DrawPolyTo (HDC hDC);
void DrawPolyPoly (HDC hDC);
void DrawPolyDraw (HDC hDC);
void DrawPolyBez (HDC hDC);
void DrawPolyBezTo (HDC hDC);
```

```c
/* Global variables */
HANDLE ghInst;
HANDLE ghWnd;
```

━━━━━━

Listing 5-19 GDI2.C—source file

```c
/* gdi2.c      Minimum program for Windows NT */

#include <windows.h>              /* include for Windows NT apps */
#include "gdi2.h"                 /* include for gdi2.c */

/* WndProc - Main Window Procedure for gdi2.c */

LONG APIENTRY WndProc (HWND hWnd, UINT message, UINT wParam, LONG lParam)
{
PAINTSTRUCT ps;
static int  DrawItem = 0;        /* set to 0 so we don't draw on startup */
HBRUSH      hBrush, hOldBrush;

    switch (message)
    {

        case WM_PAINT:               /* paint the selected figure */
            BeginPaint (hWnd, &ps);
            hBrush = CreateSolidBrush (RGB(0, 127, 127)); /* create a brush */
            hOldBrush = SelectObject (ps.hdc, hBrush);    /* select into DC and save old brush */
            switch (DrawItem)                             /* check DrawItem */
            {
                case DRAW_POLYTO:                         /* draw a PolylineTo? */
                    DrawPolyTo (ps.hdc);
                    break;
                case DRAW_POLYPOLY:                       /* draw a PolyPolyline? */
                    DrawPolyPoly (ps.hdc);
                    break;
                case DRAW_POLYDRAW:                       /* draw a PolyDraw? */
                    DrawPolyDraw (ps.hdc);
                    break;
                case DRAW_POLYBEZ:                        /* draw a PolyBezier? */
                    DrawPolyBez (ps.hdc);
                    break;
                case DRAW_POLYBEZTO:                      /* draw a PolyBezierTo? */
                    DrawPolyBezTo (ps.hdc);
                    break;
                default:                                  /* don't draw anything */
                    break;
            }
            SelectObject (ps.hdc, hOldBrush);             /* bring back old brush */
            EndPaint (hWnd, &ps);
            return (0);

        case WM_COMMAND:
```

continued on next page

continued from previous page

```
            switch (LOWORD(wParam)) /* Extract LOWORD of wParam for Win32) */
            {
                case IDM_POLYTO:                        /* user selected PolylineTo? */
                    DrawItem = DRAW_POLYTO;             /* set DrawItem */
                    break;
                case IDM_POLYPOLY:                      /* user selected PolyPolyline? */
                    DrawItem = DRAW_POLYPOLY;           /* set DrawItem */
                    break;
                case IDM_POLYDRAW:                      /* user selected PolyDraw? */
                    DrawItem = DRAW_POLYDRAW;           /* set DrawItem */
                    break;
                case IDM_POLYBEZ:                       /* user selected PolyBezier? */
                    DrawItem = DRAW_POLYBEZ;            /* set DrawItem */
                    break;
                case IDM_POLYBEZTO:                     /* user selected PolyBezierTo? */
                    DrawItem = DRAW_POLYBEZTO;          /* set DrawItem */
                    break;
                default:
                    return (0);
            }
            InvalidateRect (hWnd, NULL, TRUE);          /* force WM_PAINT */
            return (0);

        case WM_DESTROY:                    /* No cleanup necessary */
            PostQuitMessage (0);
            return (0);

        default:
            return DefWindowProc (hWnd, message, wParam, lParam);
    }

    return (0L);
}

/* DrawPolyTo() draws a polyline using current position as first point
   then updates the current position. The figure is closed creating a
   polygon, then stroked and filled with the current brush */
void DrawPolyTo (HDC hDC)
{
POINT  pPts[] = {70, 30, 100, 100, 70, 150, 30, 120};
DWORD  dwPolyPts = 4;

    BeginPath (hDC);                                /* open path bracket */
    MoveToEx (hDC, 50, 50, NULL);                   /* set current position */
    PolylineTo (hDC, pPts, dwPolyPts);              /* draw polylines */
    CloseFigure (hDC);                              /* close the figure */
    EndPath (hDC);                                  /* close the path bracket */
    StrokeAndFillPath (hDC);                        /* stroke and fill the polygon */
}

/* DrawPolyPoly() draws a three polylines. The resultant figure appears as a
   complete star; however, it is actually three polylines */
```

```
void DrawPolyPoly (HDC hDC)
{
POINT   pPts[] = {30, 50, 70, 50, 90, 20, 110, 50, 110, 50, 150, 50,
                    120, 80, 130, 120, 90, 90, 90, 90, 50, 120, 60, 80, 30, 50};
DWORD   dwPolyPts[] = {4, 5, 4};
DWORD   dwPoly = 3;

    BeginPath (hDC);                                    /* open path bracket */
    PolyPolyline (hDC, pPts, dwPolyPts, dwPoly);          /* draw PolyPolyline */
    EndPath (hDC);                                      /* close the path bracket */
    WidenPath (hDC);                                      /* widen the path */
    StrokePath (hDC);                                     /* stroke the path */
}


/* DrawPolyDraw() uses the PolyDraw() function to draw two disjointed figures.
   The first figure uses lines. The second figure uses beziers and lines */
void DrawPolyDraw (HDC hDC)
{
POINT pPts1[] = {30, 30, 30, 100, 100, 100, 100, 30};
POINT pPts2[] = {120, 30, 100, 65, 140, 65, 120, 100, 190, 100, 170, 65, 210, 65, 190, 30 };
BYTE  btMoves1[] = {PT_MOVETO, PT_LINETO, PT_LINETO, PT_LINETO | PT_CLOSEFIGURE};
BYTE  btMoves2[] = {PT_MOVETO, PT_BEZIERTO, PT_BEZIERTO, PT_BEZIERTO,
                    PT_LINETO, PT_BEZIERTO, PT_BEZIERTO, PT_BEZIERTO | PT_CLOSEFIGURE};

    BeginPath (hDC);                                    /* open path bracket */
    PolyDraw (hDC, pPts1, btMoves1, 4);                   /* draw first figure */
    PolyDraw (hDC, pPts2, btMoves2, 8);                   /* draw second figure */
    EndPath (hDC);                                      /* close path bracket */
    StrokeAndFillPath (hDC);                              /* stroke and fill figures */
}


/* DrawPolyBex() uses a for loop to call PolyBezier() 200 times. Each iteration
   Control Point #1 is incremented and Control Point #2 is decremented */
void DrawPolyBez (HDC hDC)
{
POINT pPts[] = {10, 100, 100, 0, 100, 0, 190, 100};
LONG  nControlY1, nControlY2;

    /* loop to move the control points */
    for (nControlY1 = 0, nControlY2 = 200; nControlY1 <= 200; nControlY1+=10, nControlY2-=10)
        {
        pPts[1].y = nControlY1;                            /* modify Control Point #1 */
        pPts[2].y = nControlY2;                            /* modify Control Point #2 */
        PolyBezier (hDC, pPts, 4);                          /* draw the bezier spline */
        }
}


/* DrawPolyBezTo() calls PolyBezierTo() to illustrate control points. The
   start and end points of each bezier form a square. Each side of the square
   uses different examples of control point effect. */
void DrawPolyBezTo (HDC hDC)
{
```

continued on next page

continued from previous page

```
POINT pPts[] = {100, 50, 150, 50, 150, 50,
                200, 50, 200, 150, 150, 150,
                50, 200, 150, 200, 50, 150,
                0, 50, 100, 150, 50, 50};

   BeginPath (hDC);                        /* open path bracket */
   MoveToEx (hDC, 50, 50, NULL);           /* adjust current position */
   PolyBezierTo (hDC, pPts, 12);             /* draw the bezier splines */
   EndPath (hDC);                          /* close the path bracket */
   StrokePath (hDC);                         /* stroke the path */
}
```

Overview of GDI2

The overall flow of GDI2 is fairly straightforward. We start by setting the static integer *DrawItem* to 0. This prevents drawing a figure before the user selects from the menu.

Nothing happens in GDI2 until the user selects a menu option. There are five possibilities: *PolylineTo, PolyPolyline, PolyDraw, PolyBezier,* and *PolyBezierTo.* These selections generate these menu messages: IDM_POLYTO, IDM_POLYPOLY, IDM_POLYDRAW, IDM_POLYBEZ, and IDM_POLYBEZTO, respectively. When a selection is made, we set *DrawItem* to reflect the decision. For example, if the user selects *PolylineTo,* this sends the menu message IDM_POLYTO. We set *DrawItem* to DRAW_POLYTO and break out of the *switch* statement. At the bottom of the *switch* body, we call InvalidateRect() to force a WM_PAINT message.

WM_PAINT in GDI2

We start the paint processing with the typical call to BeginPaint(). This fills the PAINTSTRUCT structure, *ps.* The next step is to create a solid brush. We call CreateSolidBrush() using the RGB macro. The color 0,127,127 is a dark cyan.

Next we select the brush into the device context with SelectObject(). Note we are storing the old brush in *hOldBrush.* If *DrawItem* is set to one of the five values defined in GDI2.H, we make a call to one of five functions. We are using separate functions to clearly define the action of the new functions. We'll cover each of these functions in a moment.

Once the function has returned, we select the original brush back into the device context using SelectObject() and the handle to the old brush. Let's look at the functions that demonstrate the new topics.

DrawPolyTo()

The DrawPolyTo() function contains code that demonstrates PolylineTo(). We define an array of four points *(pPts)*. For example, the first point in the array is 70,30. We also define *dwPolyPts,* which we will use to tell PolylineTo() how many points are in the array.

A path bracket is opened with a call to BeginPath(). We then move the current position to coordinate 50,50 using MoveToEx(). Now we make the call to PolylineTo() passing the device context, the address of the array, and the DWORD specifying the number of points. This function draws four line segments starting at the current position.

We call CloseFigure() to complete a polygon. Recall that CloseFigure() draws a line segment from the current position (now 30,120—the last point in the array) to the last MoveToEx() position (50,50). We close the path bracket and select it into the device context with EndPath().

Another new function is called in DrawPolyTo(): StrokeAndFillPath(). This function fills the completed figure using the current brush (solid—dark cyan). The function also outlines the figure with the default pen. The result appears as Figure 5-19.

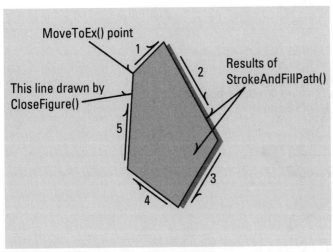

Figure 5-19 Results from PolylineTo()

DrawPolyPoly()

Our next function exercises the PolyPolyline() function. We start by filling an array of points. We also set up an array of DWORDs, *dwPolyPts*. This specifies the number of points in each polyline. The last define, *dwPoly,* is set to three; this is the number of polylines.

We start a new path and call PolyPolyline() with the addresses of the two arrays and the DWORD indicating the number of lines. After closing the path with EndPath(), we make a call to WidenPath(). Finally we draw the path on the device context with StrokePath(). Figure 5-20 illustrates the effects of this call. Note how the three individual polylines form a star.

DrawPolyDraw()

Our third function demonstrates two calls to PolyDraw(). We fill two arrays of points: *pPts1* and *pPts2*. We then fill two arrays of BYTEs, *btMoves1* and *btMoves2*. Each of these values defines a corresponding point in the first two arrays. For example, the first point in *pPts1* is 30,30 and the first byte in *btMoves1* is PT_MOVETO.

We open a path bracket and make the first call to PolyDraw() using *pPts1* and *btMoves1*. This results in the following action:

- Move the current position to 30,30 (PT_MOVETO).

- Draw a line to 30,100 (PT_LINETO).

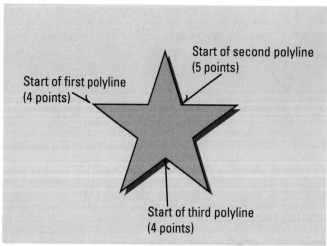

Start of second polyline
(5 points)

Start of first polyline
(4 points)

Start of third polyline
(4 points)

Figure 5-20 Results from PolyPolyline()

◢ Draw a line to 100,100 (PT_LINETO).

◢ Draw a line to 100,30 and close the figure (PT_LINETO | PT_CLOSEFIGURE).

We make another call to PolyDraw(); this time we use *pPts2* and *btMoves2*. This results in these actions:

◢ Move the current position to 120,30 (PT_MOVETO).

◢ Define a Bezier curve (two control points and one end point).

◢ Draw a line from 120,100 to 190,100 (PT_LINETO).

◢ Define another Bezier curve (two control points and one end point).

◢ Close the figure on the last Bezier point (PT_CLOSEFIGURE).

We close the path and call StrokeAndFillPath(). All of this activity results in two disjoint figures that appear as those in Figure 5-21.

DrawPolyBez()

This function demonstrates several calls to PolyBezier(). We fill an array of points that will make up the first Bezier spline. We also declare two LONG variables: *nControlY1* and *nControlY2*. A *for* loop is initialized setting

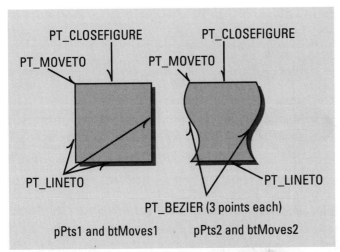

Figure 5-21 Results from 2 calls to PolyDraw()

nControlY1 to 0 and *nControlY2* to 200. The test in the *for* loop checks to see if *nControlY1* has reached 200. Since we increment *nControlY1* by 10 each iteration, the *for* loop executes 20 times. We also decrement *nControlY2* by 10 each iteration.

In the *for* body, we set the *y* member of the second point to *nControlY1*. We also set the *y* member of the third point to *nControlY2*. Recall that the second and third points in a call to PolyBezier() are the control point. This results in the first control point moving down the screen and the second control point moving up. We call PolyBezier() each iteration. The result is a symmetrical pattern shown in Figure 5-22.

DrawPolyBezTo()

Our last call demonstrates the PolyBezierTo() function. It also gives another look at the effect of control points. We define an array of points for the function (*pPts*). The points make up four Bezier splines. The start and end points of the four Beziers form a square, but the control points are placed in various coordinates around the device context.

We start a path bracket with BeginPath() and move the current position to 50,50. This is the upper-left corner of our square. Note that the points in the array are arranged in groups of three. This lets you see each set of Bezier spline coordinates. For example, the first spline uses the current position as the first point, the first two array values are control points, and the third array

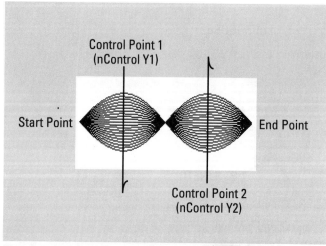

Figure 5-22 Results from 20 calls to PolyBezier()

value is the end point. The next spline uses the end point of the previous spline as its starting point, and so on.

We call PolyBezierTo() to draw the four splines. The last parameter of this function is 12. This matches the number of points in the array. Recall that this value must be divisible by three. Figure 5-23 shows the results from the call to PolyBezierTo().

The first spline has the control points on the line (between the end points); therefore, the line is not affected by the control points. The second spline has the control points to the right of the end points (CPontrol point 1 is to the right of End Point 1); therefore, the line forms a curve. The third spline's control points are crossed (Control Point 1 is closer to End Point 2). This causes the curve to come to a point. The fourth spline has the control points on opposite sides of the line.

Now that you have seen the inner workings of this application, let's build GDI2 and observe the results.

BUILDING AND USING GDI2

The GDI2 project is located in the \CHAPTER5\5.2 subdirectory, including MAKEFILE. Open a command prompt window and change to

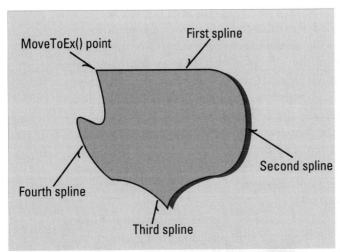

Figure 5-23 Results from PolyBezierTo()

this directory. Type NMAKE and press (ENTER). The GDI2 application compiles and links. Either use the Command Prompt window to start the program, or add the GDI2 program to an existing group in the Program Manager.

Review the code in Listings 5-16 through 5-18 while performing the following steps:

1. Start with the *Polylines* menu. Select each of the three options (PolylineTo, PolyPolyline, and PolyDraw) and observe the results. Review the listings and the descriptions of the functions (DrawPolyTo(), DrawPolyPoly(), and DrawPolyDraw()) for each option.

2. Now try the *Beziers* menu. Select each of the two options (PolyBezier and PolyBezierTo) and observe the results. Review the listings and the descriptions of the functions (DrawPolyBez() and DrawPolyBezTo()) for each option.

This completes the GDI example applications. Depending on your application needs, you may just graze the surface of these functions. If, on the other hand, you are creating an illustration or a CAD-type application, you will need to become very familiar with these new functions.

SUMMARY

The Win32 GDI has expanded significantly from previous versions of Windows. Part of the change is due to the expansion to the 32-bit operating system. You have seen some of the effects in this chapter. Handles and graphics coordinates have grown from 16 to 32 bits, but most of these changes are transparent to you. A handle to a bitmap is still a handle. You don't have to be concerned with the size of handles.

Some of the functions in the Windows 3.x API have changed slightly, others have been deleted and replaced by new functions. You have seen examples of the font resource and DIB pattern brush functions. Functions that require callbacks introduce a new keyword: CALLBACK. This replaces the FAR PASCAL from Windows 3.x.

Perhaps the most significant change in the GDI is the introduction of new functions and concepts. Wideline support is now available through functions such as ExtCreatePen(). You've seen how flexible this function is at creating virtually any pen. The topic of widelines also includes other new features like end caps and line joins. These features can be very beneficial to a programmer designing illustration and CAD software. With users of such applications demanding more elaboate features and capabilities, you have the tools and the ability to supply this demand.

You've also seen several new line drawing functions, from the extension of the existing polyline functions to the introduction of Bezier curves to the Windows API. Using combinations of these new calls, coupled with other features, you can unlock a huge potential in programs that utilize the GDI.

Let's turn to a new feature that is very specific to Windows NT: multitasking. The next chapter explores the topic of preemptive multitasking, one of the most significant changes in Windows.

Multitasking in Windows NT

6

Multitasking in Windows NT

When writing DOS applications, the programmer has control over virtually all of the system resources (memory, files, hardware, and so on). Although this seems to be quite an advantage, it means that no other application can run when a DOS program has such control. As demand for the efficient use of computer power increased, the requirement to run multiple applications emerged. Several products hit the market to address this need. Microsoft Windows immediately emerged as one of the leaders in this arena.

Among other advancements, Windows introduced the ability to run more than one application at a time. Although this was considered a multitasking environment, it was labeled nonpreemptive multitasking. This means that when an application gains control of the system, it must return control to Windows before any other event can occur. Windows cannot interrupt (preempt) the application to perform other tasks. This requires a great amount of care (on the programmer's part) to ensure that the application does not dominate the system. If the care is not taken, other running applications suffer from the loss of system resources and processor time.

The heart of the Windows NT operating system is its ability to perform *preemptive multitasking*. This allows the system to schedule sections of code, and execute them for a fixed period of time, or a *timeslice*. The sections of code are called threads. It is not a requirement for an application to create threads or manipulate the priority of *threads;* however, doing so can improve the performance of your Win32 applications significantly. In this chapter you will see how to create threads, set priorities of threads, and create processes. Let's take a look at a complete list of topics we'll cover in this chapter.

CHAPTER OVERVIEW

Concepts Covered

- Creating threads
- Setting thread priority
- Suspending and resuming threads
- Terminating and exiting threads
- Thread contention
- Starting processes
- Exiting and terminating processes
- Setting priority classes

Win32 API Functions Covered

- CreateThread()
- ResumeThread()
- SuspendThread()
- GetThreadPriority()
- SetThreadPriority()
- TerminateThread()
- ExitThread()
- GetExitCodeThread()
- CloseHandle()
- GetCurrentThread()
- CreateRemoteThread()
- Sleep()
- CreateProcess()
- GetPriorityClass()
- SetPriorityClass()
- TerminateProcess()
- ExitProcess()
- GetExitCodeProcess()
- GetCurrentProcess()

Data Types Covered

- STARTUPINFO (structure)
- PROCESS_INFORMATION (structure)

Parameters Covered

- THREAD_PRIORITY_HIGHEST
- THREAD_PRIORITY_ABOVE_NORMAL
- THREAD_PRIORITY_NORMAL
- THREAD_PRIORITY_BELOW_NORMAL
- THREAD_PRIORITY_LOWEST
- REALTIME_PRIORITY_CLASS
- HIGH_PRIORITY_CLASS
- NORMAL_PRIORITY_CLASS
- IDLE_PRIORITY_CLASS

Before we get into the details of multitasking in Windows NT, let's take a closer look at the processing differences between Windows 3.1 and NT. This background information will demonstrate the benefits of using the multitasking functions.

TYPES OF MULTITASKING

To fully appreciate what Windows NT has to offer, let's examine how previous versions of Windows handled multiple tasks. First, as mentioned, Windows 3.1 employs a nonpreemptive multitasking method. Figure 6-1 provides an overview of how this method works.

When Windows sends a message to a function in your application (WndProc( ) is used in this example), the function has control over the microprocessor. Until the function returns control to Windows, all processor time is devoted to the task. Notice that Application 1 has received a message from Windows (WM_PAINT, for example). The application message loop routes the message to WndProc( ). During this activity Application 2 also has a message in its queue. Even though Application 2 has a job to get done, it will remain idle until WndProc( ) in Application 1 returns.

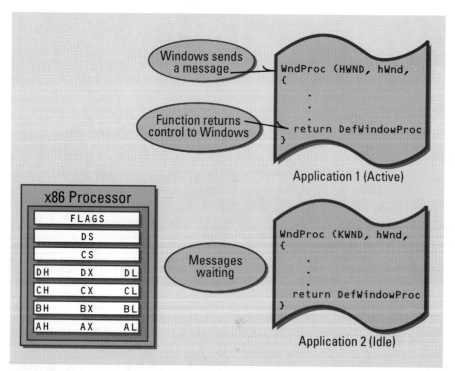

Figure 6-1 Overview of nonpreemptive multitasking

As you can see, if Application 1 takes a long time to process the WM_PAINT message, Application 2 remains idle and suffers as a result. This shows why you have to handle your messages quickly and return control to Windows promptly. This example shows only two applications. All running applications suffer when one application dominates the system.

The term "nonpreemptive" comes from the fact that Windows cannot break execution in the middle of a function and regain control. Windows NT has provided a solution to this problem in the Win32 subsystem by implementing preemptive multitasking.

Windows NT and Preemptive Multitasking

You have already seen some of the advantages of the Windows NT operating system, such as 32-bit addressing and new file management. But perhaps the biggest advancement is the introduction of preemptive multitasking. Before we take a look at the flow of applications, we need to fully define two new terms: *processes* and *threads*.

Processes and Threads

Each Windows NT application has one process and at least one thread. A process is a collection of virtual memory space, code, data, and system resources. When an application starts, a process is created. A process always consists of at least one thread, known as the *primary thread*. From this process one or more additional threads can be created. A thread is the unit of code that the NT operating system schedules to be performed. The main difference between a process and a thread is that threads *share* memory space and system resources. Processes each have their own unique memory space. What's more, the processor executes only threads, not processes. Figure 6-2 shows a breakdown of a process, and threads within a process.

When an application starts (enters the WinMain() function), a private address space is reserved in virtual memory. The initial process is also the *primary thread*. The primary thread will remain until the WinMain() function exits.

In the figure two threads are created from the initial process. Notice that the threads are not given their own private address space; instead they share the address space of the process. This example shows the threads as two separate sections of code. This does not have to be the case. You can create multiple threads that execute the same section of code. This is similar to multiple instances of applications in Window 3.x. Each thread shares the same code; however, they maintain their own stacks, as we'll see in a moment.

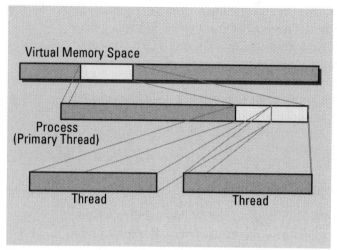

Figure 6-2 Process and threads

You must have a clear strategy in mind when creating threads. Always keep in mind that each thread is sharing global variables and resources (device contexts, pens, and so on). We will build applications that demonstrate thread strategies later in this chapter.

A Closer Look at a Thread

Let's take a closer look at threads. Figure 6-3 shows the construction of a typical instance of a thread, or *thread context*. The example shows that the thread is assigned to the ThreadProc() function. Once the thread has started, it will execute (when it gets its turn) until it exits, unless you specifically suspend or terminate the thread. A thread can also become *blocked* if there is another thread of higher priority waiting to be serviced.

There are four major sections of the thread shown in Figure 6-3. Pointers let the thread locate the code, in this case ThreadProc(). The machine registers save the state of the thread each time the timeslice for the thread expires. For example, the thread may be interrupted by the system in the middle of the function. The state of the thread is saved by storing the processor registers.

The thread context also contains a stack. The thread uses this stack to store variables during execution and idle time. Although you can specify the size of a thread's stack, usually you'll use the default stack size. The default stack size is the same as the stack size of the process that created the thread.

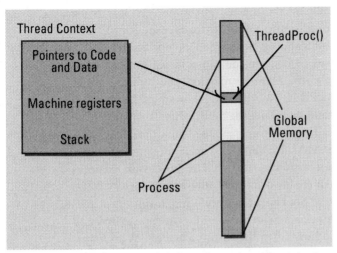

Figure 6-3 The anatomy of a thread—a thread context

When does the thread get a chance to execute? This depends on the priority of the process that created the thread and the priority of the thread itself. Table 6-1 shows the possible priorities of processes and threads.

Each process has a *priority class attribute*. The default class is NORMAL_PRIORITY_CLASS. The HIGH_PRIORITY_CLASS should be reserved for critical tasks that must be performed immediately. The

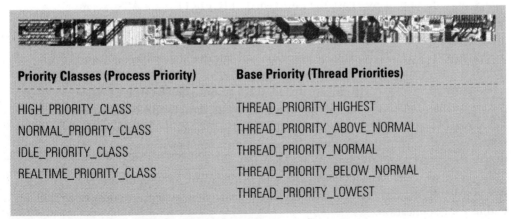

Priority Classes (Process Priority)	Base Priority (Thread Priorities)
HIGH_PRIORITY_CLASS	THREAD_PRIORITY_HIGHEST
NORMAL_PRIORITY_CLASS	THREAD_PRIORITY_ABOVE_NORMAL
IDLE_PRIORITY_CLASS	THREAD_PRIORITY_NORMAL
REALTIME_PRIORITY_CLASS	THREAD_PRIORITY_BELOW_NORMAL
	THREAD_PRIORITY_LOWEST

Table 6-1 Priority classes and thread priorities

IDLE_PRIORITY_CLASS results in the threads of the process only being executed when the system is idle (no other threads executing). The REALTIME_PRIORITY_CLASS should be avoided except for very short routines. This priority call pushes all code to the top priority, even equal to some Windows NT system functions. The user may lose the ability to move the mouse cursor when a REALTIME priority class is in effect. You can set the priority of a process at any time by calling the SetPriorityClass() function.

When you create a thread, you can set the *base priority;* it is THREAD_PRIORITY_NORMAL by default. The base priority plays a part in when the processor performs the thread. The processor executes higher priority threads first. Like the priority class, the base priority can be changed at any time by calling the SetThreadPriority() function.

A combination of the priority class of the process and the base priority of the thread determines when and how often the thread executes. Who makes these critical decisions that determine which thread gets the access to the processor? The Windows NT operating system contains a scheduler that carries out this assignment. Before we start our first multithreaded application, let's see how the scheduler makes these decisions.

The Scheduler

Today's personal computers are limited by one major factor: they can only perform one instruction at a time. Since we are trying to perform multiple tasks, each task must take its turn. If more than one application is active, their threads will take turns at the microprocessor level. The scheduler tracks all threads and assigns processor time to each.

Figure 6-4 illustrates how the scheduler handles threads with different priority values. Since most processes have the NORMAL_PRIORITY_CLASS, we are only depicting thread priorities in this example.

The scheduler maintains a queue of all threads running on the system. Threads with a HIGHEST base priority will receive attention first and therefore the greatest amount of processing time.

A temptation may exist to create all threads with a HIGHEST base priority value, but this is counterproductive to the design and purpose of Windows NT's preemptive multitasking. If your application dominates the scheduler with high priority threads, other applications (and perhaps the NT system itself) will suffer the loss in processor time.

In order to write robust, responsive NT applications, you must have a thread priority strategy. This is an essential element when you create threads within your application.

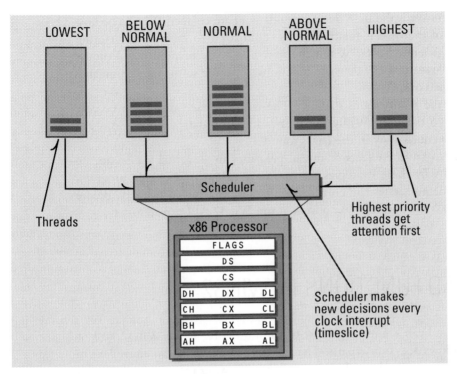

Figure 6-4 The Windows NT scheduler

Thread Priority Strategies

Thread priority can cause some confusion initially. Here are two common questions:

- Why should I assign different priorities to threads when all of the work has to get done eventually?

- If the processor can only work on one thing at a time, why does it matter which priority value I assign to a thread?

We can answer both of these questions with one example. Consider that you are writing an application that manages a large database. Like most applications, it has code that handles the user interface. There is also code that handles the database functions (searching, sorting, and so on). You create a thread to handle the user-interface routines and a thread to handle the database functions. Now you have to make a decision: Which thread should receive the higher priority?

If your answer is the user-interface code, you are correct! Why? The flow of data from the user is relatively slow compared to disk input or other computer-generated data. When the user hits a key or performs a mouse action, the lower priority database functions step aside so the user commands can be carried out.

What is the result of this strategy? The user-interface appears to be very responsive to the user. While the user is idle, the database functions can continue to churn away in the background.

It helps to see the effects of thread priorities in an actual application to understand why these strategies are necessary. The first example program, MULTI1, demonstrates the creation of threads, and thread priority. Before we get into MULTI1, let's take a look at the Win32 API thread functions.

THREAD FUNCTIONS IN WIN32

So far we've been comparing most of the functions in the Win32 API to their Windows 3.x counterparts. The subject of threads has no equivalent in prior versions of Windows, however, so the following material is uncharted territory for most Windows programmers. But there is no need to despair. With some theory and practice, you will understand the effects of preemptive multitasking in a short time.

We'll break down the thread functions into four categories: thread creation, controlling threads, thread termination, and remote threads. Let's start with thread creation.

Thread Creation

The CreateThread() function creates a thread that executes within the virtual address space of the calling process. This is the only function required to create a thread. Let's break down and examine CreateThread().

Using CreateThread()

The CreateThread() function requires six parameters: the address of a security attributes structure, the stack size, the address of the thread procedure, an optional argument, a set of creation flags, and an address to store the thread ID. CreateThread() returns a handle to the thread which you can use in other thread calls. You must define the *thread procedure* as well.

Listing 6-1 shows the syntax and an example call to CreateThread(). Also shown is an application-defined thread procedure.

Listing 6-1 CreateThread() syntax and example call

```
/* CreateThread() Syntax */
HANDLE CreateThread (LPSECURITY_ATTRIBUTES lpsa,        /* address of SA struct */
                     DWORD dwStack,                      /* initial stack size */
                     LPTHREAD_START_ROUTINE lpThreadProc, /* address of thread procedure */
                     LPVOID lpThreadArg,                 /* thread argument */
                     DWORD dwCreateFlags,                /* creation flags */
                     LPDWORD lpThreadID);                /* address to store thread ID */

/* CreateThread() Example Call */
[excerpt from WndProc()]
HANDLE hThread;
DWORD  dwThreadID;
DWORD  dwThreadArg = 5;

   hThread = CreateThread (NULL,                          /* no security attributes */
                   0,                                     /* use stack size of caller */
                   (LPTHREAD_START_ROUTINE) ThreadProc,   /* address of thread proc */
                   &ThreadArg,                            /* address of argument (5) */
                   CREATE_SUSPENDED,                      /* don't start thread */
                   &dwThreadID);                          /* address to store thread ID */
[other program lines]

DWORD ThreadProc (DWORD *ThreadArg) /* Thread procedure */
{
DWORD dwLoop;

   for (dwLoop = 0; dwLoop < *(ThreadArg); dwLoop++)
      MessageBeep (0);
   return (0);
}
```

The example above creates a thread and returns a *thread handle,* which is stored in *hThread.* This handle can be used in a number of function calls that control threads. We'll look at examples of this in the next section.

The first parameter to CreateThread() is set to NULL. This indicates that there are no security attributes for the thread. This means that any process can control the thread if it obtains the handle to the thread. We'll cover security attributes in Chapter 8, Introduction to NT System Security.

The second parameter, set to 0, is a DWORD specifying the thread stack size. Setting this parameter to 0 results in a stack size that equals that of the calling process. For example, if our application has a 16K stack, the thread we create also has a 16K stack. They are not the same stack, however; the stacks are independent. Setting this second parameter to 0 is usually sufficient because the stack will automatically grow if necessary.

The third parameter is the address of the thread procedure, in our case ThreadProc. Notice that we cast the parameter to a LPTHREAD_START_ROUTINE type. This is the data type required by CreateThread(). The actual procedure is shown below the CreateThread() call in the listing.

The fourth parameter is the address of an argument to pass to the thread procedure. In the example we are using, sending a DWORD value, *dwThreadArg*. Note that the syntax declares this parameter as type LPVOID. As a result you can send the address of virtually any data type. In our case we are sending a DWORD set to 5 to the thread procedure.

The fifth parameter is a DWORD containing the creation flags. We are sending the CREATE_SUSPENDED creation flag. This means the thread will not execute until we specifically tell it to with ResumeThread(). We'll discuss ResumeThread() in the next section.

The last parameter is the address of a DWORD, *dwThreadID*. The Win32 subsystem assigns a 32-bit value that uniquely identifies the thread and stores it at the supplied address. Some Win32 API functions require a handle to a thread, while others require the *thread ID*.

Assuming we start this thread, ThreadProc() receives the address to the argument, *ThreadArg*. We use a simple *for* loop that executes until it reaches the value stored in *ThreadArg*. Note that we are using *(ThreadArg)* to get the contents of the variable. Since *ThreadArg* is 5, the speaker beeps five times.

We'll see more calls to CreateThread() in our first multitasking application, MULTI1. Now that we know how to create a thread, let's look at some functions that control threads.

Controlling Threads

Four functions have an effect on thread execution: ResumeThread(), SuspendThread(), SetThreadPriority(), and GetThreadPriority(). Using these functions we can control threads individually, and thus create efficient multitasking applications.

Using ResumeThread() and SuspendThread()

Calling ResumeThread() and SuspendThread() is straightforward. They only require one parameter: a valid handle to a thread. Listing 6-2 shows the proper syntax and example calls to ResumeThread() and SuspendThread(). Note that the example calls assume that a thread has been created with a CREATE_SUSPENDED creation flag.

Listing 6-2 ResumeThread() and SuspendThread() syntax and example calls

```
/* ResumeThread() Syntax */
DWORD ResumeThread (HANDLE hThread);  /* valid handle to thread */

/* SuspendThread() Syntax */
DWORD SuspendThread (HANDLE hThread); /* valid handle to thread */

/* ResumeThread() and SuspendThread() Example Calls
   assumes thread was created with CREATE_SUSPENDED creation flag */
DWORD dwSuspCount;

  dwSuspCount = ResumeThread (hThread);   /* dwSuspCount == 1; thread starts running */
  dwSuspCount = SuspendThread (hThread); /* dwSuspCount == 0; thread suspended */
  dwSuspCount = SuspendThread (hThread); /* dwSuspCount == 1; thread still suspended */
  dwSuspCount = ResumeThread (hThread);   /* dwSuspCount == 2; thread still suspended */
  dwSuspCount = ResumeThread (hThread);     /* dwSuspCount == 1; thread starts running again */
  dwSuspCount = ResumeThread (hThread);     /* dwSuspCount == 0; thread continues to run */
```

Both ResumeThread() and SuspendThread() return a DWORD specifying the previous *suspension count*. The suspension count is 0 for a running thread, and greater than 0 for a suspended thread.

ResumeThread() decrements the suspension count unless the thread is already running (*dwSuspCount* == 0); in which case the count remains at 0. SuspendThread() increments the suspension count up to MAXIMUM_SUSPEND_COUNT (defined as 127 in WINNT.H).

If either function fails, the return value is 0xFFFFFFFFh. This is usually the result of an invalid thread handle or exceeding the maximum suspension count.

Let's take the example calls one at a time. Since we're assuming that the thread is initially suspended, the original suspension count is 1; the thread is suspended. The first call is to ResumeThread(). Since these functions return the previous suspension count, a value of 1 is assigned to *dwSuspCount*. The thread is running and the actual suspension count is now 0.

Next we make a call to SuspendThread(). The return value is 0 indicating that the thread was running. The suspension count is incremented to 1. We make another call to SuspendThread(). This time the return value is 1, indicating that the thread was already suspended; the suspension count is now 2.

We call ResumeThread() again. The return value is 2; this indicates that the thread is still suspended. The suspension count is decremented. Another call to ResumeThread() returns a 1. This indicates that the thread was suspended; however, the call caused the thread to start execution. The suspension count is now 0.

The last example call to ResumeThread() returns 0. This indicates that the thread was already running. The suspension count remains at 0.

Using GetThreadPriority() and SetThreadPriority()

GetThreadPriority() and SetThreadPriority() let you obtain and set the *relative* thread priority of a given thread. We say relative because of the relationship of thread priority to the priority class of the process. For example, a thread with a THREAD_PRIORITY_NORMAL in a process with a HIGH_PRIORITY_CLASS has a higher priority than a thread with a THREAD_PRIORITY_NORMAL in a process with a NORMAL_PRIORITY_CLASS.

Both calls require a valid handle to a thread. In addition, SetThreadPriority() requires an integer specifying the new thread priority value. Listing 6-3 shows the proper syntax and examples calls for GetThreadPriority() and SetThreadPriority(). Again, the example calls assume a thread has been created and assigned to *hThread*.

Listing 6-3 GetThreadPriority() and SetThreadPriority() syntax and example calls

```
/* GetThreadPriority() Syntax */
int GetThreadPriority (HANDLE hThread);    /* valid handle to thread */

/* SetThreadPriority() Syntax */
BOOL SetThreadPriority (HANDLE hThread,    /* valid handle to thread */
                        int nPriority);  /* new priority value */

/* GetThreadPriority() and SetThreadPriority() Example Calls */
int nOldPriority, nNewPriority;

   nOldPriority = GetThreadPriority (hThread);
   nNewPriority = THREAD_PRIORITY_LOWEST;
   SetThreadPriority (hThread, nNewPriority);
```

GetThreadPriority() requires a valid thread handle and returns an integer indicating the current priority of the thread. This value can be one of those listed in Table 6-1. If the function fails, it returns THREAD_PRIORITY_ERROR_RETURN.

SetThreadPriority() requires a valid thread handle and an integer specifying the new priority value. In the example call, we assign THREAD_PRIORITY_LOWEST to an integer variable. We use this variable as the second parameter to SetThreadPriority(). This function returns a Boolean value indicating success (TRUE) or failure (FALSE).

Thread Termination

There is more than one way a thread can end, or *terminate*. One way thread termination occurs is when the thread function returns. In this case the system calls ExitThread() with the return value as its parameter.

There are two function calls that explicitly terminate threads: TerminateThread() and ExitThread(). The first call terminates the thread without regard to DLLs that may be attached to the thread. The second call terminates the thread and notifies any attached DLLs that the thread has been terminated. We'll look at our first DLL later in this chapter. Another related function, GetExitCodeThread(), obtains the exit code of a specific thread. The exit code can obtain the exit code specified by TerminateThread(), ExitThread(), or the thread procedure return value.

Neither TerminateThread() nor ExitThread() removes the thread handle from the system. This must be accomplished with an explicit call to CloseHandle(). Let's look at these functions in more detail. We'll start with TerminateThread().

Using TerminateThread()

This function terminates a thread without regard to attached DLLs. This means that the thread will be interrupted and terminated regardless of the code it may be executing. TerminateThread() requires two parameters: a valid handle to the thread to terminate and an exit code. Listing 6-4 shows the syntax and an example call to this function.

Listing 6-4 TerminateThread() syntax and example call

```
/* TerminateThread() Syntax */
BOOL TerminateThread (HANDLE hThread,        /* valid thread handle */
                      DWORD  dwExitCode);  /* exit code */

/* TerminateThread() Example Call */
DWORD dwExitCode;

   dwExitCode = 0;                          /* set exit code */
   TerminateThread (hThread, dwExitCode);  /* kill thread and change termination status */
```

In this example call, the exit code is set to 0 arbitrarily. You can set the exit code to any value other than 0x103 (259 decimal). Why not use this value? If a thread is still active, the exit code is STILL_ACTIVE. STILL_ACTIVE is defined in WINBASE.H as STATUS_PENDING. STATUS_PENDING is defined in WINNT.H as 0x103. Therefore setting the exit code to this value would make the thread appear to be active.

With the exit code variable set to 0, we call TerminateThread() with a valid thread handle and *dwExitCode*. The thread termination status changes from STILL_ACTIVE to 0 and the thread is stopped. The thread's initial stack is not deallocated and no attached DLLs are notified.

TerminateThread() returns a Boolean indicating success (TRUE) or failure (FALSE). Examples of failure are an invalid thread handle or the thread is already terminated. We will see an example of the success/failure of TerminateThread() in the MULTI1 example application.

Using ExitThread()

This thread termination call is much more friendly and, as a result, is the preferred method of terminating a thread. ExitThread() is made from within the thread itself; therefore, it requires only one parameter: the exit code. Listing 6-5 shows the syntax and an example call to ExitThread(). We are using a fictitious thread procedure, ThreadProc(), in the example call.

Listing 6-5 ExitThread() syntax and example call

```
/* ExitThread() Syntax */
VOID ExitThread (DWORD dwExitCode);    /* exit code */

/* ExitThread() Example Call */
DWORD ThreadProc (DWORD *ThreadArg)
{
    [program lines for thread]

    ExitThread (0);                    /* exit thread and set termination status to 0 */
}
```

As you can see by the example call, the usage of ExitThread() is fairly straightforward. We return from the thread procedure setting the thread termination status to 0. ExitThread() does not return a value. How can we find out what exit value ExitThread(), TerminateThread(), or a thread procedure return value specified? The answer is in our next call, GetExitCodeThread().

Using GetExitCodeThread()

GetExitCodeThread() obtains the current termination status (exit code) of a specific thread. The function requires two parameters: a valid handle to a thread and an address to store the termination status. Listing 6-6 shows the syntax and an example call to GetExitCodeThread().

Listing 6-6 GetExitCodeThread() syntax and example call

```
/* GetExitCodeThread() Syntax */
BOOL GetExitCodeThread (HANDLE hThread,          /* valid thread handle */
                        LPDWORD lpdwExitCode);   /* address to store termination status */

/* GetExitCodeThread() Example Call */
DWORD dwExitCode;

   GetExitCodeThread (hThread, &dwExitCode);     /* get termination status */
   if (dwExitCode == STILL_ACTIVE)               /* is thread still active? */
      MessageBeep (0);                           /* beep if it is */
```

In this example we get the termination status of a thread. This status is placed in *dwExitCode*. We supplied the address of this DWORD in the GetExitCodeThread() call. We then compare the results to the STILL_ACTIVE define (0x103). If the thread is still active, we beep the PC speaker.

If the thread had been terminated before the call to GetExitCodeThread(), *dwExitCode* would be set to a termination status. Depending on the method of termination, this value was set by one of the following:

- the exit code specified in a call to ExitThread() (within the thread procedure)
- the exit code specified in a call to TerminateThread()
- the return value of the thread procedure (if the thread procedure had returned)
- the return value of the thread's process (in the case of process termination)

The last possibility will only occur if a separate process obtains a handle to the thread. If the thread-creating process terminates, and another process calls GetExitCodeThread(), it receives the exit code of the thread-creating process, not the thread exit code. Thread handles, and other types of handles, can be shared through *interprocess communication*. We saw one example of interprocess communication in Chapter 3. We used shared memory to exchange data between processes in MEMORY3 and MEMORY4.

Object Handles

We have been using handles in several of the applications up to this point. These handles access *objects*. The object may be a file mapping object, or in the above cases, thread objects. These objects maintain a handle count. This count is incremented if more than one process obtains a particular handle. As long as the count is non-0, the handle remains in the operating system. The CloseHandle() function decrements the handle count of an object. The GetCurrentThread() function lets a thread get a handle to itself (actually a *pseudohandle,* as we'll see shortly).

Using CloseHandle()

CloseHandle() decrements the handle count of an object. This function requires one parameter, a handle to the object (in the case of our current topic, a handle to a thread). Listing 6-7 shows the proper syntax and an example call to CloseHandle().

Listing 6-7 CloseHandle() syntax and example call

```
/* CloseHandle() Syntax */
BOOL CloseHandle (hObject);      /* handle to object */

/* CloseHandle() Example Call */

   CloseHandle (hThread);       /* close thread handle and decrement object handle count */
```

This example call closes the thread handle. If the handle count reaches 0, the object is removed from the operating system.

Using GetCurrentThread()

A thread is not aware of its own handle while it's executing, but on some occasions a thread needs to know its handle. For example, if you wanted to give a thread the ability to change its priority, the thread would need the handle required in the SetThreadPriority() call. GetCurrentThread() returns a handle to the thread making the call. It does not require any parameters. Listing 6-8 shows the syntax and an example call to GetCurrentThread().

Listing 6-8 GetCurrentThread() syntax and example call

```
/* GetCurrentThread() Syntax */
HANDLE GetCurrentThread(VOID);     /* no parameter required */

/* GetCurrentThread() Example Call */
HANDLE hThread;                            /* assumes we are in a thread procedure */

    hThread = GetCurrentThread();  /* place pseudohandle in hThread */
```

GetCurrentThread() does not return an actual handle; instead it is a *pseudohandle*. A pseudohandle is only effective in the procedure that obtained it. For example, if you use the GetCurrentThread() function in a thread, only that particular thread can use the handle. You cannot share the handle with other threads and processes. You do not have to close a pseudohandle by calling CloseHandle(); the pseudohandle disposes of itself when the thread is terminated.

Remote Threads—Creating a Thread in an External Process

A less-frequently used thread creation function creates a thread in the virtual address space of another function. The function is CreateRemoteThread(). CreateRemoteThread() requires the same parameters as CreateThread(), plus one additional parameter: a handle to the external process. Listing 6-9 shows the syntax and an example call to CreateRemoteThread().

Listing 6-9 CreateRemoteThread() syntax and example call

```
/* CreateRemoteThread() Syntax */
HANDLE CreateRemoteThread (HANDLE hProcess,             /* handle to remote process */
                   LPSECURITY_ATTRIBUTES lpsa,          /* address of SA struct */
                   DWORD dwStack,                       /* initial stack size */
                   LPTHREAD_START_ROUTINE lpThreadProc, /* address of thread procedure */
                   LPVOID lpThreadArg,                  /* thread argument */
                   DWORD dwCreateFlags,                 /* creation flags */
                   LPDWORD lpThreadID);                 /* address to store thread ID */

/* CreateThread() Example Call */
[excerpt from WndProc()]
HANDLE hThread, hProcess;
DWORD  dwThreadID;
DWORD  dwThreadArg = 3;

    hThread = CreateRemoteThread (hProcess,             /* handle to remote process */
                          NULL,                         /* no security attributes */
```

continued on next page

continued from previous page

```
                           0,                                    /* use stack size of caller */
                           (LPTHREAD_START_ROUTINE) ThreadProc,  /* address of thread proc */
                           &ThreadArg,                           /* address of argument */
                           CREATE_SUSPENDED,                     /* don't start thread */
                           &dwThreadID);                         /* address to store thread ID */
[other program lines]

DWORD ThreadProc (DWORD *ThreadArg) /* Thread procedure */
{
DWORD dwLoop;

   for (dwLoop = 0; dwLoop < *(ThreadArg); dwLoop++)
      MessageBeep (0);
   return (0);
}
```

Except for supplying a handle to a process, this example call is identical to the CreateThread() call in Listing 6-1. Although the thread procedure is defined in the current source file, it will actually execute in the address space of the process identified by the handle. You will see an example of how we obtain a handle to a remote process in the MULTI3 application later in this chapter.

THREAD CREATION AND PRIORITY DEMONSTRATION

Our first example application, MULTI1, creates five threads in a suspended state. We assign various priorities to each of the five threads and then we start the threads. Each thread has the task of drawing a rectangle that grows upward on the display. The output of MULTI1 provides a visual indication of the effects of thread priority.

Before we get into the description of the application, let's take a look at the files that make up MULTI1. Listings 6-10 through 6-13 provide the makefile, resource file, header file, and source file, respectively.

New Makefile for Multithreaded Applications

We've made a small modification to the makefile for MULTI1 (and all other multithreaded applications in this book). We've changed the command line of the compiler to use *$(cvarsmt)* instead of *$(cvars)* (see boldface entry in Listing

6-10). Recall from Chapter 2 that *$(cvars)* is defined in NTWIN32.MAK as
-DWIN32 and possibly *-DNULL=0* if defined in the current environment.
The new macro *$(cvarsmt)* is defined as *$(cvars)* plus *-D_MT*. This defines
_MT, which the header files use to properly build multithreaded applications.

Listing 6-10 The MAKEFILE for MULTI1

```
# MAKEFILE for MULTI1 (Multitasking demo in Win32)

# NMAKE macros for Win32 apps
!include <ntwin32.mak>

# all pseudotarget
all: multi1.exe

# Update the resource.

multi1.res: multi1.rc multi1.h
    rc -r -fo multi1.tmp multi1.rc
    cvtres -$(CPU) multi1.tmp -o multi1.res
    del multi1.tmp

# Update the object file-use the *(cvarsmt) macro.

multi1.obj: multi1.c multi1.h
    $(cc) $(cflags) $(cvarsmt) multi1.c

# Update the executable file and add the resource file.

multi1.exe: multi1.obj multi1.res
    $(link) $(guiflags) -IGNORE:505 -out:multi1.exe multi1.obj multi1.res $(guilibsmt)
```

The Resource Script for MULTI1

The resource script is comparable to all other RC files in this book. Nothing
is new here. We're simply defining the icon and menu resources.

Listing 6-11 MULTI1.RC—resource script

```
#include "windows.h"
#include "multi1.h"


Multi1Icon ICON multi1.ico

Multi1Menu MENU
    BEGIN
        POPUP "&Thread Control"
```

continued on next page

continued from previous page

```
    BEGIN
        MENUITEM "&Resume Threads",  IDM_RESUME
        MENUITEM "&Suspend Threads", IDM_SUSPEND, GRAYED
    END
END
```

The Header File for MULTI1

The header file for our first multithreaded application is also fairly typical; however, we've added defines that the five threads will use as arguments. We have also included a declaration for the thread procedure. Thread procedures are defined as a DWORD return type function that takes a pointer to a DWORD as its only parameter.

Listing 6-12 MULTI1.H—header file

```
/* multi1.h -- Include file for multi1.c and multi1.rc */

/* Menu defines */
#define IDM_RESUME     1
#define IDM_SUSPEND    2

/* Thread arguments */
#define HIGHEST_THREAD      0x00
#define ABOVE_AVE_THREAD    0x3F
#define NORMAL_THREAD       0x7F
#define BELOW_AVE_THREAD    0xBF
#define LOWEST_THREAD       0xFF

/* Function prototypes */
LONG APIENTRY MainWndProc (HWND, UINT, UINT, LONG);
VOID ThreadProc (DWORD *ThreadArg);

/* Global variables */
HANDLE ghInst;
HANDLE ghWnd;
```

The Source File for MULTI1

We'll go over the source code in detail in a moment, but first let's look over the source file. We have included the source in its entirety, including WinMain(). The creation of the main window has been altered slightly from previous example applications. The calls to each of the new functions has been set off in boldface.

Listing 6-13 MULTI1.C—source file

```
/* multi1.c    Demonstrate the creation and priority of threads */

#include <windows.h>
#include <stdlib.h>
#include "multi1.h"

int APIENTRY WinMain (HANDLE hInstance, HANDLE hPrevInstance, LPSTR lpCmdLine, int nCmdShow)
{
   MSG  msg;
   WNDCLASS wndclass;

   UNREFERENCED_PARAMETER (lpCmdLine);              /* Prevent compiler warnings */
   UNREFERENCED_PARAMETER (hPrevInstance);

   ghInst = hInstance;                              /* Assign global instance handle */

   wndclass.style = 0;
   wndclass.lpfnWndProc = (WNDPROC)MainWndProc;
   wndclass.cbClsExtra = 0;
   wndclass.cbWndExtra = 0;
   wndclass.hInstance = hInstance;
   wndclass.hIcon = LoadIcon (hInstance, "Multi2Icon");
   wndclass.hCursor = LoadCursor (NULL, IDC_ARROW);
   wndclass.hbrBackground = GetStockObject (WHITE_BRUSH);
   wndclass.lpszMenuName = "Multi2Menu";           /* multi2 menu */
   wndclass.lpszClassName = "Multi2Class";

   RegisterClass(&wndclass);

   ghWnd = CreateWindow ("Multi2Class",            /* Create main window */
                         "Deadlocks and Races",    /* Title bar text */
                         WS_OVERLAPPEDWINDOW,
                         CW_USEDEFAULT,
                         CW_USEDEFAULT,
                         CW_USEDEFAULT,
                         CW_USEDEFAULT,
                         NULL,
                         NULL,
                         hInstance,
                         NULL);

   ShowWindow(ghWnd, nCmdShow);                     /* Display window */

   while (GetMessage (&msg, NULL, 0, 0))            /* Message Loop */
   {
      TranslateMessage (&msg);
      DispatchMessage (&msg);
   }
```

continued on next page

continued from previous page

```
    return (msg.wParam);                              /* Return exit code */

}


/* WndProc - Main Window Procedure for multi1.c */
LONG APIENTRY MainWndProc (HWND hWnd, UINT message, UINT wParam, LONG lParam)
{
DWORD          ThreadID1, ThreadID2, ThreadID3, ThreadID4, ThreadID5;
static HANDLE  hThread1, hThread2, hThread3, hThread4, hThread5, hMasterThread;
static DWORD   ThreadArg1, ThreadArg2, ThreadArg3, ThreadArg4, ThreadArg5;
static HMENU   hMenu;

  switch (message)
  {
    case WM_CREATE:                              /* initialization */
      hMenu = GetMenu (hWnd);                    /* get handle to menu */
      hMasterThread = GetCurrentThread();        /* get handle to primary thread */
      SetThreadPriority (hMasterThread, THREAD_PRIORITY_HIGHEST); /* and set to highest */
      PostMessage (hWnd, WM_USER, 0, 0);         /* send a WM_USER message to ourselves */
      return (0);

    case WM_USER:                                /* message sent from WM_CREATE */
      ThreadArg1 = HIGHEST_THREAD;               /* assign thread argument 1 */
      hThread1 = CreateThread (NULL,                  /* create thread 1 */
                         0,                            /* default stack */
                         (LPTHREAD_START_ROUTINE)ThreadProc, /* addr of threadproc */
                         &ThreadArg1,                  /* pass the argument address */
                         CREATE_SUSPENDED,             /* don't start yet */
                         &ThreadID1);                  /* address to store thread ID */

      ThreadArg2 = ABOVE_AVE_THREAD;             /* assign thread argument 2 */
      hThread2 = CreateThread (NULL,             /* create thread 2 */
                         0,                      /* default stack */
                         (LPTHREAD_START_ROUTINE)ThreadProc, /* addr of threadproc */
                         &ThreadArg2,            /* pass the argument address */
                         CREATE_SUSPENDED,       /* don't start yet */
                         &ThreadID2);            /* address to store thread ID */

      ThreadArg3 = NORMAL_THREAD;                /* assign thread argument 3 */
      hThread3 = CreateThread (NULL,             /* create thread 3 */
                         0,                      /* default stack */
                         (LPTHREAD_START_ROUTINE)ThreadProc, /* addr of threadproc */
                         &ThreadArg3,            /* pass the argument address */
                         CREATE_SUSPENDED,       /* don't start yet */
                         &ThreadID3);            /* address to store thread ID */

      ThreadArg4 = BELOW_AVE_THREAD;             /* assign thread argument 4 */
      hThread4 = CreateThread (NULL,             /* create thread 4 */
                         0,                      /* default stack */
                         (LPTHREAD_START_ROUTINE)ThreadProc,  /* addr of threadproc */
                         &ThreadArg4,            /* pass the argument address */
                         CREATE_SUSPENDED,       /* don't start yet */
                         &ThreadID4);            /* address to store thread ID */
```

```
        ThreadArg5 = LOWEST_THREAD;                /* assign thread argument 5 */
        hThread5 = CreateThread (NULL,             /* create thread 5 */
                          0,                       /* default stack */
                          (LPTHREAD_START_ROUTINE)ThreadProc,  /* addr of threadproc */
                          &ThreadArg5,             /* pass the argument address */
                          CREATE_SUSPENDED,        /* don't start yet */
                          &ThreadID5);             /* address to store thread ID */

        /* Set variety of thread priorities */
        SetThreadPriority (hThread1, THREAD_PRIORITY_HIGHEST);
        SetThreadPriority (hThread2, THREAD_PRIORITY_ABOVE_NORMAL);
        SetThreadPriority (hThread3, THREAD_PRIORITY_NORMAL);
        SetThreadPriority (hThread4, THREAD_PRIORITY_BELOW_NORMAL);
        SetThreadPriority (hThread5, THREAD_PRIORITY_LOWEST);
        return (0);

case WM_COMMAND:
    switch (LOWORD(wParam))
    {
        case IDM_RESUME:                                /* start the threads */
            EnableMenuItem (hMenu, IDM_RESUME, MF_BYCOMMAND | MF_GRAYED);
            EnableMenuItem (hMenu, IDM_SUSPEND, MF_BYCOMMAND | MF_ENABLED);
            ResumeThread (hThread1);
            ResumeThread (hThread2);
            ResumeThread (hThread3);
            ResumeThread (hThread4);
            ResumeThread (hThread5);
            return (0);
        case IDM_SUSPEND:                               /* suspend the threads */
            SuspendThread (hThread1);
            SuspendThread (hThread2);
            SuspendThread (hThread3);
            SuspendThread (hThread4);
            SuspendThread (hThread5);
            EnableMenuItem (hMenu, IDM_SUSPEND, MF_BYCOMMAND | MF_GRAYED);
            EnableMenuItem (hMenu, IDM_RESUME, MF_BYCOMMAND | MF_ENABLED);
            return (0);
        default:
            return (0);
    }

case WM_DESTROY :                                   /* terminate threads on exit */
    if (!TerminateThread(hThread1, 0))
        MessageBeep (0);
    if (!TerminateThread(hThread2, 0))
        MessageBeep (0);
    if (!TerminateThread(hThread3, 0))
        MessageBeep (0);
    if (!TerminateThread(hThread4, 0))
        MessageBeep (0);
    if (!TerminateThread(hThread5, 0))
        MessageBeep (0);
```

continued on next page

continued from previous page

```
        PostQuitMessage (0);
        return (0);

    default:
        return DefWindowProc (hWnd, message, wParam, lParam);
    }
    return (0L);
}


/* ThreadProc()--thread procedure for five threads; called by WndProc() */
VOID ThreadProc (DWORD *ThreadArg)
{
RECT rect;
HDC   hDC;
HANDLE hBrush, hOldBrush;
DWORD dwThreadHits = 0;

    GetClientRect (ghWnd, &rect);                       /* Get client rectangle */

    do                                                  /* draw rectangle simulating activity */
    {
      dwThreadHits++;                                   /* increment times through the loop */
      hBrush = CreateSolidBrush (RGB(*(ThreadArg), 0, 0)); /* color depends on argument */
      hDC = GetDC (ghWnd);                              /* get DC */
      hOldBrush = SelectObject (hDC, hBrush);           /* set brush color */
      /* draw rectangle; based on thread argument (x-position) and loop variable (height) */
      Rectangle (hDC, *(ThreadArg), rect.bottom - (dwThreadHits/10),
                 *(ThreadArg) + 0x40 , rect.bottom);
      hBrush = SelectObject (hDC, hOldBrush);           /* get old brush */
      DeleteObject (hBrush);                            /* delete brush */
      ReleaseDC (ghWnd, hDC);                           /* release DC */

    }while (dwThreadHits < 1000);                       /* continue if under 1000 loops */

}
```

An Overview of MULTI1

Let's start with a broad overview of MULTI1. This example application creates five threads in a suspended state during startup. All five threads use the same thread function (ThreadProc()). The menu contains one popup, *Thread Control,* which has two possible selections: *Resume Threads* and *Suspend Threads.* Only the Resume Threads option is available at startup.

When the user selects *Resume Threads,* the thread procedures start to execute. Which threads get processor time depends on the individual thread priority. The thread functions draw expanding rectangles on the display, each growing upward. When the rectangle reaches 100 pixels in height, the thread function returns. The location of the rectangles and their colors is a function of each thread procedure's argument. Let's take a step-by-step look at these actions.

WinMain()

The only difference between MULTI1's and other applications' WinMain() procedures is in the call to CreateWindow(). The window creation style is WS_OVERLAPPED and WS_SYSMENU. Recall that windows created with WS_OVERLAPPED do not have a thick border, so they cannot be resized. We do not have any fancy painting strategies in this program; therefore we don't want the user resizing the window during execution. We've added the system menu because WS_OVERLAPPED does not provide it. Otherwise there would be no way to close the application (outside of using the Task Manager).

The next four parameters specify the x-y starting coordinates and the width and height of the window. This is used in the place of CW_USEDEFAULT. This presents enough client area to draw the rectangles without taking up too much desktop space.

Creating the Window and Initializing MULTI1

After the CreateWindow call, we make the typical call to ShowWindow(). This action eventually results in a WM_CREATE message being sent to the main window procedure, WndProc().

We intercept the WM_CREATE message and initialize our application. We start by getting a handle to the main menu; we store the handle in static *hMenu*. The menu handle will be used to enable and disable the menu selections.

You may not realize it yet, but we are already running one thread: the *primary thread*. Recall that every process (application) has a primary thread. Since our example will create additional threads that have high priorities, we need to set the priority of the primary thread to a high value. If we did not do this, it would be hard to select a menu option when a high priority thread is executing.

We obtain a pseudohandle to the primary thread by calling GetCurrentThread(). The return value is assigned to *hMasterThread*. We then call SetThreadPriority() with two parameters: the primary thread pseudohandle and the desired priority. In this case the priority is set to THREAD_PRIORITY_HIGHEST. Keep in mind that most applications will not require this high priority. However, since we are creating high priority threads that execute for a significant time, we must use this priority so the primary thread can compete with the high priority thread for processor time. For purposes of this demonstration, we are not worrying about the negative effects on other processes (applications).

The last step in the WM_CREATE processing is to post a message in our own message queue. We post a WM_USER message. This gives the application time to continue creating the menu before proceeding.

Processing WM_USER

When we receive the self-sent WM_USER message, we start to create the five threads. We set the static *ThreadArg1* DWORD to HIGHEST_THREAD. This value is defined in MULTI.H as 0x00. Now let's look at the first CreateThread() call in detail.

CreateThread() requires six parameters. In our case the first parameter is set to NULL indicating that the thread has no security attributes. The second parameter is set to 0. This is the stack size parameter. Since this value is set to 0, the thread allocates the same initial stack size as the calling process (the default 1 megabyte of reserved and 4K of committed stack implied in MULTI1).

The third parameter is a pointer to the thread procedure, in our case *ThreadProc*. The parameter is cast to the LPTHREAD_START_ROUTINE type, which the compiler expects. The fourth parameter is a pointer to the thread argument, *ThreadArg1*. This is the value we defined before the CreateThread() call.

The fifth parameter is the creation flag, which we set to CREATE_SUSPENDED. As a result, the thread is created in a suspended state. If we set this value to 0, the thread would start to execute immediately. The last parameter is a pointer to a DWORD. The CreateThread() function will store a unique thread ID in this variable, *ThreadID1*. At this point the first thread object is created, and the handle to the thread object (the return value of CreateThread()) is stored in *hThread1*.

The next four calls to CreateThread() create four additional threads. The differences in the additional calls are in the thread object handle, the address of the thread argument, and the address of the ThreadID. Also, the thread argument is different for each call to CreateThread(). For example, the third call uses the address of ThreadArg3 as its argument. In this case the argument is NORMAL_THREAD, which equates to 0x7F.

With our five threads in a suspended state, we call SetThreadPriority() for each of them. This call requires a handle to the thread object and the desired priority. The first thread is assigned the highest priority (THREAD_PRIORITY_HIGHEST), and each subsequent thread is assigned the next lower priority (THREAD_PRIORITY_ABOVE_NORMAL, THREAD_PRIORITY_NORMAL, and so on). Setting the first thread to the same priority as the primary thread results in the two threads competing.

You may notice that its harder to make a menu selection while the first thread is executing. Finally we return from the WM_USER processing.

Starting the Threads

Nothing else happens until the user selects *Resume Threads* from the *Thread Control* menu. When this occurs an IDM_RESUME menu message is sent to WndProc(). We start processing this message by disabling the *Resume Threads* selection and enabling the *Suspend Threads* selection. This prevents the user from selecting *Resume Threads* a second time, which would have no effect anyway.

With the menu set, we call ResumeThread() five times, one call each for the five threads. This call requires only a handle to the thread. By the time we return from the menu message, the threads (based on priority) begin to execute. Remember, we are multitasking now! The threads run independently from our primary thread.

Before we look at the other menu selection, let's take a look at what is happening in the thread procedure.

ThreadProc()

The thread procedure is responsible for drawing a growing rectangle. This procedure will execute independently for each of the five threads. Which thread gets executed is a matter of thread priority. Since the first thread has the highest priority, let's use it as an example.

The thread procedure receives the address of the thread argument. We use this argument to determine the location and color of the rectangle. First, however, we must get the coordinates of the client with a call to GetClientRect(). This fills a RECT structure with the extents of the client area.

A *do-while* loop is started. The test value for the loop is *dwThreadHits*. This variable was initialized to 0 when it was declared at the top of the procedure. The first line in the loop increments the test variable. Next, we obtain a handle to a solid brush using CreateSolidBrush(). The color of the brush is supplied in the argument, in this case an RGB macro. The first parameter in the macro is the thread argument. Notice we use *(ThreadArg)* to obtain the actual variable contents. *ThreadArg* is the *address* to the argument, not the argument itself. Since this is the first thread, the value stored in address *ThreadArg* is HIGHEST_THREAD or 0x00. This value combined with the other two RGB parameters (also 0) creates a black brush.

We follow the brush creation by getting a handle to the DC, then selecting the new brush into it. Note that we are saving the handle to the old brush in *hOldBrush*. We are now ready to draw our first rectangle.

The upper-left corner of the rectangle is defined with the second (x) and third (y) parameters. The second parameter is the thread argument address, *ThreadArg*. Again, we use indirection to gain the contents of the address. Since we're still talking about the first thread, this value is HIGHEST_THREAD, or 0x00. The third parameter is the bottom of the client area minus *dwThreadHits/10*. Since this is the first time through the loop, the upper-left corner of the rectangle is still on the bottom of the client area. The lower-right corner of the rectangle is the thread argument value plus 0x40 and the bottom of the rectangle. This creates a rectangle with a width of 65 pixels (0x00 to 0X40).

The loop body continues by selecting the old brush back into the DC, then deleting the newly created brush with DeleteObject(). We then release the DC and reach the bottom of the loop. Note that the test checks to see if *dwThreadHits* is less than 1000.

As the loop progresses, and *dwThreadHits* increases in value, the rectangle grows upward *(rect.bottom - (dwThreadHits / 10))*. This continues until *dwThreadHits* reaches 1000 and we fall out of the loop. The result? A black rectangle that stands 101 pixels high. The function returns 0. The Win32 subsystem automatically calls ExitThread() with 0 (the return value) as the exit code. This is an *implicit* thread termination. It would have been explicit if ThreadProc() called ExitThread() directly.

Normally you would place most of the code in our *do-while* loop outside of the loop. In fact, the only call that must remain inside the loop is Rectangle(). However, we are demonstrating the effects of busy threads, so we have opted to leave the brush creation and DC-related code inside the loop. This also slows the process a bit, allowing you to observe the results when we run MULTI1.

What Happens in the Other Threads?

The other threads will get their chance to execute. The only difference is the thread argument address (and its contents). The arguments get larger for each thread. For example, the second thread argument was ABOVE_AVE_THREAD, or 0x3F. This value produces a couple of changes.

First the color of the solid brush gets closer to red with each call. This is because we are increasing the R parameter in the RGB macro. Second the rectangle is shifted to the right by the argument value, since the value is used in both x values in the Rectangle() function call.

As long as we don't exit the application, or suspend the threads, we'll eventually end up with five rectangles of identical height. The leftmost rectangle is black (thread argument value == 0x00), and the rightmost rectangle is red (thread argument value == 0xFF).

Suspending the Threads

If the user selects *Suspend Threads* from the *Thread Control* menu an IDM_SUSPEND menu message is sent to WndProc(). We make five SuspendThread() calls to each of the five threads. Recall that this function requires a single parameter, a handle to the thread object. This returns the thread to a suspended state; the ThreadProc() stops executing, that is, the thread is *blocked* from reaching the processor.

If a thread has already terminated, the call to SuspendThread() will fail (return FALSE). However, we are not testing the return value in this example application.

After suspending the threads, we make two calls to EnableMenuItem; one to enable *Resume Threads,* and the other to disable *Suspend Threads.* We could have allowed the user to suspend the thread multiple times, in which case an equal number of calls to ResumeThread () would be required to restart the threads. In this example we restricted this action.

Terminating the Threads

The five threads can be terminated in two ways in MULTI1. They will terminate if the user allows them to complete their respective ThreadProc(). This is the implicit call to ExitThread() mentioned in the description above. The second possibility occurs if the user exits MULTI1 before the threads complete. This is accomplished in the WM_DESTROY code.

Processing WM_DESTROY

If the user exits MULTI1, we process the WM_DESTROY message by making five TerminateThread() calls to each of the five threads. We also check the return value of each call. If the function fails, we beep the speaker with MessageBeep().

What could cause TerminateThread() to fail? If the thread has already terminated (completed the ThreadProc() function), TerminateThread() will fail. For example, if you watch all five threads complete their respective rectangles, then exit MULTI1, the speaker will sound five times (five failures of TerminateThread()).

If you have a multimedia system with sounds enabled, you may not hear all the beeps.

How Many ThreadProc()s Are There in Memory?

Although it may seem that five copies of ThreadProc() are in memory—one for each thread—there is actually one. Recall that a thread context maintains its own priority, a stack, machine registers, and a pointer to ThreadProc(). Since each thread takes turns at the microprocessor level, they share the thread procedure. This is similar to multiple instances of applications in Windows 3.x. They share the same code, but maintain a separate data segment.

Another example of this action in MULTI1 is the variable *dwThreadHits*. Since automatic variables are placed on the stack, and each thread has its own private stack, each thread has its own private *dwThreadHits*.

This completes the description of MULTI1. Let's build our first multitasking application and observe the results.

BUILDING AND USING MULTI1

The MULTI1 program files are located in the \CHAPTER6\6.1 subdirectory. Open a Command Prompt window and change to this directory. Type NMAKE and press (ENTER). The MULTI1 application compiles and links. You can use the Command Prompt to start MULTI1 by typing MULTI1 and pressing (ENTER). However, you may want to add the application to an existing group in the Program Manager, since we will be executing the program more than once.

Review the code in Listings 6-11 through 6-13 while performing the following steps:

1. Select *Resume Threads* from the *Thread Control* menu. Observe the results in the application's client area. Note that while the first thread is executing (black rectangle), no other threads execute. This is a result of priority.

2. Let the threads complete each of their rectangles. Each thread of higher priority prevents lower priority threads from executing. The application window should look like the one shown in Figure 6-5.

3. Double-click the *System* menu (or select *Close* from the *System* menu). You should hear five beeps. These are the five calls to TerminateThread() failing. Refer to the WM_DESTROY message in WndProc() of MULTI1.C (Listing 6-13).

4. Start the MULTI1 program again. Exit MULTI1 without starting the threads. There should be no beeps this time. Since the thread objects were created and left in a suspended state, the TerminateThread() calls in WM_DESTROY terminated the threads; therefore the functions return TRUE each time.

5. Start the MULTI1 program again and select *Resume Threads* from the *Thread Control* menu.

6. While the third thread is executing, select *Suspend Threads* from the *Thread Control* menu. Your display should look similar to Figure 6-6. Keep in mind that Threads 3 through 5 have been suspended. Threads 1 and 2 have completed and terminated via an implicit call

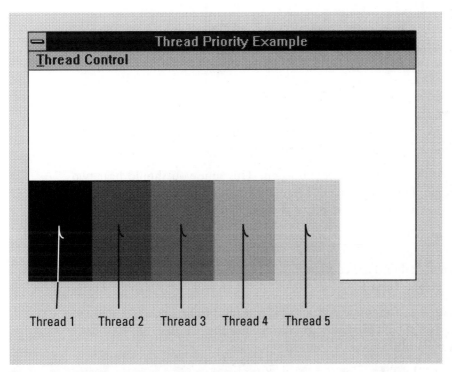

Figure 6-5 MULTI1—all threads completed

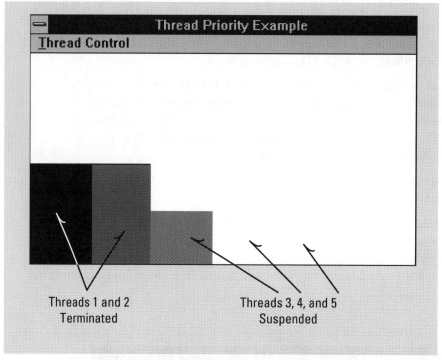

Figure 6-6 MULTI1—suspended threads

to ExitThread(). Therefore; SuspendThread() failed for the first two threads; we did not indicate this in the program with beeps.

7. Exit the MULTI1 program again. This time you should hear two beeps. This is TerminateThread() failing for the first two threads; it's successful for the three active threads, however.

8. Start MULTI1 again. Try suspending the first thread. You may experience some difficulty. The priority for Thread 1 and the primary thread are equal at this point. This makes it more difficult to interrupt Thread 1.

9. Continue to resume and suspend threads during Threads 2 through 5. This should present no problem, since the primary thread priority is higher than the other thread priorities.

10. Exit MULTI1.

What did you learn from this example? You must have a solid strategy when creating threads. You cannot simply assign a high priority to every thread you create. Here are a few tips to consider when creating threads and setting thread priorities:

- If a thread must loop infinitely (not a good idea in the first place), assign the lowest priority to the thread. If the work that the thread performs must be executed immediately, consider a new strategy to get the work done without dominating the scheduler.

- Ensure that high priority threads get in, get the work done, and get out before the rest of the system suffers.

- Pay particular attention to the way the user will interact with your application. Organize your thread strategy so the user interface has a higher priority. This will present a responsive user-interface, while continuing to perform lower priority tasks in the background.

- If a thread must perform a long calculation (requiring lots of processor time), set the priority lower. If the user becomes idle (they do that sometimes!), the lower priority thread will take advantage of the time.

Experimenting with MULTI1

Before we get deeper into the thread subject, let's try a few experiments with MULTI1. We will discuss a phenomenon that you may have already noticed: *dynamic priority.*

Dynamic Priority—Priority Boosting

You may have noticed the effects of dynamic priority during the execution of MULTI1. When you move the mouse cursor over the client area of the main window, the threads slow down. If you didn't notice these effects, run MULTI1 again, resume the threads, and run the mouse cursor over the main window client area.

What you are noticing is dynamic priority. The Windows NT scheduler can temporarily increase the priority of a thread. This occurs when the window that created the thread gains input focus; it also occurs when there is mouse movement over the client area of the window. This is also referred to as a priority boost. In this case it is boosting the priority of the primary thread, and it now has a relatively higher priority than any existing thread.

The window that has the input focus is probably important to the user as well. The scheduler realizes this importance and boosts the priority a level. Once again, the program appears to be responsive.

This is another reason that a thread priority is referred to as a *base priority:* the base priority is a starting point before any priority boost. However the priority level can never be reduced below its base priority level.

This completes the first example program using multitasking. This application provided a good foundation for the concept of threads. Let's take a look at a program that uses two separate thread functions: MULTI2.

MULTIPLE THREAD COMPETITION

Now that we understand the basics of threads, let's create an application that utilizes two separate thread functions. We can produce interesting (and sometimes undesirable) results when two thread functions rely on each other for data.

We'll demonstrate two possible problems with MULTI2: deadlock and race conditions. We'll also introduce one additional API function: Sleep(). Sleep() suspends a thread for a specified amount of time. It is used in MULTI2 to delay threads that simulate problem conditions.

Before we get into the source code for MULTI2, let's look at the two problems we will be demonstrating. We'll take a look at the Sleep() function as well.

Potential Thread Problems

Perhaps the biggest problem for a programmer new to threads is in the fact that they are independent. If you wrote programs for MS-DOS, you had to make a similar adjustment when learning Windows programming. MS-DOS programs took control of the operating system and hardware without having to worry about other programs. Windows programming, however, was message based; you had to wait for Windows to send a message. Upon receipt of a message, you could trap it and execute some code, or you could pass the message back to Windows.

Learning how to create multithreaded applications presents another shift in your mind-set. Under Windows 3.x we could predict, at any given time, what section of code is executing. However, with multiple threads running, you may not know what each thread is doing at any particular time. This can lead to unforeseen problems, especially if your threads rely on each other for data. Let's look at examples of two common thread problems: deadlocks and races.

Deadlocks

Perhaps an analogy can best describe a deadlock. Have you ever been waiting for a phone call from a friend, only to find out that your friend is waiting for a call from you? This is a deadlock. Humans, of course, have the ability to reason. Eventually one of you gets impatient and calls the other (usually followed by a ten-minute discussion of who was supposed to call).

Unfortunately threads do not have the ability to reason. As the old adage goes, a computer does exactly what it's told. Consider this example of a thread deadlock. You create Thread A, which performs a few calculations then waits for a global variable to become valid (for example, anything but NULL). You create Thread B, which also performs some calculations and waits for a different global value to become valid. Thread A is responsible for providing the global value for Thread B, but we haven't yet reached the code in Thread A that provides it. Thread B is responsible for providing the global value for Thread A, and Thread B has not reached the code that provides the value. In this case both threads are waiting for each other to provide a value. This is a deadlock. Figure 6-7 illustrates this condition.

Races

You always want to win a race, right? Not necessarily, if you are a thread. Ponder this description of a race. Once again we have two threads: Thread A and Thread B. Thread A performs some calculations. The last line in Thread A uses a global variable result from Thread B. Thread B also performs some calculations. The last line in Thread B stores the results of its calculations in the global variable referenced by Thread A. The race is on!

If Thread B wins the race, all is well. But if Thread A wins the race, it uses a bogus value because Thread B hasn't supplied it yet. How quickly each thread does its work is a function of the complexity of the code and thread priority level. We could bump up the priority of Thread B, causing it to get more processor time, but we may not know the exact moment that Thread B starts. It may not even get started before Thread A crosses the finish line and takes off with that bogus value. Remember, threads are independent. Figure 6-8 illustrates a successful and a problematic race between threads.

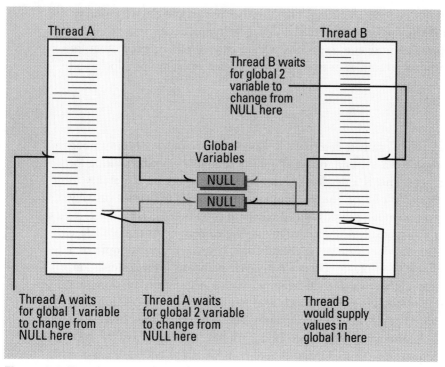

Thread A

Thread B

Thread B waits
for global 2
variable to
change from
NULL here

Global
Variables

NULL

NULL

Thread A waits
for global 1 variable
to change from
NULL here

Thread A waits
for global 2 variable
to change from
NULL here

Thread B
would supply
values in
global 1 here

Figure 6-7 Two threads in a deadlock

Solutions to Thread Deadlocks and Races

After examining these situations, you may think that rearranging the code in
the individual threads could solve these problems. However, since we can't
always predict a thread's behavior (when it starts, which line of code is
executing, and so on), doing so may not be reliable.

Also, in the deadlock example, we simply looped the thread over and over
waiting for a valid value. This is bad programming practice with threads.
Why? If a thread is constantly checking a value, it must be getting processor
time. In this case it is a waste of processor time. We need some kind of signal
when the value the thread needs is available. The best answer to our solution
is thread *synchronization,* which we will explore in Chapter 7, Synchronization
of Threads.

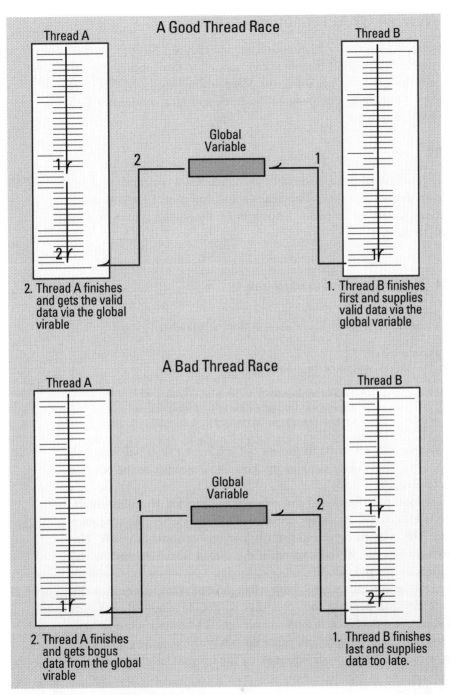

Figure 6-8 A race between threads

Another New Win32 API Function

We are introducing another API function in this chapter: Sleep(). At first glance this function appears as though it can be used to synchronize threads, but this is not the case. We are using the Sleep() function in MULTI2 to produce delays that help us demonstrate deadlock and race conditions. Let's look at the Sleep() function.

Using Sleep()

The Sleep() function suspends a thread's execution for a specified time. Its only argument defines this time. The Sleep() function must be called in the thread that you desire to suspend. Listing 6-14 shows the syntax and an example call to Sleep().

Listing 6-14 Sleep() syntax and example call

```
/* Sleep() Syntax */
VOID Sleep() (DWORD dwMilliSec)      /* milleseconds to sleep */

/* Sleep() Example Calls */
  [place in the thread procedure to suspend]

    Sleep (50);        /* thread suspended for 50 milliseconds */
    Sleep (0);         /* thread relinquishes current timeslice */
    Sleep (INFINITE);  /* thread sleeps infinitely */
```

Three example calls are given in Listing 6-14; however, you will only call one of them in a thread. The examples are shown to demonstrate the possible parameters to Sleep().

In the first example, the thread procedure will sleep for 50 milliseconds, then continue executions. As always, the thread executes when the scheduler permits it to. This is based on thread priority and other running threads. The actual delay may be over 50 milliseconds if the thread is still blocked by the scheduler after the Sleep() call.

The second example calls Sleep() with a 0 argument. This relinquishes the current timeslice and permits the scheduler to decide which thread gets control of the processor. Since threads are processed in round–robin fashion (assuming the same priority level), all other threads with the same priority get a timeslice before the thread procedure making the call gets another timeslice.

The last example causes the thread to sleep infinitely. The argument INFINITE is defined as 0xFFFFFFFF in WINBASE.H. This equates to 4,294,967,295 milliseconds (close to 50 days). This is infinity in relationship to the lifetime of most programs. In this case the thread would probably be terminated by another thread or process.

DEMONSTRATING DEADLOCKS AND RACES

The MULTI2 application demonstrates a thread deadlock and race condition. For good measure, we've also included a thread scenario that actually succeeds. Each demonstration in MULTI2 starts two threads. A growing rectangle indicates the progress of each thread on the display, and messages are supplied on the display and in message boxes.

Listings 6-15 through 6-17 contain the MULTI2 resource script, header file, and partial source file, respectively. We've omitted the makefile from this example. Except for the filenames, the makefile is identical to the one in the MULTI1 example. We've also omitted WinMain() in the source file, since it is typical of all previous examples in this book (excepting MULTI1.C).

Listing 6-15 MULTI2.RC—resource script

```
#include "windows.h"
#include "multi2.h"

Multi2Icon ICON multi2.ico

Multi2Menu MENU
    BEGIN
        POPUP "&Thread Simulation"
        BEGIN
            MENUITEM "&Race",      IDM_RACE
            MENUITEM "&Deadlock",  IDM_DEADLOCK
            MENUITEM "&Success",   IDM_SUCCESS
        END
    END
```

Listing 6-16 MULTI2.H—header file

```
/* multi2.h -- Include file for multi2.c and multi2.rc */

/* Menu defines */
#define IDM_RACE        1
#define IDM_DEADLOCK    2
#define IDM_SUCCESS     3

/* Thread arguments */
#define THREAD_RACE       0x0
#define THREAD_DEADLOCK   0x1
#define THREAD_SUCCESS    0x2

/* Function prototypes */
LONG APIENTRY MainWndProc (HWND, UINT, UINT, LONG);
VOID ThreadProc1 (DWORD *ThreadArg);
VOID ThreadProc2 (DWORD *ThreadArg);

/* Global variables */
HANDLE ghInst;
HANDLE ghWnd;
```

Listing 6-17 MULTI2.C—source file

```
/* multi2.c      Demonstrate thread contention */

#include <windows.h>
#include <stdlib.h>
#include "multi2.h"

/* WndProc - Main Window Procedure for multi2.c */
LONG APIENTRY MainWndProc (HWND hWnd, UINT message, UINT wParam, LONG lParam)
{
DWORD        ThreadID1, ThreadID2;
static HANDLE hThread1, hThread2;
static DWORD  ThreadArg;

   switch (message)
   {

   case WM_COMMAND:
      switch (LOWORD(wParam))
      {
        case IDM_RACE:                            /* demonstrate thread race condition */
           ThreadArg = THREAD_RACE;               /* assign thread argument */
           hThread1 = CreateThread (NULL,         /* create thread 1 */
                              0,
                              (LPTHREAD_START_ROUTINE)ThreadProc1,
                              &ThreadArg,
                              0,
                              &ThreadID1);
```

```
            hThread2 = CreateThread (NULL,           /* create thread 2 */
                              0,
                              (LPTHREAD_START_ROUTINE)ThreadProc2,
                              &ThreadArg,
                              0,
                              (LPDWORD)&ThreadID2);
        return (0);

    case IDM_DEADLOCK:                      /* demonstrate thread deadlock condition */
        ThreadArg = THREAD_DEADLOCK;        /* assign thread argument */
        hThread1 = CreateThread (NULL,      /* create thread 1 */
                              0,
                              (LPTHREAD_START_ROUTINE)ThreadProc1,
                              &ThreadArg,
                              0,
                              &ThreadID1);

            hThread2 = CreateThread (NULL,           /* create thread 2 */
                              0,
                              (LPTHREAD_START_ROUTINE)ThreadProc2,
                              &ThreadArg,
                              0,
                              (LPDWORD)&ThreadID2);
        return (0);

    case IDM_SUCCESS:                       /* demonstrate successful thread condition */
        ThreadArg = THREAD_SUCCESS;         /* assign thread argument */
        hThread1 = CreateThread (NULL,      /* create thread 1 */
                              0,
                              (LPTHREAD_START_ROUTINE)ThreadProc1,
                              &ThreadArg,
                              0,
                              &ThreadID1);

            hThread2 = CreateThread (NULL,           /* create thread 2 */
                              0,
                              (LPTHREAD_START_ROUTINE)ThreadProc2,
                              &ThreadArg,
                              0,
                              (LPDWORD)&ThreadID2);
        return (0);

    default:
        return (0);
    }

case WM_DESTROY :
    TerminateThread(hThread1, 0);                    /* terminate threads */
    TerminateThread(hThread2, 0);
    PostQuitMessage (0);
    return (0);

default:
```

continued on next page

continued from previous page

```
        return DefWindowProc (hWnd, message, wParam, lParam);
   }
   return (OL);
}


/* global variables--modified by thread procedures */
DWORD gdwThreadCheck, gdwDeadlock1, gdwDeadlock2;
DWORD gdwSuccess1, gdwSuccess2;

/* ThreadProc1()--first thread procedure; called by WndProc() */
VOID ThreadProc1 (DWORD *ThreadArg)
{
HDC    hDC;
HANDLE hBrush, hOldBrush;
int    i;

   hDC = GetDC (ghWnd);                            /* get handle to DC */
   hBrush = CreateSolidBrush (RGB (255, 255, 0));  /* create yellow brush */
   hOldBrush = SelectObject (hDC, hBrush);         /* select brush into DC */
   gdwDeadlock1 = gdwSuccess1 = 0;                 /* reset globals */

   switch (*(ThreadArg))                           /* which thread argument? */
   {
      case THREAD_RACE:  /* race demo */
         TextOut (hDC, 0, 0, "Thread 1 (Needs Thread 2 to complete to be successful)", 54);
         for (i = 0; i < 150; i++)
         {
            Rectangle (hDC, 0, 20, i, 40);          /* draw rectangle to simulate progress */
            Sleep (1);   /* short nap */
         }
         if (gdwThreadCheck != 100)                 /* check to see if thread 2 did its job */
            MessageBox (ghWnd,                      /* display message if not */
                     "Thread 2 did not supply the correct value in time",
                     "Thread 1 Won The Race!",
                     MB_OK | MB_ICONEXCLAMATION);
         break;

      case THREAD_DEADLOCK:                         /* deadlock demo */
         TextOut (hDC, 0, 0, "Thread 1 (Checking value from Thread 2 at count 75)", 51);
         for (i = 0; i < 150; i++)
         {
            Rectangle (hDC, 0, 20, i, 40);          /* draw rectangle to simulate progress */
            Sleep (5);   /* delay */
            if (i == 75 && gdwDeadlock2 != 100)     /* check to see if thread 2 did its job */
               TextOut (hDC, 5, 40, "FAILED", 6);   /* display message if not */
         }
         gdwDeadlock1 = 100;                        /* modify global indicating completion */
         MessageBox (ghWnd,                         /* display message indicating failure */
                  "Thread 1 was waiting for Thread 2 to modify gdwDeadLock2",
                  "DEADLOCK!",
                  MB_OK | MB_ICONEXCLAMATION);
         break;

      case THREAD_SUCCESS:                          /* success demo */
```

```
        TextOut (hDC, 0, 0, "Thread 1 (Checking value from Thread 2 in middle of loop)", 57);
        for (i = 0; i < 150; i++)
        {
            Rectangle (hDC, 0, 20, i, 40);          /* draw rectangle to simulate progress */
            Sleep (5);                              /* delay */
        }
        gdwSuccess1 = 100;                          /* modify global indicating completion */
        if (gdwSuccess2 == 100)                     /* check to see if thread 2 did its job */
            MessageBox (ghWnd,                      /* display message indicating success */
                    "Thread 1 found valid information from Thread 2",
                    "SUCCESS!",
                    MB_OK | MB_ICONEXCLAMATION);
        break;

    default:
        break;
    }
    hBrush = SelectObject (hDC, hOldBrush);         /* select old brush into DC */
    DeleteObject (hBrush);                          /* delete brush */
    ReleaseDC (ghWnd, hDC);                         /* release the DC */
    InvalidateRect (ghWnd, NULL, TRUE);             /* force WM_PAINT to cleanup */

}

/* ThreadProc2()--second thread procedure; called by WndProc() */
VOID ThreadProc2 (DWORD *ThreadArg)
{
HDC     hDC;
HANDLE hBrush, hOldBrush;
int     i;

    hDC = GetDC (ghWnd);                            /* get handle to DC */
    hBrush = CreateSolidBrush (RGB (0, 255, 255));  /* create cyan brush */
    hOldBrush = SelectObject (hDC, hBrush);         /* select brush into DC */
    gdwThreadCheck = gdwDeadlock2 = gdwSuccess2 = 0;/* reset globals */

    switch (*(ThreadArg))                           /* which thread argument? */
    {
    case THREAD_RACE:                               /* race demo */
        TextOut (hDC, 0, 60, "Thread 2 (Must complete before Thread 1 to be successful)", 57);
        for (i = 0; i < 150; i++)
        {
            Rectangle (hDC, 0, 80, i, 100);         /* draw rectangle to simulate progress */
            Sleep (10);                             /* longer nap than thread 1 */
        }
        gdwThreadCheck = 100;                       /* modify global to indicate completion */
        break;

    case THREAD_DEADLOCK:                           /*deadlock demo */
        TextOut (hDC, 0, 60, "Thread 2 (Checking value from Thread 1 at count 75)", 51);
        for (i = 0; i < 150; i++)
        {
            Rectangle (hDC, 0, 80, i, 100);         /* draw rectangle to simulate progress */
```

continued on next page

continued from previous page

```
            Sleep (5);                              /* delay */
            if (i == 75 && gdwDeadlock1 != 100)     /* check to see if thread 1 did its job */
                TextOut (hDC, 5, 100, "FAILED", 6); /* display message if not */
        }
        gdwDeadlock2 = 100;                         /* modify global indicating completion */
        MessageBox (ghWnd,                          /* display message indicating failure */
                "Thread 2 was waiting for Thread 1 to modify gdwDeadLock1",
                "DEADLOCK!",
                MB_OK | MB_ICONEXCLAMATION);
        break;

    case THREAD_SUCCESS:                            /* success demo */
        TextOut (hDC, 0, 60, "Thread 2 (Checking value from Thread 1 at end of loop)", 54);
        for (i = 0; i < 150; i++)
        {
            Rectangle (hDC, 0, 80, i, 100);         /* draw rectangle indication progress */
            Sleep (10);                             /* longer delay than thread 1 */
            if (i == 75)
                gdwSuccess2 = 100;                  /* modify global in middle of loop */
        }
        if (gdwSuccess1 == 100)                     /* check to see if thread 1 did its job */
            MessageBox (ghWnd,                      /* display message indicating success */
                "Thread 2 found valid information from Thread 1",
                "SUCCESS!",
                MB_OK | MB_ICONEXCLAMATION);
        break;

    default:
        break;
    }
    hBrush = SelectObject (hDC, hOldBrush);         /* select old brush into DC */
    DeleteObject (hBrush);                          /* delete brush */
    ReleaseDC (ghWnd, hDC);                         /* release the DC */
}
```

Overview of MULTI2

MULTI2 has one popup menu, *Thread Simulation,* that has three selections: *Race, Deadlock,* and *Success.* Each of these selections creates two threads; the same thread argument is sent to both. The thread arguments determine which problem we're simulating. For example, the THREAD_RACE argument (defined in MULTI2.H as 0x0) informs the threads to simulate a race simulation. The *Success* selection demonstrates how multiple threads can execute successfully without synchronization. You should never depend on it, however. We'll cover this in more detail in the *Success* segment that follows. Let's look at each menu selection one at a time.

The Race

When the user selects *Race* from the *Thread Simulation* menu, an IDM_RACE menu message is sent to WndProc(). We set the thread argument *(ThreadArg)* to THREAD_RACE. We then create two threads. The first uses ThreadProc1() and the second uses ThreadProc2(). Both calls to CreateThread() use 0 as the fifth parameter. This means that the threads start to execute immediately. Notice that the same thread argument is sent to both thread procedures. Let's go through ThreadProc1() first.

ThreadProc1()—THREAD_RACE

The first thing we do in ThreadProc1() is get a handle to a device context, create a solid yellow brush, and select the brush into the DC. Next, we reach a *switch* statement with *(ThreadArg)* as its expression. In this case this equates to THREAD_RACE. We also reset the global variables modified by this procedure; however, they are not used with this menu selection.

We display a message indicating that Thread 2 must complete in order for Thread 1 to be successful. We then use a *for* loop to draw the expanding rectangle. Each time we pass through the loop, we call Sleep() to delay the thread for a millisecond. This slows the thread slightly, enabling the user to see the thread progress.

Once the rectangle is complete (and the thread is virtually complete), we check a global variable *(gdwThreadCheck)* to see if it is set to 100. The globals used in MULTI2 are defined above ThreadProc1(). They are initially set to 0.

If the value is not ready (that is, does not equal 100), we display a message indicating that Thread 2 did not set the *gdwThreadCheck* in time. If *gdwThreadCheck* is 100, we simply exit the loop. Keep in mind that we are going to cause it to fail purposely.

Following the switch body, we clean up by getting the old brush, deleting the yellow brush, releasing the DC. Finally we call InvalidateRect() which redraws a clear client area. Now let's check out ThreadProc2() using the same thread argument.

ThreadProc2()—THREAD_RACE

Since both calls to CreateThread() in WndProc() used the same argument, we'll follow the code assuming *(ThreadArg)* is THREAD_RACE. Like ThreadProc1(), ThreadProc2() gets a handle to the device context, only it uses a cyan brush. We also reset the global variables.

A similar *switch* statement to that in ThreadProc1() is also used in ThreadProc2(). Since *gdwThreadArg* is THREAD_RACE, we display a message indicating that this thread must complete before Thread 1 to be successful. Next, we start a *for* loop that creates another growing rectangle. We call Sleep() each time through the loop. Since ThreadProc2() sleeps for 5 milliseconds (compared to one in ThreadProc1()), it will take ThreadProc2() longer to execute.

The last step in THREAD_RACE is to set *dwThreadCheck* to 100. By now you can tell this will occur too late, since Thread 2 sleeps longer than Thread 1. Thread 1 has already checked the value and issued the message box. Following the switch body, we clean up by getting the old brush, deleting the cyan brush, and releasing the DC. We do not call InvalidateRect() to clear the display, since ThreadProc1() is taking care of that. Let's look at the deadlock example.

A Deadlock

We don't want to create an actual deadlock; that would result in two threads that never complete. For our example we will simulate the conditions that would cause a deadlock; yet we'll allow the threads to run after checking for the appropriate values.

In this case the user selects *Deadlock* from the *Thread Simulation* menu. Again, two threads are created, only this time the thread argument is THREAD_DEADLOCK. Since we have seen most of the code in ThreadProc1() and ThreadProc2(), we'll only discuss the differences.

ThreadProc1()—THREAD_DEADLOCK

A message is displayed, indicating that this thread will check the value from Thread 1 at count 75 of the *for* loop. We use the *for* loop in a similar manner as the race example. This time we use Sleep() to suspend the thread for 5 milliseconds. When the loop reaches 75, we check *gdwDeadLock* to see if it has been set to 100 by Thread 2. Since Thread 2 is also suspended for 5 milliseconds, and modifies *gdwDeadlock2* at the end of its *for* loop, the value is not ready yet. We display some text on the DC indicating that the check failed.

In an actual deadlock, the thread would be stuck waiting for the value; therefore, it would be unable to continue. For this example, we check the global variable, then continue. At the end of the *for* loop, we set Thread 1's global, *gdwDeadLock,* to 100. Thread 2 will be checking this value at count 75 of its *for* loop.

Finally we display a message box indicating that Thread 1 was waiting for Thread 2 to modify *gdwDeadlock2.* In actuality we let the thread run past this point. Let's look at ThreadProc2() for the deadlock simulation.

ThreadProc2()—THREAD_DEADLOCK

ThreadProc2() also uses a similar *for* loop to that used in ThreadProc1(). The only difference is that it checks the value of *gdwDeadlock1* (the global variable modified by ThreadProc1()). This will fail, since Thread 1 sets *gdwDeadlock1* at the end of the loop. ThreadProc2() sets *gdwDeadlock2* to 100 following the *for* loop. This is too late, however. ThreadProc1() was checking this value earlier.

A message box is displayed indicating that Thread 2 was waiting (simulated) for Thread 1 to modify *gdwDeadlock1*.

ThreadProc1() and ThreadProc2()—THREAD_SUCCESS

The last menu selection creates a success situation. ThreadProc1() calls Sleep() for 5 milliseconds and ThreadProc2() calls Sleep() for 10 milliseconds; therefore, ThreadProc2() takes longer to execute. ThreadProc1() checks *gdwSuccess2* and sets *gdwSuccess1* at the end of its *for* loop. ThreadProc2() sets *gdwSuccess2* in the middle of its *for* loop and tests *gdwSuccess1* at the end of the loop. Even though ThreadProc2() takes longer to execute, it modifies *gdwSuccess2* before ThreadProc1() completes (which is when ThreadProc1() checks *gdwSuccess2*).

What we've done here is to create an admittedly controlled situation that guarantees success. This will not be the case in practical applications using multiple threads. There will probably be no way to gauge how much time a particular thread takes; therefore, it may be necessary to *synchronize* the threads. The thread synchronization topic is covered exclusively in Chapter 7, Synchronization of Threads. Let's build MULTI2 to see the visual effect of these multiple, nonsynchronized threads.

BUILDING AND USING MULTI2

The MULTI2 program files are located in the \CHAPTER6\6.2 subdirectory. Open a Command Prompt window and change to this directory. Type NMAKE and press (ENTER). The MULTI2 application compiles and links. You can use the Command Prompt to start MULTI2 by typing MULTI2 and pressing (ENTER). You also can add the application to an existing group in the Program Manager.

Review the code in Listings 6-15 through 6-17 while performing the following steps:

1. Select *Race* from the *Thread Simulation* menu. Observe the results in the application's client area. Also refer to the MULTI2 source file (Listing 6-17); pay particular attention to the THREAD_RACE

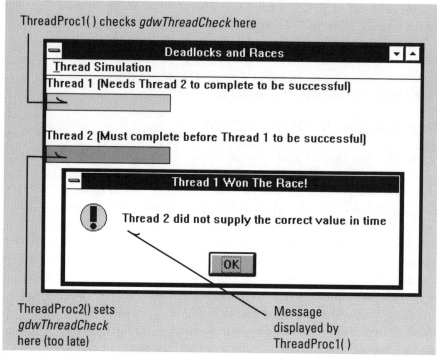

Figure 6-9 MULTI2—race simulation

cases in ThreadProc1() and ThreadProc2(). Note that ThreadProc1() wins the race; therefore, ThreadProc2() doesn't modify the global *(dwThreadCheck)* in time. Figure 6-9 shows the results from the *Race* menu selection.

2. Select *Deadlock* from the *Thread Simulation* menu. Observe the results in the application's client area. Again refer to the MULTI2 source file; this time review the THREAD_DEADLOCK cases in ThreadProc1() and ThreadProc2(). Note that ThreadProc1() and ThreadProc2() check *gdwDeadlock2* and *gdwDeadlock1,* respectively. Neither value was correct, since both thread procedures modify the global variables at the end of the loop. Figure 6-10 shows the results from the *Deadlock* menu selection.

3. Select *Success* from the *Thread Simulation* menu. Observe the results in the application's client area. Again refer to the MULTI2 source file; this time review the THREAD_SUCCESS cases in ThreadProc1() and ThreadProc2(). ThreadProc1() checks *gdwSuccess2* at the end of the loop; ThreadProc2() modified it in the middle of its *for* loop.

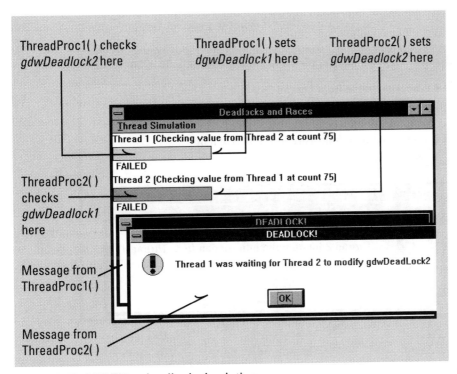

ThreadProc1( ) checks *gdwDeadlock2* here

ThreadProc1( ) sets *dgwDeadlock1* here

ThreadProc2( ) sets *gdwDeadlock2* here

ThreadProc2( ) checks *gdwDeadlock1* here

Message from ThreadProc1( )

Message from ThreadProc2( )

Figure 6-10 MULTI2—deadlock simulation

ThreadProc2() checks *gdwSuccess1* at the end of its *for* loop; ThreadProc1() has already finished and modified *gdwSuccess1*. Figure 6-11 shows the results from the *Success* menu selection.

4. Exit MULTI2.

This completes our example application demonstrating thread contention. We will need to cover more multitasking topics before we correct the problems demonstrated in this example. Let's shift the focus from threads to processes.

CREATING PROCESSES IN WIN32

Windows 3.x provided two ways for an application to start another application or module: WinExec() and LoadModule(). These functions still exist in the Win32 API, but for backward compatibility only. New Win32

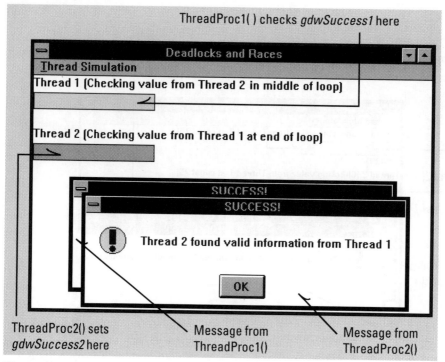

Figure 6-11 MULTI2—success simulation

applications should call CreateProcess(). This segment of this chapter discusses and demonstrates process creation. We will examine the various process-related functions, then demonstrate them in our next example application, MULTI3. Before we do that, however, let's review exactly what a process is.

Definition of a Win32 Process

A process is an application consisting of virtual address space, code, data, and other resources (such as files). Recall that a process always contains a primary thread. It is actually the primary thread that gets processor time via the scheduler. Figure 6-12 illustrates two processes in virtual memory. Each process has created two additional threads using the same thread function.

So we don't cloud the issue at hand, let's assume all threads in the figure are the same priority. The scheduler determines which thread gets a timeslice on the processor. If all threads are the same priority, the threads share timeslices in round-robin fashion. There are six thread contexts in Figure 6-12:

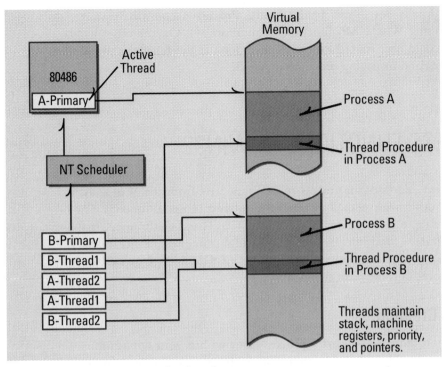

Figure 6-12 Two processes in virtual memory

◿ primary thread for Process A

◿ primary thread for Process B

◿ Thread 1 in Process A

◿ Thread 2 in Process A

◿ Thread 1 in Process B

◿ Thread 2 in Process B

The figure shows that processes have their own private space in memory, and that a process always contains a primary thread. Currently the primary thread for Process A is executing. When its timeslice expires, the primary thread for Process B starts to execute.

Threads (created with CreateThread()) on the other hand, share code, data, and resources with the process that created them. They can maintain their own private data in the form of automatic variables. This is possible because each thread maintains its own stack.

Although it is not shown in the figure, Process A could have started Process B using Win32 API function CreateProcess(). On the other hand, Process B could have started Process A. Let's look at the functions that deal with creating and managing processes in Win32.

PROCESS FUNCTIONS IN WIN32

This segment addresses six process-related functions from the Win32 API. Only one deals with actually creating a process: CreateProcess(). Two functions relate to process priority: SetPriorityClass() and GetPriorityClass(). The last three functions relate to exiting processes: ExitProcess(), TerminateProcess(), and GetExitCodeProcess(). Of these three general areas, creating processes is the most significant.

Process Creation

The function required to start a process from within your applications is CreateProcess(). This function requires several parameters, however, most of which have several possible values. Let's break down and examine the CreateProcess() function.

Using CreateProcess()

The CreateProcess() function creates a new process as its own private virtual address. It also creates the new process's primary thread. CreateProcess() requires ten parameters. Some of these parameters are simple, while others have numerous possibilities. Let's start with the syntax and an example call to CreateProcess(). Listing 6-18 contains this information. The CreateProcess() example call refers you to other listings and tables, which break down the individual parameters further.

Listing 6-18 CreateProcess() syntax and example call

```
/* CreateProcess() Syntax */
BOOL CreateProcess (LPCTSTR lpszImageName,          /* address of module name */
                    LPCTSTR lpszCommandLine,         /* address of command line */
                    LPSECURITY_ATTRIBUTES lpsaProcess, /* address of process security */
                    LPSECURITY_ATTRIBUTES lpsaThread,  /* address of thread security */
```

```
                    BOOL fInheritHandles,              /* does new process inherit handles? */
                    DWORD dwCreate,                    /* process creation flags */
                    LPVOID lpvEnvironment,             /* address of environment block */
                    LPTSTR lpszCurDir,                 /* address of current directory name */
                    LPSTARTUPINFO lpsiStartInfo,       /* address of SI structure */
                    LPPROCESS_INFORMATION);            /* address to store process information */

/* CreateProcess() Example Call */
PROCESS_INFORMATION piProcInfo;
STARTUPINFO          suiStartInfo;

    suiStartInfo.cb                  = sizeof (STARTUPINFO);   /* STARTUPINFO structure */
    suiStartInfo.lpReserved          = NULL;                   /* refer to Listing 6-19 */
    suiStartInfo.lpDeskTop           = NULL;
    suiStartInfo.lpTitle             = NULL
    suiStartInfo.dwX                 = 0;
    suiStartInfo.dwY                 = 0;
    suiStartInfo.dwXSize             = 0;
    suiStartInfo.dwYSize             = 0;
    suiStartInfo.dwXCountChars       = 0;
    suiStartInfo.dwYCountChars       = 0;
    suiStartInfo.dwFillAttribute     = 0;
    suiStartInfo.dwFlags             = 0;
    suiStartInfo.wShowWindow         = 0;
    suiStartInfo.cbReserved2         = 0;
    suiStartInfo.lpReserved2         = NULL;

    CreateProcess ("GENERIC.EXE",   /* start module GENERIC.EXE */
                NULL,               /* no command line */
                NULL,               /* no process security */
                NULL,               /* no primary thread security */
                FALSE,              /* doesn't inherit handles of caller */
                0,                  /* no creation flags (see Table 6-2) */
                NULL,               /* no new environment */
                NULL,               /* no startup directory */
                &suiStartInfo,      /* address of STARTUPINFO structure (filled above) */
                &piProcInfo);       /* address of PROCESS_INFORMATION structure (Listing 6-20) */
```

Our example call starts a process (GENERIC.EXE) in its own private
virtual address space. Note that most of the parameters in CreateProcess() and
the members of the STARTUPINFO structure are NULL or 0. In most cases
this is sufficient. To fully exploit CreateProcess(), however, we will discuss its
individual parameters.

Parameter 1—Image Name

The first parameter to CreateProcess() points to a null-terminated string
specifying the module (executable file) with which the process is created.
This can be a full path and filename, or a portion of the full path and
filename. If a full path is not supplied, the current directory is used. For

example, the call in Listing 6-18 specifies GENERIC.EXE. This assumes that this executable file is in the current directory. If this parameter is NULL, the command line pointed to by parameter 2 must specify the executable filename.

Parameter 2—Command Line

This parameter points to a null-terminated string specifying the command-line parameters for the executable file. If parameter 1 is NULL, the first token in the command-line string indicates the executable filename. In this case the system searches (in order) the current directory, the Windows system directory, the Windows directory, and directories specified in the PATH environment variable.

Parameters 3,4, and 5—Security

Parameter 3 points to a SECURITY_ATTRIBUTES structure indicating the security level of the new process. Parameter 4 points to a SECURITY_ATTRIBUTES structure indicating the security level of the primary thread of the new process. Parameter 5 is a Boolean value specifying whether or not the new process should inherit any open handles from the calling process. Security attributes are discussed in detail in Chapter 8, NT System Security.

Parameter 6—Creation Flags

Parameter 6 is a DWORD containing creation flags. There are many possible combinations for this parameter. Some deal with console (nongraphical interface) applications or debugging. Although the focus of this book is GUI applications, we'll touch on console processes lightly in MULTI3; therefore some of the basic console flags require discussion. Table 6-2 shows the creation flags for the sixth parameter of CreateProcess(). Console windows are character-based windows (such as the Command Prompt).

Parameter 7—Environment Block

This parameter points to an *environment block* for the new process. The environment block consists of a collection of null-terminated strings. The individual strings are separated by NULLs. The format for an environment string is *name=value*. For example, your system (if you are using an 80386/486 processor and you have installed the Win32 SDK) is *cpu=i386*.

Flag	Description
CREATE_SUSPENDED	Creates the primary thread of the new process in a suspended state. See Parameter 10 for more information.
DETACHED_PROCESS	For console (non-GUI) applications. New process does not have access to console of creating process. The new process must create its own console if needed. Cannot be combined with CREATE_NEW_CONSOLE.
CREATE_NEW_CONSOLE	For console (non-GUI) applications. New process creates a console (does not inherit calling process's console). Cannot be combined with DETACHED_PROCESS.
IDLE_PRIORITY_CLASS	Creates a process that will only run when the system is idle.
NORMAL_PRIORITY_CLASS	Creates a process with normal priority.
HIGH_PRIORITY_CLASS	Creates a process with high priority. Only use this attribute with processes that are very time-critical.
REALTIME_PRIORITY_CLASS	Creates a process with the highest priority. This priority level will compete with system level functions. Use only if the process will execute quickly.

Table 6-2 Creation flags—Parameter 6 of CreateProcess()

Parameter 8—Startup Directory

This parameter points to a null-terminated string indicating the full path (drive/directory) for the new process. This is similar to setting the working directory in the *File-Properties* menu of the Program Manager.

Parameter 9—STARTUPINFO structure

This parameter points to a STARTUPINFO structure. This member of this structure was filled before calling CreateProcess() in Listing 6-18. Listing 6-19 shows the members of this structures and their meaning. Most of the parameters are associated with console applications. Table 6-3 breaks down the *dwFlags* member. Table 6-4 breaks down the *wShowWindow* member.

Flag	Purpose
STARTF_USESHOWWINDOW	If NULL, ignore *wShowWindow* in STARTUPINFO.
STARTF_USEPOSITION	If NULL, ignore *dwX* and *dwY* in STARTUPINFO.
STARTF_USESIZE	If NULL, ignore *dwXSize* and *dwYSize* in STARTUPINFO.
STARTF_USECOUNTCHARS	If NULL, ignore *dwXCountChars* and *dwYCountChars* in STARTUPINFO.
STARTF_USEFILLATTRIBUTE	If NULL, ignore *dwFillAttribute* in STARTUPINFO.
STARTF_FORCEONFEEDBACK	Feedback cursor is enabled (watches console apps for GUI calls and allows them time to paint their screens).
STARTF_FORCEOFFFEEDBACK	Feedback cursor is disabled.
STARTF_SCREENSAVER	Treat application as screen saver.
STARTF_USESTDHANDLES	Set standard I/O.

Table 6-3 dwFlags member of STARTUPINFO

Listing 6-19 STARTUPINFO structure

```
typedef struct _STARTUPINFO{
    DWORD   cb;                 /* size of the structure in bytes */
    LPSTR   lpReserved;         /* reserved-must be null */
    LPSTR   lpDesktop;          /* pointer to different desktop */
    LPSTR   lpTitle;            /* title for console applications */
    DWORD   dwX;                /* x offset of upper-left corner (only with STARTF_USEPOSITION) */
    DWORD   dwY;                /* y offset of upper-left corner (only with STARTF_USEPOSITION) */
    DWORD   dwXSize;            /* width of window (only with STARTF_USESIZE) */
    DWORD   dwYSize;            /* height of window (only with STARTF_USESIZE) */
    DWORD   dwXCountChars;      /* screen buffer width (only with STARTF_USECOUNTCHARS) */
    DWORD   dwYCountChars;      /* screen buffer width (only with STARTF_USECOUNTCHARS) */
    DWORD   dwFillAttribute;    /* screen fill attributes (only with STARTF_USEFILLATTRIBUTE) */
    DWORD   dwFlags;            /* determines which member of STARTUPINFO are used (see Table 6-3) */
    WORD    wShowWindow;        /* affects ShowWindow() in WinMain() of new process (see Table 6-4) */
    WORD    cbReserved2;        /* reserved-must be 0 */
    LPBYTE  lpReserved2;        /* reserved-must be NULL */
} STARTUPINFO;
```

The values listed in Table 6-4 can be used in the *wShowWindow* member of STARTUPINFO. The *dwFlags* member must be STARTF_USESHOWWINDOW for these values to have any effect.

wShowWindow	Purpose
SW_SHOWMAXIMIZED	Shows window maximized and activates window.
SW_SHOWMINIMIZED	Shows window minimized and activates icon.
SW_SHOWMINNOACTIVE	Shows window minimized. The current active window remains active.
SW_SHOWNORMAL	Shows window using parameters in CreateWindow().
SW_RESTORE	Same as SW_SHOWNORMAL.

Table 6-4 wShowWindow member of STARTUPINFO

Parameter 10—PROCESS_INFORMATION Structure

The last parameter to CreateProcess() is a pointer to a PROCESS_INFORMATION structure. The CreateProcess() function fills this structure with handle and ID information. You can use this information in subsequent calls that require a handle to a process or a thread. For example, if you wanted to change the priority of the primary thread, you could call SetThreadPriority() using the handle from this structure along with the new priority value. Listing 6-20 shows the PROCESS_INFORMATION structure.

Listing 6-20 PROCESS_INFORMATION structure

```
typedef struct _PROCESS_INFORMATION {
    HANDLE hProcess;
    HANDLE hThread;
    DWORD dwProcessId;
    DWORD dwThreadId;
} PROCESS_INFORMATION;
```

The example call in Listing 6-18 used *piProcInfo* to pass as the tenth parameter to CreateProcess(). If you wanted to change the priority of the primary thread you could do the following:

```
SetThreadPriority (piProcInfo.hThread, THREAD_PRIORITY_ABOVE_NORMAL);
```

This would change the priority of the new process's primary thread to above normal. We'll see in a moment how to change the priority class of the new process. First, let's summarize the call to CreateProcess().

Summary of CreateProcess()

As you can see, there are many possibilities and combinations of parameters to CreateProcess(). However, for most applications, you will not need to use many of them. Most values can be NULL or 0 (depending on the data type of the member). If you find that your application requires a window to appear in a particular way, you can experiment with the various members until the desired results are achieved.

We've seen how to create a process from within an application. Now let's take a look at changing the priority *class* of the newly created process.

Priority Classes

We first discussed priority classes of processes earlier in this chapter. Table 6-1 listed the possible priority classes of processes and priorities of threads. Recall that there are four priority classes for processes:

- IDLE_PRIORITY_CLASS
- NORMAL_PRIORITY_CLASS
- HIGH_PRIORITY_CLASS
- REALTIME_PRIORITY_CLASS

Two Win32 API functions relate to priority classes: SetPriorityClass() and GetPriorityClass(). Getting and setting priority class is very similar to getting and setting thread priority level. The difference is that you are changing the priority level of the process, which in turn changes the base priority of the threads within that process. Let's look at the SetPriorityClass() and GetPriorityClass() functions.

Using GetPriorityClass() and SetPriorityClass()

GetPriorityClass() and SetPriorityClass() let you get and set the priority of a given process. Processes started with CreateProcess() have NORMAL_PRIORITY_CLASS by default. This is usually sufficient for most applications. The other priority levels are used in special cases. For example, the IDLE_PRIORITY_CLASS results in a process getting processor time only when the system is idle. Screen savers would benefit from this class since no other activity would be taking place.

Both calls require a valid handle to a process. In addition, SetPriorityClass() requires a DWORD specifying the new priority class. Listing 6-21 shows the proper syntax and example calls for GetPriorityClass() and SetPriorityClass(). The example calls assume a process has been created and assigned to *hProcess*. Recall that you can use the *hProcess* member of the PROCESS_INFORMATION structure as this handle.

Listing 6-21 GetPriorityClass() and SetPriorityClass() syntax and example calls

```
/* GetPriorityClass() Syntax */
DWORD GetPriorityClass (HANDLE hProcess);  /* valid handle to process */

/* SetPriorityClass() Syntax */
BOOL SetPriorityClass (HANDLE hThread,      /* valid handle to process */
                       DWORD dwPriority);  /* new priority class value */

/* GetPriorityClass() and SetPriorityClass() Example Calls */
DWORD nOldPriority, nNewPriority;

   nOldPriority = GetPriorityClass (hProcess);  /* save current priority */
   nNewPriority = HIGH_PRIORITY_CLASS;          /* assign new priority */
   SetPriorityClass (hProcess, nNewPriority);   /* set new priority */
```

GetPriorityClass() requires a valid process handle and returns a DWORD indicating the current priority class of the process. This value can be one of those listed in Table 6-1 earlier in this chapter. If the function fails it returns 0.

SetPriorityClass() requires a valid process handle and a DWORD specifying the new priority class. In the example call, we assign HIGH_PRIORITY_CLASS to a DWORD variable. We use this variable as the second parameter to SetPriorityClass(). This function returns a Boolean value indicating success (TRUE) or failure (FALSE).

Process Termination

Terminating, or exiting, a process is very similar to terminating threads. There are four ways a process can terminate: the process WinMain() or main() function returns, an explicit call to ExitProcess(), a call to TerminateProcess(), or an unhandled exception in the process. Of these four, the first two are the more desirable ways to exit a process. Both these methods notify attached DLLs (if any). Let's examine the TerminateProcess() function.

Using TerminateProcess()

This function terminates a process without regard to attached DLLs or user-mode code. This means that the process will be interrupted and terminated regardless of the code it may be executing. TerminateProcess() requires two parameters: a valid handle to the process to terminate and an exit code. Listing 6-22 shows the syntax and an example call to this function.

Listing 6-22 TerminateProcess() syntax and example call

```
/* TerminateProcess() Syntax */
BOOL TerminateProcess (HANDLE hProcess,     /* valid process handle */
                       DWORD  dwExitCode); /* exit code */

/* TerminateProcess() Example Call */
DWORD dwExitCode;

   dwExitCode = 0;                            /* set exit code */
   TerminateProcess (hProcess, dwExitCode);  /* kill process and change termination status */
```

In this example call, the exit code is set to 0 arbitrarily. You can set the exit code to any value other than 0x103 (259 decimal). Why not use this value? As with threads, if a process is still active, the exit code is STILL_ACTIVE. STILL_ACTIVE is defined in WINBASE.H as STATUS_PENDING. STATUS_PENDING is defined in WINNT.H as 0x103.

With the exit code variable set to 0, we call TerminateProcess() with a valid process handle and *dwExitCode.* The process termination status changes from STILL_ACTIVE to 0 and the process is stopped. No attached DLLs (if any) are notified that the process has been terminated.

TerminateProcess() returns a Boolean indicating success (TRUE) or failure (FALSE). Examples of failure are an invalid process handle or the process is already terminated.

Using ExitProcess()

This process termination call is the preferred method of terminating a process. This call is made from within the process itself. Therefore ExitProcess() requires only one parameter: the exit code. This exit code not only specifies the exit code of the process; it also specifies the exit codes for all threads within the process. Listing 6-23 shows the syntax and an example call to ExitProcess(). We are assuming the call is made in WndProc() of the process; however, you can call ExitProcess() from other functions within a process.

Listing 6-23 ExitProcess() syntax and example call

```
/* ExitProcess() Syntax */
VOID ExitProcess (UINT uExitCode);    /* exit code for process and all threads */

/* ExitProcess() Example Call */
LONG APIENTRY WndProc (HWND hWnd, UINT message, UINT wParam, LONG lParam)
{
   [program lines for process's WndProc()]

   ExitProcess (0);                   /* exit process and set termination status to 0 */
}
```

As you can see by the example call, the usage of ExitProcess() is fairly straightforward. We return from the process's WndProc() procedure setting the process termination status to 0. ExitProcess() does not return a value. How can we find out what exit value ExitProcess(), TerminateProcess(), or a process procedure (WinMain() or main()) return value specified? The answer is in our next call, GetExitCodeProcess().

Using GetExitCodeProcess()

This function obtains the current termination status (exit code) of a specific process. The function requires two parameters: a valid handle to a process and an address to store the termination status. Listing 6-24 shows the syntax and an example call to GetExitCodeProcess().

Listing 6-24 GetExitCodeProcess() syntax and example call

```
/* GetExitCodeProcess() Syntax */
BOOL GetExitCodeProcess (HANDLE hProcess,        /* valid process handle */
                         LPDWORD lpdwExitCode);  /* address to store termination status */

/* GetExitCodeProcess() Example Call */
DWORD dwExitCode;

   GetExitCodeProcess (hProcess, &dwExitCode);   /* get termination status */
   if (dwExitCode == STILL_ACTIVE)               /* is process still active? */
      MessageBeep (0);                           /* beep if it is */
```

In this example, we get the termination status of a process. This status is placed in *dwExitCode*. We supplied the address of this DWORD in the GetExitCodeProcess() call. We then compare the results to the STILL_ACTIVE define (0x103). If the process is still active, we beep the PC speaker.

If the process had been terminated before the call to GetExitCodeProcess(), *dwExitCode* would be set to a termination status. Depending on the method of termination, this value was set by one of the following:

- the exit code specified in a call to ExitProcess() (within a process's procedure)

- the exit code specified in a call to TerminateProcess()

- the return value of the process procedure (WinMain() or main())

- an exception code, if the process terminated from an unhandled exception

The last possibility would occur if an exception occurred that the application didn't handle. For example, if the application tried to write to a memory address that had not been reserved and committed, a page fault would occur. If the application did not handle the exception (for example, with structured exception handling), it would exit immediately. The exception code for this occurrence would be available in *dwExitCode* after a call to GetExitCodeProcess(). An example of structured exception handling is given in Chapter 3, Memory Management.

Using GetCurrentProcess()

A process, like a thread, is not aware of its own handle while it's executing; but on some occasions a process needs to know its handle. For example, if you wanted to give a process the ability to change its priority class, the process would need the handle required in the SetPriorityClass() call. GetCurrentProcess() returns a handle to the process making the call. It does not require any parameters. Listing 6-25 shows the syntax and an example call to GetCurrentProcess().

Listing 6-25 GetCurrentProcess() syntax and example call

```
/* GetCurrentProcess() Syntax */
HANDLE GetCurrentProcess(VOID);    /* no parameter required */

/* GetCurrentProcess() Example Call */
```

```
HANDLE hProcess;                    /* assumes we are in a process procedure */

    hProcess = GetCurrentProcess(); /* place pseudohandle in hProcess */
```

Like GetCurrentThread(), GetCurrentProcess() does not return an actual handle; instead it is a *pseudohandle*. A pseudohandle is only effective in the process that obtained it. For example, if you use the GetCurrentProcess() function in a process, only that particular process can use the handle. You cannot share the handle with other processes. You do not have to close a pseudohandle by calling CloseHandle(); the pseudohandle disposes of itself when the process is terminated.

PROCESS CREATION DEMONSTRATION

Our next example application, MULTI3, creates two processes: a GUI application (GENERIC.EXE from Chapter 2) and a console application (CMD.EXE, the Command Prompt window). This will show some of the possibilities of the usage of CreateProcess().

Before we get into the description of the application. Let's take a look at the files that make up MULTI3. Listings 6-26 through 6-28 provide the resource script, header file, and source file, respectively. Because it is typical, the WinMain() function has been omitted from the listing. You can view the file in its entirety by loading it from the \CHAPTER6\6.3 directory.

Listing 6-26 MULTI3.RC—resource script

```
#include "windows.h"
#include "multi3.h"

Multi3Icon ICON multi3.ico

Multi3Menu MENU
    BEGIN
        POPUP "&Create Process"
        BEGIN
            MENUITEM "&Generic",          IDM_GENERIC
            MENUITEM "&Command Prompt",  IDM_COMMAND
        END
    END
```

Listing 6-27 MULTI3.H—header file

```
/* multi3.h -- Include file for multi3.c and multi3.rc */

/* Menu defines */
#define IDM_GENERIC   1
#define IDM_COMMAND   2

/* Function prototype */
LONG APIENTRY WndProc (HWND, UINT, UINT, LONG);

/* Global variables */
HANDLE ghInst;
HANDLE ghWnd;
```

Listing 6-28 MULTI3.C—source file

```
/* multi3.c      Demonstrate the creation of processes */

#include <windows.h>
#include <stdlib.h>
#include "multi3.h"

/* WndProc - Main Window Procedure for multi3.c */
LONG APIENTRY WndProc (HWND hWnd, UINT message, UINT wParam, LONG lParam)
{
STARTUPINFO         suinfo;
PROCESS_INFORMATION pi;
static HANDLE       hProcess1, hProcess2;

    switch (message)
    {

    case WM_COMMAND:
       switch (LOWORD(wParam))
       {

          case IDM_GENERIC:                      /* run a GENERIC.EXE process */
             suinfo.cb            = sizeof (STARTUPINFO);
             suinfo.lpReserved    = NULL;
             suinfo.lpDesktop     = NULL;
             suinfo.lpTitle       = NULL;
             suinfo.dwX           = 0;
             suinfo.dwY           = 0;
             suinfo.dwXSize       = 0;
             suinfo.dwYSize       = 0;
             suinfo.dwXCountChars = 0;
             suinfo.dwYCountChars = 0;
             suinfo.dwFillAttribute = 0;
             suinfo.dwFlags       = 0;
             suinfo.wShowWindow   = 0;
```

```
            suinfo.cbReserved2      = 0;
            suinfo.lpReserved2      = NULL;

            if (!CreateProcess ("GENERIC.EXE", /* attempt to create process */
                               NULL,           /* no command line */
                               NULL,           /* no process security attributes */
                               NULL,           /* no primary thread security attr */
                               FALSE,          /* no handle inheritance */
                               0,              /* no creation flags */
                               NULL,           /* no new environment */
                               NULL,           /* no startup directory */
                               &suinfo,        /* address of STARTUPINFO struct */
                               &pi))           /* address of PROCESS_INFORMATION struct */
        MessageBox (hWnd, "Cannot start GENERIC.EXE", "Create Process Error", MB_OK);
            else
                hProcess1 = pi.hProcess;       /* if success, get handle to process */
            return (0);


        case IDM_COMMAND:                       /* run a CMD.EXE process (command prompt) */
            suinfo.cb               = sizeof (STARTUPINFO);
            suinfo.lpReserved       = NULL;
            suinfo.lpDesktop        = NULL;
            suinfo.lpTitle          = "MULTI3: Command Prompt Window"; /* new title */
            suinfo.dwX               = 0;
            suinfo.dwY              = 0;
            suinfo.dwXSize          = 0;
            suinfo.dwYSize          = 0;
            suinfo.dwXCountChars    = 80;       /* screen buffer width */
            suinfo.dwYCountChars    = 40;       /* screen buffer height */
            suinfo.dwFillAttribute = 0;
            suinfo.dwFlags          = STARTF_USECOUNTCHARS | STARTF_USEPOSITION; /* flags */
            suinfo.wShowWindow      = 0;
            suinfo.cbReserved2      = 0;
            suinfo.lpReserved2      = NULL;

            if (!CreateProcess (NULL,          /* no image name */
                               "CMD.EXE",       /* use command line (searches in Windows dirs) */
                               NULL,           /* no process security attributes */
                               NULL,           /* no primary thread security attr */
                               FALSE,          /* no handle inheritance */
                               CREATE_NEW_CONSOLE, /* create a new console window */
                               NULL,           /* no new environment */
                               NULL,           /* no startup directory */
                               &suinfo,        /* address of STARTUPINFO struct */
                               &pi))           /* address of PROCESS_INFORMATION struct */
            MessageBox (hWnd, "Cannot start CMD.EXE", "Create Process Error", MB_OK);
            else
                hProcess2 = pi.hProcess;       /* if success, get handle to process */
            return (0);

        default:
            return (0);
    }
}
```

continued on next page

continued from previous page

```
    case WM_DESTROY:
        TerminateProcess (hProcess1, 0);        /* terminate processes on exit */
        TerminateProcess (hProcess2, 0);
        PostQuitMessage (0);
        return (0);

    default:
        return DefWindowProc (hWnd, message, wParam, lParam);
    }
    return (0L);
}
```

Overview of MULTI3

MULTI3 has one menu popup, *Create Process,* with two selections: *Generic* and *Command Prompt.* The *Generic* selection starts a process, the minimum Win32 application we built in Chapter 2. The *Command Prompt* selection starts another process, the Windows NT Command Prompt. We position the Command Prompt window in the upper-left corner of the desktop. We also expand the screen buffer size of this application. Its default is normally 80x25; we expand it to 80x40 when we create the process. When the user exits MULTI3, both processes are terminated. Let's examine the two selections individually.

Creating the First Process—GENERIC.EXE

Although the user can start the processes in any order, we will discuss them in the order they are listed in the *Create Process* menu. The first selection, *Generic,* sends an IDM_GENERIC menu message to WndProc() of MULTI3.C.

Filling the STARTUPINFO Structure for CreateProcess()

Before calling CreateProcess() we fill a STARTUPINFO structure (declared as *suinfo* at the top of WndProc()). Since most of the members of this structure affect console (non-GUI) applications, we fill the structures with NULLs and 0s as appropriate. With the structure filled, we can make our call to CreateProcess().

CreateProcess() for GENERIC.EXE

The first parameter of CreateProcess() must specify an executable filename or a complete path and executable filename. Since the call in MULTI3.C does not specify a path, the file is assumed to be in the current directory. We supplied a copy of the executable file on disk; it is located in the \CHAPTER6\6.3 directory.

The second parameter is NULL; this indicates that there are no command line parameters to GENERIC.EXE. The third and fourth parameters are also set to NULL because we are not using security attributes for processes and threads at this point in this book. The fifth parameter is set to FALSE for the same reason. This means that GENERIC.EXE will not inherit open handles from MULTI3.

The sixth parameter is set to 0; this indicates that there are no creation flags for the new process. We will look at an example of creation flags in the next process. The seventh and eight parameters are NULL. We are not passing a new environment block nor a startup directory.

The ninth parameter is the address of *suinfo*. This is the STARTUPINFO structure we filled just prior to the CreateProcess() call. The tenth parameter is the address of a PROCESS_INFORMATION structure. We declared it as *pi* at the top of WndProc(). CreateProcess() will fill this structure with handles and thread IDs of the new process and its primary thread.

We test to see if CreateProcess() is successful in an *if* statement. If the function returns FALSE, we display a message indicating that CreateProcess() failed and on which executable module it failed.

Assuming the call to CreateProcess() is successful, we assign the process handle to a static handle, *hProcess1* (declared at the top of WndProc()). We extract this handle from the *hProcess* member of *pi*.

At this point the GENERIC.EXE process is running on its own. However, we still have some level of control because we have a handle to the process. We'll use this handle in just a moment, but first let's take a look at creating the Command Prompt window process.

Creating the Second Process—CMD.EXE (Command Prompt)

If the user chooses the *Command Prompt* selection from the *Create Process* menu, an IDM_COMMAND menu message is sent to WndProc(). Once again we must fill a STARTUPINFO structure before calling CreateProcess().

Filling the STARTUPINFO Structure for CreateProcess()

Since the CMD.EXE is a console application, we will demonstrate some of the effects of values in STARTUPINFO. The *lpTitle* member of the structure points to a string indicating the new title bar text for the process. The *dwXCountChars* and *dwYCountChars* members are assigned 80 and 40, respectively. This redefines the screen buffer for the console application. You can use this to create a scrollable Command Prompt window. It will maintain a buffer of 40 lines.

In order for the assignments to the members of the STARTUPINFO structure to take effect, we must set the creation flags. We combine STARTF_USEPOSITION and STARTF_USECOUNTCHARS using a *bitwise or.* This combination is assigned to the *dwFlags* member of *suinfo.* The remainder of the STARTUPINFO members are not used and, as a result, are set to NULL or 0 as required. We are now ready to call CreateProcess(). STARTF_USECOUNTCHARS indicates to the system that the screen buffer values are supplied in the *dwXSize* and *dwYSize* members. STARTF_USEPOSITION indicates to the system that the *dwX* and *dwY* members define the initial position of the window (in this case 0,0 or the upper-left corner of the display).

CreateProcess() for CMD.EXE (Command Prompt)

We'll use a slightly different approach to create the Command Prompt process. The first parameter to CreateProcess() is set to NULL. This indicates that the first token in the second parameter will specify the executable module name. The second parameter now contains the address of a null-terminated string specifying the filename.

Why didn't we place this string in the first parameter? If the executable filename is specified in the first parameter, it must contain a complete path and filename. Otherwise the file must be in the current directory. By placing the filename in the first token (in this case, the only token) of the second parameter, the operating system will search for the file in the current directory, the Windows system directory, the Windows directory, and every directory specified in the PATH environment variable. Since CMD.EXE is in the Windows directory, CreateProcess() will find it.

The third through fifth parameters are set to NULL and FALSE. This indicates that no security attributes or handle inheritance is used. This is the same as CreateProcess() for GENERIC.EXE.

The sixth parameter is set to CREATE_NEW_CONSOLE. If we didn't specify this parameter, CMD.EXE would have to create its own window using AllocConsole(). The seventh and eighth parameters are NULLs, indicating that neither a new environment block nor a startup directory is specified.

The ninth parameter is the address of *suinfo* (the STARTUPINFO structure), which was filled just prior to the CreateProcess() call. The last parameter is the address of a PROCESS_INFORMATION structure, *pi.* As in our previous call to CreateProcess(), this structure is filled if CreateProcess() is successful.

We check to see if the CreateProcess() call succeeds or fails by using an *if* statement. If the function fails, we display a message indicating the failure. If the function succeeds, we assign the handle to the process to static handle *hProcess2*. This is extracted from the *hProcess* member of the *pi* (PROCESS_INFORMATION) structure.

At this point a Command Prompt (CMD.EXE) process is started. The only difference in this instance of Command Prompt is the title bar text and the size of the screen buffer. These differences were caused by the entries to the STARTUPINFO structure. Now that we have created the two processes, let's see how they are terminated.

Terminating the Processes

The processes created by MULTI3 can be terminated in two ways. The user can exit either of the processes using the system menu (or in the case of CMD.EXE, you can type EXIT and press (ENTER). However, the processes will also be terminated if the user exits MULTI3. This generates a WM_DESTROY message as the main window is about to be destroyed.

While processing the WM_DESTROY message, we call TerminateProcess() with each of the processes' handles. These calls will fail if the user exited the processes directly, or if they were not created in the first place. Since we are not testing the return value from TerminateProcess(), there is no indication of this failure in MULTI3.

In MULTI3, we do not prevent the user from starting more than one GENERIC.EXE or CMD.EXE. Since we do not allocate additional handles during MULTI3 (we just have *hProcess1* and *hProcess2*), the handles will reflect the last instance of its respective application. For example, if the user selects *Generic* twice from the *Create Process* menu, *hProcess1* will have the handle to the second instance. Having done this, if the user exits MULTI3, only the second instance of GENERIC.EXE will be terminated. We will demonstrate this effect after we build and run MULTI3. Let's get started.

BUILDING AND USING MULTI3

The MULTI3 program files are located in the \CHAPTER6\6.3 subdirectory. A copy of GENERIC.EXE also resides in this directory. Open a Command Prompt window and change to this directory. Type NMAKE and press (ENTER). The MULTI3 application compiles and links. You can use the Command Prompt to start MULTI3 by typing MULTI3 and pressing (ENTER). You can also add the application to an existing group in the Program Manager.

Review the code in Listings 6-26 through 6-28 while performing the following steps:

1. Select *Generic* from the *Create Process* menu. A process is started for GENERIC.EXE. Review the code in Listing 6-28 (IDM_GENERIC menu message). Click on the MULTI3 window to bring it to the front. Figure 6-13 shows the MULTI3, GENERIC, and CMD applications (the windows have been moved).

2. Select *Command Prompt* from the *Create Process* menu. A process is started for CMD.EXE. Review the code in Listing 6-38 (IDM_COMMAND menu message). Note the following:

   The Command Prompt window starts in the upper-left corner of the desktop (*dwX* = 0, *dwY* = 0, and *dwFlags* = STARTF_USEPOSITION).

   The title bar is different from a standard Command Prompt window *(lpTitle* = "MULTI3: Command Prompt Window").

   The window has a scroll bar *(dwXCountChars* = 80, *dwYCountChars* = 40, and *dwFlags* = STARTF_USECOUNTCHARS).

3. Exit MULTI3 without closing GENERIC.EXE or CMD.EXE. Notice that both processes are terminated along with MULTI3. This occurs while processing the WM_DESTROY message in WndProc() of MULTI3.C

4. Start MULTI3 again and create a *Generic* and *Command Prompt* process. Minimize the new process windows.

5. Create an additional *Generic* and a *Command Prompt* process.

6. Exit MULTI3 and observe the results. The most recent processes are terminated with MULTI3; however, the first set of processes remains. This is a result of only having two process handles: *hProcess1* and *hProcess2*. These handles only reflect the most recently created processes.

7. Using the system menu, close the remaining instances of *Generic* and *Command Prompt* individually.

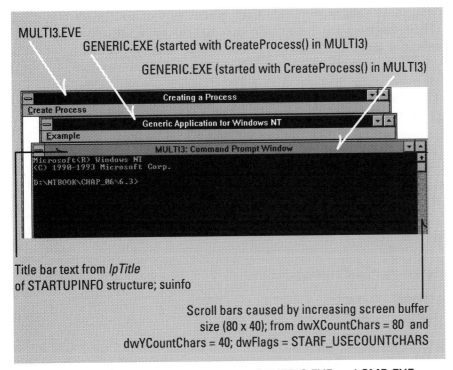

Figure 6-13 MULTI3 and two processes—GENERIC.EXE and CMD.EXE

This completes our example application demonstrating process creation. Let's look at an example program that shows the differences between Windows 3.x and Win32 DLLs. We'll also take a look at how threads and processes relate to DLLs.

DYNAMIC LINK LIBRARIES (DLL) IN WIN32

Creating a dynamic link library, or DLL, in Windows 3.x was a fairly straightforward process. If you created and used DLLs in your Windows 3.x projects, moving to Win32 DLLs is even more straightforward. If you have never created a DLL, you may want to read this section anyway. You'll find that DLLs are fairly simple to create. They also can be very beneficial to your programming projects.

DLLs let you make calls to functions that are not part of your main application. These functions are dynamically linked at run time. Once you have your application and DLLs created, you can change code within them without affecting your original application; only the function parameters and the return type must remain the same. Also, different applications can use the same DLL. This allows multiple applications to call functions within a DLL, yet only one DLL file must be present on the system.

To access a function in a DLL, you can use one of two methods: *load-time linking* and *run-time linking*. In load-time linking, you link the DLL along with your executable file. The actual code from the DLL is not compiled with your application's code; only the references to the DLL code. The DLL must be installed on the system in order for the application to find it at run time. The operating system will search the following places on the system:

- the directory of the calling process
- the current directory
- the Windows directory
- the Windows system directory
- all directories in the PATH environment variable

Once the DLL is loaded successfully, you can make calls to the functions in the DLL. These functions must have been defined in the IMPORTS section of a module definition file, or using an import library. Our example in this chapter will use an import library to resolve the external references to DLL functions.

Using run-time linking means that you must load the DLL from within your application. This is accomplished with LoadLibrary(). Once the DLL is loaded, you must get an address to the DLL functions using GetProcAddress(). Having done this, you can call the DLL functions using a pointer to the function (return value of GetProcAddress().

If you have written DLLs in Windows 3.x, most of this information appears to be the same. Let's look at the changes to DLLs in Win32.

New to DLLs in Win32

Three areas have been affected in Win32 DLLs: the LibMain() function, the WEP() function, and data for individual processes and threads. Let's look at the changes to LibMain().

The LibMain() Function

The name of the LibMain() function and its arguments have changed in
Win32 DLLs. Recall that the LibMain() function arguments in Windows 3.x
resemble the WinMain function arguments. Compare the two function
prototypes:

```
/* Win32 version */
int WINAPI DLLEntryPoint(HANDLE hInst, ULONG umessage, LPVOID lpReserved)

/* Windows 3.x version */
int FAR PASCAL LibMain(HANDLE hInst, WORD wDataSeg, WORD wHeapSize, LPSTR lpstrCmdLine);
```

Note that FAR PASCAL has been replaced by WINAPI. Recall that
WINAPI and APIENTRY (used in WinMain) are essentially the same type
(in 80386/486 systems). They both declare the function calling convention
(_stdcall).

We are also using DLLEntryPoint() instead of LibMain(). The name of
this function is defined when linking the DLL by the -entry switch. You can
continue to use LibMain() as long as it's defined on the link command line.

The first argument is still the instance handle, but that is where the
similarity ends. The Windows 3.x version has arguments for the address of
the DLL's data segment, heap size, and a pointer to command-line
parameters. These arguments are determined by the LIBENTRY assembler
code. The only time command-line parameters are used is when the DLL is
started by using LoadModule() in the executable. LIBENTRY is an assembler
file; therefore it is processor dependent. Since Windows NT can run on
multiple platforms, LIBENTRY can no longer be used.

The Win32 version receives an instance handle and a message from the
Win32 subsystem. Possible messages are DLL_PROCESS_ATTACH when a
process attaches to the DLL, DLL_PROCESS_DETACH when it detaches,
DLL_THREAD_ATTACH when a thread attaches to the DLL, and
DLL_THREAD_DETACH when it detaches. You can test for these
messages by adding a switch statement with umessage as its test argument. This
is how DLLEntryPoint() can be used as both a startup and ending DLL
function. We will demonstrate this in MULTIDLL. The last parameter is
reserved by the operating system.

The Demise of WEP()

In Windows 3.x DLLs, the WEP() function was called as the DLL was being
removed. Like LibMain(), applications did not call this function directly.
When the last application freed the DLL, the system called the WEP()

function. You could perform any last minute cleanup that may have been required (freeing allocated memory, and so on).

In Win32 the WEP() function has been removed. You can trap the DLL_PROCESS_DETACH message in LibMain() as an equivalent.

Data in Win32 DLLs, Processes, and Threads

In Windows 3.x static variables created a problem. If more than one application accessed the DLL and modified static variable, the other application would not be aware that the variable changed. In Win32 this is not a problem. Each calling application has its own instance of the DLL in its virtual memory addresses. Figure 6-14 illustrates the difference between Windows 3.x DLLs and Win32 DLLs using static variables.

Recall that each application in Win32 has its own private set of virtual addresses. Each application that loads a DLL obtains addresses to the functions in its own virtual memory addresses.

Now that we've seen the differences in DLLs, let's try a few example applications to demonstrate them.

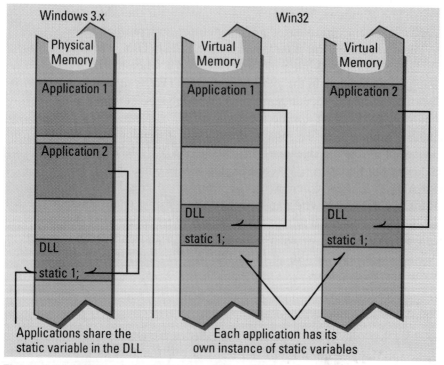

Figure 6-14 Windows 3.x and Win32 DLLs—static variable scope

MULTI4, MULTI5, AND MULTIDLL

The last example of this chapter consists of three projects: MULTI4, MULTI5, and MULTIDLL. MULTI4 is an application that loads a DLL at run time. MULTI5 is an application that links a DLL at compile time. MULTIDLL is the DLL module that the applications load (or link).

Both applications have a menu option that creates a thread. We will observe how the applications (processes) attach and detach to the DLL. We will also see how the additional threads attach and detach from the DLL. The makefile contains some new information for the DLL. Let's start by examining the additions to the makefile

MAKEFILE for MULTI4, MULTI5, and MULTIDLL

In Chapter 4 we used a makefile that built two applications. The makefile for this example builds two executable applications and a dynamic link library. Several lines in the makefile are devoted to compiling the DLL and building an import library. Listing 6-29 shows the makefile for this example project.

Listing 6-29 MAKEFILE for MULTI4, MULTI5, and MULTIDLL

```
# MAKEFILE for MULTI4 (multitasking and DLLs)

# Nmake macros for Win32 apps
!include <ntwin32.mak>

#all pseudotarget
all: multi4.exe multi5.exe multidll.dll

# Update the object files.
multi4.obj: multi4.c
    $(cc) $(cflags) $(cvarsmt) multi4.c

multi5.obj: multi5.c
    $(cc) $(cflags) $(cvarsmt) multi5.c

multidll.obj: multidll.c
    $(cc) $(cflags) $(cvarsmtdll) multidll.c

# Update the resource.
multi4.res: multi4.rc multi4.h
    rc -r -fo multi4.tmp multi4.rc
    cvtres -$(CPU) multi4.tmp -o multi4.res
```

continued on next page

continued from previous page

```
    del multi4.tmp

multi5.res: multi5.rc multi5.h
    rc -r -fo multi5.tmp multi5.rc
    cvtres -$(CPU) multi5.tmp -o multi5.res
    del multi5.tmp

# Update the import library.
multidll.lib: multidll.obj multidll.def
    $(implib) -machine:$(CPU) \
    -def:multidll.def          \
    multidll.obj               \
    -out:multidll.lib          \

# Update the dynamic link library.
multidll.dll: multidll.obj multidll.def
    $(link)             \
    -IGNORE:505         \
    -base:0x1C000000    \
    -dll                \
    -entry:DLLEntryPoint$(DLLENTRY)    \
    -out:multidll.dll   \
    multidll.exp multidll.obj $(guilibsdll)


# Update the executable and add the resource file.

multi4.exe: multi4.obj multi4.res
    $(link) $(guilflags) -IGNORE:505 -out:multi4.exe multi4.obj multi4.res $(guilibsmt)

multi5.exe: multi5.obj multidll.lib multi5.res
    $(link) $(guilflags) -IGNORE:505 -out:multi5.exe multi5.obj multidll.lib multi5.res
$(guilibsmt)
```

The first segment of the makefile compiles the executable and DLL source files. Compiling the DLL requires the *$(cvarsmtdll)* macro. This equates to placing *-DWIN32 -D_MT -D_DLL* on the compiler command line.

Building the Import Library and Export Module

The next step is to build an import library. The dependent files for the import library are the DLL's module definition file and object file. The command line starts with the *$(implib)* macro, which equates to LIB32 (the import librarian executable). This is followed by switches for the machine type (in our case i386) and the module definition file (MULTIDLL.DEF).

Next on the command line is the object file for MULTIDLL. Finally we use a switch to designate the output file from the librarian (MULTIDLL.LIB). This file is used by MULTI5 to resolve external conflicts for the DLL functions. MULTI5 uses link-time binding to the DLL.

What you don't see here is that LIB32 will create a file with an .EXP extension. This is an export module that is required when linking the DLL. This is our next step.

Linking the DLL

The *$(link)* macro is first on the command line. This equates to LINK32. This is followed by several switches. These switches and their purposes are

- *-IGNORE: 505* (suppress *No module extracted from xxx* warnings)
- *-base: 0x1C000000* (base address to locate the DLL if available)
- *-dll* (create a DLL)
- *-entry:DLLEntryPoint$(DLLENTRY)* (define entry point— equates to DLLEntryPoint@12)
- *-out:multidll.dll* (output file is MULTIDLL.DLL)

The command-line switches are followed by the export module created by LIB32, the object file for the DLL, and the libraries for DLLs (defined by the *$(guilibsdll)* macro), which are given in Table 6-5.

Linking the Executables

Linking MULTI4 is no different than linking the other applications in this chapter. Since it loads the DLL at run time, it does not require an import library. MULTI5 on the other hand, requires the import library (MULTIDLL.LIB) to resolve external conflicts at link time. Therefore it's included on the command line to the linker. It also is on the dependency line of MULTI5.EXE.

CRTDLL.LIB	NTDLL.LIB	KERNEL32.LIB
USER32.LIB	GDI32.LIB	WINSPOOL.LIB
COMMDLG.32LIB		

Table 6-5 Libraries in the $(GUILIBSDLL) macro

The Big Picture

There is a lot going on is this makefile. It is best to see an overall picture of what is taking place in this project. Figure 6-15 provides a pictorial for the makefile.

Resource files and the resource compiler are not shown in the figure, but MULTI4 and MULTI5 use them. MULTI4 is typical of most applications we've seen up to this point. MULTI4 doesn't link to MULTIDLL.LIB; it just gets references to it at run time. MULTI5 requires a LIB file at link time in addition to its own object file. MULTIDLL requires an export module in addition to its object file.

The library manager (LIB32) is responsible for generating MULTIDLL.LIB and MULTIDLL.EXP. The inputs to the library manager are the object file from the DLL and the DLL module definition file.

Now that we've seen how the overall project is built, let's examine the individual modules in the project. We'll start with the DLL.

MULTIDLL

Since our two applications (MULTI4 and MULTI5) in this project rely on the DLL to function properly, we'll start by examining MULTIDLL. The DLL in our example consists of three files. Listings 6-30 through 6-32 provide the module definition file, the header file, and the complete source file for MULTIDLL.

The DEF file contains four entries. The LIBRARY entry specifies the DLL filename. The CODE entry specifies the attributes for the DLL's code: EXECUTE and READ. The DATA entry specifies the attributes for the DLL's data: READ WRITE. The EXPORTS section specifies the exported function (GenDLLCall()) with an ordinal value of 1. Module definition files are covered in detail in Chapter 2.

Listing 6-30 MULTIDLL.DEF—module definition file

```
LIBRARY     MULTIDLL

CODE EXECUTE READ
DATA READ WRITE

EXPORTS
    GenDLLCall    @1
```

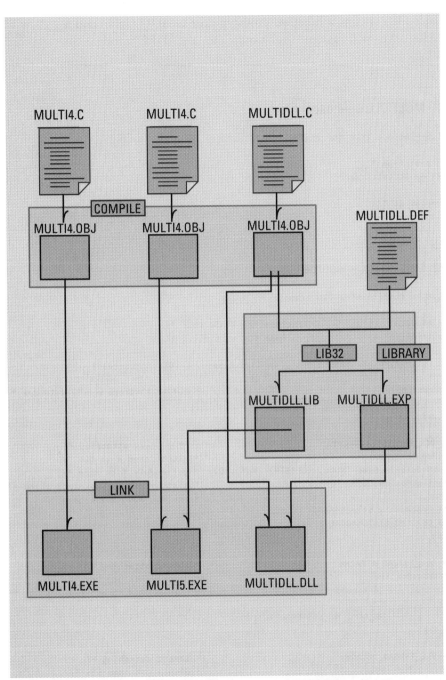

Figure 6-15 Overview of MAKEFILE for MULTI4, MULTI5, and MULTIDLL

The header file contains a function prototype for GenDLLCall() and a global handle. We will assign the handle to the DLL module in MULTIDLL.C.

Listing 6-31 MULTIDLL.H—header file

```
/* multidll.h--include file for multidll.c */

/* Function prototype */
INT APIENTRY GenDLLCall(HWND);

/* Global variables */
HANDLE ghModule;
```

Listing 6-32 MULTIDLL.C—source file

```
/* multidll.c -- Multitasking DLL example */

#include "windows.h"              /* include for Win32 DLLs */
#include "multidll.h"             /* include for multidll.c */

BOOL WINAPI DLLEntryPoint (HANDLE hDLL, DWORD dwReason, LPVOID lpReserved)
{
static char cBuf[80];                              /* buffer to store module filename */

    switch (dwReason)
    {
        case DLL_PROCESS_ATTACH:                   /* process attaching */
            ghModule = hDLL;                       /* global handle to DLL */
            GetModuleFileName (NULL, (LPTSTR) cBuf, 80); /* get module file name */
            MessageBox (NULL,                      /* display message box indicating */
            cBuf,                                  /* the DLL module filename */
            "A Process is attaching",
            MB_OK | MB_SYSTEMMODAL);
        break;

        case DLL_THREAD_ATTACH:                    /* thread attaching */
            MessageBox (NULL,                      /* display message box */
                    "A Thread is attaching",       /* indicating a thread is attaching */
                    "",
                    MB_OK | MB_SYSTEMMODAL);
            break;

        case DLL_THREAD_DETACH:                    /* thread detaching */
            MessageBox (NULL,                      /* display message box */
                    "A Thread is detaching",       /* indicating a thread is detaching */
                    "",
                    MB_OK | MB_SYSTEMMODAL);
```

```
          break;

      case DLL_PROCESS_DETACH:                    /* process detaching */
          MessageBox (NULL,                       /* display message box */
                      "A Process is detaching",   /* indicating a process is detaching */
                      "",
                      MB_OK | MB_SYSTEMMODAL);
      break;
    }
    return TRUE;
}


/* GenDLLCall--an exported DLL function which displays a message
   indicating that the message is coming from a DLL */
INT APIENTRY GenDLLCall(HWND ghWnd) /* Exported function */
{
                                    /* Message box displays that the */
    MessageBox (ghWnd,              /* activity is occuring in the DLL */
                "This message is from MULTIDLL.DLL",
                "GenDLLCall()", MB_OK | MB_SYSTEMMODAL);
    return (1);
}
```

DLLEntryPoint()

When a process attaches to the DLL, DLLEntryPoint() receives a DLL_PROCESS_ATTACH message via its *dwReason* parameter. We use this parameter in a *switch* statement to determine why DLLEntryPoint() is being called. Since a process is attaching, the code in the DLL_PROCESS_ATTACH case is executed.

The first line gets the name of the calling process with GetModuleFileName(). The results are stored in a char buffer, *cBuf.* Next we display a message box. The text in the message box indicates that a process is attaching to the DLL. The title bar displays the path and filename of the attaching process *(cBuf).*

The remaining cases also display a message indicating what action is taking place. For example, when an attached process creates a thread, a DLL_THREAD_ATTACH message is sent to DLLEntryPoint(). We display a message indicating that a thread is attaching. An identical method is used for DLL_THREAD_DETACH and DLL_PROCESS_DETACH; only the message is altered to reflect the situation at hand.

GenDLLCall()

GenDLLCall() is a generic function that the attached processes and threads can call. We display another message box indicating that we have actually called the function in the DLL. The calling process provides a handle to its window as the only parameter to this call. This handle is used in the MessageBox() call.

That's it for the DLL. Let's look at the two example applications that will use MULTIDLL. MULTI4 loads the DLL at run time and MULTI5 employs the link-time method.

MULTI4

MULTI4 is an application that loads MULTIDLL at run time. Since it loads the DLL and gets the address of its function at run time, there is no need to link the import library to the executable. Listings 6-33 through 6-35 provide the resource script, header file, and source file for MULTI4.

The resource script defines four menu selections; only the Load DLL option is enabled.

Listing 6-33 MULTI4.RC—resource script

```
#include "windows.h"
#include "multi4.h"

Multi4Icon ICON Multi4.ico
Multi4Menu MENU
    BEGIN
        POPUP "&DLL Demonstration"
        BEGIN
            MENUITEM "&Load DLL",          IDM_LOAD_DLL
            MENUITEM "&Call DLL Function",  IDM_CALL_DLL, GRAYED
            MENUITEM "&Start Thread",       IDM_START_THREAD, GRAYED
            MENUITEM "&Remove DLL",         IDM_REMOVE_DLL, GRAYED
        END
    END
```

In addition to the typical defines, this header file contains a function prototype for the thread procedure used in MULTI4.C. Is also uses a typedef which defines a pointer to a function that returns an integer *(PFNDLL)*. We declare a global of this type and set it to NULL. We will use this variable to store a pointer to the DLL function in MULTI4.C. Finally we define a global character string. This message will be used by the thread procedure in MULTI4.C.

Listing 6-34 MULTI4.H—header file

```
/* multi4.h--include file for multi4.c and multi4.rc */

/* Menu defines */
#define IDM_LOAD_DLL      1
#define IDM_CALL_DLL      2
#define IDM_START_THREAD  3
#define IDM_REMOVE_DLL    4

/* Function prototypes */
LONG APIENTRY WndProc (HWND, UINT, UINT, LONG);
void MenuSet (WORD);
void ThreadProc (char *);

/* Typedefs */
typedef int (*PFNDLL) ();

/* Global variables */
HANDLE ghInst;
HANDLE ghWnd;
PFNDLL gpfnDLLFunc = NULL;
char   gThreadArg[] = "This message is from the thread";
```

Listing 6-35 MULTI4.C—source file

```
/* multi4.c     Loads a DLL in Windows NT - run time linking */

#include <windows.h>
#include "multi4.h"
#include "multidll.h"

LONG APIENTRY WndProc (HWND hWnd, UINT message, UINT wParam, LONG lParam)
{
static HANDLE hDLL = NULL;                            /* Handle for DLL */
DWORD   ThreadID;

   switch (message)
   {
     case WM_COMMAND:
        switch (LOWORD(wParam))          /* Extract LOWORD of wParam (message from menu) */
        {
           case IDM_LOAD_DLL:                          /* user selected Load DLL */
             if (hDLL = LoadLibrary ("MULTIDLL.DLL")) /* load DLL and assign to handle */
             {
                                                       /* get pointer to DLL function */
                 gpfnDLLFunc = (PFNDLL) GetProcAddress (hDLL, "GenDLLCall");
                 MenuSet (IDM_LOAD_DLL);
             }
             return (0);
```

continued on next page

continued from previous page

```
            case IDM_CALL_DLL:                          /* user selected Call DLL function */
                (gpfnDLLFunc) (ghWnd);                  /* call DLL function */
                return (0);

            case IDM_START_THREAD:                      /* user selected Start Thread */
                CreateThread (NULL,                     /* Create a Thread */
                              0,
                              (LPTHREAD_START_ROUTINE) ThreadProc,
                              &gThreadArg,
                              0,
                              &ThreadID);

                return (0);

            case IDM_REMOVE_DLL:                        /* user selected Remove DLL */
                FreeLibrary (hDLL);                     /* release DLL */
                gpfnDLLFunc = (PFNDLL) NULL;            /* set DLL function pointer to NULL */
                MenuSet (IDM_REMOVE_DLL);               /* update the menu */
                return (0);

            default:
                return (0);
        }

    case WM_DESTROY:
        PostQuitMessage (0);
        return (0);

    default:
        return DefWindowProc (hWnd, message, wParam, lParam);
    }

    return (0L);
}


/* MenuSet()--Enables and disables menu selections */
void MenuSet (WORD MenuSelect)
{
HMENU hMenu;
int   i;

    hMenu = GetMenu (ghWnd);                            /* get handle to menu */

    for (i = IDM_LOAD_DLL; i <= IDM_REMOVE_DLL; i++)    /* disable all menu selections */
        EnableMenuItem (hMenu, i, MF_BYCOMMAND | MF_GRAYED);

    if (MenuSelect == IDM_LOAD_DLL)                     /* if DLL is loaded, gray Load DLL */
        for (i = IDM_CALL_DLL; i <= IDM_REMOVE_DLL; i++)  /* and enable the rest */
            EnableMenuItem (hMenu, i, MF_BYCOMMAND | MF_ENABLED);
    else
    {                                                   /* DLL is removed */
        EnableMenuItem (hMenu, IDM_LOAD_DLL, MF_BYCOMMAND | MF_ENABLED);
        for (i = IDM_CALL_DLL; i <= IDM_REMOVE_DLL; i++)  /* disable all but Load DLL */
```

```
            EnableMenuItem (hMenu, i, MF_BYCOMMAND | MF_GRAYED);
    }

}

/* ThreadProc()--attaches to DLL, displays message box, and calls DLL function */
void ThreadProc (char *ThreadArg)
{                                                          /* display message box */
    MessageBox (ghWnd, ThreadArg,"Ready to call GenDLLCall()", MB_OK);
    (gpfnDLLFunc) (ghWnd);                              /* call exported DLL function */
}
```

Overview of MULTI4

MULTI4 has one popup menu, *DLL Demonstration,* that contains four options: *Load DLL, Call DLL Function, Start Thread,* and *Remove DLL.* Initially only the *Load DLL* option is enabled. The others are grayed in the resource script. Once the DLL is loaded, we call MenuSet(). This function receives the menu message and updates the menu as required. If the user selects *Load DLL,* that option is grayed and all others are enabled. If the user selects *Remove DLL,* the *Load DLL* option is enabled and all others are grayed. Let's examine the actions of each menu selection individually.

Load DLL

When the user selects *Load DLL,* an IDM_LOAD_DLL message is sent to WndProc(). We make a call to LoadLibrary() to load the DLL. The library must be in the current directory, the startup directory, the Windows directory, the Windows system directory, or in a directory specified by the PATH environment variable. In our case it is in the current directory, since we built MULTI4 and MULTIDLL in the same directory.

We test the return value of LoadLibrary() in an *if* statement. If the function fails, we simply return without updating the menu. In your applications you may provide other means to help the user to get the program running. At the very least, you should specify that the application could not locate the DLL. We assign the return value of the LoadLibrary() call to static handle *hDLL.* This handle is declared as static since we will use it later in a call to free the DLL.

If the LoadLibrary() function is successful, we call GetProcAddress() to obtain the address of the function in the DLL. The parameters to GetProcAddress() are the handle to the DLL and a null-terminated string identifying the DLL function name. We cast the return value to PFNDLL (typedef in MULTI4.H) and store the result in *gpfnDLLFunc.* We call MenuSet() to update the menu.

337

Call DLL Function

If the user selects *Call DLL Function,* the IDM_CALL_DLL menu message needs to be processed. This consists of one line. We call the DLL function using the pointer *(gpfnDLLFunc)* assigned in IDM_LOAD_DLL. The argument to this function is a handle to the MULTI4's window.

Start Thread

If the user selects *Start Thread,* we create a simple thread. The CreateThread() call specifies ThreadProc() and the thread procedure. We pass *gThreadArg* as the argument to the thread procedure. This value is a pointer to a null-terminated string. The assignment of *gThreadArg* is in MULTI4.H.

ThreadProc()

We've created a thread, so let's take a look at the thread procedure. ThreadProc() receives the argument described in the previous paragraph. Since the process (MULTI4) is attached to the DLL at this point, any threads that are created within the MULTI4 result in a DLL notification. The DLL is notified that the thread is attaching to the DLL. This action is not visible in the source code; we will observe this when we build and run MULTI4 and MULTIDLL.

The next step is to display a message indicating that we are in the thread procedure. The message also indicates that we are about to call the DLL function. As soon as the user closes the message box, we call the DLL function again. Since the pointer to the DLL function and the handle to MULTI4's window are global, both are still valid at this point.

When the DLL function returns, we've reached the end of the thread procedure. When the thread procedure exits, the DLL is notified that the thread is detaching from the process.

Removing the DLL

The last menu selection removes the DLL from memory. The first line in the IDM_REMOVE_DLL case is a call to FreeLibrary(). We use the static handle to the DLL as its only argument. This action results in the DLL being notified that a process is detaching from the DLL. At this point the DLL is removed from the virtual memory space of this instance of MULTI4.

We set the pointer to the DLL function to NULL since it is no longer valid. Finally we call MenuSet() to update the menu. This concludes the description of MULTI4. Let's examine the code for MULTI5.

MULTI5

MULTI5 resolves the external references to the DLL at link time. This requires that the import library (generated from MULTIDLL.OBJ and MULTIDLL.DEF) be linked with the MULTI5 object file. Listings 6-36 through 6-38 provide the resource script, header file, and source file for MULTI5.

This resource script defines two menu selections. The DLL will be loaded automatically, so there is no need to load and remove DLL menu selections. The selections are not grayed, since the MULTI5 process will be attached before the main window and menu are created.

Listing 6-36 MULTI5.RC—resource script

```
#include "windows.h"
#include "multi5.h"

Multi5Icon ICON Multi5.ico
Multi5Menu MENU
    BEGIN
        POPUP "&DLL Demonstration"
        BEGIN
            MENUITEM "&Call DLL Function", IDM_CALL_DLL,
            MENUITEM "&Start Thread",      IDM_START_THREAD,
        END
    END
```

The main difference between this header file and MULTI4.H is the absence of the function pointer. Since this application is bound to the DLL at link time, we will call the function directly in MULTI5.C.

Listing 6-37 MULTI5.H—header file

```
/* multi5.h--include file for multi5.c and multi5.rc */

/* Menu defines */
#define IDM_CALL_DLL     1
#define IDM_START_THREAD 2

/* Function prototypes */
LONG APIENTRY WndProc (HWND, UINT, UINT, LONG);
void ThreadProc (char *);
```

continued on next page

continued from previous page

```
/* Global variables */
HANDLE ghInst;
HANDLE ghWnd;
char   gThreadArg[] = "This message is from the thread";
```

Listing 6-38 MULTI5.C—source file

```
/* multi5.c     Loads a DLL in Windows NT - load time linking */

#include <windows.h>
#include "multi5.h"
#include "multidll.h"

LONG APIENTRY WndProc (HWND hWnd, UINT message, UINT wParam, LONG lParam)
{
DWORD   ThreadID;

   switch (message)
   {
      case WM_COMMAND:
         switch (LOWORD(wParam))        /* Extract LOWORD of wParam (message from menu) */
         {

            case IDM_CALL_DLL:                       /* user selected Call DLL function */
               GenDLLCall(ghWnd);                    /* call DLL function */
               return (0);

            case IDM_START_THREAD:                   /* user selected Start Thread */
               CreateThread (NULL,                   /* Create a Thread */
                        0,
                        (LPTHREAD_START_ROUTINE) ThreadProc,
                        &gThreadArg,
                        0,
                        &ThreadID);

               return (0);

            default:
               return (0);
         }

      case WM_DESTROY:
         PostQuitMessage (0);
         return (0);

      default:
         return DefWindowProc (hWnd, message, wParam, lParam);
   }

   return (0L);
}
```

```
/* ThreadProc()--attaches to DLL, displays message box, and calls DLL function */
void ThreadProc (char *ThreadArg)
{                                                    /* display message box */
   MessageBox (ghWnd, ThreadArg,"Ready to call GenDLLCall()", MB_OK);
   GenDLLCall (ghWnd);                               /* call DLL function */
}
```

When Is the DLL Loaded?

In MULTI4 we loaded the DLL with a call to LoadLibrary(). This is not necessary in MULTI5, since we linked the MULTIDLL import library along with MULTI5.OBJ. When we start MULTI5, MULTIDLL is automatically loaded and MULTI5 attaches to the DLL. This occurs before the main window of MULTI5 is created.

For this same reason, we only have two menu selections: *Call DLL Function* and *Start Thread*. Let's examine the code that handles these selections.

Call DLL Function

This menu option only requires one line of code in this example. We simply call the DLL function using the function name GenDLLCall(). As in MULTI4 we pass a handle to the main window to the DLL function. How does MULTI5 know the function's name? It was resolved at compile time by including the header file of MULTIDLL. The function name was resolved at link time because we linked MULTIDLL's import library along with MULTI5's object file.

Start Thread

The code that creates the thread in WndProc() is identical to that in MULTI4. There is a slight difference in the thread procedure, however. We are now able to call the function directly, since MULTI5 knows the DLL function name. Similar to MULTI4, the DLL is notified when the thread attaches (after successful CreateThread() call) and detaches (when ThreadProc() returns).

When Does MULTI5 Detach from MULTIDLL?

In MULTI4 we detached from the DLL with a call to FreeLibrary(). In MULTI5, we detach when the process exits. This is after the window for MULTI5 is destroyed. We will see this effect in our next step: building and running MULTI4, MULTI5, and MULTIDLL.

BUILDING MULTI4, MULTI5, AND MULTIDLL

All the required program files for this project are located in the \CHAPTER6\6.4 subdirectory. This includes files for MULTI4, MULTI5, and MULTIDLL. Open a Command Prompt window and change to this directory. Type NMAKE and press (ENTER). The applications and DLL are compiled, the import library is created, the DLL is linked, and the applications are linked. You can use the Command Prompt to start MULTI4 or MULTI5 by typing the filename and pressing (ENTER). You may want to add the applications to an existing group in the Program Manager. Let's start with the MULTI4 program.

Review the code in Listings 6-30 through 6-32 for MULTIDLL, and 6-33 through 35 for MULTI4 while performing the following steps:

1. Select Load DLL from the DLL Demonstration menu in MULTI4. Since this selection loads the DLL, MULTIDLL receives a DLL_PROCESS_ATTACH message via its DLLEntryPoint() function (Listing 6-32). The DLL displays a message box indicating that a process has attached. The title bar indicates the path and filename of the attaching module. Figure 6-16 shows the output at this point.

2. Close the message box and select *Call DLL Function* from the *DLL Demonstration* menu. Another message box is displayed. This message is from the DLL function (GenDLLCall()). This message box is shown in Figure 6-17.

3. Close the message box and select *Start Thread* from the *DLL Demonstration* menu. This sets off a sequence of four message boxes (you must close each message box in order to view the next):

   The first occurs after a successful call to CreateThread() (the thread attaches to the DLL).

   The second is from a call within ThreadProc().

   The third occurs in GenDLLCall(), since ThreadProc() makes a call to the DLL function.

   The last occurs as ThreadProc() returns and, as a result, the DLL is notified that the thread is detaching from the DLL.

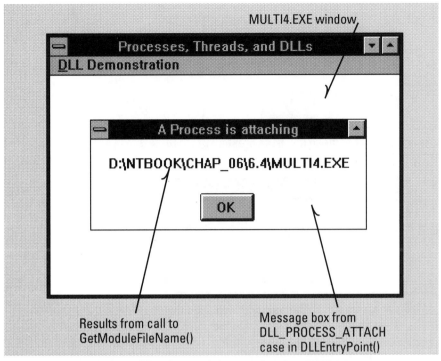

Figure 6-16 A process (MULTI4.EXE) attaches to MULTIDLL

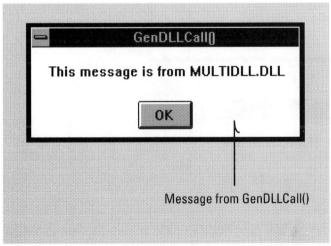

Figure 6-17 A call to GenDLLFunc

343

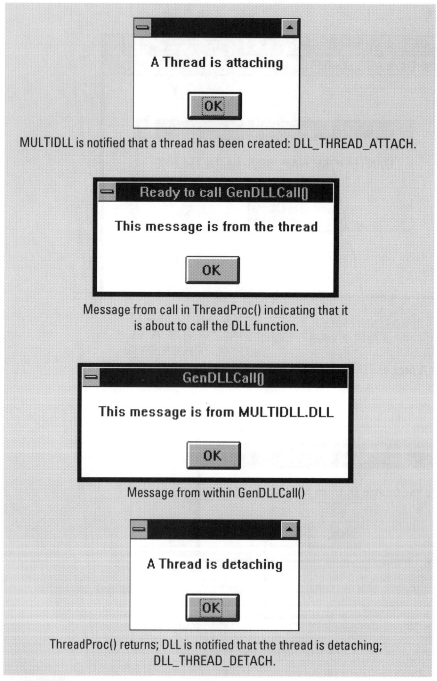

MULTIDLL is notified that a thread has been created: DLL_THREAD_ATTACH.

Message from call in ThreadProc() indicating that it
is about to call the DLL function.

Message from within GenDLLCall()

ThreadProc() returns; DLL is notified that the thread is detaching;
DLL_THREAD_DETACH.

Figure 6-18 Start thread in MULTI4

Figure 6-18 shows the message boxes and the sequence of events.

4. Close the final message box from *Start Thread*. Select *Remove DLL* from the *DLL Demonstration* menu. This results in a call to FreeLibrary() which detaches MULTI4.EXE from the DLL. Figure 6-19 shows this message from MULTIDLL.

5. Close the process detach message box and exit MULTI4.

Now let's give MULTI5 a try. Start MULTI5 using the Command Prompt (or double-click its icon if you added it to a group in the Program Manager). Review the code in Listings 6-30 through 6-32 for MULTIDLL and Listings 6-36 through 6-38 for MULTI5 while continuing with the steps.

6. Notice that you receive a message from MULTIDLL before the main window for MULTI5 is created. Why did this occur? With link-time DLLs, the process attaches as the program starts. This is before the call to CreateWindow() in MULTI5.C.

7. Close the process attach message box and try the *Call DLL Function* and *Start Thread* selections from the *DLL Demonstration* menu. The selections should behave identically to MULTI4. The only difference is the method in which they are called.

8. Exit MULTI5. The main window of MULTI5 is destroyed, then you get a message indicating that the process is detaching. This is also a

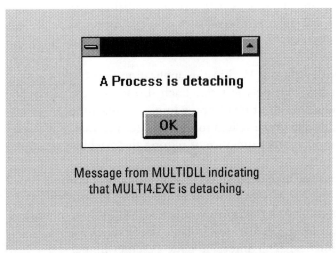

Message from MULTIDLL indicating
that MULTI4.EXE is detaching.

Figure 6-19 MULTI4.EXE detaches from MULTIDLL

function of the link-time binding to the DLL. The DLL is notified that MULTI5 is detaching after MULTI5's window is destroyed.

This completes our final example for this chapter. You can use the example programs as a starting point for your experimentation. Try creating multiple threads within an application. You will see that each successful call to CreateThread() generates a message from the DLL.

The messages to the DLL are usually not used to display message boxes. You can perform initialization and cleanup for each process and thread as they attach and detach.

SUMMARY

This chapter has introduced many new topics, concepts, and techniques. If you understand the basics provided here, you're well on your way to multitasking in Windows NT. Let's review some of the highlights of this chapter.

Windows NT supports preemptive multitasking. No longer can an application gain arbitrary control of the processor. The operating system can preempt the application at the end of its timeslice. The NT scheduler allocates timeslices to each application. In order to determine which application gets processor time, you have to understand threads and processes. A process is an executing program that has its own private virtual address space. It consists of code, data, and other resources (such as files). A process does not receive the timeslice to execute; it is the thread that is the actual unit of execution.

Each application has a primary thread. Within the application you can create individual threads to carry out specific tasks. Each thread context contains its own stack, a pointer to the thread procedure, and machine registers. Having this information allows the system to interrupt (or preempt) a thread. Once the thread receives another timeslice, it restores the machine registers and continues.

How often a thread gets processor time depends on priority—not only the priority of your threads, but the priority of other threads waiting for the processor. You've seen how to get and set the priority of threads within your process. Threads that perform long calculations and number crunching should be assigned lower priorities. User-interface code deserves higher priority to ensure that your application is responsive. As soon as the user is idle, the lower threads receive processor time to continue their tasks.

You've also seen some of the problems that can crop up with multiple threads. Deadlocks can occur when two threads are waiting for each other to supply a specific value. A thread race can be a problem if one thread finishes first, yet it depends on a value from a thread that isn't ready to supply it.

You've also seen how to create another process from within your own process. In fact, you can start any process that the Windows NT operating system supports (Win32 GUI applications, Win32 console applications, DOS applications, and so on). You can start any process for which Windows NT provides a subsystem.

In our last example, you saw how to create a DLL in Win32. You also saw how to call functions within the DLL using two methods: link time and run time. DLL source files have changed in Win32. The entry function of the DLL can determine if a process or a thread is attaching or detaching by examining a message passed from the system. The WEP() function from Windows 3.x is no longer valid. Instead you can trap the message that indicates a process is detaching.

Continue to experiment with the examples in this chapter to broaden your understanding of multitasking. You'll find that this difficult subject becomes easier with practice, experience, and imagination.

The second example program, MULTI2, left us with examples of thread problems. The next chapter will address these problems with a new topic: thread synchronization.

CHAPTER 7

Synchronization of Threads and Processes

bits
bits

ABC123

1

2

3

GENERIC.C

WINDOWS.H

INDEF.H

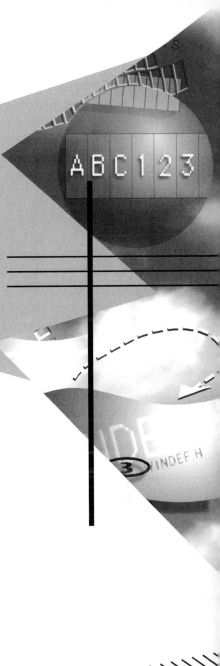

Synchronization of Threads and Processes

Multithreaded applications have many benefits. You can design your programs to take advantage of preemptive multitasking, which the Windows NT operating system provides. For example, if your application must perform lengthy, number-crunching tasks, you can create a low priority thread to do the work. At the same time, a higher priority thread is handling interaction with the user. When the user is idle, the number-crunching thread churns away. When the user is active (selecting a menu option, moving the mouse, and so on), the higher priority thread kicks in and the lower priority threads stops. This scenario gets the most out of the microprocessor's time.

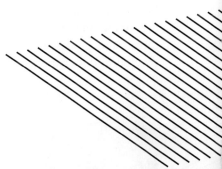

Along with the benefits of multitasking appear potential problems. Writing a multithreaded application requires care and attention to detail. To see what types of problems can arise, let's look at how the programming approach is altered in moving from DOS applications, to Windows applications, to multithreaded applications.

If you have written programs for MS-DOS, you may recall the total control you had over the system. Basically you could assume that your program was the only one running. Although this allowed a great amount of freedom, you often had to determine the specific hardware that the program was running on. For example, you couldn't assume that the system had an EGA or VGA card installed, or that a particular printer was connected. Your program had to test for each case and act accordingly. Many programs were limited to specific types of hardware for this reason.

Windows 3.x programming took over some of the programmer's responsibilities. For example, Windows had already determined what types of peripheral equipment were installed on a particular system before your application started. Using APIs you could examine capabilities of the peripherals from within the application. On the downside (initially), you had a learning curve to climb. Windows 3.x is a message-based operating system that allows more than one application to run at a time. Your applications had to wait for a message from Windows. These messages varied, depending on the particular task (you need to paint the screen, the mouse moved, a key was pressed, and so on).

Windows NT is very similar to Windows 3.x—both are message-based operating systems. The similarity ends when a Win32 application creates threads to take advantage of preemptive multitasking. At any given time in Windows 3.x, you could point to a line of code and say, "This is where my application is executing right now." In a multithreaded application, however, you can't always predict the point of execution with accuracy. If you have multiple threads running, all threads (based on priority) are receiving timeslices at the microprocessor level. When different threads rely on each other for data, problems with thread *synchronization* can result.

In this chapter we will introduce the *synchronization objects* available to your Win32 applications. You can use different types of synchronization objects depending on the synchronization problem. Before we look at the individual thread and process synchronization objects, let's take a look at the topics covered in this chapter.

CHAPTER OVERVIEW

Concepts Covered

◢ Creating event objects

◢ Setting, pulsing, and resetting events

◢ Waiting on a single object

◢ Waiting on multiple objects

◢ Using critical sections

◢ Creating mutexes

◢ Creating named objects

◢ Creating anonymous objects

◢ Opening mutexes

◢ Releasing mutexes

◢ Creating semaphores

◢ Opening semaphores

◢ Releasing semaphores

Win32 API Functions Covered

◢ CreateEvent()

◢ OpenEvent()

◢ SetEvent()

◢ ResetEvent()

◢ PulseEvent()

◢ WaitForSingleObject()

◢ InitializeCriticalSection()

◢ EnterCriticalSection()

◢ LeaveCriticalSection()

◢ DeleteCriticalSection()

◢ CreateMutex()

◢ OpenMutex()

◢ ReleaseMutex()

◢ CreateSemaphore()

◢ OpenSemaphore()

◢ ReleaseSemaphore()

◢ WaitForMultipleObjects()

Data Types Covered

◢ CRITICAL_SECTION (structure)

Parameters and Values Covered

◢ SYNCHRONIZE

◢ EVENT_MODIFY_STATE

◢ EVENT_ALL_ACCESS

◢ WAIT_OBJECT_0

◢ WAIT_OBJECT_0 + n

◢ WAIT_ABANDONED

◢ WAIT_ABANDONED_0

◢ WAIT_ABANDONED_0 + n

◢ WAIT_TIMEOUT

◢ MUTEX_ALL_ACCESS

◢ SEMAPHORE_MODIFY_STATE

◢ SEMAPHORE_ALL_ACCESS)

--- ---

THE NEED FOR SYNCHRONIZATION

We demonstrated two thread synchronization problems in Chapter 6 (MULTI2): deadlocks and races. You can avoid these pitfalls in your multithreaded applications by using a combination of synchronization objects and program organization. Synchronization objects alone will not protect your applications from multiple thread bugs; you can still create deadlocks and races if you are not careful. In most cases, however, these objects will correct problems that otherwise would have no solution.

Objects—Signaled and Not-Signaled

There are many types of objects in Win32 programming. Many of these objects maintain a state known as *signaled* or *not-signaled*. For example, an individual thread has a state of not-signaled while it's executing. When the thread function returns, the state of the thread is signaled. Other threads can wait for this signal before starting their own execution. If Thread 2 requires a value that is only valid if Thread 1 returns, it can test to see if Thread 1 is signaled before proceeding.

Threads are not the only objects with which you can synchronize other threads. The Win32 API lets you create objects specifically to control synchronization. Similar to threads, three of these objects also have a signaled or not-signaled state, depending on the situation.

Types of Synchronization Objects

There are four types of thread/process synchronization objects in Win32 programming: events, critical sections, mutexes, and semaphores. It is necessary to understand the purpose of each type of object in order to implement it in your applications. Let's look at an overview of each object before discussing the APIs that create and manipulate them.

Events

An event object provides a way of signaling one or more threads that a particular event has occurred. The object can have a signaled or not-signaled state at any given time. The Win32 API provides functions for creating, setting, resetting, and pulsing (setting and resetting) an event object. Also, you can create two types of event objects: *manual reset* and *automatic reset*.

Who creates the event object? Any thread within a process can create an event object. A handle to the object is returned by the event creating API.

Once created, threads can wait on the object using another API function, provided they have a handle to the event object. Figure 7-1 illustrates an example of three threads waiting for an event object. Thread 1 has been released by setting the event object; this assumes an automatic reset event object.

Processes in Win32 are labeled as related (created by a call to CreateProcess()) or unrelated. You can create events that can be opened by unrelated processes by naming them. As long as the other process knows the name of an event, it can open it.

We'll cover the details of event objects and demonstrate their capabilities in SYNCH1. For now, think of an event object as a traffic cop; the cop (event) can let one or more cars (threads) continue, given certain conditions.

Critical Sections

If you need to prevent threads from performing an action simultaneously (writing to a file, drawing on the device context, accessing shared memory, and so on), consider initializing a critical section. Critical sections can only be accessed by one thread at a time. Other threads attempting to enter a critical section are blocked. A *blocked* thread consumes very little processor time.

Critical sections do not use handles like the other synchronization objects in our discussion. Instead you must initialize a critical section structure. The first thread that enters a critical section modifies the structure (through an API function). Any other thread trying to enter the same critical section area

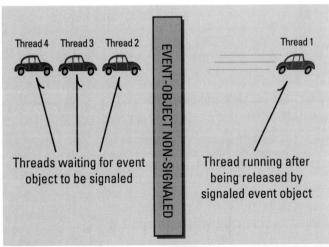

Figure 7-1 Event object—released a single thread

will be blocked until the first thread leaves its critical section. Critical sections can only be used with threads that belong to the same process.

A critical section is not specific lines of code; it is a structure that any thread can check to see if it can continue. For example, a critical section structure is initialized in the primary thread of a process. Thread 1 enters a critical section in its own code and calls the API function that modifies the structure. While Thread 1 is in the critical section, Thread 2 also enters a critical section in its code. Thread 2 is blocked and cannot continue until Thread 1 leaves its critical section. Figure 7-2 illustrates a critical section scenario. In this case Thread 1 is in a critical section; Thread 2 must wait for Thread 1 to exit its critical section before continuing. Thread 3 has not yet reached its critical section and continues to run at this point.

A critical section is like a single-track section of a railroad which only one train can occupy at a time. As soon as one train leaves the section, another train can enter. We'll demonstrate critical section APIs in our second example program of this chapter, SYNCH2.

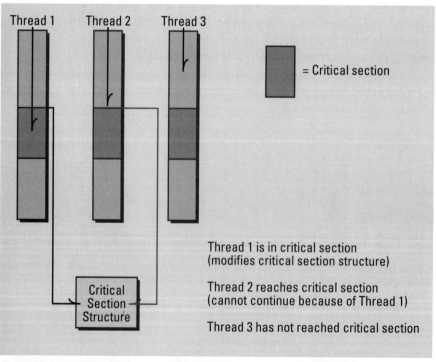

Figure 7-2 Critical sections—Thread 1 in critical section (Thread 2 is blocked)

Mutexes

A *mutex* object is very similar to critical sections. The name mutex is a contraction of *mutual exclusion*. The main difference between a critical section and a mutex object is that the latter can be used by threads of different processes. The mutex creation API also returns a handle to the object.

Once a mutex object is created, a thread can request ownership of the object. If no other thread owns the mutex object, the thread is granted ownership. Any other threads requesting ownership must wait until the original thread gives up ownership of the object. The next thread to receive ownership of the mutex object is the first thread to request it (after the original thread took ownership). Think of this as a first-come, first-serve ownership basis.

The functionality of a mutex object is similar to the critical section illustrated in Figure 7-2. Instead of attempting to enter a critical section, the thread would wait on a mutex object. If the mutex object is signaled, the thread can continue. If the object is non-signaled, the thread is blocked. We'll cover mutex objects in our third example program of this chapter, SYNCH3.

Semaphores

The last synchronization object we will be covering is the *semaphore*. Semaphores act as gates that let a specified number of threads execute at a given time. The number of threads that can own a semaphore object at one time is determined when the object is created. This number can be modified by any thread that has a handle to the object and the handle has the appropriate permissions to modify the count.

When the maximum number of threads own the semaphore, any other threads requesting ownership are blocked. When an owner thread releases the semaphore, another thread gains ownership. In the case of multiple threads waiting for the semaphore object, the first thread to request ownership is the next thread to obtain the ownership. Figure 7-3 shows a simple overview of a semaphore object.

This example assumes we have created a semaphore object with a maximum count of three. The top half of the figure shows that Threads 1, 2, and 3 have requested and obtained ownership of the semaphore. The remaining threads are blocked. The bottom half of the figure shows that Thread 1 has released the semaphore object. This allows a waiting thread (in this case Thread 4) to gain ownership of the object.

You can use semaphores to limit the number of threads that can execute simultaneously. However a thread will not become blocked if it does not wait

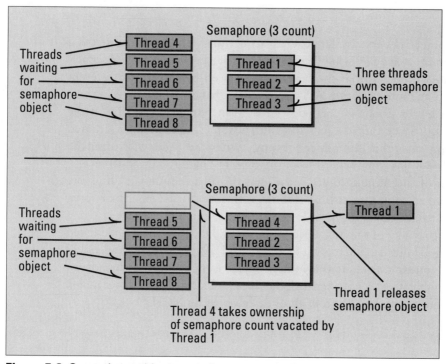

Figure 7-3 Semaphore object—maximum count = 3

on the semaphore object. You must specifically request ownership of the semaphore in each thread you wish to depend on the object. Use semaphore objects when you want to restrict a resource to a certain number. For example, a multiple document interface (MDI) application could use semaphore objects to limit the number of open windows. We'll provide an example in SYNCH4 that demonstrates the behavior of semaphore objects.

EVENT OBJECTS AND WAITING

Our first example program demonstrates the creation of an event object. It also shows how you can make a thread wait for the object to become signaled. Event objects have five related API functions. Two API functions that permit a thread to wait on an object or objects: WaitForSingleObject()

and WaitForMultipleObjects(). We'll discuss the first function in this segment. Multiple object waits are covered in the last segment of this chapter. Let's start with the event API functions.

Event API Functions in Win32

There are five event API functions: CreateEvent(), OpenEvent(), SetEvent(), ResetEvent(), and PulseEvent(). Any thread can create an event object. Depending on the access level of the handle, a thread can also modify the state of the event. Events are used to synchronize a thread or multiple threads with a particular event. For example, if three threads needed a particular value, they could wait for a signaled event object. The thread providing that value could set the event when the value is ready.

Events function differently depending upon how they are created. In order to understand the different event objects, we must look closely at the function that creates them: CreateEvent().

Using CreateEvent()

You can create an event object in a number of different ways, depending on the parameters supplied in the call to CreateEvent(). CreateEvent() requires four parameters: a pointer to an optional SECURITY_ATTRIBUTES structure, a Boolean value indicating if the event is manual-reset or automatic-reset, a Boolean value specifying the initial state of the object, and an optional pointer to a null-terminated string indicating the name for the object. Listing 7-1 shows the proper syntax and an example call to CreateEvent().

Listing 7-1 CreateEvent() syntax and example call

```
/* CreateEvent() Syntax */
HANDLE CreateEvent (LPSECURITY_ATTRIBUTES lpsa, /* optional pointer to security attributes */
            BOOL bManualReset,          /* manual-reset or automatic-reset */
            BOOL bInitialState,         /* initial state (signaled/not-signaled) */
            LPTSTR lpszName);           /* pointer to string containing optional name */


/* CreateEvent() Example Call */
HANDLE hEvent;

   hEvent = CreateEvent (NULL,           /* no security for event */
               FALSE,                    /* automatic-reset */
               FALSE,                    /* initially reset (not-signalled */
               "TheBigEvent");  /* the name of the event */
```

Let's take the example call a parameter at a time. The first parameter is set to NULL, indicating that the event handle has no security associated with it. We'll take a look at security issues in the next chapter. The second parameter is set to FALSE, indicating that the event is automatically reset after a waiting thread is released. The third parameter is FALSE, indicating that the event starts out reset. We'll explain what this means in a moment. The fourth parameter gives the event a name that other processes can use. We'll look at a use for this parameter in the description of the next function: OpenEvent().

The CreateEvent() function returns a handle to the new event object. Threads can use this handle to wait on the event object. You can also modify the state of the event using API functions and this handle. The handle created by CreateEvent() has an access level of EVENT_ALL_ACCESS. This means that any thread using this handle can wait on, change the state of, or close the event object. The return value of CreateEvent() is NULL if the function fails.

What is the difference between automatic and manual reset? Let's look at a few examples. Say that three threads are waiting on an event object. If the event object is automatic-reset, *setting* the event releases one thread (the one that started to wait on the event object first). After the thread is released, the state of the event object automatically changes back to a reset (not-signaled) state. Any threads that started to wait on the object after the reset would be blocked.

If the same three threads were waiting on a manual-reset event object, setting the event would cause all threads to be released and the event object would remain in the signaled state. Any threads starting to wait on the object would continue immediately because of the set (signaled) state of the event. We will see in a moment how a thread can manually set or reset an event object's state. You can use an automatic-reset event for more controlled execution, or a manual-reset event when you want to release all waiting threads.

Creating an event object with CreateEvent() results in a handle that is only visible to the creating process. In order to create an event that can be used by other unrelated processes, you need to name the event in the creating process (as in the example call). Let's look at an API function that opens an event by name: OpenEvent().

Using OpenEvent()

A process can open an event object from an unrelated process by using the name of the object. This function requires three parameters: a DWORD indicating the desired access level for the event handle, a Boolean value indicating whether or not new processes will inherit this handle, and a pointer to a null-terminated string indicating the name of the object. Listing 7-2 shows the syntax and an example call to OpenEvent(). The example call assumes that another process created an event object under the given name (as in the example call in Listing 7-1).

Listing 7-2 OpenEvent() syntax and example call

```
/* OpenEvent() Syntax */
HANDLE OpenEvent (DWORD dwAccess,      /* access level for new handle */
                 BOOL bInherit,        /* will new processes inherit this handle? */
                 LPTSTR lpszName);     /* a pointer to the name of the event object */

/* OpenEvent() Example Call */
HANDLE hEvent;

    hEvent = OpenEvent (SYNCHRONIZE,    /* used for waits only--no modification allowed */
                   FALSE,               /* no inheritance of handle */
                   "TheBigEvent");      /* name of event object created in other process */
```

The first parameter of this call specifies the *desired* access level for the new handle. If the security descriptor on the original object does not permit this level of access, OpenEvent() will fail. In this example call, we are requesting the SYNCHRONIZE access level. This means that this process can use this handle to wait on the event object, but it cannot set or reset the event object. There are two other possible access levels for parameter. The EVENT_MODIFY_STATE access level permits the process to change the state of the event object, but it cannot use the handle for synchronization (waits). The EVENT_ALL_ACCESS level permits the highest level of access. In this case you can use the handle for synchronization as well as modifying its state.

The second parameter determines whether or not new processes will inherit this handle. For example, Process A creates an event object named TheBigEvent. Process B opens the event by name, and the second parameter is FALSE. If Process B creates a new process, with CreateProcess(), the new process will not inherit the handle. If the second parameter to OpenEvent() were TRUE, the new process would inherit the handle. We'll cover more on this subject in the next chapter.

The last parameter to OpenEvent() is a pointer to a null-terminated string containing the name of the object. The name must match a name of an existing event object in the system (object names are not case-sensitive).

If the function succeeds, OpenEvent() returns a handle to the event object. If the function fails, it returns NULL. Possible failures are: the name of the object doesn't exist on the system, or the desired access level cannot be provided.

Now that we can create or open a handle to an event object, let's look at three functions that modify the state of the event object.

Using SetEvent(), ResetEvent(), and PulseEvent()

These three API functions modify the state of an event object. All three functions require a single parameter—a valid handle to an event object—but each function modifies the event object differently. Listing 7-3 shows the proper syntax and example calls for these functions. The example calls assume a valid event has been created or opened.

— — — — — —

Listing 7-3 SetEvent(), ResetEvent(), and PulseEvent() syntax and
example calls

```
/* SetEvent(), ResetEvent(), and PulseEvent() Syntax */
BOOL SetEvent (HANDLE hEvent);     /* handle to valid event object */
BOOL ResetEvent (HANDLE hEvent);
BOOL PulseEvent (HANDLE hEvent);

/* SetEvent(), ResetEvent(), and PulseEvent() Example Calls */

   SetEvent (hEvent);     /* sets event object to a signaled state */

   ResetEvent (hEvent);  /* resets event object to a not signaled state */

   PulseEvent (hEvent);  /* sets then immediately resets event object */
```

Each of these event-modifying functions returns a Boolean value; you can test this value to determine if the function succeeds (returns TRUE) or fails (returns FALSE). Passing a handle that does not identify a valid event object results in a failure. Also, the handle to the event object must have the EVENT_MODIFY_STATE or EVENT_ALL_ACCESS permissions to use these functions.

The effects of these functions vary depending on the type of event object: manual- or automatic-reset. Let's discuss some scenarios for each function for both event object types.

If you call SetEvent() on a manual-reset event object, it changes the state of the object to signaled. If the event is already signaled, the function has no effect. The event will remain signaled until it is reset with a call to ResetEvent() or PulseEvent(). In this case all waiting threads are released. If you call SetEvent() on an automatic-reset event object, it changes the state to signaled, after which, the event object resets itself to a not-signaled state. In this case one waiting thread is released. If multiple threads are waiting, the thread that started to wait first is released.

If you call ResetEvent() on a manual-reset event object, it changes the state of the object to not-signaled. All threads that start to wait for the object after this call are blocked. This state continues until changed by SetEvent() or PulseEvent(). Calling ResetEvent() on an automatic-reset event object has no effect, since the event automatically resets itself.

If you call PulseEvent() on a manual-reset event object, it changes the state of the object to signaled, all waiting threads are released, then it changes the state of the object to not-signaled. If the manual-reset event object is already signaled, PulseEvent() resets the event object. If you call PulseEvent() on an automatic-reset event object, it changes the state of the object to signaled, one waiting thread is released, then it changes the state of the object to not-signaled. If an event is not-signaled and no threads are waiting, calling PulseEvent() has no effect. It still sets and resets the event object, but since no threads are waiting, nothing happens. Table 7-1 summarizes the effects of SetEvent(), ResetEvent(), and PulseEvent() on automatic and manual-reset event objects.

Function	Effects on Manual-Reset	Effects on Automatic-Reset
SetEvent()	Changes state to signaled; all threads are released.	Changes state to signaled; one thread is released; event object automatically resets.
ResetEvent()	Changes state to not-signaled; subsequent threads calling a wait function are blocked.	No effect.
PulseEvent()	Changes state to signaled; all waiting threads are released; changes state back to not-signaled.	Changes state to signaled; one thread is released; changes state back to not-signaled.

Table 7-1 Effects of setting, resetting, and pulsing events (automatic and manual-reset)

We've talked a lot about waiting threads, but we haven't seen how a thread actually waits on an event object (or other types of objects). The next segment shows you how to cause a thread to wait on a single object.

Using WaitForSingleObject()

This API function has a lengthy yet descriptive name. WaitForSingleObject() causes a thread to wait until a specified object becomes signaled. When a thread is waiting, it uses very little processor time. If you sent a thread into a loop that tested for an event to occur, the loop would consume a large amount of processor time and your application's performance would suffer as a result. WaitForSingleObject() requires two parameters: a valid handle to an object and a DWORD indicating a timeout. Listing 7-4 shows the syntax and an example call to WaitForSingleObject(). The example call assumes a valid event object has been created or opened.

Listing 7-4 WaitForSingleObject() syntax and example call

```
/* WaitForSingleObject() Syntax */
DWORD WaitForSingleObject (HANDLE hObject,   /* valid handle to object */
                           DWORD  dwTimeout); /* timeout value (measured in milliseconds) */

/* WaitForSingleObject() Example Call */
DWORD dwResult;

   dwResult = WaitForSingleObject (hEvent, 60000); /* wait for signaled event for 60 seconds */
```

This example call waits for an event object to become signaled for 60 seconds. The timeout value is specified in milliseconds. If the event object is signaled, or the timeout is reached, the function returns. The return value is stored in *dwResult* in the example call. Even though this example is waiting for an event object, there are several object types that you can make a thread wait for. Here is a list of the objects and what causes them to be signaled:

- thread (signaled when the thread function returns)
- process (signaled when the process terminates)
- event (signaled by SetEvent() or PulseEvent())
- mutex (signaled when the mutex is not owned)
- semaphore (signaled when its count is greater than zero)
- change notification (signaled when a change is made in a directory)

We haven't yet seen the last three of the above object types. Mutex and semaphore objects are described later in this chapter. A change notification handle can be obtained by a call to FindFirstChangeNotification(). This Win32 API function returns a handle to an object that monitors a directory (and optionally its subdirectories). If a change is made (a new file or directory is created, a file is deleted, and so on), the object attains a signaled state. Change notifications are not covered in this book. We'll stay on course with the basic synchronization objects for now.

If the event specified by the first parameter to WaitForSingleObject() does not become signaled before the timeout, the function returns anyway. We can test the return value to determine what caused the function to return.

There are three possible successful return values from WaitForSingleObject(). If this function returns because the object is signaled, the return value is WAIT_OBJECT_0. If the function returns because the timeout limit has been reached (without the object being signaled), the return value is WAIT_TIMEOUT. The other possible return value is WAIT_ABANDONED. We'll discuss this return value in the third segment of this chapter: Mutex Objects.

You can pass INFINITE instead of a timeout value in the second parameter to WaitForSingleObject(). This causes the thread to wait infinitely for the object to become signaled. The timeout value however, is useful in cases where an object cannot reach a signaled state. Testing for all possibilities will produce a more robust multithreaded application.

Let's use the information we've covered up to this point in an example application. SYNCH1 demonstrates creating event objects, event modification, and waiting threads.

EVENTS AND WAIT DEMONSTRATION

Our first example application, SYNCH1, demonstrates the creation and modification of an event object. We will create two threads; both threads will wait occasionally for an event to occur. The example application allows you to see the effects of manual- and automatic-reset events objects.

SYNCH1 has two popup menus: *Threads* and *Events*. The *Threads* menu has one option, *Start Threads*, which creates two threads. The *Events* menu has four options. Three of these options (*Set Event, Reset Event,* and *Pulse Event*) modify the event object. The event object itself is created when the application is started. The fourth option is *Manual Reset;* this selection toggles the event type from manual- to automatic-reset. In this action it deletes the previous event object.

The files for this project are located in the \CHAPTER7\7.1 subdirectory. Since the WinMain() function is one we commonly use, it is omitted from the source listing. Listings 7-5 through 7-7 show the resource script, header file, and source file for SYNCH1. Calls to the event and wait-related API functions are in boldface.

Listing 7-5 SYNCH1.RC—resource script

```
#include "windows.h"
#include "synch1.h"


Synch1Icon ICON synch1.ico

Synch1Menu MENU
    BEGIN
        POPUP "&Threads"
        BEGIN
            MENUITEM "&Start Threads",  IDM_START_THREADS
        END
        POPUP "&Events"
        BEGIN
            MENUITEM "&Set Event",      IDM_SET_EVENT
            MENUITEM "&Pulse Event",    IDM_PULSE_EVENT
            MENUITEM "&Reset Event",    IDM_RESET_EVENT
            MENUITEM "&Manual Reset",   IDM_MANUAL_RESET
        END
    END
```

The header file for SYNCH1 contains a few new entries. Function prototypes are included for the two thread procedures: ThreadProc1() and ThreadProc2(). A global handle is declared, *ghEvent;* we will store the handle to the event object in this variable. Two global character buffers (*gcThread1Status* and *gcThread2Status*) are declared; these buffers will store messages which we will write to the display. We've also declared two global integers (*nThread1Progress* and *nThread2Progress*), which we will use to monitor the progress of each thread.

Listing 7-6 SYNCH1.H—header file

```
/* synch1.h -- Include file for synch1.c and synch1.rc */

/* Menu defines */
```

```
#define IDM_START_THREADS  1
#define IDM_SET_EVENT       2
#define IDM_PULSE_EVENT     3
#define IDM_RESET_EVENT     4
#define IDM_MANUAL_RESET    5


/* Function prototypes */
LONG APIENTRY MainWndProc (HWND, UINT, UINT, LONG);
VOID ThreadProc1 (DWORD *);
VOID ThreadProc2 (DWORD *);


/* Global variables */
HANDLE ghInst;
HANDLE ghWnd;
HANDLE ghEvent;
char   gcThread1Status[40], gcThread2Status[40];
int    nThread1Progress, nThread2Progress;
```

━━ ━━ ━━ ━━ ━━

Listing 7-7 SYNCH1.C—source file

```
/* synch1.c      Demonstrates the use of event synchronization objects */

#include <windows.h>
#include <stdlib.h>
#include "synch1.h"

/* WndProc - Main Window Procedure for synch1.c */
LONG APIENTRY MainWndProc (HWND hWnd, UINT message, UINT wParam, LONG lParam)
{
static HANDLE hThread1, hThread2;
static BOOL   bManualReset = FALSE;
DWORD         ThreadArg1, ThreadArg2, ThreadID1, ThreadID2;
PAINTSTRUCT   ps;
char          cBuf[80];

   switch (message)
   {
      case WM_CREATE:                              /* initialization */
         ghEvent = CreateEvent (NULL, bManualReset, FALSE, NULL); /* create event object */
         lstrcpy (gcThread1Status, "does not exist"); /* set thread 1 status message */
         lstrcpy (gcThread2Status, "does not exist"); /* set thread 2 status message */
         return (0);

      case WM_PAINT:
         BeginPaint (hWnd, &ps);
         lstrcpy (cBuf, "Thread 1 ");                /* first part of thread 1 status message */
         lstrcat (cBuf, gcThread1Status);            /* append the status to the message */
         TextOut (ps.hdc, 0, 0, cBuf, lstrlen (cBuf)); /* draw message */
         Rectangle (ps.hdc, 0, 20, nThread1Progress, 40); /* draw thread 1 progress rectangle */
         lstrcpy (cBuf, "Thread 2 ");                /* first part of thread 2 status message */
         lstrcat (cBuf, gcThread2Status);            /* append the status to the message */
```

continued on next page

continued from previous page

```
                TextOut (ps.hdc, 0, 60, cBuf, lstrlen (cBuf)); /* draw message */
                Rectangle (ps.hdc, 0, 80, nThread2Progress, 100); /* draw thread 2 progress rectangle */
                EndPaint (hWnd, &ps);
                return (0);

        case WM_COMMAND:
            switch (LOWORD(wParam))
            {
                case IDM_START_THREADS:                       /* start the threads */
                    ThreadArg1 = 1;                           /* assign the thread argument */
                    hThread1 = CreateThread (NULL,            /* create thread 1 */
                                        0,
                                        (LPTHREAD_START_ROUTINE)ThreadProc1,
                                        &ThreadArg1,
                                        0,
                                        &ThreadID1);
                    lstrcpy (gcThread1Status, "is running");  /* update status message */

                    ThreadArg2 = 2;                           /* assign the thread argument */
                    hThread2 = CreateThread (NULL,            /* create thread 2 */
                                        0,
                                        (LPTHREAD_START_ROUTINE)ThreadProc2,
                                        &ThreadArg2,
                                        0,
                                        &ThreadID2);
                    lstrcpy (gcThread2Status, "is running");  /* update the status message */
                    InvalidateRect (hWnd, NULL, TRUE);        /* force WM_PAINT to update messages */
                    return (0);

                case IDM_SET_EVENT:
                    SetEvent (ghEvent);                       /* set event */
                    return (0);

                case IDM_PULSE_EVENT:
                    PulseEvent (ghEvent);                     /* pulse event */
                    return (0);

                case IDM_RESET_EVENT:
                    ResetEvent (ghEvent);                     /* reset event */
                    return (0);

                case IDM_MANUAL_RESET:
                    {
                    HMENU hMenu = GetMenu (hWnd);             /* get menu handle */
                    bManualReset = !bManualReset;             /* toggle manual reset Boolean */
                    if (bManualReset)                 /* if manual reset...check the menuitem */
                        CheckMenuItem (hMenu, IDM_MANUAL_RESET, MF_BYCOMMAND | MF_CHECKED);
                    else                              /* otherwise... uncheck the menuitem */
                        CheckMenuItem (hMenu, IDM_MANUAL_RESET, MF_BYCOMMAND | MF_UNCHECKED);
                    CloseHandle (ghEvent);                    /* close the old event handle */
                    ghEvent = CreateEvent (NULL, bManualReset, FALSE, NULL); /* and create the new event */
                    }
                    return (0);
```

```
            default:
                return (0);
        }

    case WM_DESTROY:
        CloseHandle (ghEvent);                      /* close the event object handle */
        PostQuitMessage (0);
        return (0);

    default:
        return DefWindowProc (hWnd, message, wParam, lParam);
    }
    return (0L);
}

/* ThreadProc1()--thread procedure for first thread */
VOID ThreadProc1 (DWORD *Arg)
{
HDC   hDC;

    for (nThread1Progress = 1; nThread1Progress <= 250; nThread1Progress++) /* loop global */
    {
        if (nThread1Progress%50 == 0)                    /* if progress is a multiple of 50 */
        {
            lstrcpy (gcThread1Status, "is waiting for event"); /* update status message */
            InvalidateRect (ghWnd, NULL, TRUE);          /* force WM_PAINT to display message */
            WaitForSingleObject (ghEvent, INFINITE);     /* wait for event */
            lstrcpy (gcThread1Status, "is running");     /* event occurred...update status message */
            InvalidateRect (ghWnd, NULL, TRUE);          /* force WM_PAINT to display message */
        }
        hDC = GetDC (ghWnd);                             /* get handle to DC */
        Rectangle (hDC, 0, 20, nThread1Progress, 40);   /* draw progress rectangle */
        ReleaseDC (hDC, ghWnd);                          /* release the DC */
        Sleep (10);                                      /* sleep to simulate work */
    }
    nThread1Progress = 0;                                /* reset progress global */
    lstrcpy (gcThread1Status, "is terminated");          /* update status message */
    InvalidateRect (ghWnd, NULL, TRUE);                  /* force WM_PAINT to erase old status rect */
}

/* ThreadProc2()--thread procedure for second thread */
VOID ThreadProc2 (DWORD *Arg)
{
HDC   hDC;

    for (nThread2Progress = 1; nThread2Progress <= 250; nThread2Progress++) /* loop global */
    {
        if (nThread2Progress%50 == 0)                    /* if progress is a multiple of 50 */
        {
            lstrcpy (gcThread2Status, "is waiting for event"); /* update status message */
            InvalidateRect (ghWnd, NULL, TRUE);          /* force WM_PAINT to display message */
            WaitForSingleObject (ghEvent, INFINITE);     /* wait for event */
```

continued on next page

continued from previous page

```
        lstrcpy (gcThread2Status, "is running");     /* event occurred...update status message */
        InvalidateRect (ghWnd, NULL, TRUE);          /* force WM_PAINT to display message */
    }
    hDC = GetDC (ghWnd);                              /* get handle to DC */
    Rectangle (hDC, 0, 80, nThread2Progress, 100);   /* draw progress rectangle */
    ReleaseDC (hDC, ghWnd);                          /* release the DC */
    Sleep (10);                                      /* sleep to simulate work */
  }
  nThread2Progress = 0;                              /* reset progress global */
  lstrcpy (gcThread2Status, "is terminated");        /* update status message */
  InvalidateRect (ghWnd, NULL, TRUE);                /* force WM_PAINT to erase old status rect */
}
```

Overview of SYNCH1

This program creates one event object and two threads. Each thread simulates work by drawing an expanding rectangle on the display. A *for* loop in each of the thread procedures performs this task. Each time the loop variable reaches a multiple of 50, the thread waits for the event object to be signaled. When the loop reaches the end, the thread terminates.

During the thread procedures' execution, the user can modify the state of the event object. The results depend on the event type and the given situation. The event object type (manual or automatic-reset) is also selectable by the user. Let's look into SYNCH1.C in more detail.

Creating the Event Object

SYNCH1 creates the event object by calling CreateEvent(). This occurs while processing the WM_CREATE message in WndProc(). The first parameter in CreateEvent() is NULL; this indicates that no security identifier is supplied. The second parameter is a static Boolean, *bManualReset*. This value is initially set to FALSE in the declaration at the top of WndProc(). This means the initial event object is the automatic-reset type.

The third parameter to CreateEvent() is FALSE. This indicates that the event object will start out in a not-signaled state. The last parameter is NULL, indicating that the event type is *anonymous* (has no name). Since the event will not be opened by another process, using OpenEvent(), naming the event is not necessary. We will demonstrate opening a synchronization object later when we cover mutex objects.

The next two lines in the WM_CREATE processing copy strings into the global character buffers. These strings are the end of a message that we will display in the processing of WM_PAINT. One message is for the first thread's status, the other is for the second thread's status. Let's look at the WM_PAINT processing.

Processing WM_PAINT

This message needs to be processed as SYNCH1 creates its main window. The message will also occur when we call InvalidateRect() at various points in the program. The processing basically writes two status messages to the display and redraws the thread progress rectangles. These rectangles provide a visual cue as to where the thread procedures are in their execution.

After the call to BeginPaint(), we copy "Thread 1 " into a local character buffer. We then append the status character buffer (a global) to the local buffer. Since this is the first time through WM_PAINT, the message indicates that Thread 1 does not exist (which is true at this point). Later in the application, the global message changes. Each time the message changes we call InvalidateRect() to update the message. We display the message for Thread 1 with a call to TextOut().

The next line draws a rectangle. The left, top, and bottom of the rectangle are constants. The right side of the rectangle is determined by the global integer *nThread1Progress*. The first time through the loop, this integer is 0; therefore the rectangle has a width of 0 (no rectangle is visible at all).

The remaining lines repeat a similar action, only for Thread 2. The message data depends on the second character buffer and the rectangle depends on the second global integer. The second rectangle's y-constants are higher; therefore drawing it lower on the display. Let's get the thread procedures started.

Starting the Thread Procedures

When the user selects *Start Threads* from the *Threads* menu, an IDM_START_THREADS menu message is sent to WndProc(). We assign a thread argument and call CreateThread(). Note that the thread procedure is ThreadProc1 (third parameter in CreateThread()). After the thread is created, we copy new information into the global thread status buffer, *gcThread1Status*. This time we indicate the thread is running. The same sequence is repeated for the second thread, only the thread procedure is ThreadProc2 and the status buffer is *gcThread2Status*. A call to InvalidateRect() forces a WM_PAINT, which updates the messages on the display. Both threads are now running.

What Is Happening in the Thread Procedures?

Let's take ThreadProc1() and follow it through to see what is going on in the thread procedures. Except for modifying different globals and drawing rectangles in different places on the display, the thread procedures basically do the same thing.

The first section of the thread procedure is a *for* loop. The loop variable is the global variable *nThread1Progress*. The first thing we do inside the loop is check to see if *nThread1Progress* is a multiple of 50 (using the modulus operator). Since this won't occur for a while, we'll skip this section for now.

Next we obtain a handle to the device context and draw a rectangle with a width based on the global variable *nThread1Progress*. We release the device context and call the Sleep() function for 10 milliseconds. These are two reasons for the presence of the Sleep() call. We are simulating that the thread is doing actual work, and the delay makes it easier to see what is going on in the loop. In most cases your programs will not have to call Sleep() from within its threads. In fact, you will most likely want to get the work done as fast as possible. Sleep() also makes it easier to experiment by modifying the event reset status while the threads are still running—otherwise they would zip on by!

The loop continues and the rectangle grows. When the loop reaches the first multiple of 50 (*nThread1Progress* == 50), we copy a new status message into the buffer and call InvalidateRect() to update the display. This is an interesting feature of multiple threads. In Windows 3.x you could call InvalidateRect(); however, you had to return control to Windows before you could start processing the WM_PAINT message. Now, with preemptive multitasking, you can call InvalidateRect(). WndProc() is a different thread (the primary thread); therefore we can continue inside the thread procedure without returning control to Windows.

This new message indicates that the thread is waiting for an event object. We have to change this message before calling WaitForSingleObject(). Why? Because when WaitForSingleObject() returns, the thread is no longer waiting.

Examine the WaitForSingleObject() call. The first parameter is the global handle to the event object. The second parameter is INFINITE, indicating that we are willing to wait forever for this object to become signaled (we'll see how in a moment). When the event object eventually is signaled, the WaitForSingleObject() function returns, we change the message, and update the display once again. The loop continues until it reaches the next multiple of 50.

Determining the state of the event object while examining the code on paper is difficult. You will see the various effects of the event object state when we build and run SYNCH1.

When the loop falls through (*nThread1Progress* > 250), we reset the progress global, copy a terminated message into the global status buffer, and update the display. At this point the rectangle disappears (width == 0) and the message indicates that Thread 1 has terminated. Thread 2 terminates the same way.

Setting, Resetting, and Pulsing the Event

Three menu selections in the *Events* popup can modify the state of the event. The *Set Event* selection generates the IDM_SET_EVENT menu message. In this case we call SetEvent() with the global handle to the event object as its parameter. The function of the *Reset Event* and *Pulse Event* selections are similar. The only variance is the type of API call (ResetEvent() and PulseEvent(), respectively). The effect on the thread procedures is hard to see on paper, but we'll see the full effects at run time.

The Manual/Automatic-Reset Toggle

The fourth selection on the *Events* popup menu is *Manual Reset*. Recall that our original call to CreateEvent() created an automatic event object. When the user selects *Manual Reset,* an IDM_MANUAL_RESET menu message is sent to WndProc(). This case of the *switch* statement is enclosed in braces, allowing us to define a local variable for the menu handle.

We toggle the status of *bManualReset* with the logical NOT operator. In other words if it was FALSE, now it is TRUE, or vice versa. If *bManualReset* is TRUE we check the *Manual Reset* menu item; otherwise we uncheck it. Next we close the handle to the old event object and create a new one using the current status of *bManualReset*. Note that this is for demonstration purposes only. You should never close a handle when a thread has a possibility of waiting on the object. We will only use this selection when both threads are terminated (or haven't been created yet).

Let's see how all of this works in actual practice. The next step is to experiment with the various states and types of event objects.

BUILDING AND USING SYNCH1

The files for SYNCH1 are located in the \CHAPTER7\7.1 subdirectory. Open a Command window and change to this directory. Type NMAKE and press (ENTER). The program is compiled and linked. Either use the Command Prompt to start SYNCH1, or add SYNCH1 to an existing Program Manager group. Review Listings 7-5 through 7-7 while performing the following steps:

1. Note that there are two messages indicating that the threads do not exist. This is a result of the first call to WM_CREATE and WM_PAINT. Open the *Events* menu and look at its options. At this point *Manual Reset* is unchecked (recall the original event object created in WM_CREATE is the automatic-reset type).

2. Select *Start Threads* from the *Threads* menu. This creates two threads; both threads progress until they reach the first call to WaitForSingleObject(). Both thread loop variables (*nThread1Progress* and *nThread2Progress*) are 50 at this point. The messages above the thread rectangles indicate that the threads are running until the wait is reach; at this point the messages indicate that the threads are waiting for an event object. Figure 7-4 shows the status of SYNCH1 at this point.

3. Select *Set Event* from the *Events* menu. This sets the event object, which releases the thread that started the wait first (most likely this is Thread 1). The released thread continues to the next wait point (100 in the loop variable). Why didn't both threads start? Because this is an automatic-reset event object. As soon as a thread is released the event automatically changes to not-signaled. Figure 7-5 shows the status at this point.

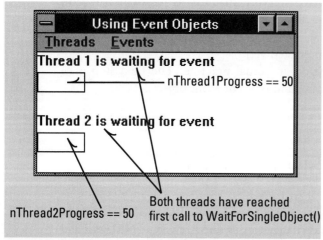

Figure 7-4 Both threads have reached the first WaitForSingleObject() call

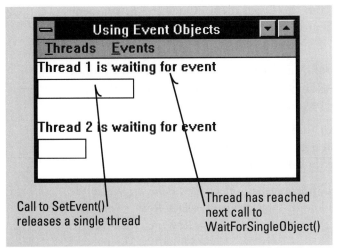

Figure 7-5 One thread is released with call to
SetEvent()—thread has reached next wait

4.   Select *Set Event* again. This time the other thread is released; it also
     continues until the next wait.

5.   Try selecting *Reset Event*. Nothing happens. The event is already
     reset; calling ResetEvent() has no effect with automatic-reset
     objects.

6.   Select *Pulse Event;* a single thread is released. Calling PulseEvent()
     sets and resets an event object; however, an automatic-reset object
     resets itself anyway.

7.   Select *Set Event* twice quickly (before the first released thread
     reaches the next wait). This releases each of the threads. Both
     threads continue to the next wait.

8.   Try *Pulse Event* twice quickly. Again, with automatic-reset events,
     calling PulseEvent() has a similar effect as SetEvent().

9.   Continue to select *Set Event* until both threads are terminated.
     When this occurs the thread progress rectangles disappear and the
     message indicates thread termination.

This concludes demonstrating the effects of setting, resetting, and pulsing
automatic event objects. Since we can change the type of event object when
the threads are terminated, let's observe the same effects on manual-reset
event objects. Continue with the following steps:

375

10.   Select *Manual Reset* from the *Events* menu. Open the *Events* menu and observe the checkmark indicating that the event object is now a manual-reset type.

11.   Select *Start Threads* from the *Threads* menu. Both threads continue to the first wait point. They stop and wait because the event object was created with a not-signaled initial state.

12.   Select *Set Event;* both threads progress until they are terminated. The event object no longer resets automatically (manual-reset type). Figure 7-6 shows the threads in the middle of their progress.

13.   With the event object still signaled, select *Start Threads.* While the threads are in the middle of their progress, select *Reset Event.* The threads stop at the next wait point following the call to ResetEvent( ).

14.   Select *Set Event* to signal the event object and let the threads continue to termination.

15.   Select *Reset Event* to reset the event object. Now select S*tart Threads.* Both threads advance to the first wait point.

16.   Now select *Pulse Event.* Both threads are released and they progress to the next wait point. The threads stopped at the wait point, yet we didn't reset the event! With a manual-reset event object, a call to PulseEvent( ) releases all waiting threads and then resets the object to a not-signaled state.

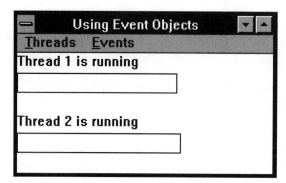

Figure 7-6 Both threads running free—manual reset event object is signaled

17.   Select *Pulse Event* twice quickly. The threads continue to the next wait and stop. Only the first call to PulseEvent() releases the threads. The second call does nothing. Calling PulseEvent() while all threads are running really has no effect; it simply sets and resets the event object.

18.   Select *Set Event* a final time and allow the threads to progress until they are terminated.

19.   Close SYNCH1.

You may want to repeat the steps and follow the example code listings until you are comfortable with event objects. Understanding how event manual- and automatic-reset objects behave will help you decide which type of event to use in your programs.

Although we have been setting, resetting, and pulsing the event objects using menu selections, in most applications you will have a thread signal (set) the event to indicate to a waiting thread that it may continue.

This completes our description and demonstration of event objects. The next segment looks at a different type of synchronization: *critical sections.*

CRITICAL SECTION OBJECTS

The next example program demonstrates the use of critical sections. You can initialize a critical section object within your applications. Only one thread can use the critical section at a time. A critical section is not a specific area of code; it is an object. The object is used for mutual-exclusion (that is, only one thread can *own* the object at any given time). This is virtually the same functionality as the topic in the next segment: mutex objects. The differences between the two are (1) a critical section can only be used within a single process; and (2) critical section objects use a structure, while mutex objects use handles.

You can use critical sections to ensure that two or more threads do not conflict in an operation. For example, if you have three threads that all write to a single file, you want to avoid multiple threads writing at the same time. As soon as a thread needs to write to the file, it can attempt to enter a critical section. If a second thread has entered the critical section first and is writing to the file, the first thread must wait until the second thread leaves the critical section. The bottom line is that only one thread can own the critical section object at a time.

Critical Section API Functions in Win32

Four API functions relate to critical sections: InitializeCriticalSection(), EnterCriticalSection(), LeaveCriticalSection(), and DeleteCriticalSection(). Any thread can initialize a critical section object. Any thread can attempt to gain ownership of the critical section. Once owned, a thread must leave the critical section object before another thread can gain ownership. When no longer needed, any thread can delete the critical section.

More than one critical section object can be initialized within a process. For example, one critical section object can be used to prevent two threads from writing to the same file simultaneously, while another prevents two threads from writing to a specific area of memory simultaneously. Let's look at the first function: InitializeCriticalSection().

Using InitializeCriticalSection()

This function initializes a critical section object. Before this function is called, no thread can use the critical section object. All critical section API functions require a single parameter: a pointer to a CRITICAL_SECTION object. The object is actually a structure. You must not modify this structure (object) manually. Instead you must use one of the four critical section functions to modify the object. Listing 7-8 shows the syntax and an example call to InitializeCriticalSection().

Listing 7-8 InitializeCriticalSection() syntax and example call

```
/* InitializeCriticalSection() Syntax */
VOID InitializeCriticalSection (LPCRITICAL_SECTION lpcsCSObject); /* pointer to CRITICAL_SECTION object */

/* InitializeCriticalSection() Example Call */
CRITICAL_SECTION CSObject;                /* declare CRITICAL_SECTION variable */

   InitializeCriticalSection (&CSObject); /* pass address to initialize CRITICAL_SECTION object */
```

As you can see, the call to InitializeCriticalSection() is straightforward. You simply pass the address of a CRITICAL_SECTION variable to the function. At this point the critical section object is initialized; this means we can make the remaining calls. This function does not return a value.

Using EnterCriticalSection() and LeaveCriticalSection()

Threads can call EnterCriticalSection() to request ownership of the critical section object. Once a thread owns the object, all other threads attempting to gain ownership of the same object are blocked. When the thread has completed its critical processing tasks, you can call LeaveCriticalSection() to release ownership of the object. Listing 7-9 shows the syntax and example calls for EnterCriticalSection() and LeaveCriticalSection(). The calls assume that the critical section object has been initialized.

--- --- --- --- --- --- --- ---

Listing 7-9 EnterCriticalSection() and LeaveCriticalSection() syntax and example call

```
/* EnterCriticalSection() and LeaveCriticalSection() Syntax */
VOID EnterCriticalSection (LPCRITICAL_SECTION lpcsCSObject); /* pointer to initialized CS object */
VOID LeaveCriticalSection (LPCRITICAL_SECTION lpcsCSObject); /* pointer to initialized CS object */

/* EnterCriticalSection() and LeaveCriticalSection() Example Calls */
VOID SampleThreadProc (DWORD *Arg)
{
    [non-critical lines of code]

    EnterCriticalSection (&CSObject); /* request ownership of CS object */

    [critical lines of code]          /* perform critical operations */

    LeaveCriticalSection (&CSObject); /* release ownership of CS object */

}
```

This set of example calls shows a thread procedure that performs both noncritical and critical operations. When the critical area of the thread is reached, we make a call to EnterCriticalSection(). This requests ownership of the critical section object. If the object is not owned by another thread, the function returns and the object is modified to indicate that this thread owns the object. We can continue with our critical calls with confidence that no other thread procedure can enter this critical section. Other threads that perform the same critical calls must also make a call to EnterCriticalSection().

If the critical section object is owned by another thread, our thread procedure is blocked and must wait until the owning thread releases ownership. As with the WaitForSingleObject() call, threads that call EnterCriticalSection() gain ownership in order of the requests: first come, first served.

Once the critical operations are completed in our thread procedure, we call LeaveCriticalSection() to release ownership of the critical section object.

Using DeleteCriticalSection()

Once a critical section object is no longer needed, you can delete the object with this call. Listing 7-10 shows the syntax and an example call to DeleteCriticalSection(). Again, this call assumes that the critical section object is initialized.

Listing 7-10 DeleteCriticalSection() syntax and example call

```
/* DeleteCriticalSection() Syntax */
VOID DeleteCriticalSection (LPCRITICAL_SECTION lpcsCSObject); /* pointer to initialized CS object */

/* DeleteCriticalSection() Example Call */

   DeleteCriticalSection (&CSObject);   /* deletes CRITICAL_SECTION object */
```

After the call to DeleteCriticalSection(), the critical section object is deleted and cannot be used in EnterCriticalSection() and LeaveCriticalSection() calls. It is important to ensure that none of the threads that use the critical section are waiting on the object. One method of doing this is to use WaitForMultipleObjects() to wait for all of the threads to become signaled (terminate) before deleting the critical section. We will cover WaitForMultipleObjects() in the last segment of this chapter.

Now that we've seen the four functions that pertain to critical section objects, let's try them out in a sample application.

A CRITICAL SECTION DEMONSTRATION

The next example application, SYNCH2, demonstrates the initialization and use of critical section objects. First we will initialize a critical section object. Then we will create two threads; both threads attempt to enter the critical section at different points in a loop.

The files for this project are located in the \CHAPTER7\7.2 subdirectory. The WinMain() function is typical; therefore it is omitted from the source listing. Listings 7-11 through 7-13 show the resource script, header file, and source file for SYNCH2. Calls to the critical section related API functions are in boldface.

Listing 7-11 SYNCH2.RC—resource script

```
#include "windows.h"
#include "synch2.h"

Synch2Icon ICON    synch2.ico

Synch2Menu MENU
    BEGIN
        POPUP "&Threads"
        BEGIN
            MENUITEM "&Start Threads",  IDM_START_THREADS
        END
    END
```

The header file for SYNCH2 contains function prototypes for two threads: ThreadProc1() and ThreadProc2(). A global CRITICAL_SECTION variable is declared *(CtrclSect)*; this is the critical section object used in SYNCH1. Two global integers are declared *(nThread1Progress* and *nThread2Progress)*; we will use these values as thread procedure loop variables. Two Boolean values are also declared here *(bThread1CS)* and *(bThread2CS)*. The WM_PAINT processing in SYNCH2.C uses these values to determine what message to display while the threads are running.

Listing 7-12 SYNCH2.H—header file

```
/* synch2.h -- Include file for synch2.c and synch2.rc */

/* Menu defines */
#define IDM_START_THREADS 1

/* Function prototypes */
LONG APIENTRY MainWndProc (HWND, UINT, UINT, LONG);
VOID ThreadProc1 (DWORD *);
VOID ThreadProc2 (DWORD *);

/* Global variables */
HANDLE           ghInst;
HANDLE           ghWnd;
CRITICAL_SECTION CrtclSect;
int              nThread1Progress; nThread2Progress;
BOOL             bThread1CS;
BOOL             bThread2CS;
```

Listing 7-13 SYNCH2.C—source file

```
/* synch2.c      Demonstrates the use of critical section objects */

#include <windows.h>
#include <stdlib.h>
#include "synch2.h"

/* WndProc - Main Window Procedure for synch2.c */
LONG APIENTRY MainWndProc (HWND hWnd, UINT message, UINT wParam, LONG lParam)
{
static HANDLE    hThread1, hThread2;
DWORD            ThreadArg1, ThreadArg2, ThreadID1, ThreadID2;
PAINTSTRUCT      ps;
HBRUSH           hBrush, hOldBrush;
char             cBuf[80];

    switch (message)
    {
        case WM_CREATE:                              /* initialization */
            InitializeCriticalSection (&CrtclSect);  /* initialize critical section */
            bThread1CS = FALSE;                      /* thread 1 is not in CS yet */
            bThread2CS = FALSE;                      /* thread 2 is not in CS yet */
            return (0);

        case WM_PAINT:
            BeginPaint (hWnd, &ps);
            lstrcpy (cBuf, "Thread 1 is ");          /* first part of status message for thread 1 */
            if (bThread1CS == FALSE)                 /* if thread 1 is not in CS... */
            lstrcat (cBuf, "not ");                  /*  then append "not " to the message */
            lstrcat (cBuf, "in a critical section"); /* append the rest of the message */
            TextOut (ps.hdc, 0, 0, cBuf, lstrlen (cBuf));    /* draw the message */
            Rectangle (ps.hdc, 0, 20, nThread1Progress, 40);    /* draw thread 1 progress rect */
            lstrcpy (cBuf, "Thread 2 is ");          /* first part of status message for thread 2 */
            if (bThread2CS == FALSE)                 /* if thread 2 is not in CS... */
            lstrcat (cBuf, "not ");                  /*  then append "not " to the message */
            lstrcat (cBuf, "in a critical section"); /* append the rest of the message */
            TextOut (ps.hdc, 0, 60, cBuf, lstrlen (cBuf));   /* draw the message */
            Rectangle (ps.hdc, 0, 80, nThread2Progress, 100);   /* draw thread 2 progress rect */
            hBrush = CreateSolidBrush (RGB (0x7F, 0x00, 0x00)) /* create a red brush */
            hOldBrush = SelectObject (ps.hdc, hBrush); /* select brush into DC */
            Rectangle (ps.hdc, 100, 41, 200, 50);    /* draw critical section identifiers */
            Rectangle (ps.hdc, 125, 101, 225, 110);
            SelectObject (ps.hdc, hOldBrush);        /* bring back old brush */
            DeleteObject (hBrush);                   /* delete the new brush */
            EndPaint (hWnd, &ps);
        return (0);

        case WM_COMMAND:
```

```
        switch (LOWORD(wParam))
        {
            case IDM_START_THREADS:                 /* start the threads */
                ThreadArg1 = 1;                      /* assign thread argument */
                hThread1 = CreateThread (NULL,       /* create thread 1 */
                                0,
                                (LPTHREAD_START_ROUTINE)ThreadProc1,
                                &ThreadArg1,
                                0,
                                &ThreadID1);
                ThreadArg2 = 2;                      /* assign thread argument */
                hThread2 = CreateThread (NULL,       /* create thread 2 */
                                0,
                                (LPTHREAD_START_ROUTINE)ThreadProc2,
                                &ThreadArg2,
                                0,
                                &ThreadID2);
                return (0);

            default:
                return (0);
        }

    case WM_DESTROY :
        DeleteCriticalSection (&CrtclSect):        /* delete the critical section */
        PostQuitMessage (0);

                return (0);

    default:
            return DefWindowProc (hWnd, message, wParam, lParam);
    }
    return (OL);
}

/* ThreadProc1()--thread procedure for first thread */
VOID ThreadProc1 (DWORD *Arg)
{
HDC      hDC;

    hDC = GetDC (ghWnd);                            /* get handle to DC */
    for (nThread1Progress = 1; nThread1Progress <=250; nThread1Progress++) /* loop with global */
    {
        Sleep (30);                                 /* delay to simulate work */
        if (nThread1Progress==100)                  /* are we up to 100? */
        {
            bThread1CS = TRUE;                       /* set global to indicate thread is in CS */
            InvalidateRect (ghWnd, NULL, TRUE);      /* force WM_PAINT to output message */
            EnterCriticalSection (&CrtclSect);       /* enter the critical section if avail */
        }
```

continued on next page

continued from previous page

```
     if (nThread1Progress==200)                    /* are we up to 200? */
     {
     bThread1CS = FALSE;                            /* reset global — out of critical section */
     InvalidateRect (ghWnd, NULL, TRUE);            /* force WM_PAINT to output message */
      LeaveCriticalSection (&CrtclSect);             /* leave the critical section */
     }
     Rectangle (hDC, 0, 20, nThread1Progress, 40);  /* draw progress rectangle */
  }
  nThread1Progress = 0;                             /* reset progress global to 0 */
  InvalidateRect (ghWnd, NULL, TRUE);               /* force WM_PAINT to erase old progress rect */
  ReleaseDC (ghWnd, hDC);                           /* release the DC */
}


/* ThreadProc2()--thread procedure for second thread */
VOID ThreadProc2 (DWORD *Arg)
{
HDC       hDC;

  hDC = GetDC (ghWnd);                              /* get handle to DC */
  for (nThread2Progress = 1; nThread2Progress <=250; nThread2Progress++) /* loop with global */
  {
     Sleep (30);                                    /* delay to simulate work */
     if (nThread2Progress==125)                     /* are we up to 125? */
     {
        bThread2CS = TRUE;                           /* set global to indicate thread is in CS */
        InvalidateRect (ghWnd, NULL, TRUE);          /* force WM_PAINT to output message */
        EnterCriticalSection (&CrtclSect);           /* enter the critical section if available */
     }
     if (nThread2Progress==225)                     /* are we up to 225? */
     {
        bThread2CS = FALSE;                          /* reset global — out of critical section */
        InvalidateRect (ghWnd, NULL, TRUE);          /* force WM_PAINT to output message */
        LeaveCriticalSection (&CrtclSect);           /* leave the critical section */
     }
     Rectangle (hDC, 0, 80, nThread2Progress, 100); /* draw progress rectangle */
  }
  ReleaseDC (ghWnd, hDC);                           /* release the DC */
  nThread2Progress = 0;                             /* reset progress global to 0 */
  InvalidateRect (ghWnd, NULL, TRUE);               /* force WM_PAINT to erase old progress rect */
}
```

Overview of SYNCH2

In this example application, we will initialize a critical section object. Upon a menu selection, we create two threads. Both thread procedures are similar to those in SYNCH1. They both consist of a *for* loop that counts from 1 to 250. Both threads attempt to enter a critical section. Thread 1 tries earlier in the loop, therefore it will own the critical section object first. Thread 2 will attempt to enter the critical section after Thread 1 has gained ownership; therefore Thread 2 will be forced to wait until Thread 1 leaves the critical section releasing ownership of the object; this permits Thread 2 to gain ownership and continue. Let's look at SYNCH2 in more detail.

SYNCH2 Initialization

When the main window is being created, WndProc() traps the WM_CREATE message. Here we call InitializeCriticalSection() and pass the address of the global critical section object. We also set the two global Booleans to FALSE; we are using these values to determine whether or not a thread procedure is in a critical section.

The next step is to process the first WM_PAINT message. After calling BeginPaint(), we copy a string into a local character buffer, *cBuf.* This is the first portion of a message that we will display in a moment. The next line checks to see if the Boolean *(bThread1CS)* for Thread 1 is FALSE. This time it is FALSE, since we just set it in WM_CREATE. Therefore we append the word "not" onto the end of the message. The next line appends the rest of the message. The full message is, "Thread 1 is not in a critical section." If *bThread1CS* were TRUE, the word "not" would not appear in the message. We finally show the message to the user with a call to TextOut().

The next line draws a rectangle whose width is determined by the progress of the global integer for Thread 1. Since the thread procedure has not modified this value yet, it is still 0. We'll see in a moment that the thread procedure also draws this rectangle. The only reason the same call is here is to avoid having the rectangle disappear when WM_PAINT is used to update the screen messages.

The same scenario is repeated for Thread 2. The only difference is in which globals we use and the vertical location of the progress rectangle.

The remaining lines in WM_PAINT create a red brush, select it into the DC, draw two rectangles, select the old brush back into the DC, and delete the red brush. These two red rectangles will help us identify the location of the critical areas of each thread while we are running the program.

The Thread Procedures

We create two threads when the user selects *Start Threads* from the *Threads* menu. This is also the only menu selection in SYNCH2. The first and second thread point are ThreadProc1() and ThreadProc2(), respectively.

ThreadProc1()

Since both thread procedures are very similar, we'll take a close look at the first one and then point out the differences in the other. The first line in ThreadProc1() gets a handle to the device context. Next we enter the *for* loop, which simulates thread progress. We use *nThread1Progress* as the loop variable. It is initialized to 1 and counts to 250.

The first line in the *for* loop calls Sleep() for 30 milliseconds. This slows the thread procedure both to simulate work and to make it easier to see what's happening when we run SYNCH2. Two *if* statements check to see if the loop variable is 100 and 200, respectively. Since the loop just started, neither statement is TRUE. The only other call in the loop is Rectangle(). This draws a growing rectangle as the thread progresses.

When the *for* loop reaches 100, the first *if* statement is TRUE. This is where we are simulating that critical work is about to be performed. We set Boolean *bThread1CS* to TRUE. The code in WM_PAINT uses this value to determine the message. We then call InvalidateRect() to force the WM_PAINT message. Finally we call EnterCriticalSection() to request ownership of the critical section object. Since no other thread has ownership at this time, EnterCriticalSection() returns and the loop continues.

When the *for* loop reaches 200, the second *if* statement is TRUE. Now we are simulating that the critical work has been completed. We set *bThread1CS* to FALSE and call InvalidateRect(). We call LeaveCriticalSection() to give up ownership of the critical section object. The loop is now free to continue until it reaches 251 and falls through.

After the *for* loop body, we release the device context, reset the thread progress global integer, and call InvalidateRect() to erase the rectangle (*nThread1Progress* == 0).

ThreadProc2()

The second thread procedure is almost identical to ThreadProc1(). Other than the global variables used and the location of the rectangle, the significant difference is the point where we request ownership of the critical section object. Instead of 100, this procedure attempts to gain ownership at 125. Since ThreadProc1() owns the object at this point, ThreadProc2() will be forced to wait until ThreadProc1() gives up ownership of the object. Once it gains ownership, the loop continues to a loop count of 225. ThreadProc2() gives up ownership of the object at this point. No other threads are waiting at this point.

Deleting the Critical Section Object

We delete the critical section object when the user exits SYNCH2. This is performed by a simple call to DeleteCriticalSection() while processing WM_DESTROY. Now let's see the effects of SYNCH2.

BUILDING AND USING SYNCH2

The files for SYNCH2 are located in the \CHAPTER7\7.2 subdirectory. Open a Command window and change to this directory. Type NMAKE and press (ENTER). The program is compiled and linked. Either use the Command Prompt to start SYNCH2, or add SYNCH2 to an existing Program Manager group. Review Listings 7-11 through 7-13 while performing the following steps:

1. Notice that WM_PAINT has displayed two messages indicating that neither thread is in a critical section. Two red rectangles simulate the regions where the two threads will attempt to gain ownership of the critical section object.

2. Select *Start Threads* from the *Threads* menu. The threads start to run. Note: You may have to restart the threads several times to observe the following events.

3. When ThreadProc1() reaches a loop variable of 100, the message changes to indicate that the thread is in the critical section; ThreadProc2() continues. The fact that one thread gains ownership does not stop the other thread.

4. With ThreadProc1() in the critical section, ThreadProc2() reaches its critical section and stops. This is because ThreadProc1() owns the critical section object at this point. Figure 7-7 illustrates SYNCH2 at this point.

5. When ThreadProc1() leaves its critical section, ThreadProc2() can gain ownership of the object and continue. Note that ThreadProc1() does not stop, since it no longer needs the critical section to continue.

6. Both threads can continue to the end of their loop.

7. Exit SYNCH2.

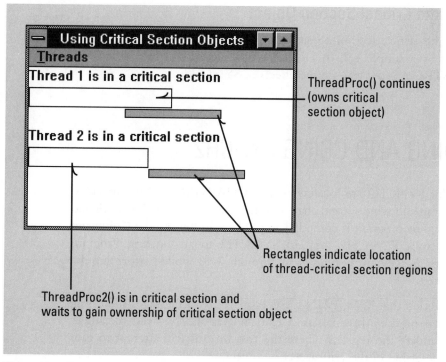

Using Critical Section Objects

Threads

Thread 1 is in a critical section

ThreadProc() continues (owns critical section object)

Thread 2 is in a critical section

Rectangles indicate location of thread-critical section regions

ThreadProc2() is in critical section and waits to gain ownership of critical section object

Figure 7-7 ThreadProc1() owns the critical section object—ThreadProc2() waits

This demonstrates how you can use critical section objects to prevent more than one thread at a time from performing a particular action. Critical section objects, however, can only be used for a single process. No other running processes can use this object for synchronization. If this is necessary, you will have to use a mutex object. Mutex objects are the subject of the next segment in this chapter.

MUTEX OBJECTS

The next example program demonstrates the use of mutex synchronization objects. Functionally mutex objects are very similar to critical section objects. There are two basic differences: (1) we must *create* a mutex object (as opposed to initializing it) which returns a handle to the object (which means we can use the wait API functions); and (2) mutex objects can be named and, as a result, be opened by an unrelated process.

Like critical section objects, mutex objects ensure that two or more threads do not conflict in an operation. Let's look at the functions that relate to mutex objects in Win32.

Mutex API Functions in Win32

There are three API functions that relate to mutex objects: CreateMutex(), OpenMutex(), and ReleaseMutex(). Any thread within a process can create or open a mutex object. Any thread can wait for a mutex object to become signaled (not owned) before continuing. This is accomplished by passing the handle of the mutex object to the WaitForSingleObject() or WaitForMultipleObject() functions. Once owned, a thread must release the mutex object before another thread can satisfy its wait and gain ownership.

Using CreateMutex()

This function creates a mutex object. The object can be named or unnamed, depending on whether another process will need to open it or not. CreateMutex() requires three parameters: an optional pointer to a SECURITY_ATTRIBUTES structure, a Boolean value indicating whether the creating thread wants to own the object immediately, and an optional name. Listing 7-14 shows the syntax and an example call to CreateMutex().

Listing 7-14 CreateMutex() syntax and example call

```
/* CreateMutex() Syntax */
HANDLE CreateMutex (LPSECURITY_ATTRIBUTES lpsa,   /* optional pointer to SECURITY_ATTRIBUTES */
                BOOL bInitialOwn,                 /* does creating thread gain ownership? */
                LPTSTR lpszMutexName);            /* optional name for mutex */


/*  CreateMutex() Example Call */
HANDLE hMutex;

    hMutex = CreateMutex (NULL,        /* no security on mutex object */
                    FALSE,             /* mutex object is not owned initially */
                    "MyMutex");        /* name the mutex "MyMutex" */
```

This example call creates a named mutex object. The first parameter is set to NULL, indicating that the object has no security attributes. The second parameter is FALSE; this indicates that the calling thread does not wish to gain immediate ownership of the mutex object. If this parameter were set to

TRUE, the calling thread would take ownership until it released the mutex object with a call to ReleaseMutex().

The last parameter in the example call is a null-terminated string containing the name of the mutex. If you plan for an unrelated process to open up the mutex object, you must specify a name. If the mutex object will only be used in one process, you can pass NULL to create an unnamed mutex object.

If the call to CreateMutex() is successful, it returns a handle to a mutex object. This handle can be used for synchronization in other calls to WaitForSingleObject(), WaitForMultipleObjects(), and ReleaseMutex().

Using OpenMutex()

This function opens a preexisting mutex object. A named mutex object must be created by another process before calling this function. You can open a mutex object from within the same process; however, you can use unnamed mutex objects instead. OpenMutex() requires three parameters: a DWORD indicating the desired access level to the object, a Boolean value that specifies whether or not other processes will inherit the handle to the mutex object, and a pointer to a null-terminated string containing the name of the pre-existing mutex object. Listing 7-15 shows the syntax and an example call to OpenMutex().

Listing 7-15 OpenMutex() syntax and example call

```
/* OpenMutex() Syntax */
HANDLE OpenMutex (DWORD dwAccess,          /* desired access level */
                  BOOL bInherit,            /* do related processes inherit the handle */
                  LPTSTR lpszMutexName);    /* name of the preexisting mutex */

/*  OpenMutex() Example Call */
HANDLE hMutex;

    hMutex = OpenMutex (SYNCHRONIZE,   /* requesting SYNCHRONIZE access to mutex object */
                   FALSE,              /* mutex handle is not inheritable */
                   "MyMutex");         /* name of the preexisting mutex object, "MyMutex" */
```

This example call opens a named mutex object that was previously created by another process. The first parameter is set to SYNCHRONIZE. This indicates that we are requesting access to use the object for synchronization. In other words we will use the call in WaitForSingleObject() of WaitForMultipleObjects(). The only other possible value for the first parameter is MUTEX_ALL_ACCESS. This sets all possible access flags for the mutex object. This would allow the process to use the mutex for synchronization as well as close the handle of the mutex object.

The second parameter in our example call is set to FALSE. This indicates that related processes (processes created by a call to CreateProcess() from the current process) will not inherit the handle to the mutex. Use TRUE if you want related processes to inherit the handle.

The last parameter is a pointer to a null-terminated string containing the name of the existing mutex object. In our example call, we are specifying a string constant. This object name is the same as our example call to CreateMutex().

Upon success, OpenMutex() returns a handle to the mutex object. As with CreateMutex(), this handle can be used for synchronization in other calls to WaitForSingleObject(), WaitForMultipleObjects(), and ReleaseMutex(). We provide an example of creating and opening a named synchronization object in the next application, SYNCH3.

Using ReleaseMutex()

This function releases ownership of a mutex object. A thread gains ownership of a mutex object by calling one of the two wait functions: WaitForSingleObject() (covered in SYNCH1) and WaitForMultipleObjects() (covered in SYNCH4). ReleaseMutex() requires only one parameter: a handle to the owned mutex object. Listing 7-16 shows the syntax and an example call to ReleaseMutex().

Listing 7-16 ReleaseMutex() syntax and example call

```
/* ReleaseMutex() Syntax */
BOOL ReleaseMutex (HANDLE hMutex);   /* handle to owned mutex object */

/*  ReleaseMutex() Example Call */

   [somewhere in a thread procedure—assumes a valid mutex object has been created or opened]

   WaitForSingleObject (hMutex, INFINITE); /* wait until mutex object is not owned */

   [other lines of code]

   ReleaseMutex (hMutex);
```

This example releases ownership of the mutex object. The ownership was obtained in this case by a call to WaitForSingleObject(). Once the wait is satisfied, we call the lines of code that are dependent upon owning the mutex object. For example, if you are using the object to prevent multiple threads from writing to a file, these lines of code would call the API functions required to write to the file. Since the mutex object must be owned to reach these lines of code, and other threads cannot own the object at the same time, there is no danger of multiple threads writing to the file at the same time. All threads that contend for the permission to write to the file must contain similar calls to the wait and release functions using the same handle.

There is one interesting anomaly to the wait and release functions. The Win32 subsystem allows a thread to call WaitForSingleObject() or WaitForMultipleObjects() more than once. To prevent a deadlock situation, another call is allowed without blocking the thread. For example, one of your thread procedures calls a wait function and waits for ownership. Once the mutex object is free (unowned), the wait is satisfied and the function returns. If you make another call to a wait function later in the procedure using the same handle, the operating system knows that the thread is owned and in normal cases blocks your thread from continuing. However, since the system knows that it is in the same thread procedure that owns the object, it permits the thread to continue. Why bring this up? Because you must make sure that for every wait function encountered, there must be a matching call to ReleaseMutex().

You can see that the functions of a mutex object and a critical section are very similar; they both prevent multiple threads from performing a potentially damaging event by executing simultaneously (such as two threads writing to a file at the same time).

Recall that even though an 80386/486 microprocessor can only execute one instruction at a time, the NT operating system is preemptive. Threads receive timeslices to perform their work. For example, Thread 1 could receive a timeslice, open a file, and start writing to the file. Then Thread 1's timeslice expires and Thread 2 gets a chance. Thread 2 opens the same file and starts to write. As the timeslices are shared back and forth between the two threads, the alternating writes to the file could cause havoc. Using mutual exclusion synchronization objects (critical sections and mutex objects) prevents this from occurring. Let's look at an example of mutex objects in an example application.

A MUTEX DEMONSTRATION

The next set of example applications, SYNCH3 and SYNCH3A, demonstrate mutex objects and opening named objects. The two applications are nearly identical. Both applications have two thread procedures that draw progress rectangles similar to those in SYNCH1 and SYNCH2. SYNCH3, however, creates a named mutex object that is used in the thread's wait functions and SYNCH3A opens the named mutex object and uses it in the same manner.

The files for this project are located in the \CHAPTER7\7.3 subdirectory. The WinMain() function is typical, so it is omitted from the source listing. Listings 7-17 through 7-19 show the resource script, header file, and source file for SYNCH3. Listing 7-20 shows an excerpt from SYNCH3A.C. This excerpt contains the code that is significantly different to that in SYNCH3.C. You can review the entire listing of SYNCH3A by printing it or using a text editor. Calls to the mutex related API functions are in boldface.

Listing 7-17 SYNCH3.RC—resource script

```
#include "windows.h"
#include "synch3.h"

Synch3Icon ICON    synch3.ico

Synch3Menu MENU
    BEGIN
        POPUP "&Threads"
        BEGIN
            MENUITEM "&Start Threads",  IDM_START_THREADS
        END
    END
```

The header files for SYNCH3 and SYNCH3A are identical except for their names. We are providing separate include files because we are simulating unrelated processes. If you experiment and modify one of the application's header files, the other application will not be affected.

Both header files contain function prototypes for two thread procedures: ThreadProc1() and ThreadProc(). Three global variables are also declared here: a handle to a mutex object (*ghMutex*) and two integers to track the thread's progress (*nThread1Progress* and *nThread2Progress*).

Listing 7-18 SYNCH3.H—header file

```
/* synch3.h -- Include file for synch3.c and synch3.rc */

/* Menu defines */
#define IDM_START_THREADS 1

/* Function prototypes */
LONG APIENTRY MainWndProc (HWND, UINT, UINT, LONG);
VOID ThreadProc1 (DWORD *);
VOID ThreadProc2 (DWORD *);

/* Global variables */
HANDLE ghInst;
HANDLE ghWnd;
HANDLE ghMutex;
int    nThread1Progress; nThread2Progress;
```

Listing 7-19 SYNCH3.C—source file

```
/* synch3.c      Demonstrates the use of mutex objects - creating process */

#include <windows.h>
#include "synch3.h"

/* WndProc - Main Window Procedure for synch3.c */
LONG APIENTRY MainWndProc (HWND hWnd, UINT message, UINT wParam, LONG lParam)
{
static HANDLE   hThread1, hThread2;
DWORD           ThreadArg1, ThreadArg2, ThreadID1, ThreadID2;

    switch (message)
    {
    case WM_CREATE:                                /* initialization */
        ghMutex = CreateMutex (NULL, FALSE, "The_Mutex"); /* create named mutex */
        return (0);

    case WM_COMMAND:
        switch (LOWORD(wParam))
        {
            case IDM_START_THREADS:                /* start the threads */
                ThreadArg1 = 1;                    /* assign thread argument */
                hThread1 = CreateThread (NULL,     /* create thread 1 */
                                0,
                                (LPTHREAD_START_ROUTINE)ThreadProc1,
                                &ThreadArg1,
                                0,
                                &ThreadID1);

                ThreadArg2 = 2;                    /* assign thread argument */
                hThread2 = CreateThread (NULL,     /* create thread 2 */
                                0,
```

```
                                    (LPTHREAD_START_ROUTINE)ThreadProc2,
                                    &ThreadArg2,
                                    0,
                                    &ThreadID2);

            return (0);

        default:
            return (0);
    }

  case WM_DESTROY :
    CloseHandle (ghMutex);                        /* close handle to mutex object */
    PostQuitMessage (0);
    return (0);

  default:
    return DefWindowProc (hWnd, message, wParam, lParam);
  }
  return (0L);
}

/* ThreadProc1()--thread procedure for first thread */
VOID ThreadProc1 (DWORD *Arg)
{
HDC     hDC;

  WaitForSingleObject (ghMutex, INFINITE);         /* wait for mutex to be signaled */
  hDC = GetDC (ghWnd);                              /* get handle to DC */
  for (nThread1Progress = 1; nThread1Progress <=250; nThread1Progress++) /* loop with global */
  {
     Sleep (10);                                   /* delay to simulate work */
     Rectangle (hDC, 0, 20, nThread1Progress, 40); /* draw progress rectangle */
  }
  ReleaseDC (ghWnd, hDC);                           /* release the DC */
  InvalidateRect (ghWnd, NULL, TRUE);              /* erase the rectangle */
  ReleaseMutex (ghMutex);                           /* release the mutex object */
}


/* ThreadProc2()--thread procedure for second thread */
VOID ThreadProc2 (DWORD *Arg)
{
HDC     hDC;

  WaitForSingleObject (ghMutex, INFINITE);         /* wait for mutex to be signaled */
  hDC = GetDC (ghWnd);                              /* get handle to DC */
  for (nThread2Progress = 1; nThread2Progress <=250; nThread2Progress++) /* loop with global */
  {
     Sleep (10);                                   /* delay to simulate work */
     Rectangle (hDC, 0, 80, nThread2Progress, 100); /* draw progress rectangle */
  }
  ReleaseDC (ghWnd, hDC);                           /* release the DC */
  InvalidateRect (ghWnd, NULL, TRUE);              /* erase the rectangle */
  ReleaseMutex (ghMutex);                           /* release the mutex object */
}
```

Listing 7-20 SYNCH3A.C—source file excerpt

```
/* synch3a.c        Demonstrates the use of mutex objects - opening process */

/* excerpt from WndProc() in SYNCH3A.C */

    switch (message)
    {
    case WM_CREATE:                                     /* initialization */
        ghMutex = OpenMutex (MUTEX_ALL_ACCESS, FALSE, "The_Mutex"); /* open named mutex */
        return (0);
```

Overview of SYNCH3 and SYNCH3A

SYNCH3 and SYNCH3A both have one menu, *Threads,* with one selection, *Start Threads.* Selecting this menu item creates two threads. SYNCH3 creates a named mutex object and assigns the result to a global handle when the main window is created. SYNCH3A opens the named mutex object created by SYNCH3 when its main window is created.

Each application has two thread procedures. All four thread procedures depend on owning the mutex object in order to satisfy a wait function. This wait is at the start of each thread procedure. The first thread to gain ownership of the mutex object draws a progress rectangle using a *for* loop. When the loop is complete, it releases ownership of the mutex object. This allows another thread procedure to gain ownership of the object. Let's look at these applications in more detail.

Creating and Opening Named Mutex Objects

While processing the WM_CREATE message in SYNCH3, we create a named mutex object by calling CreateMutex(). The first parameter to this function is NULL, indicating that there are no security attributes for the object. The second parameter is FALSE; this indicates that the creating thread (in this case the primary thread) does not want to gain ownership of the mutex object. The third parameter is the address of a null-terminated string, which contains the name of the mutex object ("The_Mutex").

While processing WM_CREATE in SYNCH3A, we open the named mutex object created by SYNCH3. This is accomplished with a call to OpenMutex(). The first parameter is MUTEX_ALL_ACCESS. This means we are requesting the maximum access level to the mutex object. This is an arbitrary decision at this time. The second parameter is FALSE, indicating that any processes created by SYNCH3 will not inherit the mutex object handle. The third parameter is the address of a null-terminated string containing the name of the mutex object to be opened ("The_Mutex"). Neither SYNCH3 nor SYNCH3A has ownership of the object at this time.

The Thread Procedures

All four thread procedures (two in SYNCH3 and two in SYNCH3A) are basically the same. The only difference is the location of the progress rectangles. Let's look at ThreadProc1() in SYNCH3.

The first line of ThreadProc1() is a call to WaitForSingleObject(). The first parameter is *ghMutex;* therefore, we are requesting ownership of the mutex object. The second parameter is INFINITE; this indicates that we are willing to wait indefinitely for the object to become signaled (unowned). Since this is the first thread procedure to request ownership of the object, and the object is not owned yet, the function returns and the state of the mutex object changes to not-signaled. Any other threads calling a wait function will become blocked at this point.

Since WaitForSingleObject() returned, we can continue with the remainder of the thread procedure. The next line gets a handle to the device context. Note that we obtain this handle after the wait. Otherwise, we would obtain a system resource (a handle to a DC) and simply have to wait. This is a waste of the resource.

The next portion of ThreadProc1() is a *for* loop that draws an expanding progress rectangle. This is very similar to the methods used in SYNCH1 and SYNCH2. A Sleep() call of 10 milliseconds delays the loop to provide a visually appealing output. It also simulates work being done in the thread. Once the rectangle reaches an x-coordinate of 250, the loop falls through. At this point we release the handle to the DC and call InvalidateRect() to erase the rectangle. We also call ReleaseMutex() to give up ownership of the mutex object. Another thread that is currently blocked will gain ownership of the object.

The Waiting Threads

While the first thread is drawing its progress rectangle, the other threads are sitting at the first line of their respective procedures. They are waiting for the mutex object to become signaled (unowned). When the first thread completes and releases ownership of the mutex object, a waiting thread gains ownership of the mutex objects. Threads gain ownership in the same order they called the wait function. Let's observe the effects of creating, opening, waiting on, and releasing mutex objects.

BUILDING AND USING SYNCH3 AND SYNCH3A

The files for SYNCH3 and SYNCH3A are located in the \CHAPTER7\7.3 subdirectory. Open a Command window and change to this directory. Type NMAKE and press (ENTER). The makefile contains entries to compile and link both applications. Either use the Command Prompt to start SYNCH3 and SYNCH3A, or add the applications to an existing Program Manager group. Review Listings 7-18 through 7-20 while performing the following steps:

1. Arrange the windows for SYNCH3 and SYNCH3A so both are visible on the desktop. Make sure that the windows are large enough to show the progress rectangles. Figure 7-8 shows a typical arrangement. You may have to run the applications several times to see the effects of the following steps.

2. Select *Start Threads* from the *Threads* menu for SYNCH3. Quick select *Start Threads* from SYNCH3A as well. Notice that only the first thread in SYNCH3 starts to run; the other threads are blocked while they are waiting for the ThreadProc1() in SYNCH3 to release the mutex object.

3. As soon as ThreadProc1() completes and releases ownership of the mutex object, ThreadProc2() in SYNCH3 gets ownership. The progress rectangle for this thread starts to grow. Figure 7-8 shows ThreadProc2() from SYNCH3 running. There is still no activity on the client area of SYNCH3A. These threads are still blocked while waiting for the mutex object to become signaled. ThreadProc1()'s rectangle is erased by the call to InvalidateRect().

4. Once ThreadProc2() completes and releases ownership, ThreadProc1() (in SYNCH3A) gains ownership. The process continues until all four threads have gained ownership of the mutex object, completed the loop, and released the mutex object.

5. Close both applications and restart SYNCH3A by itself. We'll demonstrate what will happen if an application attempts to open a nonexistent named mutex object. Since SYNCH3 is not running, no mutex object is created.

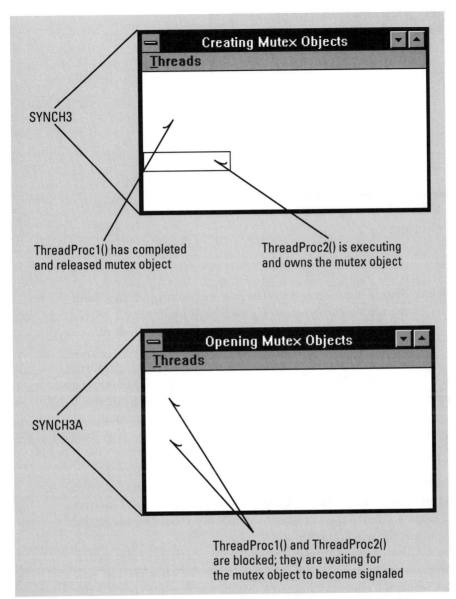

Figure 7-8 ThreadProc2() in SYNCH3 running—threads in SYNCH3A are blocked

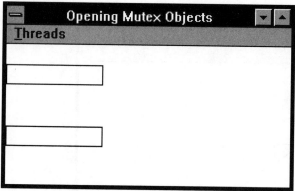

Figure 7-9 SYNCH3A running without a valid
named mutex object

6. Select *Start Threads* from the Threads menu. Notice that both threads are running as shown in Figure 7-9. Why? Since SYNCH3 was not started, no named mutex object was created. When SYNCH3A tried to open the object with OpenMutex(), the function failed (we did not test for this case in this example). When the WaitForSingleObject() call is reached in either thread procedure, the function also fails because the handle to the mutex is not valid. Thus neither thread is blocked from running to completion.

7. Close SYNCH3A.

This completes our example application on mutex objects. You can see that the purpose of mutex objects is the same as that of critical section objects; the difference lies in the fact that the mutex objects can be opened by unrelated processes for synchronization.

Even though our example threads maintained ownership of the mutex object throughout the thread, this does not have to be the case. You can wait on or release a mutex object anywhere in a thread. The key is to bracket the code that must be mutually excluded with a call to a wait function and ReleaseMutex(). We'll shift the focus of synchronization to a different type of object: the semaphore.

SEMAPHORE OBJECTS

The next example program demonstrates the use of semaphore synchronization objects. Semaphores are unique in comparison to the synchronization objects we've seen up to this point. A semaphore is something like a busy parking garage. Have you ever had to wait at a large parking garage that is full? A gate blocks your car from entering the structure until another car leaves. The car leaving generates a signal that raises the gate and allows one car in. This situation continues; for every car leaving, another car is admitted. If the lot is half full, the gate lets every car in until the lot is full again.

Semaphore objects are very similar to the parking garage scenario. Whenever you have a need to limit the number of threads that execute a particular action, you can create a semaphore object to control the number of threads allowed to perform that action. For example, an MDI application could limit the number of open child windows using a semaphore object. You can specify the maximum number of threads allowed to own the semaphore at any given time. In other words you can define the capacity of the parking garage.

In this segment we will examine the functions that create, open, and release semaphore objects. We will also take a look at the WaitForMultipleObjects() function, both in the text and in an example application.

Semaphore API Functions in Win32

Three API functions relate to semaphore objects: CreateSemaphore(), OpenSemaphore(), and ReleaseSemaphore(). Any thread within a process can create or open a semaphore object. Any thread can call a wait function to request ownership of the semaphore. If the semaphore is owned by the maximum number of threads, the thread is blocked. If the number of threads that own the semaphore is less than the maximum, the wait function returns and thread execution continues. Once owned, a thread must release the semaphore object and increment the semaphore count to make "space" available for a waiting thread.

Using CreateSemaphore()

This function creates a semaphore object. The object can be named or unnamed. If you intend to open the semaphore in an unrelated process, you must create a named semaphore object. CreateSemaphore() requires four parameters: an optional pointer to a security attributes structure, a LONG value specifying the initial count, a LONG value specifying the maximum count, and an optional pointer to a null-terminated string containing the semaphore name. Listing 7-21 shows the proper syntax and an example call to CreateSemaphore().

Listing 7-21 CreateSemaphore() syntax and example call

```
/* CreateSemaphore() Syntax */
HANDLE CreateSemaphore (LPSECURITY_ATTRIBUTES lpsa,   /* optional pointer to SECURITY_ATTRIBUTES */
                        LONG lInitialCount,           /* initial semaphore count */
                        LONG lMaximumCount,           /* maximum semaphore count */
                        LPTSTR lpszName);             /* optional pointer to semaphore name */

/* CreateSemaphore() Example Call */
HANDLE hSemaphore;

    hSemaphore = CreateSemaphore (NULL,             /* no security for semaphore object */
                        5,                          /* initial count of 5 */
                        5,                          /* maximum count of 5 */
                        "My_Semaphore");  /* named semaphore */
```

This example call creates a semaphore object with no security attributes, an initial count of five, a maximum count of five, and a name ("My_Semaphore"). The third parameter (maximum number) sets the quantity of threads that can own the thread at any given time. Threads request ownership by calling a wait function using the handle returned by CreateSemaphore(). The second parameter (initial count) sets the starting count of the semaphore object.

The count of a semaphore object is decremented each time a thread calls a wait function. When the count reaches 0, subsequent thread calling wait functions (with the same semaphore handle) are blocked. Note that the initial count does not have to equal the maximum (as it does in our example call). The valid range of the initial count is from 0 to the maximum value specified in the third parameter.

This function returns a handle to the semaphore object if successful and NULL on failure. You can use the resultant handle in calls to wait functions and ReleaseSemaphore().

Using OpenSemaphore()

You can open a semaphore object from an unrelated process if two conditions exist: the semaphore was created as a named semaphore object, and you know the name of the semaphore object. OpenSemaphore() requires three parameters: a DWORD that represents the access flags, a Boolean value that determines handle inheritance, and a pointer to a null-terminated string containing the name of the object to open. Listing 7-22 shows the syntax and an example call to OpenSemaphore(). The example call assumes another process created a semaphore object with the name My_Semaphore.

Listing 7-22 OpenSemaphore() syntax and example call

```
/* OpenSemaphore() Syntax */
HANDLE OpenSemaphore (DWORD dwAccess,         /* desired access */
                      BOOL bInherit,          /* do related processes inherit the handle */
                      LPTSTR lpszName);       /* name of the preexisting semaphore */

/* OpenSemaphore() Example Call */
HANDLE hSemaphore;

    hSemaphore = OpenSemaphore (SYNCHRONIZE,    /* request object for synchronization */
                                FALSE,          /* related processes cannot inherit handle */
                                "My_Semaphore"); /* name of preexisting semaphore object to open */
```

This example call opens a semaphore object named My_Semaphore. The object must be created beforehand with a call to CreateSemaphore(). This call matches up with the example call to CreateSemaphore() in Listing 7-22.

The first parameter to OpenSemaphore() is the desired access level to the object. In this case we specified SYNCHRONIZE. This means we can use the resultant handle to synchronize threads. Other possible values for this first parameter are SEMAPHORE_MODIFY_STATE and SEMAPHORE_ALL_ACCESS. The former permits a thread to modify the state of the semaphore object using a ReleaseSemaphore() call; however, the thread cannot use the handle for synchronization. The latter allows both synchronization and modification using the handle.

The second parameter is a Boolean value that specifies whether or not the handle is inherited by related processes. The second parameter in our example call is set to FALSE. This means if the calling application created another process (with CreateProcess()), the new process would not inherit the handle to the semaphore object.

The third parameter is a pointer to a null-terminated string containing the name of the semaphore object to open. If the name does not exist in the system, the call to OpenSemaphore() fails.

When OpenSemaphore() is successful, a handle is returned; when the function fails, it returns NULL. You can use a valid handle to a semaphore object in wait functions and ReleaseSemaphore().

Using ReleaseSemaphore()

This function releases ownership of a semaphore object. It also provides the opportunity to modify the count of the semaphore object. A thread gains ownership of a semaphore object by calling one of the two wait functions: WaitForSingleObject() (covered in SYNCH1) and WaitForMultipleObjects() (covered in the next example application). ReleaseSemaphore() requires three parameters: a handle to the semaphore object, a LONG value indicating the amount to increment the count of the semaphore, and an optional pointer to a LONG value to store the old semaphore count. Listing 7-23 shows the syntax and an example call to ReleaseSemaphore().

------ -- -- -- -- --

Listing 7-23 ReleaseSemaphore() syntax and example call

```
/* ReleaseSemaphore() Syntax */
BOOL ReleaseSemaphore (HANDLE hSemaphore,     /* handle to owned mutex object */
                       LONG lReleaseCount,    /* amount to increment semaphore count */
                       LPLONG lplPrevCount); /* a pointer to a LONG to store old count */

/*  ReleaseSemaphore() Example Call */
DWORD dwOldCount;

  [somewhere in a thread procedure—assumes a valid semaphore object has been created
  or opened. This example assumes the current count of the semaphore object is 5 and
  the maximum count is 5].

  WaitForSingleObject (hSemaphore, INFINITE); /* wait function returns and decrements
                                         count of semaphore—count == 4 */

  [other lines of code]

  ReleaseSemaphore (hSemaphore, 1, &dwOldCount); /* semaphore object is incremented by one
                                    and old count (4) is stored in dwOldCount */
```

This example releases ownership of the semaphore object. The ownership was obtained by a call to WaitForSingleObject(). Since we assumed that the count of the semaphore object was five, the wait function returns immediately and decrements the count of the object to four.

Once the code that relies on the semaphore object is completed, we call ReleaseSemaphore(). The first parameter is the handle of the semaphore object. The second parameter is the amount to increment the object. The thread parameter is a pointer to *dwOldCount*. In this example the count of the semaphore object is four before the call to ReleaseSemaphore(). After the call the semaphore count is back up to five because the second parameter adds one to the count. The old count (four in this case) is stored in *dwOldCount*.

Two conditions must be met for ReleaseSemaphore() to be successful. First the handle used in the call must have at least SEMAPHORE_MODIFY_ACCESS. Second, if the maximum count of the semaphore object is exceeded by the call, the function fails and the count of the semaphore object is not modified.

The return value from ReleaseSemaphore() is a Boolean value. It returns TRUE on success and FALSE on failure.

Waiting for Multiple Objects

Earlier in this chapter, we examined the Win32 API function that allowed a thread to wait for a single object to become signaled. Now let's look at a function that allows a thread to wait for multiple objects. The types of objects a thread can wait for are the same as the single-wait function (threads, processes, events, semaphores, and so on). The main difference is we specify more than one handle to wait for. Let's examine the WaitForMultipleObjects() API function.

Using WaitForMultipleObjects()

This function is very versatile. You can cause a thread to wait for multiple objects to become signaled, or you can specify that the function return if any of the objects are signaled. In the latter case, you can also determine which of the objects caused the function to return. WaitForMultipleObjects() requires four parameters: a DWORD indicating the number of objects to wait for, a pointer to an array of object handles, a Boolean value specifying whether or not to wait for all of the objects, and a DWORD specifying a timeout in milliseconds. Listing 7-24 shows the syntax and two example calls to WaitForMultipleObjects(). One example call requires that all objects are signaled. The other call returns if any of the objects are signaled. Both example calls assume three objects exist: two thread handles (*hThread1* and *hThread2*) and one mutex object handle (*hEvent*).

Listing 7-24 WaitForMultipleObjects() syntax and example calls

```
/* WaitForMultipleObjects() Syntax */
DWORD WaitForMultipleObjects (DWORD dwObjects,      /* number of objects in handle array */
                              LPHANDLE lphObjects, /* pointer to array of object handles */
                              BOOL bWaitAll,        /* wait for all objects to become signaled? */
                              DWORD dwTimeout);     /* timeout value in milliseconds */


/* WaitForMultipleObjects() Example Call (wait for all objects) */
DWORD dwResult;
```

continued on next page

continued from previous page

```
HANDLE lphObjects[3];

    lpObjects[0] = hThread1;
    lpObjects[1] = hThread2;
    lpObjects[2] = hMutex;

    dwResult = WaitForMultipleObjects (3, lpObjects, TRUE, 60000);

    switch (dwResult)
    {
       case WAIT_OBJECT_0:
          [hThread1 was the last signaled];
          break;
        case WAIT_OBJECT_0 + 1:
          [hThread2 was the last signaled];
          break;
       case WAIT_OBJECT_0 + 2:
          [hMutex was the last signaled];
          break;
       case WAIT_ABANDONED_0:
          [hThread1 was the last signaled and hMutex was abandoned];
          break;
       case WAIT_ABANDONED_0 + 1:
          [hThread2 was the last signaled and hMutex was abandoned];
          break;
       case WAIT_TIMEOUT:
          [timeout occurred before all objects were signaled];
          break;
    }

/* WaitForMultipleObjects() Example Call (wait for any one objects) */
DWORD dwResult;
HANDLE lphObjects[3];

    lpObjects[0] = hThread1;
    lpObjects[1] = hThread2;
    lpObjects[2] = hMutex;

    dwResult = WaitForMultipleObjects (3, lpObjects, FALSE, INFINITE);

    switch (dwResult)
    {
       case WAIT_OBJECT_0:
          [code to handle hThread1 signaled];
          break;
        case WAIT_OBJECT_0 + 1:
          [code to handle hThread2 signaled];
          break;
       case WAIT_OBJECT_0 + 2:
          [code to handle hMutex signaled];
          break;
    }
```

The two example calls perform two distinct operations. The first example call waits for all objects to become signaled while the second example waits for one of the objects to become signaled. Let's examine the first example call.

An array of object handles is initialized before making the first example call. The first parameter to WaitForMultipleObjects() is the number of handles in the array; in this case it is three. The second parameter is the address of the handle array. The third parameter is a Boolean TRUE, indicating that all objects must be signaled before the wait function returns. The last parameter is a timeout; in this case it is 60,000 milliseconds or 60 seconds.

When WaitForMultipleObjects() returns, the return value (a DWORD) indicates the reason for the return. If all objects have been signaled, the return value is WAIT_OBJECT_0 + n; where n is the array index of the last signaled object. For example, if *hThread2* was the last object signaled (the other objects were signaled first), the return value would be WAIT_OBJECT_0 + 1 because *hThread2's* array index is 1. Only one of the first three cases is possible in this example call.

Another possibility (only involving mutex objects) is if all objects are signaled and a mutex object is *abandoned*. An abandoned mutex occurs if another thread gains ownership of a mutex object, and fails to release the object before the owning thread procedure terminates. For example, if the mutex object identified by *hMutex* is abandoned by another thread, then *hThread2* is signaled followed by *hThread1,* the return value is WAIT_ABANDONED_0. This indicates that the handle array, index 0, was the last to become signaled and a mutex object identified in the array was abandoned. WAIT_ABANDONED_0 + 2 is not a possibility in this example call. Why? Because this would indicate that *hMutex* was signaled *and* abandoned; this is impossible.

The last possible return value is WAIT_TIMEOUT. This simply means that the timeout value occurred before all the objects were signaled. In the case of the example call, this would occur after 60 seconds.

The second example call fills the same handle array as the first call, only this time we pass FALSE as the third parameter to WaitForMultipleObjects(). This value indicates that we want the function to return if any objects in the array are signaled. We are also specifying INFINITE as a timeout value, although this is not mandatory for this call.

If any of the objects identified in the handle array are signaled, the wait function returns. The DWORD return value indicates the object that was signaled. Again, the return value is WAIT_OBJECT_0 + n, where n is the handle index in the array. For example, if *hMutex* was signaled, the function would return WAIT_OBJECT_0 + 2 (the array index for *hMutex* is 2).

We did not include the WAIT_TIMEOUT in this *switch* statement because INFINITE was specified in the timeout parameter. In other words a timeout cannot occur in this situation.

The last example application demonstrates multiple object waits and semaphore objects. Let's examine SYNCH4.

A SEMAPHORE AND MULTIPLE WAIT DEMONSTRATION

The last example application of this chapter, SYNCH4, demonstrates semaphore objects and multiple-object waits. This application creates ten threads, each using the same thread procedure. Each thread's execution relies on a semaphore object. The semaphore object will allow a maximum of three threads to execute at any given time. An eleventh thread is also created using a separate thread procedure. This thread will demonstrate a multiple wait. The wait function builds an array using the thread handles from Threads 3 through 6. When all four threads are signaled (terminated), the wait is satisfied.

The files for this project are located in the \CHAPTER7\7.4 subdirectory. The WinMain() function is typical; therefore, it is omitted from the source listing. Listings 7-25 through 7-27 show the resource script, header file, and source file for SYNCH4. Calls to the semaphore and multiple-wait-related API functions are in boldface.

Listing 7-25 SYNCH4.RC—resource script

```
#include "windows.h"
#include "synch4.h"

Synch4Icon ICON    synch4.ico

Synch4Menu MENU
    BEGIN
        POPUP "&Threads"
        BEGIN
            MENUITEM "&Start Threads",   IDM_START_THREADS
        END
    END
```

The header file for SYNCH4 contains two thread function prototypes: ThreadProc() (used for ten threads) and WaitThreadProc() (used for one thread). We also define MAX_THREADS, which will limit the number of threads using ThreadProc() to ten. Two global variables are also declared in the header file: *ghSemaphore* (a global handle to the semaphore object) and *ghThread* (the address for an array of thread handles).

Listing 7-26 SYNCH4.H—header file

```
/* synch4.h -- Include file for synch4.c and synch4.rc */

/* Menu defines */
#define IDM_START_THREADS 1

/* Set maximum number of threads */
#define MAX_THREADS        10

/* Function prototypes */
LONG APIENTRY MainWndProc (HWND, UINT, UINT, LONG);
VOID ThreadProc (DWORD *);
VOID WaitThreadProc (DWORD *);

/* Global variables */
HANDLE ghInst;
HANDLE ghWnd;
HANDLE ghSemaphore;
HANDLE ghThread[MAX_THREADS];
```

Listing 7-27 SYNCH4.C—source file

```
/* synch4.c      Demonstrates the use of semaphore objects */

#include <windows.h>
#include "synch4.h"

/* WndProc - Main Window Procedure for synch4.c */
LONG APIENTRY MainWndProc (HWND hWnd, UINT message, UINT wParam, LONG lParam)
{
static HANDLE hWaitThread;
static DWORD   ThreadArg[MAX_THREADS], ThreadID[MAX_THREADS];
static DWORD   WaitThreadArg, WaitThreadID;
int            i;

   switch (message)
   {
   case WM_CREATE:                          /* initialization */
      ghSemaphore = CreateSemaphore (NULL, 3, 3, NULL); /* create semaphore object */
```

continued on next page

continued from previous page

```
            return (0);

    case WM_COMMAND:
        switch (LOWORD(wParam))
        {
            case IDM_START_THREADS:                    /* start the threads */
                for (i = 0; i < MAX_THREADS; i++)      /* create MAX_THREADS threads */
                {
                    ThreadArg[i] = i;                  /* assign thread argument */
                    ghThread[i] = CreateThread (NULL,  /* create thread */
                                        0,
                                        (LPTHREAD_START_ROUTINE)ThreadProc,
                                        &ThreadArg[i],
                                        0,
                                        &ThreadID[i]);
                }

                WaitThreadArg = 0;                     /* assign thread argument */
                hWaitThread = CreateThread (NULL,      /* create waiting thread */
                                    0,
                                    (LPTHREAD_START_ROUTINE)WaitThreadProc,
                                    &WaitThreadArg,
                                    0,
                                    &WaitThreadID);
                return (0);

            default:
                return (0);
        }

    case WM_DESTROY:
        CloseHandle (ghSemaphore);                     /* close semaphore handle */
        PostQuitMessage (0);
        return (0);

    default:
        return DefWindowProc (hWnd, message, wParam, lParam);
    }
    return (0L);
}

/* ThreadProc()--thread procedure for ten threads */
VOID ThreadProc (DWORD *Arg)
{
HDC   hDC;
char cBuf[80];
int   i;

    WaitForSingleObject (ghSemaphore, INFINITE);   /* wait until semaphore is signaled */
    hDC = GetDC (ghWnd);                            /* get handle to DC */
    for (i = 1; i <=250; i++)                       /* loop to simulate thread progress */
    {
        Sleep (*(Arg) * 15);                                /* later threads sleep longer */
```

```
        Rectangle (hDC, 0, *(Arg) * 20, i, (*(Arg) * 20) + 19);     /* draw progress rectangle */
        wsprintf (cBuf, "Thread %d", *(Arg)+1);              /* format title for thread # */
        TextOut (hDC, 10, (*(Arg) * 20) + 1, cBuf, lstrlen (cBuf)); /* draw title on rectangle */
    }
    ReleaseDC (ghWnd, hDC);                              /* release the DC */
    ReleaseSemaphore (ghSemaphore, 1, NULL);              /* release the semaphore and increment 1 */
}

/* Thread Procecdure that waits on threads 3 through 6 */
VOID WaitThreadProc (DWORD *Arg)
{
HANDLE dwObjects[4];

    dwObjects[0] = ghThread[3];                          /* fill array of thread handles */
    dwObjects[1] = ghThread[4];
    dwObjects[2] = ghThread[5];
    dwObjects[3] = ghThread[6];

    MessageBox (ghWnd,                                  /* notify the user that we are going to wait */
            "Entering wait for threads 3 through 6",
            "WaitForMultipleObjects()",
            MB_OK);

    WaitForMultipleObjects (4, dwObjects, TRUE, INFINITE); /* wait for four threads */

    MessageBox (ghWnd,                                  /* notify that the four threads are signaled */
            "Threads 3, 4, 5, and 6 are signaled",
            "The WAIT is over", MB_OK);
}
```

Overview of SYNCH4

The first thing we do in SYNCH4 is create a semaphore object. This object will ultimately control the number of threads executing simultaneously. Next we create ten threads, all of which depend of the semaphore object. At the same time, we create another thread that uses a multiple wait call to see if four specific threads are signaled (terminated).

Creating the Semaphore Object

We create a semaphore object when the main window is created. This is accomplished while processing the WM_CREATE message. The first parameter to CreateSemaphore() is NULL, indicating that the resultant handle does not have security attributes. The second and third parameters are 3. This specifies the initial and maximum count for the semaphore object. The last parameter is NULL, indicating that we are not naming the semaphore object. This is fine in this application, since no unrelated processes will open the semaphore object.

The return value from CreateSemaphore() is assigned to *ghSemaphore*. We now have a global handle to the semaphore object, which the threads will use in their wait functions.

Starting the Threads

When the user selects *Start Threads* from the *Threads* menu, an IDM_START_THREADS menu message is sent to WndProc(). We create ten threads all using the same thread procedure (ThreadProc()). This is accomplished by a *for* loop with a CreateThread() call in its body. Notice that the *for* loop starts at 0 and continues to MAX_THREADS. MAX_THREADS is defined as 10 in SYNCH4.H. The address of the argument is passed to each thread. This address contains the number of the thread (the argument of the first thread created is 0, the second is 1, and so on).

The return value of each call to CreateThread() is assigned to a global handle array: *ghThread*. For example, the first thread is *ghThread*[0], the second is *ghThread*[1], and so on.

When the *for* loop is completed, we create another thread using the WaitThreadProc() procedure. This thread procedure will demonstrate the WaitForMultipleObjects() function. Let's look at both thread procedures.

ThreadProc()

This thread procedure is used by the ten threads created in WndProc(). How the thread behaves depends on the argument passed to the thread procedure. Let's go through the thread procedure assuming this is the first thread; therefore the argument is 0.

The first line in ThreadProc() is a call to WaitForSingleObject(). Its arguments are *ghSemaphore* and INFINITE. If the semaphore object is signaled (its count is above 0), this function will return.

Now that the thread has permission to continue, we start drawing the infamous progress rectangle. We get a handle to the DC and start a *for* loop. The loop counts from 1 to 250. The first line in the *for* body is a call to Sleep(). The amount of sleep depends on the thread argument. We extract the thread argument (recall that the argument passed to ThreadProc() is actually the address of the argument) and multiply it by 15. This results in the first thread sleeping for 15 milliseconds, the second thread sleeps for 30 milliseconds, and so on. This will simulate the thread working, and will also spread out the thread so they do not end at the same time. We'll see this effect when we run SYNCH4.

The next step is to draw the rectangle. The left coordinate is 0, and the right depends on the loop variable. This results in a rectangle that grows from left to right. The vertical location depends on the value stored in the thread argument address. For example, the top of the first thread rectangle will be *(Arg) * 20, or 0 * 20, which evaluates to 0. The bottom of the first thread rectangle is (*(Arg) * 20 +19), or (0 * 20) +19, or 19. Each successive thread procedure draws its progress rectangle farther down on the display.

We format a string indicating which thread procedure this is and store the results in a character buffer, *cBuf*. We call TextOut() to display the string on top of the expanding rectangle.

When the *for* loop is complete, we release the DC and call ReleaseSemaphore(). The first parameter to ReleaseSemaphore() is *ghSemaphore*. This identifies the semaphore object that we are releasing. The second parameter is 1. This is the amount to increase the count of the semaphore object. This allows another thread to gain ownership of the semaphore object. The last parameter is NULL, indicating that we are not storing the old semaphore count value. Let's examine how the semaphore count is affected in SYNCH4.

The Semaphore Count

While processing the WM_CREATE message, we created a semaphore object with a maximum count of 3 and an initial count of three. We created ten threads when a menu choice was made. The first three threads will reach their *for* loops immediately, since the semaphore object allows three threads to own it at a given time. The count starts at 3 and is decremented three times by the first three threads. The count drops to 0. This blocks any other waiting threads (initially this is seven threads).

When a thread terminates, it releases the semaphore object and increments the semaphore count. Now the count is 1. This satisfies the wait of the next waiting thread and the count drops down to 0 again. As each thread completes, another thread satisfies its wait. It is important to note that the threads may not execute in order. For example, the order may be 1, 2, 3, 5, 4, 6, and so on. Waits are satisfied in the order they were received by the operating system. When the last thread releases the semaphore object, the count is back to 3. Let's look at the other thread procedure which demonstrates multiple-object waits.

WaitThreadProc()

The thread that uses this procedure was created immediately following the creation of the original ten threads. Its purpose is to monitor four objects and let us know when they are all signaled. In this case the four objects are threads 3, 4, 5, and 6. Recall that when a thread is running it is not-signaled. When a thread terminates, it is signaled.

The first four lines of WaitThreadProc( ) fill an array of objects. The objects are the thread handles from threads 3, 4, 5, and 6. Next we display a message box to let the user know we are entering the wait. You must close this box before the wait function is reached.

Next we call WaitForMultipleObjects( ). The first parameter is the 4, the number of objects in the array. The second parameter is the address of the object array. The third parameter is TRUE, which indicates that the function will not return until all four objects are signaled. The fourth parameter is INFINITE, which indicates that the function will not timeout. The only way out is if all four objects become signaled.

When the four threads specified in the object array terminate, the WaitForMultipleObjects( ) function returns. We display another message box indicating that the wait had ended and all four threads are signaled. Let's observe the semaphore object and the multiple-wait function in action.

BUILDING AND USING SYNCH4

The files for SYNCH4 are located in the \CHAPTER7\7.4 subdirectory. Open a Command Window and change to this directory. Type NMAKE and press (ENTER). The application compiles and links. Either use the Command Prompt to start SYNCH4, or add the application to an existing Program Manager group. Review Listings 7-25 through 7-27 while performing the following steps:

1. Select *Start Threads* from the *Threads* menu. Three threads start to draw their rectangles and a message box pops up (see Figure 7-10). Close this message box by clicking on OK.

Figure 7-10 MessageBox() from WaitThreadProc()—the wait has started

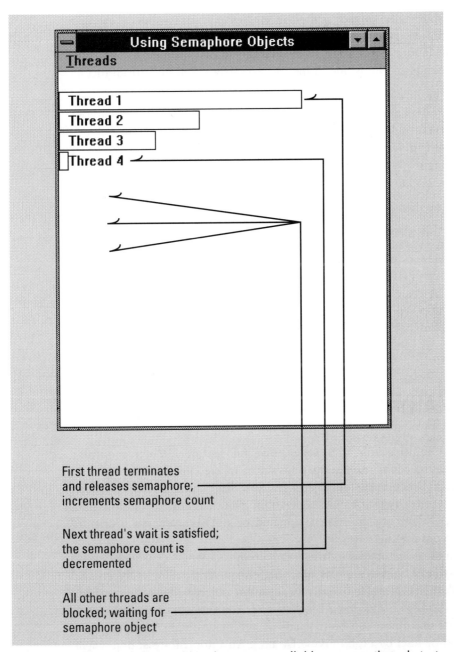

Figure 7-11 The semaphore object becomes available—a new thread starts

2. Observe the threads as their rectangles expand. As soon as the first thread terminates, another thread begins. This action is illustrated in Figure 7-11. Each successive thread takes longer to draw the rectangle. This is due to the variable Sleep() call in ThreadProc().

3. The threads continue. As one thread terminates and increments the semaphore count, another thread starts and decrements the count back to 0. When threads 3, 4, 5, and 6 have terminated, the wait in WaitThreadProc() is satisfied. A message box is displayed (Figure 7-12) indicating the wait is over. Close this message box by clicking OK.

4. The threads continue until the last thread procedure terminates.

5. Close SYNCH4.

This concludes our example on semaphore objects and multiple-object waits. You can continue to experiment with SYNCH4 by modifying the semaphore object, changing the initial and maximum count to various values. You can also try modifying the WaitForMultipleObjects() call in WaitThreadProc() to wait for a different group of threads.

SUMMARY

Preemptive multitasking is a very powerful feature. When multiple, independent threads are executing, however, it is often necessary to establish some control. Synchronization objects give you that control in Win32. There are basically three types of synchronization: events, mutual exclusion, and semaphores. Most objects have a signaled or not-signaled state (critical sections do not use this state).

You can use event objects to trigger certain threads when a particular event occurs. A thread must call a wait function, either WaitForSingleObject() or WaitForMultipleObjects(), to wait for an event object to become signaled. Waiting threads are considered blocked and consume very little processor time. The event object can be manual- or automatic-reset. A manual-reset object must be reset by a call to ResetEvent(). An automatic-reset object will reset itself upon releasing a waiting thread. Event objects can be named and opened by unrelated processes, as long as the process knows the name of the object.

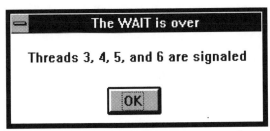

Figure 7-12 The wait in WaitThreadProc() is satisfied

Mutual-exclusion objects prevent more than one thread from performing an action at a given time. There are two methods of mutual exclusion. Critical section objects perform mutual exclusion in a single process. Instead of creating a critical section object, you must initialize it with InitializeCriticalSection(). Critical sections do not use handles, so the wait functions are not used for these objects. Instead you must enter or leave the critical section with the EnterCriticalSection() and LeaveCriticalSection() API calls. When the critical section object is no longer needed, you can delete the object with a call to DeleteCriticalSection().

The other method of mutual exclusion is the mutex object. You can create a named or anonymous mutex object. As with event and semaphore objects, named mutex objects can be opened by unrelated processes. Only one thread can own a mutex object at any given time. A thread can request ownership by calling one of the wait functions. When the thread no longer needs the object, it releases the mutex, changing its state to signaled. At this point the next waiting thread gains ownership of the mutex object.

The last type of synchronization object is the semaphore. You can create a semaphore object with a maximum count. This count determines how many threads can own the object at any given time. When this count reaches 0, all other waiting threads are blocked until a thread releases ownership of the semaphore object. A thread requests ownership of a semaphore object by calling a wait function. Semaphore objects can also be named or anonymous. Use named semaphores if the object must be opened by an unrelated process.

Up to this point in the book, we've been passing NULL to all functions that use a security attributes parameter. In the next chapter, we'll take a look at an introduction to Windows NT System Security.

Introduction to Windows NT System Security

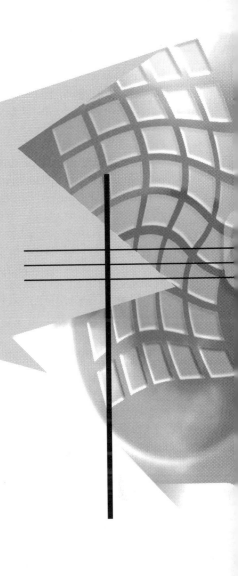

Introduction to Windows NT System Security

Security is a vast topic in Windows NT and there are numerous API functions that support the NT security system. We will cover some of these new API functions in this chapter. To cover them all in detail would fill a book in itself, but we will do more than scratch the surface of this topic. After reading this chapter, and examining the example application, you will have a good grasp of the design, purpose, and functionality of NT security.

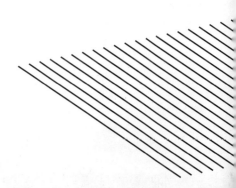

We have created several *objects* in our previous applications, such as files, threads, processes, and synchronization objects. Each time we created an object, we passed a NULL value to a parameter that could have specified security attributes. These attributes are one of the two major topics of this chapter. You (and other people in your organization) are the other major topic—you are all *users* of Windows NT. It is the user-object relationship that is at the heart of NT security. These security attributes will specify what a user, or group of users, can or cannot do with the object.

Security is not mandatory when you create objects. You can create an application without regard to security issues. All you have to do is to continue passing the NULL value in the security attributes argument to the object creation API functions. If you need built-in security in your applications, however, these topics provide a starting point so you can do just that.

We will start with an overview of the NT security system in which we describe the goals and the scope of our discussion. After this overview we will examine some of the key API functions that aid you in implementing security features within your applications. Finally we will create a sample application that creates a file with security in mind. Let's start with a list of topics that you will be learning in this chapter.

CHAPTER OVERVIEW

Concepts Covered

⊿ Security identifiers (SID)

⊿ Finding an account SID by name

⊿ Finding an account name by SID

⊿ Access control lists (ACL)

⊿ Initializing discretionary ACLs (DACL)

⊿ Iinitializing system ACLs (SACL)

⊿ Access control entries (ACEs)

⊿ Using access allowed ACEs

⊿ Using access denied ACEs

⊿ Using system audit ACEs

Win32 API Functions Covered

⊿ LookupAccountName()

⊿ LookupAccountSid()

⊿ GetLengthSid()

⊿ InitializeAcl()

⊿ InitializeSecurityDescriptor()

⊿ AddAccessAllowedAce()

⊿ AddAccessDeniedAce()

⊿ AddAuditAccessAce()

⊿ InitializeSecurityDescriptor()

⊿ SetSecurityDescriptorOwner()

⊿ SetSecurityDescriptorSacl()

⊿ SetSecurityDescriptorDacl()

Data Types Covered

⊿ SECURITY_ATTRIBUTES structure

⊿ SECURITY_DESCRIPTOR structure

⊿ SID_NAME_USE enumerated type

⊿ ACL_SIZE_INFORMATION structure

⊿ ACCESS_ALLOWED_ACE structure

⊿ ACCESS_DENIED_ACE structure

⊿ SYSTEM_AUDIT_ACE structure

⊿ ACCESS_MASK

⊿ SECURITY_INFORMATION

OVERVIEW OF WINDOWS NT SECURITY

Windows NT was designed to meet the requirements of United States Department of Defense C2 security measurement criteria. This means that the NT security system must provide *discretionary* security protection. The owner of a resource (file, semaphore, and so on) can control the access to the resource, and he or she can also permit access to other users on the system at his or her discretion. Windows NT promises to be extensible to division B

423

security; this security division demands *mandatory* security protection. In this scenario an owner of a resource can only permit another user's access to an object if the user is permitted access by the system. For now, Windows NT has discretionary access control.

It is not a requirement for a Win32 application to have security implemented. However, if you find that security would benefit your application, this chapter provides the example API calls to get you going. Before examining the security function calls, let's examine the two basic elements in NT security: *users* and *objects*.

USERS AND OBJECTS—SID AND SD

We can more easily grasp the complex subject of security by concentrating on two fundamental elements: users and objects. A user is represented by a security identifier or SID. This unique identifier is generated when the user logs on to Windows NT. As an analogy, think of the SID as a key. Users must always log on to Windows NT, even on a single-user system.

THE WINDOWS NT LOGON PROCESS

When a Windows NT system is powered on, a dialog box informs the user to press CONTROL-ALT-DEL to log on. After pressing this key combination, another dialog box appears, allowing user to enter his or her user name and password. If the logon is successful, an access token is created consisting of the user's SID and group SIDs.

The other fundamental element of security is the object. An object can be a file or other system resource, such as a semaphore, thread, and process. Every time we created an object in previous applications, we passed NULL as one of the creation arguments. Passing NULL indicated that we did not wish to pass security attributes to the object. This left the object unprotected in the system. If this object was a file, any other process could access the file for any reason (provided the process knows the name of the file). Likewise, if we create a named semaphore object, other processes can open the object.

SIDs represent more than users. Groups and the NT operating system also have SIDs. For example, an SID exists to represent groups (Power Users, Backup Operators, and so on) created by the system administrator.

In order to protect the object, we must pass a SECURITY_ATTRIBUTES structure to the function that creates the object. This structure is declared in WINBASE.H. Here is the SECURITY_ATTRIBUTES declaration:

```
typedef struct _SECURITY_ATTRIBUTES {
    DWORD nLength;
    LPVOID lpSecurityDescriptor;
    BOOL bInheritHandle;
} SECURITY_ATTRIBUTES;
```

The first member of SECURITY_ATTRIBUTES is *nLength*. This member specifies the length of the structure in bytes. This is normally set to *sizeof* (SECURITY_ATTRIBUTES). The second member, *lpSecurityDescriptor* is a pointer to a *security descriptor,* or SD. This security descriptor determines who can access the object it is applied to. It also specifies the level of access-allowed to the object (for example read only, write, and so on). To complete our analogy, the security descriptor is the lock on the object. SIDs (the key) can access certain objects provided they are allowed access by the object's security descriptor (the lock).

The third member of the structure specifies whether or not the resultant handle to the object is inherited by child processes. For example, suppose you create a file and pass a security attributes structure in which *bInheritHandle* is TRUE. You then spawn a new process using CreateProcess(). The new process will inherit the handle to the file.

Our two fundamental security elements are users and objects. Internally to the Windows NT operating system, the elements are SIDs and SDs. Figure 8-1 shows the analogy for security identifiers and security descriptors.

If a security identifier (SID) can open a lock on the object's security descriptor, it can gain access to the object. Notice that locks can be different depending on the level of access (read, write, synchronize). In fact, there are more types of access than those shown in Figure 8-1. We will examine the security descriptor later in this chapter. Before describing the makeup of an SD, we must first look at SIDs.

The Access Token

When a user logs on to Windows NT, an access token is created by the system. This token can be broken up into three areas: the user SID, group SIDs, and privileges. Figure 8-2 shows the access token.

As you can see in the figure, the access token provides you with a set of keys. These keys are your personal SID, a set of group SIDs, and a list of privileges. Just because an object does not specify your SID doesn't mean you won't be able to access the object. For example, suppose a file object does not specifically

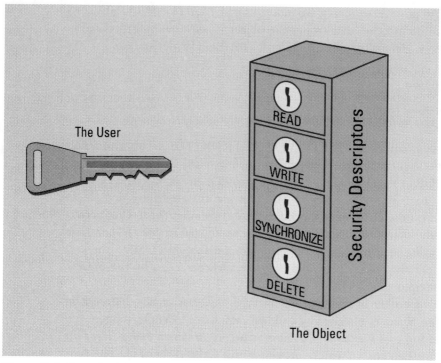

Figure 8-1 Security identifiers and security descriptors (users and objects)

give you permission to write to the file. Your SID will not be able to open the file (or do anything else with it, for that matter). However, if you belong to the Power Users group, and the file's security descriptor allows read and write access, you will gain access because you are a member of the group (even though you do not gain access through your personal SID). The system administrator controls which users make up the group.

Privileges also extend the security power of a user. If a user's access token contains one or more privileges, this may permit the user to access a resource that otherwise would have been inaccessible. Some examples of privileges are

- SeBackupPrivilege (lets the user to back up files and directories)

- SeShutdownPrivilege (lets the user shut down the system)

- SeTakeOwnershipPrivilege (lets the user take ownership of files)

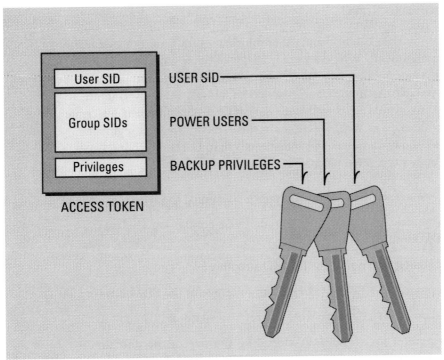

Figure 8-2 The access token—user SID, group SIDs, and privileges

A complete list of privileges is listed in WINNT.H. These privileges are called *well-known* privileges, meaning they are predefined. There are also well-known SIDs such as NT Authority and Network Logon. We won't be dissecting SIDs and access tokens in this book. There are several API functions, however, that interact with SIDs. In the next segment, we'll look at two functions: one that obtains an SID given the user name, and another that obtains a user name given a valid SID.

Security Identifier API Functions

A number of API functions relate to SIDs. You can create and manipulate SIDs using several of these functions, but for this discussion we will examine two particular API functions; one obtains an SID given a user name, and the other function the user name given a valid SID.

Using LookupAccountName()

This function retrieves an SID and other information by passing a user name as one of its arguments. Why do we need SIDs of other users on the system? Because SIDs are used in security descriptors to allow or deny access to a specific object. For example, if we wanted to allow a user, say BSmith, to access a file, we would need to specify the SID for BSmith when we create the security descriptor. We'll see more on this topic in the next segment.

Listing 8-1 shows the syntax and an example call to LookupAccountName(). This function requires seven parameters:

- a pointer to a null-terminated string containing the system name

- a pointer to a null-terminated string containing the user (account) name

- a pointer to a buffer for the SID structure

- a pointer to a DWORD indicating the size of the SID buffer

- a pointer to a string to store the referenced domain

- a pointer to a DWORD indicating the size of the domain string buffer

- a pointer to a SID_NAME_USE enumerated type

Listing 8-1 LookupAccountName() syntax and example call

```
/* LookupAccountName() Syntax */
BOOL LookupAccountName (LPTSTR lpszSystem,      /* name of system to search */
                        LPTSTR lpszAccount,     /* name of user to search for */
                        PSID psid,              /* pointer to SID buffer */
                        LPDWORD pdwSid,         /* pointer to DWORD indicating length of buffer */
                        LPTSTR lpszDomain,      /* name of domain in which user was found */
                        LPDWORD lpdwDomain,     /* pointer to DWORD indicating length of buffer */
                        PSID_NAME_USE psnu);    /* pointer to type of SID */

/* LookupAccountName() Example Call */
UCHAR        cSidBuffer [500], cDomain [80];
SID_NAME_USE SidNu;
DWORD        dwSidLength = 500, dwDomainLength = 80;

    LookupAccountName ("",           /* Null string indicates to search on current system */
                "RJones",            /* search for RJones account */
                &cSidBuffer,         /* address to store the RJones SID structure */
                &dwSidLength,        /* length of SID buffer */
```

```
&cDomain,              /* address to store the RJones domain */
&dwDomainLength,       /* Length of domain buffer */
&SidNu);               /* address of SID_NAME_USE enum type */
```

In this example call, we are trying to get the SID for user "RJones." The first parameter is the name of the system on which to search. We've placed a NULL string here, which results in a search of the local system. In cases where you would want to search for a user on a remote system, you would specify the name of the remote system in this argument. System names are established during the Windows NT installation process.

The second parameter is the name of the user (in our case RJones) to search for. The account name is not case-sensitive. The third parameter is a buffer to store the retrieved SID. An SID structure is variable in length. Our buffer, *cSidBuffer,* is 500 bytes in length. The fourth parameter lets the function know the length of the SID buffer.

The fifth parameter is a second buffer to store the domain of the retrieved SID. The sixth parameter specifies the length of the domain buffer. In our example we are using a buffer of 80 bytes. Your domain and user name are on the title bar of the Program Manager. This is in the format of /DomainName/UserName. Domains are usually created and administered by a network administrator.

The last parameter is a pointer to a SID_NAME_USE enumerated type. This type is defined in WINNT.H. The following is the portion of this file that defines the SID_NAME_USE type:

```
typedef enum _SID_NAME_USE {
    SidTypeUser = 1,
    SidTypeGroup,
    SidTypeDomain,
    SidTypeAlias,
    SidTypeWellKnownGroup,
    SidTypeDeletedAccount,
    SidTypeInvalid,
    SidTypeUnknown
} SID_NAME_USE, *PSID_NAME_USE;
```

This parameter will end up with an enumerated value representing the type of SID found. If RJones is a user, this value would be 1; if RJones indicated a group, this value would be 2; and so on.

LookupAccountName() returns a Boolean value that you can test for success or failure. If the function returns FALSE (failure), you can call GetLastError() for extended error information. If the buffer for the SID is not large enough, a pointer to the required buffer size is returned by the fourth parameter (in our case *&dwSidBuffer).* Likewise, if the buffer for the domain name is not large enough, a pointer to the required buffer length is returned by the sixth parameter. We will demonstrate a use for this function in SECURE1 later in this chapter.

Using LookupAccountSid()

This function is the reciprocal of the previous function. LookupAccountSid() retrieves a user name and other information by passing an SID as one of its arguments. Listing 8-2 shows the syntax and an example call to LookupAccountSid(). This function requires seven parameters:

- a pointer to a null-terminated string containing the system name
- a pointer to a SID structure containing the SID
- a pointer to a buffer to store the retrieved name
- a pointer to a DWORD indicating the size of the account name buffer
- a pointer to a string to store the referenced domain
- a pointer to a DWORD indicating the size of the domain string buffer
- a pointer to a SID_NAME_USE enumerated type

Listing 8-2 LookupAccountSid() syntax and example call

```
/* LookupAccountSid() Syntax */
BOOL LookupAccountSid (LPTSTR lpszSystem,    /* name of system to search */
                       PSID psid,            /* pointer to SID to find account for */
                       LPTSTR lpszAccount,   /* buffer to store name of user */
                       LPDWORD pdwAccount,   /* pointer to DWORD indicating length of buffer */
                       LPTSTR lpszDomain,    /* name of domain in which user was found */
                       LPDWORD lpdwDomain,   /* pointer to DWORD indicating length of buffer */
                       PSID_NAME_USE psnu);  /* pointer to type of SID */

/* LookupAccountSid() Example Call */
UCHAR        cAccountBuffer [100], cDomain [80];
SID_NAME_USE SidNu;
DWORD        dwAccountLength = 100, dwDomainLength = 80;
PSID         pSid;

/* This example call assumes that pSid points to a valid SID structure */

    LookupAccountSid ("",                   /* Null string indicates to search on current system */
```

```
        pSid,               /* points to a valid SID structure */
        &cAccountBuffer,    /* address to store account name for above SID */
        &dwAccountLength,   /* length of account name buffer */
        &cDomain,           /* address to store the SID domain */
        &dwDomainLength,    /* length of domain buffer */
        &SidNu);            /* address of SID_NAME_USE enum type */
```

In this example call, we are trying to get the account name for the specified SID. We are assuming that *pSid* actually points to an existing SID structure. As with the LookupAccountName() function, the first parameter is the name of the system on which to search. Again we've placed a NULL string here, resulting in a search of the local system. In cases where you would want to search for an SID on a remote system, you would specify the name of the remote system in this argument.

The second parameter is a pointer to a valid SID structure. This tells the function which to search for. The third parameter is the buffer to store the retrieved account name. The buffer in the example call, *cSidBuffer,* is 100 bytes in length. The fourth parameter lets the function know the length of the account name buffer.

The fifth parameter is a second buffer to store the domain of the retrieved account name. The sixth parameter specifies the length of the domain buffer. In our example we are using a buffer of 80 bytes. The last parameter is a pointer to a SID_NAME_USE enumerated type.

LookupAccountSid() also returns a Boolean value you can test for success or failure. If the function returns FALSE (failure), you can call GetLastError() for extended error information.

Using GetLengthSid()

This function returns the length in bytes of an SID structure. We will call this function in SECURE1 to get the length of several SIDs. GetLengthSid() requires one parameter: a pointer to a valid SID structure. Listing 8-3 shows the syntax and an example call to GetLengthSid().

Listing 8-3 GetLengthSid() syntax and example call

```
/* GetLengthSid() Syntax */
DWORD GetLengthSid (PSID pSid);  /* a pointer to a valid SID structure */

/* GetLengthSid() Example Call */
DWORD dwSidLength;

   [assumes pSid points to a valid SID structure]
   dwSidLength = GetLengthSid (pSid);
```

The use of this function is fairly straightforward. When and why should you use it? We will see later in this chapter that the SID structure is a part of an access control entry (ACE), which in turn is a part of an access control list (ACL). In order to allocate enough memory to store an ACL, we must know the size of the SID structure.

NT Objects and Security Descriptors

Now that we have an understanding of the user side (SIDs, groups, and so on) of the security equation, let's look at the object side. Each object in Windows NT can contain a security descriptor, or SD. The SD can specify what users can and cannot do to the object. Before we get deeper into the security descriptor, let's look at some of the objects.

Types of Objects in Windows NT

There are many types of objects in Windows NT. Every time you call an object creation API function that contains a SECURITY_ATTRIBUTES argument, you can specify security for the object. Examples of these objects are

- file
- event
- mutex
- semaphore
- thread
- process

Several other objects can be protected by security. All the object creation functions have one thing in common: you can pass a pointer to a SECURITY_ATTRIBUTES structure. We briefly looked at this structure earlier in the chapter. The following is an excerpt of the WINBASE.H file, where this structure is declared.

```
typedef struct _SECURITY_ATTRIBUTES {
    DWORD nLength;
    LPVOID lpSecurityDescriptor;
    BOOL bInheritHandle;
} SECURITY_ATTRIBUTES;
```

The second member of this structure is a pointer to a security descriptor. The SD will contain information that will allow or deny users the right to perform specific actions on the resultant object. Figure 8-3 shows how the

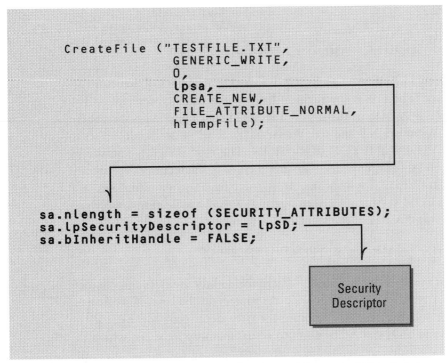

```
CreateFile ("TESTFILE.TXT",
            GENERIC_WRITE,
            0,
            lpsa,
            CREATE_NEW,
            FILE_ATTRIBUTE_NORMAL,
            hTempFile);



sa.nlength = sizeof (SECURITY_ATTRIBUTES);
sa.lpSecurityDescriptor = lpSD;
sa.bInheritHandle = FALSE;
```

Security Descriptor

Figure 8-3 Object creation, security attributes, and the security descriptor

object creation function (in this case CreateFile()), relates to the security descriptor. To complete this scenario illustrated in the figure, we must examine the contents of the security descriptor.

The Security Descriptor

A security descriptor is a structure containing security information for an object. This information consists of flags, an owner, a group, a system access control list, and a discretionary access control list. Figure 8-4 shows a graphical representation of a security descriptor structure followed by an excerpt from WINNT.H. This is the declaration of the SECURITY_DESCRIPTOR structure.

```
typedef struct _SECURITY_DESCRIPTOR {
    BYTE   Revision;                          /* revision of SD */
    BYTE   Sbz1;                              /* must be zero */
    SECURITY_DESCRIPTOR_CONTROL Control;      /* flags for SD */
    PSID Owner;                               /* owner SID of SD */
```

continued on next page

continued from previous page

```
    PSID Group;                      /* not used in Win32 */
    PACL Sacl;                       /* system access control list */
    PACL Dacl;                       /* discretionary access control list */
    } SECURITY_DESCRIPTOR, *PISECURITY_DESCRIPTOR;
```

The first two members of the SECURITY_DESCRIPTOR structure are
BYTE values. The first is the revision level of the security descriptor. The
revision level is defined in the header files and may change with subsequent
releases of Windows NT and the Win32 SDK. This value should be set to
SECURITY_DESCRIPTOR_REVISION. The next BYTE is reserved by
the system and should remain 0. The group entry in the security descriptor is
not used in Win32 applications. It is used by another Windows NT
subsystem, POSIX. Since we are targeting Win32 applications, we won't
look further at this area of the security descriptor.

Flags—The Control Member of SECURITY_DESCRIPTOR

The *Control* member of the security descriptor defines the type and contents
of the security descriptor. A security descriptor can be one of two types:
absolute or self-relative. An absolute security descriptor means that the
pointers to the SIDs and ACLs point to actual memory locations where the
information resides. A self-relative security descriptor means that the
information immediately follows the security descriptor structure in memory
or on disk. As a result self-relative security descriptors can be transmitted over

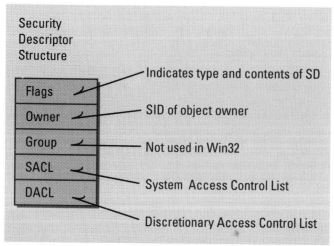

Figure 8-4 The security descriptor

a network. Absolute security descriptors cannot be transmitted because the pointers point to information on the local system. We will create an absolute security descriptor in the example that follows. The operating system creates a *self-relative* security descriptor from the absolute security descriptor. This is a more efficient method of storing the security descriptor, since it lies in contiguous memory, rather than using pointers.

There are also flags in the Control member that specify whether a DACL or SACL is present. The flags can also indicate that the owner, DACL, or SACL as created by a defaulting mechanism. This mechanism must be created in advance. We will specify a DACL when creating a security descriptor in SECURE1. Default mechanisms are not covered in this introduction to NT security. We'll discuss DACLs and SACLs in detail in a moment.

About the Owner of the Security Descriptor

The owner of an object can perform virtually any action on the security descriptor. The owner is represented in the security descriptor by the owner's SID. Shortly we will look at a function that allows you to set the owner of a security descriptor. It is important to note that you cannot assign an owner that is not in the current access token. An *access token* represents a user and consists of the user's SID, group SIDs, and other privileges. For example, user TSmith is logged on to the system. TSmith belongs to two groups: Users and Power Users. In this case you can assign the owner as a pointer to an SID for TSmith, Users, or Power Users. All other attempts will result in problems when you use the security descriptor. We'll show an example of these problems in SECURE1. If the pointer in the owner member of the security descriptor points to the SID for Power Users, all members of Power Users would be considered the owner of the security descriptor.

Access Control Lists—System and Discretionary ACLs

The last two members of the security descriptor are both access control list types (ACLs). The system *access control list* (SACL) contains access control entries (ACEs) that generate audit messages for successful and unsuccessful attempts to access the object. The discretionary access control list (DACL) contains ACEs that determine which users or groups can access the object. Figure 8-5 shows examples of a SACL and a DACL in a security descriptor.

You can see that an access control list (ACL) is made up of access control entries (ACEs). Let's look at the structure declarations for ACL and an access–allowed ACE:

```
typedef struct _ACL {
    BYTE    AclRevision;        /* ACL Revision--set to ACL_REVISION */
    BYTE    Sbz1;               /* reserved--must be zero */
    WORD    AclSize;            /* size of the ACL */
    WORD    AceCount;           /* number of access control entries */
    WORD    Sbz2;               /* reserved--must be zero */
} ACL;


typedef struct _ACCESS_ALLOWED_ACE {
    ACE_HEADER Header;          /* ACE header structure */
    ACCESS_MASK Mask;           /* desired access */
    DWORD SidStart;             /* allow access to this SID */
} ACCESS_ALLOWED_ACE;
```

For the first example in Figure 8-5, we need to specify that BSmith should have read/write access to the object. To do this we need to add an access-allowed ACE to the DACL for the object. If this was the first ACE added to the DACL, the *AclCount* member of the ACL would be 1. The ACE would immediately follow the ACL structure. The *AclSize* member of the ACL would be increased to accommodate the access-allowed ACE.

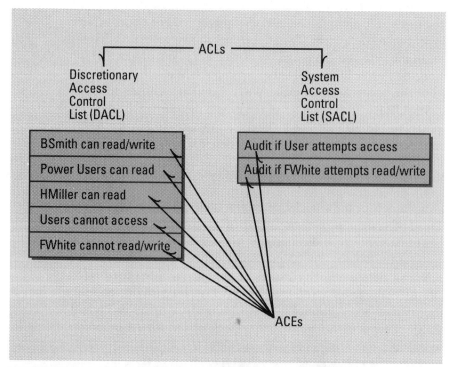

Figure 8-5 Access control lists—system and discretionary

The access-allowed ACE contains two important members. The *Mask* member is a bitmask showing the access level to grant (in the above example, read/write). The *SidStart* member is the SID of the user or group to grant access to (BSmith in the example).

Fortunately we don't have to manipulate these structures at this level. The Win32 API provides a set of functions that let us build a security descriptor. The structures are filled and maintained by these functions. Before we look at the functions that create the security descriptors, access control lists, and access control entries, let's look at an overview of the process. Figure 8-6 shows the process of creating a security descriptor.

There are several steps involved in creating a security descriptor. You must first initialize a security descriptor structure. Optionally you can initialize a DACL and/or a SACL and add access control entries to them. Once the DACL and SACL are completed, you can set the owner of the SID as well as attach the DACL and SACL (if any). You perform these steps using several API functions. Let's examine some of the security descriptor and access control list functions.

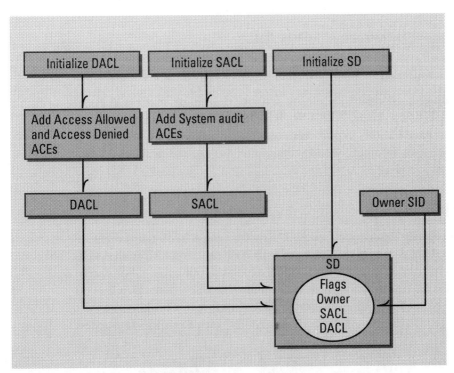

Figure 8-6 Creating a security descriptor

Building a Security Descriptor

The first step in building a security descriptor is to initialize a security descriptor structure. An initialized SD structure contains no DACL, no SACL, no owner, and all flags are set to FALSE. This is considered an empty security descriptor. If you applied this security descriptor to an object, any user could access the object for any type of access.

Using InitializeSecurityDescriptor()

This function creates an empty security descriptor. The function requires two parameters: a pointer to a security descriptor structure and a DWORD specifying the revision of the SD. Listing 8-4 shows the syntax and an example call to InitializeSecurityDescriptor().

Listing 8-4 InitializeSecurityDescriptor()

```
/* InitializeSecurityDescriptor() Syntax */
BOOL InitializeSecurityDescriptor (PSECURITY_DESCRIPTOR pSd, /* pointer to SD stucture */
                                   DWORD dwRevision);        /* revision of SD */

/* InitializeSecurityDescriptor() Example Call */
SECURITY_DESCRIPTOR SecDesc;

   InitializeSecurityDescriptor (&SecDesc, SECURITY_DESCRIPTOR_REVISION);
```

This example call creates an empty security descriptor at the address of *SecDesc*. SECURITY_DESCRIPTOR_REVISION is defined in WINNT.H. This value is passed as the second parameter to InitializeSecurityDescriptor(). Now that we have an empty security descriptor, we can create access control lists, or a DACL and a SACL.

Creating ACLs

Similar to security descriptors, an ACL structure must be initialized before you use it. This is accomplished with one API function. After the ACL structure is initialized, you can start adding access control entries. For system ACLs (SACLs), you can add *system audit* ACEs. For discretionary ACLs you can add *access-allowed* and *access-denied* ACEs. Before we look at the API functions that initialize ACLs and add ACEs, let's examine the access bitmask.

The Access Mask

An access bitmask is paired up with an SID in each access control entry. For example, if we wanted user CThomas to have read and write access to an object, the SID for CThomas would become one member of the ACE, and a bitmask would indicate the access-allowed (read and write). Figure 8-7 shows the access mask that is used in all types of ACEs.

The bitmask in each ACE is a DWORD. The low word of the DWORD is used for access levels specific to the object. For example, this portion of the bitmask for a file would specify access levels to a file object. For a semaphore the bitmask would contain access levels for a semaphore object. Fortunately the high word of the access mask contains generic bits for *generic mapping*. For example, setting a GENERIC_READ access level sets the appropriate bits in the low word depending on the type of object. Generic access bits are:

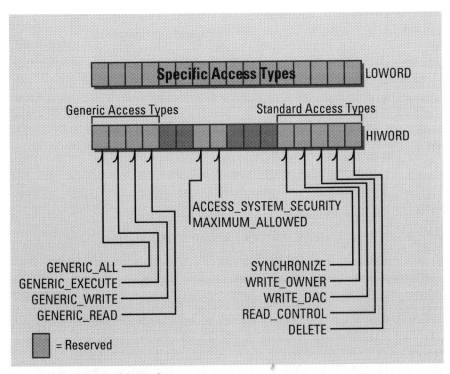

Figure 8-7 Access bitmask

GENERIC_ALL (allow all access), GENERIC_READ (read only), GENERIC_WRITE (allow write access), and GENERIC_EXECUTE (allow execution if executable). In most cases these will be all you'll need.

The lower 5 bits of the access mask provide standard access rights if set. SYNCHRONIZE allows the object to be used in a wait function. WRITE_OWNER grants write access to the owner of the object, WRITE_DAC provides the group or user SID the ability to change or replace the DACL. READ_CONTROL allows read access to the owner of the object, or additionally, a group or user SID.

There are many possible combinations of access levels. We will demonstrate the access mask in SECURE1 using the generic bits. Now that we have seen the access mask, we can initialize an ACL and add some ACEs to it.

Using InitializeAcl()

This function creates a new access control list (ACL) structure. It requires three parameters: a pointer to the ACL structure to be initialized, a DWORD specifying the size of the ACL structure, and a DWORD indicating the revision level of the ACL. Listing 8-5 shows the syntax and an example call to InitializeAcl().

Listing 8-5 InitializeAcl() syntax and example call

```
/* InitializeAcl() Syntax */
BOOL InitializeAcl (PACL pAcl,         /* pointer to ACL structure to initialize */
                    DWORD dwAcl,        /* size of ACL structure */
                    DWORD dwAclRev);    /* revision of ACL structure */

/* InitializeAcl() Syntax */
DWORD dwDaclSize;

    dwDaclSize = sizeof (ACL) + sizeof (ACCESS_ALLOWED_ACE) + GetLengthSid (pSid);

    /* assumes that Dacl points to allocated memory (at least dwDaclsize) */
    InitializeAcl (Dacl, dwDaclSize, ACL_REVISION);
```

This example call initializes a DACL. The only difference between a DACL and a SACL is in the access control entries added after initialization. Note that the first parameter to InitializeAcl() is a pointer to memory. Enough memory must be allocated to store the resultant ACL. We calculate the size of this example DACL by adding the size of the ACL structure (also known as the ACL header), the size of an ACCESS_ALLOWED structure, and the length of the SID. The sum is assigned to *dwDaclSize* and used as the second parameter to InitializeAcl(). We are assuming that this ACL will only contain one ACE (an access-allowed ACE). Each additional ACE requires additional space in the ACL. The last parameter to InitializeAcl() is the revision of the ACL. ACL_REVISION is defined in WINNT.H. This value should be passed when initializing an ACL.

Now that we have an ACL initialized, we can add an ACE to it. There are three functions that add ACEs to ACLs: AddAccessAllowedAce(), AddAccessDeniedAce(), and AddAuditAccessAce(). The first two functions are used to add entries to a discretionary access control list (DACL), while the latter function is used to add entries to a system access control list (SACL).

Using AddAccessAllowedAce()

This function adds an access-allowed ACE structure to an ACL. The function requires four parameters: a pointer to an ACL structure, a DWORD indicating the revision level, a DWORD containing the access bitmask, and a pointer to the SID gaining the access. Listing 8-6 shows the syntax and an example call to AddAccessAllowedAce(). This example assumes that an ACL has been initialized and a valid pointer to an SID exists. You can get a pointer to an SID using the LookupAccountName() function.

Listing 8-6 AddAccessAllowedAce() syntax and example call

```
/* AddAccessAllowedAce() Syntax */
BOOL AddAccessAllowedAce (PACL pAcl,        /* pointer to ACL receving ACE */
                          DWORD dwAclRev,   /* revision of ACL */
                          DWORD dwAccess,   /* access level to grant */
                          PSID pSid);       /* pointer to SID gaining access */

/* AddAccessAllowedAce() Example Call */

    AddAccessAllowedAce (pAcl,              /* pointer to initialized ACL structure */
                         ACL_REVISION,      /* revision of ACL */
                         GENERIC_READ,      /* allow generic read access */
                         pSid);             /* pointer to SID structure */
```

This example call adds an access-allowed ACE to an initialized ACL. We pass a pointer to this ACL as the first parameter. The second parameter is the revision level; this should be set to ACL_REVISION. The third parameter is a DWORD specifying the access level to be granted. The fourth parameter is a pointer to an SID. This SID represents the user or group gaining access.

For example, if the SID in the example call represented BSmith (an individual user), BSmith would gain GENERIC_READ access. This DACL (including the access-allowed ACE) must be set into a security descriptor. You can then use the security descriptor on an object. If this example DACL were set into a security descriptor and applied to a file object, BSmith would be able to access the file for read only.

You can add additional access-allowed ACEs. Keep in mind that ACEs will be evaluated sequentially, starting with the first entry. For example, the first access-allowed ACE permits BSmith read only access, and the second ACE grants every user GENERIC_ALL access. If BSmith attempts to open the object for GENERIC_READ access, the first ACE is satisfied and the evaluation stops. If BSmith attempts to open the object for GENERIC_WRITE access, the first ACE fails, but the second ACE is satisfied. Therefore the order of the access control entries can affect the level of access granted. We'll discuss this more in detail later in this chapter.

We've seen how we can give a group or user a specific access level. Now let's look at a function that denies a group or user a specific access level.

Using AddAccessDeniedAce()

This function adds an access-denied ACE structure to an ACL. The function requires four parameters: a pointer to an ACL structure, a DWORD indicating the revision level, a DWORD containing the denied access bitmask, and a pointer to the SID being restricted. Listing 8-7 shows the syntax and an example call to AddAccessDeniedAce(). Again, this example assumes that an ACL has been initialized and a valid pointer to an SID exists.

Listing 8-7 AddAccessDeniedAce() syntax and example call

```
/* AddAccessDeniedAce() Syntax */
BOOL AddAccessDeniedAce (PACL pAcl,         /* pointer to ACL receving ACE */
                         DWORD dwAclRev,    /* revision of ACL */
                         DWORD dwAccess,    /* access level to deny */
                         PSID pSid);        /* pointer to SID losing access */

/* AddAccessDeniedAce() Example Call */

   AddAccessDeniedAce (pAcl,            /* pointer to initialized ACL structure */
                       ACL_REVISION,    /* revision of ACL */
                       GENERIC_ALL,     /* deny all access */
                       pSid);           /* pointer to SID structure */
```

This function is identical to AddAccessAllowedAce(), except it denies access instead of granting access. The first parameter is a pointer to the initialized ACL structure receiving the ACE. The second parameter is the revision level of the ACL. The third parameter is an access level to deny (in this case all access). The fourth parameter is a pointer of the user or group SID to deny access.

If the SID represented BSmith, that user would not be able to access the object in any way. Again, this ACL structure must be set in a security descriptor, and the security descriptor must be applied to the object.

Like access-allowed ACEs, the order of access-denied ACEs can affect the protection of the object. For example, if an ACE allowed BSmith the desired access before this example ACE, BSmith would gain access to the object. The security check stops when the desired access has been granted. Let's look at a function that adds an ACE to a system access control list.

Using AddAuditAccessAce()

AddAuditAccessAce() lets you add an "automatic notifier" when certain attempts are made on an object. The administrator can monitor security breaches in the Event Viewer. This function adds an audit access ACE structure to an ACL. The purpose of the audit access ACE is to generate an audit message if a user (or a user in a group) accesses the object (based on an access mask). You can set up an ACE to generate an audit message on successful or unsuccessful attempts. For example, you could create an audit access ACE that says, "Generate an audit message if any user in the Power Users group tries to gain GENERIC_WRITE access and fails."

Since this is a security-related ACL, it is termed a system access control list (SACL). This function requires six parameters: a pointer to an ACL structure, a DWORD indicating the revision level, a DWORD containing the audit access bitmask, and a pointer to the SID being audited, and two Boolean values that indicate whether successful or unsuccessful access should generate an audit entry. Listing 8-8 shows the syntax and an example call to AddAuditAccessAce(). Once again, this example call assumes that an ACL has been initialized and a pointer to a valid SID structure exists.

Listing 8-8 AddAuditAccessAce() syntax and example call

```
/* AddAuditAccessAce() Syntax */
BOOL AddAuditAccessAce (PACL pAcl,        /* pointer to ACL receiving ACE */
                        DWORD dwAclRev,   /* revision of ACL */
                        DWORD dwAccess,   /* access level to audit */
                        PSID pSid,        /* pointer to SID to audit */
                        BOOL bSuccess,    /* generate audit on success? */
                        BOOL bFailure);   /* generate audit on failure? */


/* AddAuditAccessAce() Example Call */

    AddAuditAccessAce (pAcl,              /* pointer to initialized ACL structure */
                       ACL_REVISION,      /* revision of ACL */
```

continued on next page

continued from previous page

```
        GENERIC_EXECUTE,   /* check to see if SID executes the object */
        pSid,              /* pointer to SID structure to audit */
        FALSE,             /* do not generate audit on success */
        TRUE);             /* generate audit on failure */
```

The first parameter to this function is a pointer to an initialized ACL structure; in this case it is a system ACL, or SACL. The second parameter is the typical revision value used in previous ACL functions. The third parameter is a DWORD specifying the audit access mask. In the example call, we've set this value to GENERIC_EXECUTE. We'll explain the effects of this value after looking at the remaining parameters.

The fourth parameter is a pointer to the user or group SID to audit. The fifth and sixth parameters are set to FALSE and TRUE, respectively. This indicates that we want audit messages on failure only.

To see how the access audit ACE works, consider this scenario. Let's assume *pSid* points to an SID structure representing the Managers group. If a member of this group tries to execute the object, and the Managers are not granted access in the DACL, a system audit message is added. This message can be viewed by the system administrator in the Event Viewer.

Another system ACE type may be introduced in a future version of Windows NT: the system alarm ACE. This ACE would generate a real-time audit message to the administrator. The structure for this type of ACE is declared in the header files; however, there is no implementation of it at this time.

Setting Owners, DACLs, and SACLs into the Security Descriptor

Now that we've created a SACL and a DACL, we can finish the security descriptor. Three functions perform this final stage. SetSecurityDescriptorOwner() sets the owner information (SID) into the security descriptor. The other functions, SetSecurityDescriptorDacl() and SetSecurityDescriptorSacl(), set the DACL and SACL information into the security descriptor. Let's start with the owner of the security descriptor

Using SetSecurityDescriptorOwner()

This function establishes the owner of the security descriptor. Recall that the owner can perform virtually any action on an object, including setting a new DACL or SACL. This function requires three parameters: a pointer to an initialized security descriptor, a pointer to an SID structure indicating a user or group, and a Boolean value that indicates whether the owner is derived from a defaulting mechanism. In our examples we will specify the owner. Listing 8-9 shows the syntax and an example call to SetSecurityDescriptorOwner(). The example call assumes that *pSd* points to an initialized security descriptor and *pSid* points to a valid SID structure.

Listing 8-9 SetSecurityDescriptorOwner() syntax and example call

```
/* SetSecurityDescriptorOwner() Syntax */
BOOL SetSecurityDescriptorOwner (PSECURITY_DESCRIPTOR pSd, /* pointer to initialized SD */
                                 PSID pSidOwner,           /* pointer to SID to make owner */
                                 BOOL bOwnerDefault);      /* is owner defaulted? */


/* SetSecurityDescriptorOwner() Example Call */

    SetSecurityDescriptorOwner (pSd,    /* pointer to SD */
                                pSid,   /* pointer to valid SID */
                                FALSE); /* owner is specified */
```

This example call makes the user or group represented by an SID the owner of a security descriptor. The first parameter is a pointer to an initialized security descriptor structure. The second parameter is a pointer to the user or group SID that will become the owner. The third parameter is set to FALSE; this indicates that the owner is specified in the previous argument.

If NULL is specified in the second parameter, the security descriptor is said to have *no owner.* In this case any user or group can take ownership of the SD. Remember, the current user on the system cannot create an object and give ownership to another user. A user can only give ownership to himself or herself, or to a group to which he or she belongs. For example, if BSmith is logged on to the system (access token includes user SID) and tries to create an object and give ownership to HJones, the object creation function (such as CreateFile()) fails. Note that it is not the SetSecurityDescriptorOwner() function that fails. No user (not even the Administrator) can give ownership to another user. Other users can take ownership, but never give it.

Now that we have the owner of the security descriptor set, let's set the SACL and DACL structures.

Using SetSecurityDescriptorSacl()

This function sets a system access control list (SACL) into a security descriptor. The function requires four parameters: a pointer to an initialized security descriptor, a Boolean value indicating whether a SACL is present or not, a pointer to a system access control list, and a Boolean value indicating whether the SACL is supplied by this call or a defaulting mechanism. Listing

8-10 shows the syntax and an example call to SetSecurityDescriptorSacl(). The example call assumes that *pSacl* points to a valid system access control list and *pSd* points to an initialized security descriptor.

Listing 8-10 SetSecurityDescriptorSacl() syntax and example call

```
/* SetSecurityDescriptorSacl() Syntax */
BOOL SetSecurityDescriptorSacl (PSECURITY_DESCRIPTOR pSd,/* pointer to an initialized SD */
                                BOOL bSaclPresent,       /* is SACL present */
                                PACL pAcl,               /* pointer to system access control list */
                                BOOL bSaclDefault);      /* is SACL defaulted? */

/* SetSecurityDescriptorSacl() Example Call */

    SetSecurityDescriptorSacl (pSd,     /* pointer to an initialized SD */
                               TRUE,    /* yes, the SACL is present */
                               pSacl,   /* pointer to valid system ACL */
                               FALSE);  /* SACL is not from defaulting mechanism */
```

Recall that you can create a system access control list by initializing an ACL structure and adding audit ACEs to it. Once this list is built, you can set the SACL into the security descriptor. The first parameter in the example call is a pointer to the initialized SD. The second parameter is TRUE, indicating that the SACL is present. The third parameter is a pointer to a SACL structure. The last parameter is set to FALSE; this indicates that the SACL is specified in the third parameter, not from a default. Now let's add the discretionary access control list to the security descriptor.

Using SetSecurityDescriptorDacl()

This function sets the discretionary access control list (DACL) into a security descriptor. The function requires the same four parameters as the last function. The only difference is in the third parameter. In this case we are pointing to a DACL structure instead of a SACL. Listing 8-11 shows the syntax and an example call to SetSecurityDescriptorDacl().

Listing 8-11 SetSecurityDescriptorDacl() syntax and example call

```
/* SetSecurityDescriptorDacl() Syntax */
BOOL SetSecurityDescriptorDacl (PSECURITY_DESCRIPTOR pSd,/* pointer to an initialized SD */
                                BOOL bDaclPresent,       /* is DACL present */
                                PACL pAcl,               /* pointer to system access control list */
                                BOOL bDaclDefault);      /* is DACL defaulted? */
```

```
/* SetSecurityDescriptorDacl() Example Call */

   SetSecurityDescriptorDacl (pSd,      /* pointer to an initialized SD */
                              TRUE,      /* yes, the DACL is present */
                              pDacl,     /* pointer to valid discretionary ACL */
                              FALSE);    /* DACL is not from defaulting mechanism */
```

The discretionary access control list is created by initializing an ACL structure and adding access-allowed and/or access-denied ACEs. We are assuming in this example call that *pDacl* points to a valid DACL and that *pSd* points to an initialized security descriptor. As in the previous function, the second parameter is set to TRUE, indicating a DACL exists, and the fourth parameter is set to FALSE, indicating that the DACL is specified.

At this point we've seen how to initialize a security descriptor and an access control list. We also have seen how to add access control entries to an access control list (system or discretionary). Finally we set the owner, DACL, and SACL of the initialized security descriptor. We'll see how much of this takes place in SECURE1. Before we look at the sample program, let's examine how security is evaluated by the Windows NT operating system.

How Windows NT Evaluates Security

The security descriptor controls the access to an object by a user. The discretionary access control list (DACL) contains access control entries (ACEs) that allow or deny specific access. The DACL is the primary focus of the object side of security evaluation. The other side is the user attempting to access the object. This user is represented in the operating system by the access token. An access token contains the user's SID and any group SIDs that he or she may belong to. To illustrate the security evaluation process, let's look at a few examples.

Figure 8-8 shows an example where a user (represented by an access token) is attempting to access a file object. The desired access is GENERIC_WRITE. The object has a security descriptor which contains a DACL with three ACE entries. This example demonstrates how the order of the ACEs can affect security.

The first ACE in the DACL is evaluated. This ACE does grant HMiller read access, but he is not requesting it. The search continues. The second ACE is evaluated. This ACE allows all members of Power Users to access the file with GENERIC_WRITE access. HMiller gains access to the object not because of his user SID, but one of his group SIDs (Power Users).

Notice that the third ACE is not evaluated because the second ACE granted the desired access. This is a problem, however. The third ACE

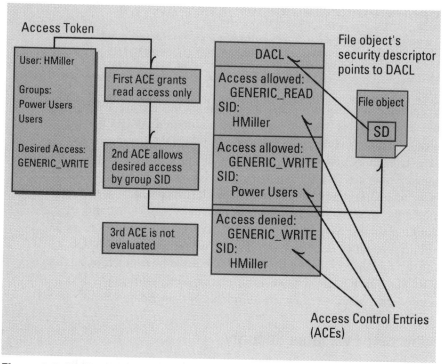

Figure 8-8 HMiller attempts GENERIC_WRITE on a file object

intended to deny HMiller GENERIC_WRITE access to the object. It is safer to place access-denied ACEs at the top of the list. This way, if an ACE denies access, the evaluation stops and the user cannot access the object—even though an ACE later in the list may have granted the access.

Let's look at another example. Figure 8-9 shows HMiller requesting GENERIC_READ and GENERIC_WRITE access. This illustrates that multiple ACEs can satisfy the desired access.

In this attempt the first ACE grants HMiller GENERIC_READ access, but this does not satisfy HMiller's request. The second ACE is evaluated. This ACE grants all access to the Administrator, which does not affect HMiller. The third ACE denies GENERIC_EXECUTE access to all members of Power Users. Since HMiller is a member of this group, he is denied this type of access. However, HMiller is not requesting GENERIC_EXECUTE access, so the evaluation process continues.

The last ACE grants Power Users GENERIC_WRITE access. Since HMiller is a member, this completes his request and gains the desired access to the file object. Here's the bottom line: as long as a user is not denied a

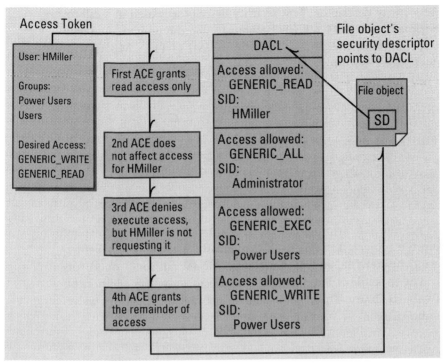

Figure 8-9 HMiller attempts GENERIC_READ and GENERIC_WRITE on a file object

desired access, the scan continues until the access is granted. If a desired access is denied, the scan is stopped and the user is denied all access (even previously satisfied ACEs). Also, if a scan reaches the end of the DACL without satisfying the desired access, the user is denied all access. There are many combinations of access levels and ACEs. You must understand the importance of the order of ACEs within a DACL to effectively implement security in your programs.

Let's look at a short example program that demonstrates the use of some of the Win32 API security functions.

A SECURITY DEMONSTRATION—SECURE1

This example application initializes a security descriptor and an ACL structure, builds a DACL and sets into the security descriptor, and sets the owner of the security descriptor. This security descriptor is used in a call to create a file named SECURITY.TXT. Before running the program, we will create two accounts on the system: MBIG and MLITTLE. MBIG will belong to the Power Users group. After running the program, we will log on using these new accounts and demonstrate the effects of the DACL.

NTFS REQUIRED

This example program requires an NTFS partition to work correctly. If you are using the FAT file system, the program will run, but security will have no effect. Warning: If you convert a FAT partition to an NTFS partition you cannot convert it back without reformatting the drive.

Before we get into a description of SECURE1, let's take a look at the files that make up the project. Listings 8-12 through 8-15 show the makefile, resource script, header file, and partial source file (WndProc() only) for SECURE1. The makefile is listed in this example to show the addition of the ADVAPI32.LIB library. This contains the security related functions we've discussed in this chapter.

Listing 8-12 MAKEFILE—makefile for SECURE1

```
# MAKEFILE for SECURITY1 (Security in Windows NT)

# NMAKE macros for Win32 apps
!include <ntwin32.mak>

# all pseudotarget
all: secure1.exe

# Update the resource.
secure1.res: secure1.rc secure1.h
    rc -r -fo secure1.tmp secure1.rc
    cvtres -$(CPU) secure1.tmp -o secure1.res
    del secure1.tmp

# Update the object file.
secure1.obj: secure1.c secure1.h
    $(cc) $(cflags) $(cvars) secure1.c


# Update the executable file and add the resource file.
secure1.exe: secure1.obj secure1.res
    $(link) $(guilflags) -IGNORE:505 -out:secure1.exe secure1.obj secure1.res $(guilibs)
advapi32.lib
```

The resource file is typical. It defines a simple menu resource. Notice that the *Create File* option is grayed initially. We don't want to create the file before the security descriptor is completed.

Listing 8-13 SECURE1.RC—resource file

```
#include "windows.h"
#include "secure1.h"

Secure1Icon ICON secure1.ico

Secure1Menu MENU
   BEGIN
      POPUP "&Security"
      BEGIN
         MENUITEM "&Build DACL",  IDM_BUILD_DACL
         MENUITEM "&Create File", IDM_CREATE_FILE, GRAYED
      END
   END
```

Listing 8-14 SECURE1.H—header file

```
/* secure1.h -- Include file for secure1.c and secure1.rc */

/* Menu defines */
#define IDM_BUILD_DACL  1
#define IDM_CREATE_FILE 2

/* Function prototypes */
LONG APIENTRY MainWndProc (HWND, UINT, UINT, LONG);

/* Global variables */
HANDLE ghInst;
HANDLE ghWnd;
```

Listing 8-15 SECURE1.C—source file

```
/* secure1.c     Demonstrates NT Security */

#include <windows.h>
#include "secure1.h"

/* WndProc - Main Window Procedure for secure1.c */
LONG APIENTRY MainWndProc (HWND hWnd, UINT message, UINT wParam, LONG lParam)
{
HANDLE hFile;
```

continued on next page

continued from previous page

```
HMENU    hMenu;
BOOL     bResult;
UCHAR    cWriteData[]="This file is protected by NT Discretionary Access Control\x0D\x0A";
UCHAR    pSidAdminBuf[500], pSidBigBuf[500], pSidPUsersBuf[500];
PSID     pSidAdmin, pSidBig, pSidPUsers;
UCHAR    cDomain[32];
DWORD    dwDomainLength, dwSIDLength;
DWORD    dwNumBytes;
PACL     Dacl;
LPSTR    lpMem;
INT      i;
DWORD    dwDaclSize;
SID_NAME_USE              SIDnu;
static HANDLE             hHeap;
static SECURITY_DESCRIPTOR SecDesc;
static SECURITY_ATTRIBUTES sa;


    switch (message)
    {
        case WM_CREATE:
            hHeap = HeapCreate (0, 0x1000, 0);      /* create a private heap */
            break;

        case WM_COMMAND:
            switch (LOWORD(wParam))
            {
                case IDM_BUILD_DACL:                  /* build the DACL for SECURITY.TXT */
                    dwDomainLength = 32;              /* set buffer length to store domain */
                    dwSIDLength = 500;                /* set buffer length to store SID */
                    LookupAccountName ((LPTSTR)"",    /* look up Administrator to obtain SID */
                                        "Administrator",
                                        &pSidAdminBuf,
                                        &dwSIDLength,
                                        cDomain,
                                        &dwDomainLength,
                                        &SIDnu);
                    dwDomainLength = 32;              /* reset buffer lengths */
                    dwSIDLength = 500;
                    LookupAccountName ((LPTSTR)"",    /* look up MBIG to obtain SID */
                                        "MBIG",
                                        &pSidBigBuf,
                                        &dwSIDLength,
                                        cDomain,
                                        &dwDomainLength,
                                        &SIDnu);
                    dwDomainLength = 32;              /* reset buffer lengths */
                    dwSIDLength = 500;
                    LookupAccountName ((LPTSTR)"",    /* look up Power Users to obtain group SID */
                                        "Power Users",
                                        &pSidPUsersBuf,
                                        &dwSIDLength,
                                        cDomain,
                                        &dwDomainLength,
```

```
                  &SIDnu);

pSidAdmin = pSidAdminBuf;          /* assign SID buffers to PSIDs */
pSidBig = pSidBigBuf;
pSidPUsers = pSidPUsersBuf;

 /* initialize a security descriptor */
 InitializeSecurityDescriptor (&SecDesc,
                          SECURITY_DESCRIPTOR_REVISION);


/* compute size of discretionary access control list */
dwDaclSize = sizeof (ACL) + (3 * sizeof (ACCESS_ALLOWED_ACE)) +
      GetLengthSid (pSidAdmin) + GetLengthSid (pSidBig) +
      GetLengthSid (pSidPUsers) - sizeof (ULONG);


/* allocate memory to store DACL */
lpMem = HeapAlloc (hHeap, 0, dwDaclSize);
Dacl = (PACL) lpMem;


/* initialize DACL */
InitializeAcl (Dacl, dwDaclSize, ACL_REVISION);


/* add permissions to Adminstrator, MBIG, and Power Users */
bResult = AddAccessAllowedAce (Dacl, ACL_REVISION, GENERIC_ALL, pSidBig);
bResult = AddAccessAllowedAce (Dacl, ACL_REVISION, GENERIC_ALL, pSidAdmin);
bResult = AddAccessAllowedAce (Dacl, ACL_REVISION, GENERIC_READ, pSidPUsers);


if (IsValidAcl (Dacl))              /* is this a valid DACL? */
{                                   /* if so, display a success message */
  MessageBox (hWnd, "A valid Discretionary Access Control List (DACL) has been created",
          "ACL Status", MB_OK);
  hMenu = GetMenu (hWnd);           /* enable the Create File menuitem */
  EnableMenuItem (hMenu, IDM_CREATE_FILE, MF_BYCOMMAND | MF_ENABLED);
}
else                                /* otherwise, display a failure message */
{
  MessageBox (hWnd, "DACL creation failed",
          "ACL Status", MB_OK);
  return (0);                       /* and exit */
  }


/* apply DACL to security descriptor */
SetSecurityDescriptorDacl (&SecDesc, TRUE, Dacl, FALSE);


/* set owner of security descriptor */
SetSecurityDescriptorOwner (&SecDesc, pSidAdmin, FALSE);


/* fill SECURITY_ATTRIBUTES structure */
sa.nLength = sizeof (SECURITY_ATTRIBUTES);
sa.lpSecurityDescriptor = &SecDesc;
sa.bInheritHandle = FALSE;
return (0);
```

continued on next page

continued from previous page

```
            case IDM_CREATE_FILE:                    /* create file with security */
                hFile = CreateFile ("SECURITY.TXT",
                                    GENERIC_READ | GENERIC_WRITE,
                                    0,
                                    &sa,             /* pointer to SECURITY_ATTRIBUTES struct */
                                    CREATE_NEW,
                                    FILE_ATTRIBUTE_NORMAL,
                                    NULL);

                if (hFile != INVALID_HANDLE_VALUE) /* if successful, display a message */
                MessageBox (hWnd, "SECURITY.TXT has been created", "CreateFile() Success", MB_OK);

                /* Write data to file */
                for (i = 0; i < 5; i++)              /* write five lines of data to file */
                    WriteFile (hFile, cWriteData, lstrlen (cWriteData), &dwNumBytes, NULL);

                CloseHandle (hFile);                  /* Close file handle */
                return (0);

            default:
                return (0);
        }

    case WM_DESTROY:
            HeapFree (hHeap, 0, lpMem);            /* free the allocated heap space */
            HeapDestroy (hHeap);                   /* destroy the heap */
            PostQuitMessage (0);
            return (0);

    default:
        return DefWindowProc (hWnd, message, wParam, lParam);
    }
    return (0L);
}
```

Overview of SECURE1.C

This program has two menu options: *Build DACL* and *Create File*. The first menu option is the only one available at startup. The goal is to create a security descriptor and apply it to a file creation function. The resultant file is protected by security; the file can be accessed by the administrator, a designated user, and a designated group.

As the main window is created, we process the WM_CREATE message. Here we create a private heap from which we will allocate memory for the DACL structure. We don't know in advance how large the DACL will be.

Getting the SIDs

When the user selects *Build DACL*, a host of activity occurs. This menu selection generates an IDM_BUILD_DACL menu message. The first two lines set two DWORD values to the length of the Domain Length and SID Length buffers. The actual buffers are declared at the top of WndProc().

We call LookupAccountName() to get the SID of the administrator. The SID structure is stored in a buffer, *pSidAdminBuf.* The name of the domain (cDomain) and the SID type (SIDnu) are also filled by this function; however, we are only interested in the SID in this program.

Notice that the first parameter to LookupAccountName() is a null string. This means to search the local system. The second parameter is string containing the account name.

This function is repeated to obtain the SIDs for MBIG and the Power Users group. Note that we must reset the buffer length values each time we call LookupAccountName(). This is because the previous call to this function modifies these values. For example, the first call obtains the SID for the administrator; therefore, *&dwSIDLength* contains the length of the administrator's SID. If the next SID is larger in size, LookupAccountName() will fail.

After the three SIDs are found and placed in buffers, we assign the address of these buffers to pointers to a SID type (*pSidAdmin, pSidBig,* and *pSidPUsers*). We will use these SID pointers when adding access-allowed ACEs in a moment.

Initializing the Security Descriptor and DACL

It is fairly simple to activate the security descriptor. We merely call InitializeSecurityDescriptor(), thus passing a pointer to a SECURITY_DESCRIPTOR structure (and the revision level). The DACL is a little more complicated. We must first calculate the size of the DACL.

We obtain the size of the DACL by adding sizes of the ACL structure, three access-allowed ACEs, and the cumulative lengths of the three SIDs. Note that we obtain SID lengths with GetLengthSid(). We are using these values because we will add three access-allowed ACEs to the DACL. The number of bytes required is assigned to *dwDaclSize.*

The next line allocates memory for the DACL using HeapAlloc() with *dwDaclSize* as its size parameter. Next we assign this pointer to a DACL pointer type (PACL). Note that we cast the memory pointer to the PACL type.

Now that we have the memory space available, we initialize the DACL by calling InitializeAcl(). The first parameter is the pointer to the memory address to store the DACL information. The second parameter is the size of the DACL *(dwDaclSize).* The remaining parameter specifies the revision level of the ACL.

Adding Access-Allowed ACEs

Our next step is to add three access-allowed ACEs. The first call adds an ACE that gives a user (MBig) GENERIC_ALL access. This allows the highest level of access to the object. The next call grants the administrator the GENERIC_ALL access. The third call gives the Power Users group the ability to open the object for GENERIC_READ access.

In each call to AddAccessAllowedAce(), the first parameter is a pointer to the DACL, the second parameter is the revision of the ACL, the third parameter is the access level to allow, and the fourth parameter is a pointer to the SID gaining access.

The next line tests the DACL for validity. If IsValidDacl() returns TRUE, the DACL is valid and we display a message box indicating the success. We also can enable the menu item that will allow the user to select *Create File*. If IsValidDacl() returns FALSE, the DACL is invalid and we display a message indicating failure. We also return immediately in this case.

Setting the DACL and the Owner into the Security Descriptor

The next two lines set the DACL and the owner into the security descriptor. The first call is to SetSecurityDescriptorDacl(). The first parameter is a pointer to the security descriptor structure. We initialized this structure earlier. The second parameter is set to TRUE, indicating that a DACL is present. The third parameter is a pointer to the DACL, and the fourth parameter is FALSE, indicating that the DACL was not derived from a defaulting mechanism.

The next call is to SetSecurityDescriptorOwner(). The first parameter is a pointer to the security descriptor structure. The second parameter is a pointer to the group or user SID (in this case the Administrator). The third parameter is FALSE, indicating that the owner is not derived from a defaulting mechanism.

Filling the SECURITY_ATTRIBUTES Structure

The last three lines in the IDM_BUILD_DACL case body fill the security attributes structure, *sa*. This structure contains three members. The first is the size of the structure in bytes. The second member is a pointer to a security descriptor; in our case we'll use the address of our security descriptor, *&SecDesc*. The third member is the handle inheritance Boolean. We'll set this member to FALSE, indicating that child processes will not inherit the handle to an object protected by this structure.

Creating the File

When the user selects *Create File,* an IDM_CREATE_FILE menu message is sent to WndProc(). In processing this message, we attempt to create a file and display a message if the creation is successful.

The first line calls CreateFile() to create a new file called SECURITY.TXT. The desired access level is GENERIC_READ and GENERIC_WRITE. The fourth parameter to CreateFile() is a pointer to the security attributes structure. This applies the security descriptor to the file object.

We test to see if the file is created by making sure the file handle does not contain INVALID_HANDLE_VALUE. Otherwise we can assume the file handle is valid. In the latter case, we display a message box indicating that SECURITY.TXT has been created successfully.

The next step writes five identical lines of data into SECURITY.TXT. The data is a static string containing "This file is protected by NT Discretionary Access Control," followed by a carriage return–line feed. We then close the file handle and return.

The effects of the security descriptor will become evident when we attempt to open the file using the Notepad program. The results will depend on which user tries to open the file and whether or not that user attempts to write to the file. Let's build and run SECURE1.

BUILDING AND USING SECURE1

The files for SECURE1 are located in the \CHAPTER8\8.1 subdirectory. Open a Command Prompt window and change to this directory. Type NMAKE and press (ENTER). The SECURE1 application compiles and links. Do not start the application yet, we must create some new accounts before running SECURE1. You must be the administrator of your system to use this example program. You become the administrator when installing Windows NT on a single system. The file system must be NTFS. Perform the following steps to create two new accounts:

1. If you are not logged on as the Administrator, log off and log back on using the Administrator user ID.

2. Open the *Administrative Tools* group and start the *User Manager.*

3. Select *New User* from the *User* menu. Use MBIG as the user name and Mr. Big as the full name. You can also provide a description and a password, although it is not necessary for this example.

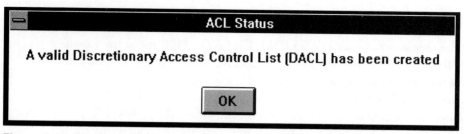

Figure 8-10 The discretionary access control list (DACL) has been created

4. Select *Groups* (lower left corner of *User Properties* dialog). Notice that MBIG belongs to Users. Select Power Users from the *Not member of*: list and click on *Add*. MBIG is now a member of Power Users.

5. Select *OK* to accept the groups. Select *OK* to accept the user properties. MBIG's account is now complete.

6. Create another user with MLITTLE as the user name and Mr. Little as the full name. Do not add this user to the Power User group.

Now that we have the accounts created, let's start SECURE1 and create the file. Review the code in Listings 8-13 through 8-15 while performing the following steps:

7. Open up a Command Prompt window; type SECURE1 and press (ENTER).

8. Select *Build DACL* from the *Security* menu. A security descriptor is initialized and the DACL with three access–allowed ACEs is created. SECURE1 displays a message box indicating that the DACL has been created. This is shown in Figure 8-10.

9. Select OK to close the message box. The owner and DACL are set into the security descriptor and the security information structure is filled.

10. Select *Create File* from the *Security* menu. SECURITY.TXT is created using the security attributes structure, *sa*. Figure 8-11 shows the message box that indicates the file has been created.

11. Select OK to close the message box and exit SECURE1.

Now we have created a file protected by security. The file is located in the same directory as SECURE1.EXE. The remaining steps will use three accounts (Administrator, MBIG, and MLITTLE) to try to gain access to the file. We will be using the Notepad program to open SECURITY.TXT.

Figure 8-11 SECURITY.TXT file has
been created

12. Let's see if the Administrator account can open SECURITY.TXT. Start the *File Manager* (located in the Main group).

13. Locate the directory that contains the file (\CHAPTER8\8.1). Select the file and press (ENTER) or double-click on it to start the *Notepad* and open the file. The file opens because the second ACE allows the Administrator GENERIC_ALL access. Figure 8-12 shows the open file in *Notepad*.

14. Close the *Notepad* and log off the system.

15. Log back on the system as MBIG. We'll attempt to open the file as this user.

16. Start the *File Manager*, locate SECURITY.TXT, and attempt to open it. MBIG can also open the file. This is because of the first ACE in the DACL. Figure 8-13 shows this activity. Notice that the first ACE satisfies the request even though MBIG belongs to Power Users. Power Users are granted GENERIC_READ access by the third ACE.

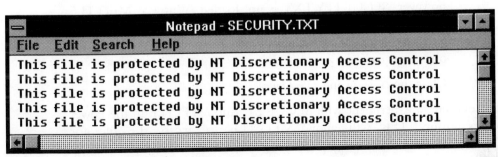

Figure 8-12 Opened SECURITY.TXT in Notepad

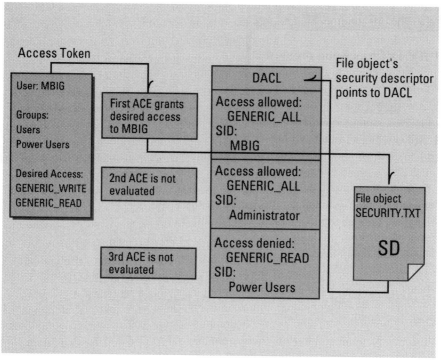

Figure 8-13 MBIG attempting to access SECURITY.TXT

17. Close the *Notepad* and the *File Manager* and log off.

18. Log back on as MLITTLE, start the *File Manager,* locate SECURITY.TXT and attempt to open it. The system displays a message box indicating that this user cannot access the file. This message box is shown in Figure 8-14.

19. Click on *OK* to close the message box. The *Notepad* program starts; however, SECURITY.TXT is not loaded. Why was MLITTLE denied access? Figure 8-15 shows the reason. None of the three ACEs permitted MLITTLE any kind of access, so access to the file object was denied.

20. Close the *Notepad* and *File Manager.*

Continue to experiment with SECURE1. Add MLITTLE to the Power Users group. This will allow MLITTLE to access the file for GENERIC_READ access. The access is granted by the third ACE.

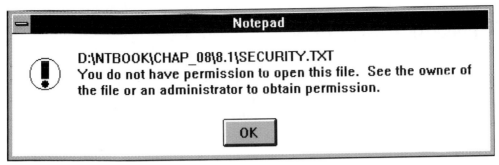

Figure 8-14 Access SECURITY.TXT is denied to MLITTLE

Another experiment is to delete SECURITY.TXT and run SECURE1 while you are logged on as MBIG. The CreateFile() call will fail because you are trying to create an object and give ownership to another user. Recall that we hard-coded the owner of the object as the administrator.

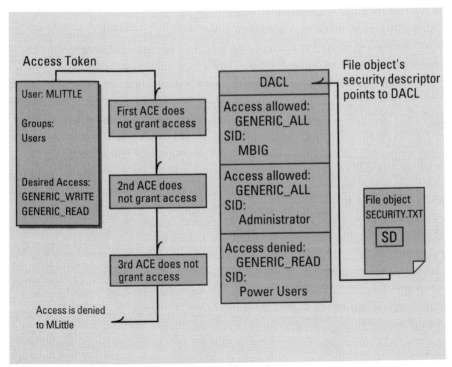

Figure 8-15 Why access is denied to MLITTLE

SUMMARY

As you can see, security is a large topic in Windows NT. Although this introduction only scratched the surface of the capabilities of security, you've gained a basic understanding of the relationship between objects and users. This should provide a foundation on which you can build as you delve deeper into the Win32 security API.

The user side of the security equation is represented by a security identifier, or SID. The SID is a unique number that represents a user or group of users. You can think of SIDs as keys to open certain objects. When a user logs on to the system, he or she is represented by an *access token*. This token contains the user's SID as well as the group SIDs he or she belongs to.

The object side of the security equation is the security descriptor. A security descriptor structure contains an owner, a discretionary access control list (SACL), and a system access control list (SACL). Both SACLs and DACLs are ACL type structures. An ACL structure contains access control entries (ACEs). The type of ACEs is what sets SACLs and DACLs apart.

A SACL can contain zero or more access audit ACEs. A DACL can contain zero or more *access-allowed* and *access-denied* ACEs. The specific access in an ACE is represented by an *access bitmask*. The range of access levels is wide, from ACEs that are specific (for example, SYNCHRONIZE) or very broad (GENERIC_ALL).

The security descriptor is applied to an object when the object is created. For example, we applied a security descriptor to SECURITY.TXT when we created the file. Any user trying to access an object is subject to the access control entries in the DACL. If the user is denied any portion of the requested access level, the system informs the user that access is denied and evaluation of ACEs ceases. If the user is granted the desired access level, the user gains access to the object and evaluation of ACEs also ceases. If all ACEs are evaluated, and the user has not been granted the requested access, access is denied to the user.

This concludes our introduction to security, users, groups, and objects. Let's look at some issues that will come up if you plan to use your applications in both Windows 3.1 and Windows NT. Chapter 9 covers portability concerns.

Portability Issues in Windows NT

CHAPTER 9

Portability Issues in Windows NT

If the target system for your applications is specific, portability may not seem to be a large concern. One of Windows NT's strong points, however, is the ability to run different types of programs (Win32, OS/2, Windows 3.x, MS-DOS, and so on) on different types of hardware (for example, Intel 80386/486 and Pentium, MIPS, DEC Alpha). Both of these aspects bring up portability issues that must be addressed in order to create robust applications that run on multiple platforms.

Windows NT isolates itself and its subsystems from the processor with a hardware abstraction layer, or HAL. The HAL is a DLL that provides a layer of code in between the processor and the NT executive. In general, the effect on this arrangement is minimal to the programmer. Difficulty can arise, however, if you attempt to use techniques that manipulate the processor directly. Doing so restricts the application to a specific type of processor. Any run-time library code written for a particular platform must be avoided.

The other portability concern comes from the Windows NT subsystems (such as Win32, OS/2, POSIX, and so on) and Windows 3.x. This book targets Windows programmers, our discussion concentrates on running Windows 3.x applications under Windows NT, running Win32 applications under Windows 3.x, and converting Windows 3.x applications to Win32. Since Windows 3.x programs normally run in a DOS environment, we'll look at virtual-DOS machines, or VDMs. We'll also take a look at the Windows on Win32 (WOW) subsystem.

Portability becomes a larger topic if you intend to design your Win32 applications to run on both Windows NT (via the Win32 subsystem) and Windows 3.x (via Win32s). Win32s is a mapping layer that lets you call most Win32 API functions if a Win32 application is running under Windows 3.x. Win32s extends the API for Windows 3.x; not all Win32 API functions, however, are supported by Win32s. These functions must be avoided (or recoded) if your application targets both Windows 3.x and Windows NT. We'll look at a short example program that enables or disables certain functions, depending on the platform.

This chapter describes the interaction between these two platforms and their applications, points out potential problem areas, and suggests techniques to solve and prevent portability problems. Let's look at the topics we will cover in this chapter.

PORTABILITY ISSUES

We are going to focus on three portability issues that face Windows/Windows NT programmers. Basically these issues relate to running either Windows 3.x or Win32 applications on Windows 3.x and/or Windows NT. We'll break this down into three scenarios; two of these scenarios require the attention of the programmer to ensure that the resultant applications behave properly. The first demonstrates a possible need to port a Windows 3.x application to Win32.

Three Scenarios

Figure 9-1 shows two of three scenarios that bring up portability concerns. The first scenario describes the behavior that takes place when a user runs an existing Windows 3.x program in Windows NT. This involves a Windows NT subsystem (Win32) that creates a virtual DOS machine (VDM). The VDM starts a process called Windows on Win32, or WOW. The WOW process can run multiple Windows 3.x applications after it is loaded. We'll see in a moment how this method can be restrictive to some applications.

The second scenario illustrates running Win32 applications on Windows 3.x. With so many systems running Windows 3.1, and (initially) fewer running NT, you may want to consider Win32s. Win32s is an extension of the Windows 3.x operating system. It allows some Win32 applications to run under Windows 3.x. Not all Win32 API functions are supported by Win32s, however.

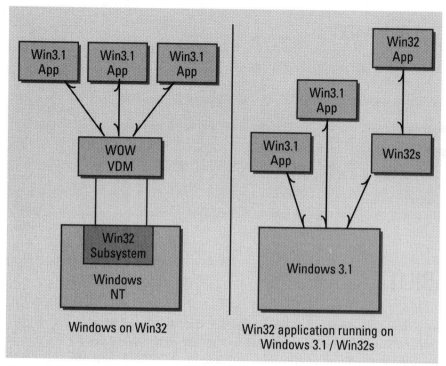

Windows on Win32   Win32 application running on
Windows 3.1 / Win32s

Figure 9-1 Two of three portability scenarios

The final scenario involves porting your existing Windows 3.x applications to Win32. This may involve changes in API calls and data types depending on the complexity of your programs. We'll look at methods you can use to convert your code. In addition, we'll keep in mind that the new Win32 application may run on Windows 3.1 systems as well. Let's first look at how a Windows 3.1 application runs under Windows NT.

WINDOWS 3.1 APPLICATIONS ON WINDOWS NT

One of the primary goals of Windows NT is to have backward compatibility. With literally thousands of existing MS–DOS and Windows applications on the market, this feature is essential. We'll take a brief look at how both

MS-DOS and Windows applications run on Windows NT. This will also expose some of the limitations that face these programs.

Virtual DOS Machine (VDM)

In order to understand how a Windows 3.x application runs on Windows NT, we must first discuss how MS-DOS applications run. After all, Windows 3.x itself runs in the MS-DOS environment. This brings up the concept of a virtual DOS machine, or VDM. The VDM allows MS-DOS applications to run in Windows NT. Figure 9-2 shows a view of a VDM.

When a user starts an MS-DOS application in Windows NT, the Win32 subsystem detects the application type. As a result the Win32 subsystem creates a VDM process. This is essentially a process that executes the MS-DOS application. Recall that DOS applications had virtually total control over the system. The purpose of the VDM is to make the DOS program think it has total control, yet yield (preemptively) to other running applications on the system.

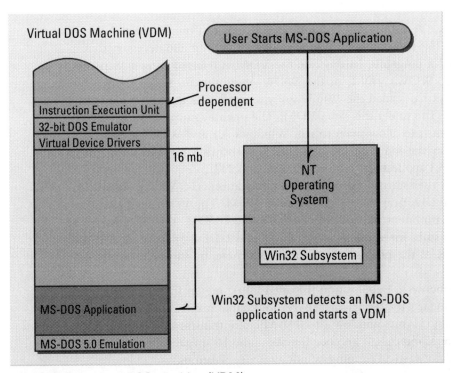

Figure 9-2 A virtual DOS machine (VDM)

The VDM is made up of MS-DOS 5.0 emulation (except for file management) and a range of virtual addresses for the program itself. Located above the process 16-megabyte boundary are the *instruction execution unit, a 32-bit MS-DOS emulator,* and *virtual device drivers.* The instruction execution unit binds the code to a specific processor. For example, this code would be different for an Intel 80386/486 and a DEC Alpha processor. The 32-bit MS-DOS emulator permits applications to take advantage of the 32-bit function calls. The virtual device drivers provide emulation so that MS-DOS I/O operations are carried out successfully.

A VDM is created for each running MS-DOS application, thus enabling the user to run multiple DOS sessions. Only one copy of the instruction execution unit, 32-bit DOS emulator, and virtual device drivers exists in memory. The NT virtual memory manager allows the multiple DOS sessions to share this copy. At the processor level, each MS-DOS application must share timeslices with all other running applications (and the operating system itself). Most activity is taken care of by the operating system and is of little concern to the programmer.

Windows on Win32 (WOW)

Now that we've seen how MS-DOS applications run on Windows NT, we can extend this to Windows 3.x applications. A VDM is also necessary to run Windows 3.x programs. In this case the VDM is referred to as a Windows on Win32 (WOW) VDM, or the WOW environment. Once the WOW environment has loaded the Win32 subsystem, all subsequent Windows 3.x applications run under this same VDM. The primary purpose of the WOW environment is to allow users to run Windows 3.1 and Win32 applications together on the same desktop. Figure 9–3 shows a representation of a Windows 3.1 application running on Windows NT.

When a user starts a Windows 3.x application, the Win32 subsystem detects it as a DOS application and starts a VDM. The VDM then loads the WOW environment. In addition to the typical VDM, the Windows 3.1 kernel and stubs for window management and GDI calls are loaded in the lower 640K of the process. Remember that these are virtual, not physical addresses.

The Windows 3.1 application is loaded into a region that spans from the 640K boundary to the 16-megabyte boundary. Any calls that are made to (normally 16-bit) window or GDI APIs are transformed (thunked) to appropriate 32-bit calls. This code lies above the 16-megabyte boundary and it is shared between all running Windows 3.x applications.

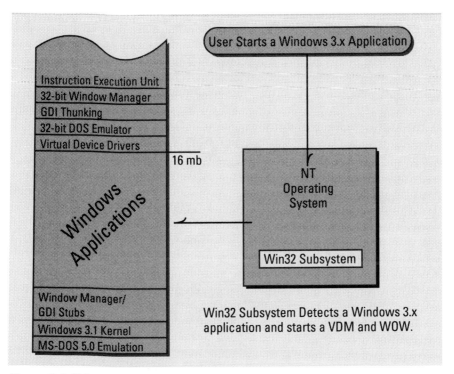

Figure 9-3 Windows on Win32 (WOW)

The WOW VDM is only loaded on the first instance of a Windows 3.x application, so the first application may take longer to load. Subsequent applications are loaded directly in the WOW VDM address space.

At first glance it may seem like Windows NT can run Windows 3.x applications with no drawbacks. However, these applications still run in a synchronized fashion; while one Windows 3.x application is processing a message, no other Windows 3.x application receives any processing time. These applications cannot take advantage of preemptive multitasking. Figure 9-4 shows the NT operating system (and the Win32 subsystem) running two Win32 applications, a Windows 3.x application, and an MS–DOS application.

The figure illustrates how the applications of different types are scheduled at the processor level. Recall that each Win32 application has its own private address space. The Win32 application receives processor timeslices based on its own priority and the priority of other applications. MS–DOS applications also receive individual timeslices since each application starts another VDM.

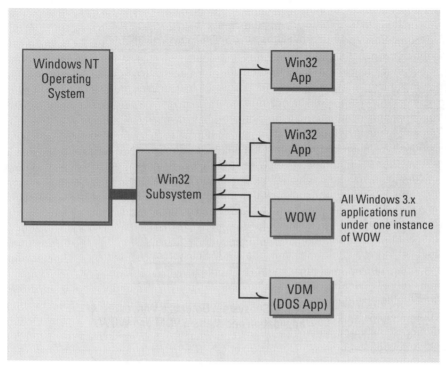

Figure 9-4 Win32, Windows 3.x, and MS-DOS

Windows 3.x applications all run in a single VDM, the WOW environment. This environment is scheduled processor time as a whole inside the VDM; however, Windows 3.x applications have a single input queue. For example, assume that two Windows 3.x applications (WinApp A and WinApp B) are running under the WOW environment. WinApp A is in the middle of processing a message. WinApp B will continue to be blocked until WinApp A checks the message queue. This is identical to the nonpreemptive multitasking employed in Windows 3.1.

If your Windows 3.x applications would benefit from the advanced features of Windows NT (preemptive multitasking, security, and so on), you may want to consider porting your existing code to Win32. Once you have your existing code up and running, you can add the new functionality. You may not want to port simple programs that would not benefit from multiple threads, the extended GDI, or other new features. We'll look at some of the issues that arise when porting 3.x code to Win32 later in this chapter. Now let's look at how Win32 applications run in the Windows 3.x environment.

WIN32 APPLICATIONS ON WINDOWS 3.1

You can increase the target audience of your Win32 applications by testing and ensuring that they run on Windows 3.x platforms. This involves including Win32s with your product. Win32s extends the Windows 3.x API to include the Win32 API; however, not all of the API is supported under Win32s. Let's look at an overview of Win32s followed by the types of Win32 functions not supported.

Win32s

Win32s is a product of Microsoft that allows Win32 applications to run on Windows 3.1. Other compilers plan to implement their own solutions as well. Win32s offers many benefits. Perhaps the largest benefit lies in the current number of copies of Windows 3.x in existence today. Writing your applications so they run on Windows3.x/Win32s and Windows NT greatly increases your potential audience. Win32s also provides the advantages of 32-bit processing and the full Win32 API (although some portions of the API are not implemented at this time).

Win32s consists of several DLLs and other files, most of which are installed in a subdirectory \WIN32s under the Windows system directory. Another Win32 DLL is installed in the Windows system directory. The Win32 Software Development Kit contains the files necessary to install Win32s on a Windows 3.x system. You can modify these setup files to install your own Win32 applications on a Windows 3.1 system.

Figure 9-5 shows a portion of Win32s and a general overview of how it works. The Win32 components are shaded in the figure. Notice that a Windows 3.1 applications calls the Windows Kernel, GDI, and User directly. Most of the calls from a Win32 application call Kernel32, GDI32, and User32. These are DLL modules located in the \Win32s directory (beneath the Windows system directory).

The heart of Win32s is the *thunking DLL,* WIN32S16. This module resides in the Windows system directory. It is responsible for resolving 16/32-bit issues, managing the stack, and mapping message parameters. We've already seen how the WM_COMMAND message is packed differently in Windows 3.x and Win32. This module resolves these types of issues and calls the appropriate API in Windows 3.x (Kernel, GDI, and User).

There is actually a lot more going on in Win32s. Fortunately the programmer is isolated from most of it; however, there are some Win32

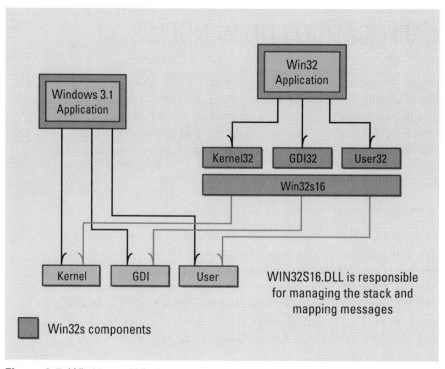

Figure 9-5 Win32s on Windows 3.1

functions that are not presently supported by Win32s. It is important to write your programs to account for this.

Functions Not Supported in Win32s

If you are writing an application that targets both Windows NT and Windows 3.x/Win32s, it is important to understand the API limitations. The entire Win32 API is represented by Win32s, but not all API calls are implemented. Although the level of support may change in subsequent releases, the following areas are currently not supported by Win32s:

- security APIs
- thread APIs
- GDI path APIs
- GDI Bezier APIs
- asynchronous file I/O

- enhanced metafiles

- console APIs

- unicode APIs

- comm APIs

We have covered the first four areas on the list in this book. For this reason some of the example programs in this book will not run properly on Win32s. For example, the GDI application that draws Bezier curves will not function properly under Win32s. The only calls that will work are supported Win32 APIs, like MoveToEx() and LineTo().

Win32s—Nonpreemptive Multitasking

Win32 applications are subject to the constraints of the Windows 3.1 system while running under Win32s. You cannot design your application with preemptive multitasking in mind; in other words the application must be single-threaded. It is also important to process messages quickly and return control to Windows. Figure 9-6 shows two Win32 and two Windows 3.x applications running under Windows 3.x/Win32s.

The figure shows the constraints placed on Win32 applications running on Windows 3.x. Application 1 is currently processing a message. As a result all other applications are blocked until Application 1 checks its message queue. This is identical to the nonpreemptive nature of Windows 3.x. It is important to consider this when writing applications that target both Windows NT and Windows 3.1

Dynamic Functionality

There are two methods to help the user get the most out of your applications in both Windows NT and Windows 3.1. Both involve making decisions at run time as to what functionality is available to the user. The first method examines the error code generated by functions that are not supported in Win32s. The second method involves a Win32 API function that determines the version and platform on which the application is running.

Testing Error Codes

If a Win32 API function is not supported by Win32s, the call fails and generates the error code ERROR_CALL_NOT_IMPLEMENTED. You can obtain the error code by calling GetLastError(). Here is an excerpt of code attempting to call a Win32 API function, and testing the results:

```
hThread = CreateThread (NULL,
                        0,
                        (LPTHREAD_START_ROUTINE) lpThreadProc,
                        &Arg
                        0,
                        &ThreadID);
if (hThread == NULL)                                /* test for failure */
{
    dwError = GetLastError();                       /* get error code */
    if (dwError == ERROR_CALL_NOT_IMPLEMENTED);     /* failing in Win32s? */
    {
        /* code to handle alternate method */;      /* handle with alternate code */
    }
}
```

This example tries to create a thread, something not supported in Win32s. If the application that contains this excerpt is run on Windows NT, the entire Win32 API is valid; therefore a thread is created as a result of the call (assuming there is no other type of failure). If the same application is run on Windows 3.1, the CreateThread() function will fail (return NULL) and the error code is ERROR_CALL_NOT_IMPLEMENTED. In this case, you

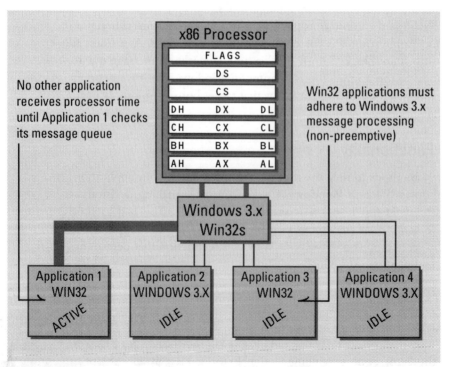

Figure 9-6 Synchronized message processing in Windows3.x/Win32s

could use an alternate method to handle the situation. This may end up causing a decrease in performance for Win32 applications running under Win32s. Let's look at another method that tests to see which platform the application is running on: Windows NT or Windows 3.x.

Using GetVersion()

This Win32 API function lets you find out what platform your application is running on. It also returns the major and minor versions of the platform. This function does not require any parameters and returns a DWORD specifying the platform, major, and minor versions. Listing 9-1 shows the syntax and an example call to GetVersion().

Listing 9-1 GetVersion() syntax and example call

```
/* GetVersion() Syntax */
DWORD GetVersion (VOID);              /* returns platform and version numbers */

/* GetVersion() Example Call */
BOOL gbNTDetect=TRUE;                 /* declared as a global Boolean */
,
DWORD dwVersion;

    dwVersion = GetVersion();         /* get the platform and version */
    if (dwVersion & 0x80000000)       /* test for platform */
        gbNTDetect = FALSE;           /* reset Boolean if Win32s or Windows 3.1 */
```

This example assumes a global Boolean variable, *gbNTDetect,* exists. The Boolean value is initialized to TRUE (meaning we are assuming the application in running on Windows NT at first). We call GetVersion() and assign its return value to *dwVersion.* By *bitwise and*-ing this value with 0x80000000 as a mask, we can determine if the application is running on Windows NT or Windows 3.x. The high bit of the high word in *dwVersion* is 0 for Windows NT and 1 for Win32s or Windows 3.1.

The low word of *dwVersion* contains the version information, although we are not testing for it here. The low byte of the low word contains the major revision level while the high byte of the low word contains the minor revision level. Figure 9-7 shows the breakdown of the DWORD return value of GetVersion().

If your applications target both Win32s and Windows NT, you can use this function to determine the platform, then assign a global Boolean to represent it throughout the program. For example, if we continue with our example call in Listing 9-1, we can use the global *gbNTDetect* to determine whether or not to implement specific code. If we were creating a drawing

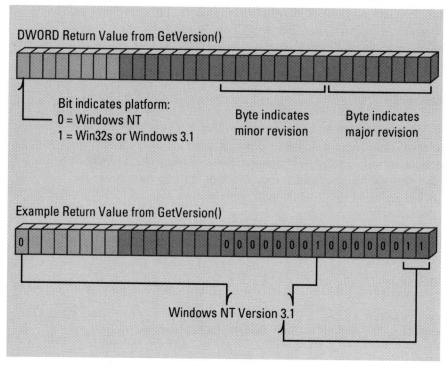

Figure 9-7 DWORD return value from GetVersion()

package, we could test to see if Bezier curves are permitted. If the platform is Windows NT, we know the Bezier API functions are supported. If the platform is Win32s, we must either take the Bezier functionality away from the user (by graying or removing menu items) or implement our own code to handle Bezier curves. The following example applications demonstrate this technique.

PORT1—WIN32 / WIN32S EXAMPLE APPLICATION

PORT1 is a hybrid of the GDI1 and GDI2 example applications from Chapter 5. It has two top-level menu items: *Figures* and *Beziers*. The *Figures* popup menu contains two menu items: *Lines* and *Square*. Both of these selections use APIs supported by Win32 and Win32s. The *Beziers* popup also contains two menu items: *PolyBezier* and *PolyBezierTo*. These selections use APIs that are not supported in Win32s. We'll test for the current platform using GetVersion() and adjust the menu. If the platform is Win32s, we must gray the *Bezier* menu item.

Listings 9-2 through 9-4 show the resource script, header file, and source file for PORT1. The call to GetVersion() and associated code are listed in boldface.

Listing 9-2 PORT1.RC—resource script

```
#include "windows.h"
#include "Port1.h"


Port1Icon ICON  Port1.ico

Port1Menu MENU
BEGIN
    POPUP "&Figures"
    BEGIN
        MENUITEM "&Lines",       IDM_LINES
        MENUITEM "&Square",      IDM_SQUARE
    END
    POPUP "&Beziers"
    BEGIN
        MENUITEM "Poly&Bezier",   IDM_POLYBEZ
        MENUITEM "PolyBezier&To", IDM_POLYBEZTO
    END
END
```

Listing 9-3 PORT1.H—header file

```
/* port1.h -- Include file for port1.c and port1.rc */

/* Menu defines */
#define IDM_LINES     1
#define IDM_SQUARE    2
#define IDM_POLYBEZ   3
#define IDM_POLYBEZTO 4

/* Object to draw defines */
#define DRAW_LINES      1
#define DRAW_SQUARE     2
#define DRAW_POLYBEZ    3
#define DRAW_POLYBEZTO  4
```

continued on next page

continued from previous page

```
/* Function prototype */
LONG APIENTRY WndProc (HWND, UINT, UINT, LONG);
void DrawPolyBez (HDC hDC);
void DrawPolyBezTo (HDC hDC);

/* Global variables */
HANDLE ghInst;
HANDLE ghWnd;
```

Listing 9-4 PORT1.C—source file

```
/* port1.c      Win32s / Win32 Portability */

#include <windows.h>              /* include for Win32 apps */
#include "port1.h"                /* include for port1.c */

/* WndProc - Main Window Procedure for port1.c */

LONG APIENTRY WndProc (HWND hWnd, UINT message, UINT wParam, LONG lParam)
{
PAINTSTRUCT    ps;
static int     nDraw = 0;
static DWORD   dwVersion;
HMENU          hMenu;

    switch (message)
    {
        case WM_CREATE:
            hMenu = GetMenu (hWnd);
            dwVersion = GetVersion();
            if (dwVersion & 0x80000000)               /* is this Win32s? */
                                                      /* then gray the bezier menu */
                EnableMenuItem (hMenu, 1, MF_GRAYED | MF_BYPOSITION);
            return (0);

        case WM_PAINT:                                /* paint depending on nDraw */
            BeginPaint (hWnd, &ps);
            switch (nDraw)
            {
                case DRAW_LINES:                      /* draw two horizontal lines */
                    MoveToEx (ps.hdc, 50, 50, NULL);  /* move to coordinate 50,50 */
                    LineTo (ps.hdc, 150, 50);         /* draw first line */
                    MoveToEx (ps.hdc, 50, 150, NULL); /* move to coordinate 50, 150 */
                    LineTo (ps.hdc, 150, 150);        /* draw second line */
                    break;
                case DRAW_SQUARE:                     /* draw square */
                    MoveToEx (ps.hdc, 50, 50, NULL);  /* move to coodinate 50,50 */
                    LineTo (ps.hdc, 150, 50);         /* draw top of square */
                    LineTo (ps.hdc, 150, 150);        /* draw right side of square */
                    LineTo (ps.hdc, 50, 150);         /* draw bottom of square */
                    LineTo (ps.hdc, 50, 50);          /* complete the square */
```

```
                    break;
                case DRAW_POLYBEZ:                    /* draw a PolyBezier? */
                    DrawPolyBez (ps.hdc);
                    break;
                case DRAW_POLYBEZTO:                  /* draw a PolyBezierTo? */
                    DrawPolyBezTo (ps.hdc);
                    break;
                default:
                    break;
            }
            EndPaint (hWnd, &ps);
            break;

        case WM_COMMAND:
            switch (LOWORD(wParam)) /* Extract LOWORD of wParam for Win32) */
            {
                case IDM_LINES:                    /* user selected Lines */
                    nDraw = DRAW_LINES;            /* set nDraw to DRAW_LINES */
                    break;
                case IDM_SQUARE:                   /* user selected Square */
                    nDraw = DRAW_SQUARE;           /* set nDraw to DRAW_SQUARE */
                    break;
                case IDM_POLYBEZ:                  /* user selected PolyBezier */
                    nDraw = DRAW_POLYBEZ;          /* set nDraw to DRAW_POLYBEZ */
                    break;
                case IDM_POLYBEZTO:                /* user selected PolyBezierTo */
                    nDraw = DRAW_POLYBEZTO;        /* set nDraw to DRAW_POLYBEXTO */
                    break;
                default:
                    return (0);
            }
            InvalidateRect (hWnd, NULL, TRUE);    /* force WM_PAINT */
            return (0);

        case WM_DESTROY:                          /* No cleanup necessary */
            PostQuitMessage (0);
            return (0);

        default:
            return DefWindowProc (hWnd, message, wParam, lParam);
    }

    return (0L);
}


/* DrawPolyBez() uses a for loop to call PolyBezier() 200 times. Each iteration
   Control Point #1 is incremented and Control Point #2 is decremented */
void DrawPolyBez (HDC hDC)
{
POINT pPts[] = {10, 100, 100, 0, 100, 0, 190, 100};
LONG  nControlY1, nControlY2;

    /* loop to move the control points */
```

continued on next page

continued from previous page

```
    for (nControlY1 = 0, nControlY2 = 200; nControlY1 <= 200; nControlY1+=10, nControlY2-=10)
      {
      pPts[1].y = nControlY1;                           /* modify Control Point #1 */
      pPts[2].y = nControlY2;                           /* modify Control Point #2 */
      PolyBezier (hDC, pPts, 4);                        /* draw the bezier spline */
      }
}

/* DrawPolyBezTo() calls PolyBezierTo() to illustrate control points. The
   start and end points of each bezier form a square. Each side of the square
   uses different examples of control point effect. */
void DrawPolyBezTo (HDC hDC)
{
POINT pPts[] = {100, 50, 150, 50, 150, 50,
                200, 50, 200, 150, 150, 150,
                50, 200, 150, 200, 50, 150,
                0, 50, 100, 150, 50, 50};

    BeginPath (hDC);                                    /* open path bracket */
    MoveToEx (hDC, 50, 50, NULL);                       /* adjust current position */
    PolyBezierTo (hDC, pPts, 12);                       /* draw the bezier splines */
    EndPath (hDC);                                      /* close the path bracket */
    StrokePath (hDC);                                   /* stroke the path */
}
```

Checking for Win32/Win32s

While processing the WM_CREATE message, we call GetVersion() and assign its return value to *dwVersion*. We check to see if the platform is Windows NT or Windows 3.x/Win32s by checking the high bit of the high word in *dwVersion*. To accomplish this we *bitwise and* 0x80000000 and *dwVersion*. If this result is TRUE, it means that the platform is Win32s; if it is FALSE, the platform is NT.

If the platform is Win32s, we gray out the *Beziers* menu item. If the platform is Windows NT, we don't make any adjustment; all functionality is implemented. Let's look at which functions are allowed and which functions are denied in Win32s.

API Functions Allowed/Not Allowed in Win32s

The code that processes the *Figures* menu selections (*Lines* and *Square*) consists of two calls: LineTo() and MoveToEx(). These calls are supported under both Win32 and Win32s; therefore, there is no reason to gray out the *Figures* menu item.

On the other hand, the code that processes the *Beziers* menu selection (PolyBezier and PolyBezierTo) consists of several calls (PolyBezier(),

PolyBezierTo, BeginPath(), EndPath, and StrokePath()) that are not supported under Win32s. Therefore, if the platform is Win32s, we gray out the *Beziers* menu item.

Alternative Methods

There are many ways to dynamically adjust the functionality of your programs depending on the type of platform. Instead of graying menu items, you could remove unsupported functionality completely. You could also build a menu from within your application, only adding items that are supported by the current platform.

BUILDING AND RUNNING PORT1

The files for PORT1 are located in the \CHAPTER9\9.1 subdirectory. Open a Command window and change to this directory. Type NMAKE and press (ENTER). The program is compiled and linked. Either use the Command Prompt to start PORT1, or add PORT1 to an existing Program Manager group. Review Listings 9-2 through 9-4 while performing the following steps:

1. Select each of the menu selections while running under Windows NT. You'll notice that all functionality is available. Figure 9-8 shows PORT1 running on Windows NT—*PolyBezier* has been selected from the *Beziers* menu.

2. Copy PORT1.EXE to a FAT-partitioned drive if you are using NTFS.

3. Close the PORT1 application and shut down Windows NT.

WIN32S REQUIREMENT

The remaining steps require that you have the capability to run Windows 3.1 and have installed Win32. Installation instructions for Win32s are provided in the Win32 SDK documentation.

4. Start Windows 3.1.

5. Start PORT1 using the Run command in the Program Manager, the File Manager, or add the PORT1 program to an existing group

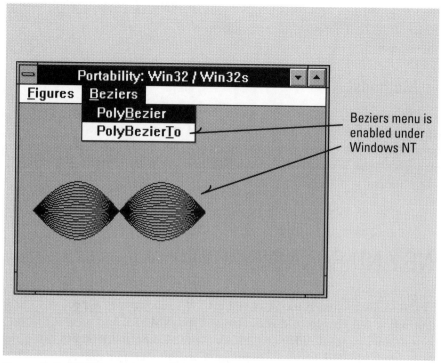

Figure 9-8 PORT1 running on Windows NT

in the Program Manager and start it by double-clicking its icon. Figure 9-9 shows PORT1 running under Win32s. Note that the *Beziers* menu item has been grayed.

6.   Close PORT1 and exit Windows 3.1

TESTING, TESTING, TESTING

The best way to ensure your applications work on both platforms is to test them extensively. The types of problems that crop up depend on the complexity of your programs and the level of their reliance on Win32 API functions *not* supported by Win32s. If your application is single-threaded, and does not use security features, advanced GDI functions, or any of the other API that is not supported by Win32s, it will likely work under Win32s

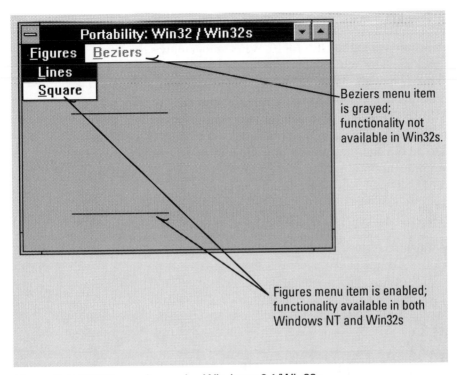

Figure 9-9 PORT1 running under Windows 3.1/Win32s

without problems. Now let's look at this issue of taking existing Windows 3.1 programs and converting them to Win32 applications.

CONVERTING WINDOWS 3.1 APPLICATIONS TO WIN32

In Chapter 2 we showed the basic differences between a Windows 3.1 and a Win32 generic application. This illustrated some of the differences, such as the WINAPI return typedef replacing FAR PASCAL and different parameter types for the main window procedure. We will look deeper into the API and messaging to see other areas of concern: message packing, data type, API function, and message differences.

Message Packing

Another issue illustrated in the GENERIC Win32 program was the difference in message packing. This was due to the window handle growing to 32 bits. Figure 9-10 shows how the WM_COMMAND message was affected.

In Windows 3.x the window handle was in the low word of *lParam* for the WM_COMMAND message. The notification code was in the high word of *lParam*. In Win32 handles are 32 bits. To accommodate this *wParam* is lengthened to 32 bits and the notification code is moved to the high word of *wParam*. This brought on the usage of the LOWORD macro when trapping WM_COMMAND messages with a *switch* statement:

```
case WM_COMMAND:
  switch (LOWORD(wParam))    /* extract the low word of wParam (message id) */
  {
      case IDM_ANYSELECTION:
```

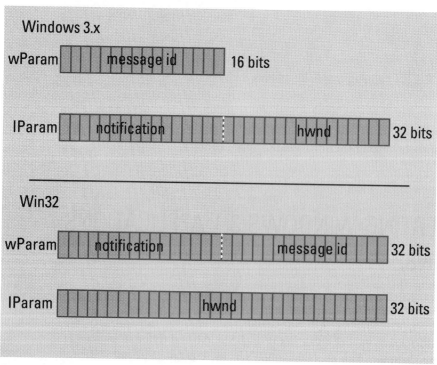

Figure 9-10 Windows 3.x and Win32 message packing—WM_COMMAND

This method works for both Windows 3.x and Win32 programs. Since *wParam* is a UINT, it is 16 bits in Windows 3.x and 32 bits in Win32. Applying the LOWORD macro in both platforms achieves the same result, but this becomes more difficult when extracting the notification code or window handle. For example, we could not use the following code for Win32:

```
notification = HIWORD (lParam);  /* works in Windows 3.x, not in Win32 */
```

Likewise the following code would not work in Windows 3.x:

```
notification = HIWORD (wParam);  /* works in Win32, not in Windows 3.x */
```

If you intend to use conditional compilation and build separate Windows 3.x and Win32 applications, you could use the following to remedy the situation:

```
#ifdef WIN32
    notification = HIWORD (wParam);      /* Win32 notification */
    hWnd =  lParam;                      /* Win32 window handle */
#else
    notification = HIWORD (lParam);      /* Windows 3.x notification */
    hWnd = LOWORD (lParam);              /* Windows 3.x window handle */
#endif
```

This coding extracts the correct values, depending on the target platform. Windows 3.x programs can run on Windows NT in a virtual DOS machine. Win32 applications can run on Windows 3.x using Win32s. Therefore using conditional compilation is not a requirement.

You can design applications that target Windows NT and still run the same program on Win32s (Windows 3.x), regardless of conditional compilation. It is only necessary when producing two executables: one specifically for Windows 3.x, the other for Win32. Let's look at the effects of differences in data types between Windows 3.x and Win32 applications.

Data Types

Most data type differences between Windows 3.x and Win32 are transparent to the programmer. For example, a handle to a window (hWnd) is 16 bits wide in Windows 3.x and 32 bits wide in Win32; however, a handle is a handle, you do not have to be concerned with its length (except how it affects the message packing described above). Table 9-1 shows the basic types for Microsoft C and their size in a 16-bit and 32-bit environment; other compilers' basic types may vary.

Data Type	Length in a 16-Bit Environment	Length in a 32-Bit Environment
char/unsigned char	1 byte	1 byte
short/unsigned short	2 bytes	2 bytes
int/unsigned int	**2 bytes**	**4 bytes**
long/unsigned long	4 bytes	4 bytes
float	4 bytes	4 bytes
double	8 bytes	8 bytes
long double	10 bytes	10 bytes
near pointer	**2 bytes**	**4 bytes**
far pointer	**4 bytes**	**8 bytes**

Table 9-1 Microsoft data types in 16-bit and 32-bit environments

The data types that are affected by the 16/32-bit platform are in boldface. These types are integers, NEAR pointers, and FAR pointers. Since the 32-bit Win32 environment has a flat 32-bit address space, the pointers do not actually come into play. In fact, they are defined as nothing in WINDEF.H for Win32 applications. The integer can become a problem spot, though, depending how you use them.

For example, if you rely on an unsigned integer to overflow after 65535 (which is normal in a 16-bit environment) in a 32-bit environment, you will have problems. An integer will not overflow until after the count of 4,294,967,295 in a 32-bit environment. The solution to this problem is to avoid depending on overflow of integers and test for specific values instead. Let's look at an overview of the Windows API functions that have changed in Win32.

API Differences

Most of the Windows 3.x API calls have 32-bit equivalents in Win32. You can simply call the API as you did in Windows 3.x and achieve the same result. A handful of functions, however, needed modification. These functions relate to the GDI. The modification was necessary because of the Windows 3.x API function returned graphics coordinates (packed x/y) in a

DWORD. Now that graphics coordinates are 32 bits (as opposed to 16 bits in Windows 3.x), a POINT structure becomes part of the Win32 API equivalent function. To illustrate this point, Listing 9-5 shows the Windows 3.x API function, MoveTo(), and the Win32 replacement, MoveToEx().

Listing 9-5 MoveTo() and MoveToEx() syntax and example calls

```
/* MoveTo() and MoveToEx() Syntax */
DWORD MoveTo (HDC hDC, int X, int Y);                    /* Windows 3.x call */
BOOL  MoveToEx (HDC hDC, int X, int Y, LPPOINT lp Point);  /* Win32 call */

/* MoveTo() Example Call */
DWORD dwOldPosition;
int    nOldX, nOldy;                      /* int is 16 bits in Windows 3.x */

    dwOldPosition = MoveTo (hDC, 10, 10);  /* move to position 10, 10--return old position */
    nOldX = LOWORD (dwOldPosition);         /* extract old X coordinate */
    nOldY = HIWORD (dwOldPosition);         /* extract old Y coordinate */

/* MoveToEx() Example Call */
POINT OldPoints;
LONG  nOldX, nOldY;                       /* LONG is 32 bits */

    MoveToEx (hDC, 10, 10, &OldPoints);    /* move to position 10,10--return old position */
    nOldX = OldPoints.x;                    /* get old X coordinate */
    nOldY = OldPoints.y;                    /* get old Y coordinate */
```

Since graphics coordinates have grown to 32 bits, the DWORD return value of MoveTo() cannot accommodate both coordinates. The solution to this problem is the Win32 API function MoveToEx(). MoveTo() is obsolete to Win32 applications. New functions (suffixed with *Ex*) work in both Windows 3.x and Win32 applications.

In the example call to MoveTo(), we assign the return value to a DWORD *(dwOldPosition)*. We obtain the previous position by applying the HIWORD and LOWORD macros to *dwOldPosition*. The high word of this return value contains the prior Y value while the low word contains the prior X value.

The call to MoveToEx() accepts an optional parameter: a pointer to a POINT structure. This structure can hold two 32-bit coordinate values. The call carries out the same function as in MoveTo()—it moves the current position to (10,10); but the method in obtaining the old position is different. MoveToEx() fills the point structure identified by the third parameter (in our case the address of *OldPoints*). We can then get the individual x-y coordinates by accessing the *x* and *y* members of the point structure (*OldPoints.x* and *OldPoints.y*).

Windows 3.x Function	Win32 Function
MoveTo()	MoveToEx()
OffsetViewPortOrg()	OffsetViewPortOrgEx()
OffsetWindowOrg()	OffsetWindowOrgEx()
ScaleViewportExt()	ScaleViewportExtEx()
ScaleWindowExt()	ScaleWindowExtEx()
SetBitmapDimension()	SetBitmapDimensionEx()
SetMetaFileBits()	SetMetaFileBitsEx()
SetViewportExt()	SetViewportExtEx()
SetViewportOrg()	SetViewportOrgEx()
SetWindowExt()	SetWindowExtEx()
SetWindowOrg()	SetWindowOrgEx()
GetBitmapDimension()	GetBitmapDimensionEx()
GetBrushOrg()	GetBrushOrgEx()
GetCurrentPosition()	GetCurrentPositionEx()
GetTextExtent()	GetTextExtentPoint()
GetTextExtentEx()	GetTextExtentPointEx()
GetViewportExt()	GetViewportExtEx()
GetViewportOrg()	GetViewportOrgEx()
GetWindowExt()	GetWindowExtEx()
GetWindowOrg()	GetWindowOrgEx()

Table 9-2 Windows 3.x API functions—Win32 replacements

MoveTo() is not the only API function modified because of the larger coordinate values. Table 9-2 shows a list of Windows 3.x API functions and their Win32 equivalents.

Notice how the majority of Win32 replacement functions append an *Ex* suffix to the Windows 3.x function it is replacing. The only exceptions are GetTextExtent() and GetTextExtentEx() (both Windows 3.x API functions). Since GetTextExtentEx() already has an *Ex* suffix, the word *Point* is added the function name in Win32. Therefore GetTextExtent()

becomes GetTextExtentPoint() and GetTextExtentEx() becomes
GetTextExtentPointEx(). Again, the replacements are necessary to
accommodate 32-bit graphics coordinates. Now let's see how messages are
affected in the crossover from Windows 3.x to Win32.

Message Differences

The last topic that relates to porting Windows 3.x code to Win32 is
differences in messages. You have already seen how the 32-bit window handle
forced repacking of the notification code. Here is a list of the messages
affected by repacking of *wParam* and *lParam* values.

MESSAGES AFFECTED BY WIN32 MESSAGE PACKING

- WM_ACTIVATE
- WM_CHARTOITEM
- WM_COMMAND
- WM_MENUSELECT
- WM_MDIACTIVAT
- WM_MDISETMENU
- WM_MENUCHAR
- WM_PARENTNOTIFY
- WM_VKEYTOITEM
- WM_HSCROLL
- WM_VSCROL L
- EM_GETSEL
- EM_LINESCROLL
- EM_SETSET

The WM_CTLCOLOR message is also affected in Win32. In Windows
3.x WM_CTLCOLOR contained a HDC in *wParam,* and a HWND and
type in *lParam*. Since both handles (HDC and HWND) are 32 bits, there is
no longer room for the type of WM_CTLCOLOR message. Figure 9-11
illustrates this point.

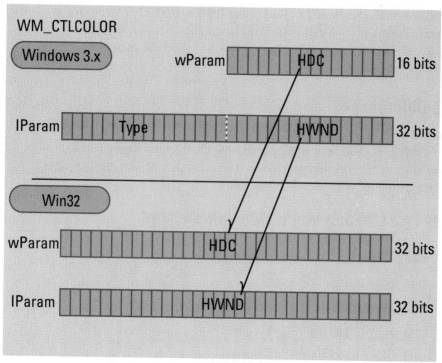

Figure 9-11 WM_CTLCOLOR message (Windows 3.x/Win32)

As the figure illustrates, there is no room for the type in *lParam* because the window handle is 32 bits in Win32. There is also no room in *wParam* for the same reason. This results in a need for multiple messages to differentiate the types of WM_CTLCOLOR messages. Here is a list of the Win32 messages; there is one for every type of Windows 3.x WM_CTLCOLOR message.

- WM_CTLCOLORBTN
- WM_CTLCOLORDLG
- WM_CTLCOLORLISTBOX
- WM_CTLCOLORMSGBOX
- WM_CTLCOLORSCROLLBAR
- WM_CTLCOLORSTATIC
- WM_CTLCOLOREDIT

If your applications do not use any of the affected API functions or messages, porting the Windows 3.x code to Win32 should be fairly easy. However, if your existing applications use these messages or API functions extensively, porting the code will be more difficult and will require a greater attention to detail.

SUMMARY

Writing portable applications is a must if you want to reach the largest audience. This chapter attempted to smooth over the rough edges between Windows 3.x and Win32 programming. We described three scenarios that related to portability. The first scenario showed how existing Windows 3.x applications run on Windows NT. The second scenario demonstrated how Win32 applications can run on Windows 3.x. Finally we looked at porting existing Windows 3.x code to Win32.

In order to see how Windows 3.x applications run on Windows NT, you must first understand the virtual DOS machine, or VDM. The VDM is what allows Windows NT to run multiple MS-DOS applications. A VDM is started for each MS-DOS application.

In order to run a Windows 3.x application on Windows NT, the Win32 subsystem starts a VDM with a WOW (Windows on Win32) environment. All Windows 3.x applications use the same VDM. They are also subject to the same limitations of nonpreemptive multitasking experienced on the Windows 3.x platform.

Win32 applications can run on Windows 3.1 systems with a little help. This help is provided by Win32s, a Microsoft product that extends the existing API of Windows 3.1 to include Win32 API functions. Win32s does not support the entire Win32 API. Functions that create threads, use Bezier curves, create graphics paths, and others are not implemented in the current version of Win32s. If a Win32 function fails in Win32s, you can call GetLastError() to determine if the function is not implemented in Win32s. You can also call GetVersion() to determine the platform your application is running on. With this information you can add or take away functionality from the user.

The last segment addressed issues that arise when porting existing Windows 3.x code to Win32. You saw how message packing and data types vary from the two platforms. You also saw several Windows 3.x API functions that have been modified due to the expansion of graphics coordinates to 32 bits. Finally you saw how messages have been affected by repacking, due to the expansion of handles (such as HWND and HDC) to 32 bits.

The next chapter introduces a new slant on an old topic: *Multiple Document Interface,* or MDI. We'll use a simple program to demonstrate a multithreaded MDI application.

CHAPTER 10

Multithreaded
MDI

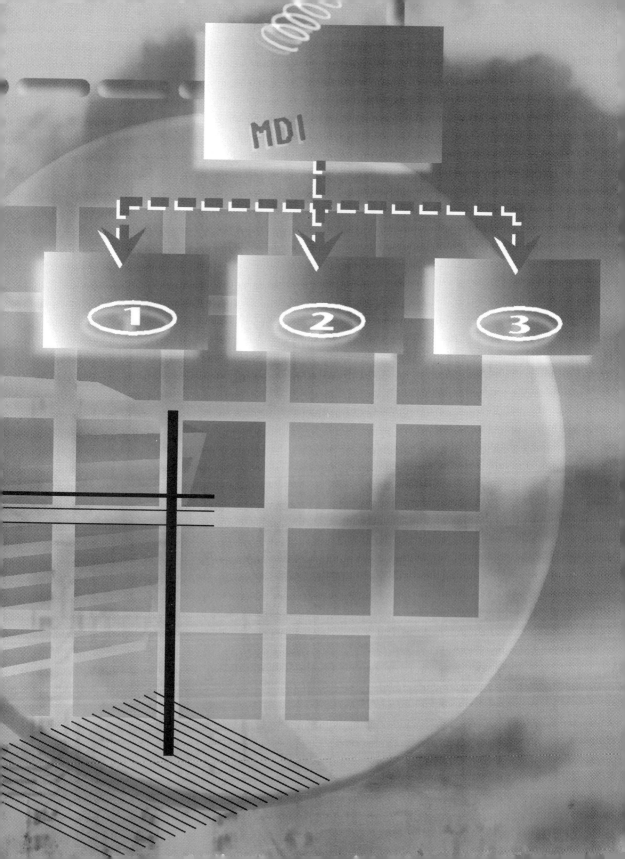

CHAPTER 10

Multithreaded

MDI

The majority of Windows programs on the shelves of software stores today are multiple document interface (MDI) applications. Whether or not MDI enhances an application depends on the types of tasks the application needs to carry out. For example, a simple program such as the Windows Calculator would not gain much if it employed MDI. However, there are many applications that could benefit from MDI features: paint programs, integrated software packages, and word processors to name a few.

An MDI application starts with a main window, called the *frame* window. Inside the frame window is an MDI *client window*. This window is the central point for processing MDI messages. The client window can contain multiple *child windows*. These windows are confined to the frame window at all times. A child window can be maximized to take up the entire client area, or minimized to an icon. Child windows are not required to contain the same type of information. For example, an integrated MDI application could create a child window for a word processor, another for a spreadsheet, and yet another to display graphs. You can also create a different menu for each type of child window.

There are other benefits to MDI applications. For example, the frame menu maintains a list of all active child windows. This enables the user to access any window by making a menu selection. MDI messages allow the user (and programmer) to arrange the child windows into tiles or cascades, or arrange the minimized windows (icons) into a neat row at the bottom of the client area.

This chapter explores the topic of MDI as it relates to Win32 programming. The MDI messages have been affected slightly, mostly because of the expansion of handles to 32 bits. We'll examine a simple, single-thread MDI application and discover some of its limitations. We'll also take a look at an MDI application that employs multiple threads; each child window is associated with its own thread. This overcomes the serial nature of MDI in Windows 3.1, but it restricts the application to the Windows NT platform.

If you are familiar with MDI applications from Windows 3.1, the transition to Win32 MDI should be no problem. Let's take a look at the topics covered in this chapter.

CHAPTER OVERVIEW

Concepts Covered

◁ Overview of MDI applications

◁ Creating a frame window

◁ Creating an MDI client window

◁ Creating MDI child windows

◁ Sending MDI messages

◁ Creating a single-thread MDIapplication

◁ Creating a multithreaded MDI application

Win32 API Functions Covered

◁ DefFrameProc()

◁ DefChildProc()

Messages Covered

◁ WM_MDIACTIVATE

◁ WM_MDICASCADE

◁ WM_MDICREATE

◁ WM_MDIDESTROY

◁ WM_MDIGETACTIVE

◁ WM_MDIICONARRANGE

◁ WM_MDIMAXIMIZE

◁ WM_MDINEXT

◁ WM_MDIREFRESHMENU

◁ WM_MDIRESTORE

◁ WM_MDISETMENU

◁ WM_MDITILE

AN OVERVIEW OF MDI

The basic function of an MDI application is the same for Windows 3.x and Win32. Each MDI program must contain a frame window, an MDI client window, and child windows. Figure 10-1 shows the relationship between these windows.

The Frame Window

The frame window is similar to the main window in most Windows applications. An MDI program starts out by registering a window class (WNDCLASS) for the frame window in WinMain. We create the frame window with a call to CreateWindow(). The only difference in this call is the addition of the window class attribute WS_CLIPCHILDREN, which

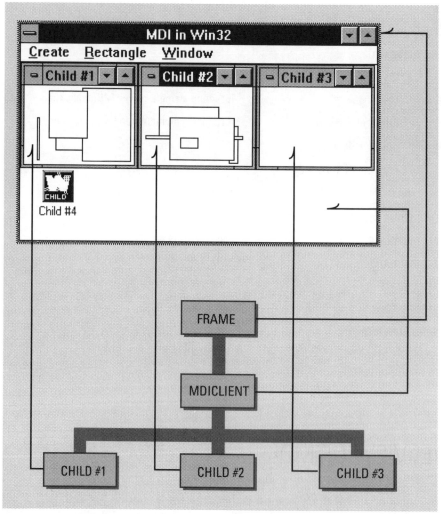

Figure 10-1 Window relationship of an MDI application

confines child windows to the boundary of the parent: in this case the parent is the frame.

When filling the WNDCLASS structure for the frame window, we designate a frame window procedure in the *lpfnWndProc* member. The frame window procedure is the same as a typical, non–MDI window procedure except for three things: creation of a client window, creation of child windows, and the default message processing.

The Client Window

During the creation of the frame window, an MDI application must create a client window. This is done while processing the WM_CREATE message in the window procedure of the frame. A CLIENTCREATESTRUCT structure must be filled and passed along with other parameters to CreateWindow(). This structure contains two members: a handle to the frame window's popup menu and the ID for the first child window.

The child window ID is used by the frame menu when a user selects a child window from the menu; therefore no other menu selections can conflict with child window IDs. For example, if we set the first child ID to 100, Windows will increment this number for each successive window. If a child is destroyed, Windows reassigns the child IDs to keep them contiguous, starting with the application-supplied first child ID.

The other member of CLIENTCREATESTRUCT is a handle to the frame window's popup menu, which will contain the child window list. We can obtain this handle with calls to GetMenu() (to get the top level menu) and GetSubMenu(). Listing 10-1 shows an excerpt from a frame window procedure (WM_CREATE processing). Note that the structure is filled and passed to CreateWindow().

Listing 10-1 Frame window procedure excerpt—creating the client window

```
LONG APIENTRY FrameWndProc (HWND hWnd, UINT message, UINT wParam, LONG lParam)
{
CLIENTCREATESTRUCT clientcreate;
HMENU              hMenu, hSubMenu;

   switch (message)
   {
     case WM_CREATE:
        hMenu = GetMenu (hWnd);                           /* get handle to top level menu */
        hSubMenu = GetSubMenu (hMenu, 1);                 /* get handle to popup */

        clientcreate.hWindowMenu = hSubMenu;              /* fill CLIENTCREATESTRUCT */
        clientcreate.idFirstChild = 100;

        ghWndClient = CreateWindow ("MDICLIENT",          /* predefined window class */
                      NULL,                               /* no window proc */
                      WS_CHILD | WS_CLIPCHILDREN | WS_VISIBLE, /* window style */
                      0, 0, 0, 0,                         /* x, y, width, height */
                      hWnd,                               /* handle to parent window (frame) */
                      NULL,                               /* no menu handle */
                      ghInstance,                         /* program module instance */
                      &clientcreate);                     /* address of CLIENTCREATESTRUCT */
```

Notice that there is no window procedure or menu for the client window. This is because the client window is simply a vehicle for MDI message processing. For example, if we wish to tile the active child windows, we can issue a message to the client window to do so.

Child Windows

With the frame and client windows in place, we can start to create child windows. A window class for the child window must be registered before creating the child window. We do not create MDI child windows using the CreateWindow() call; instead we fill an MDICREATESTRUCT structure and send a message to the client window. The structure contains members similar to the parameters of a CreateWindow() call. There is no definition of a parent window, since the parent is assumed to be the client window. There is also no definition of a menu, since the menu is on frame. We'll change the frame menu in the child window procedure. The style member of MDICREATESTRUCT can contain one or more style definitions. The possible style values and their effects are

- WS_MINIMIZE—create the child in a minimized state
- WS_MAXIMIZE—create the child in a maximized state
- WS_HSCROLL—create the child with a horizontal scroll bar
- WS_VSCROLL—create the child with a vertical scroll bar

The code excerpt in Listing 10-2 shows the creation of a child window. This excerpt assumes that a window class named "MDIChild" has been registered.

Listing 10-2 Creating an MDI child window

```
MDICREATESTRUCT mdicreate;

    mdicreate.szClass = "MDIChild";          /* child window class */
    mdicreate.szTitle = "The Child Window";  /* child window title */
    mdicreate.hOwner = ghInstance;           /* owner instance */
    mdicreate.x = CW_USEDEFAULT;             /* position and size */
    mdicreate.y = CW_USEDEFAULT;
    mdicreate.cx = CW_USEDEFAULT;
    mdicreate.cy = CW_USEDEFAULT;
    mdicreate.style = 0;                     /* no style definition */
    mdicreate.lParam = NULL;                 /* no user defined data */

    hWndChild = SendMessage (ghWndClient,    /* send message to client */
                       WM_MDICREATE,         /* message to send */
```

```
Ol,                     /* not used in this message type */
&mdicreate);            /* address to MDICREATESTRUCT */
```

To create the child, a WM_MDICREATE message is sent to the client window. In this example we are assuming that the client window has the handle name *ghWndClient*. What we don't see in the listing is the window procedure for the child. This procedure is specified in the *lpfnWndProc* member of a WNDCLASS structure when the child window class is created and registered.

The WM_MDICREATE message is one of many MDI messages. This is where Windows 3.x and Win32 MDI applications differ slightly. Some of the messages have been affected slightly in the transition. We will discuss these differences shortly.

Default Message Processing and Accelerators

Another difference between non-MDI and MDI Windows applications is the way that default message processing and accelerators are handled. In a non-MDI application, we normally pass unprocessed messages to a default message processing function: DefWindowProc(). Listing 10-3 shows the default message processing for a non-MDI, MDI frame, and MDI child window procedure. We use these functions in place of DefWindowProc() for the frame and child windows.

Listing 10-3 Default message processing functions

```
return DefWindowProc (hWnd, message, wParam, lParam); /* non-MDI default message processing */

return DefFrameProc (hWnd, message, wParam, lParam);  /* frame default message processing */

return DefChildProc (hWnd, message, wParam, lParam);  /* child default message processing */
```

We must provide a method of accommodating keyboard accelerators in MDI applications. This is accomplished by extending the message loop using the TranslateMDISysAccel() function. Listing 10-4 shows the modified message loop for MDI applications.

Listing 10-4 MDI message loop

```
while (GetMessage (&msg, NULL, 0, 0))
{
    if (!TranslateMDISysAccel (ghWndClient, &msg) &&      /* MDI accelerators */
        !TranslateAccelerator (ghWndFrame, hAccel, &msg))  /* standard accelerators */
```

continued on next page

continued from previous page

```
    {
        TranslateMessage (&msg);                        /* common message loop */
        DispatchMessage (&msg);
    }
}
```

Note that the topics we've discussed to this point are the same for both Windows 3.x and Win32 applications. Some of the MDI window messages are affected slightly, however, since they are now using 32-bit window handles. Let's take a look at the MDI window messages.

MDI WINDOW MESSAGES

We can use MDI messages in two ways in our MDI applications: sending and receiving. For example, we sent a WM_MDICREATE message to the client window to create an MDI child window. If you are familiar with these messages from Windows 3.x, the transition to Win32 MDI is fairly easy; however, there are some slight differences to consider between the two platforms.

Windows 3.x vs Win32 MDI Window Messages

The following information discusses the purpose, usage, and Windows 3.x/Win32 differences (if any) of MDI Window messages. The messages are listed in alphabetical order.

WM_MDIACTIVATE

We can send this message to the client window to activate a specific MDI child window. The child window procedure can receive this message from the client window to determine whether it is being activated or deactivated. Listing 10-5 shows the Windows 3.x and Win32 versions of sending and receiving this message.

Listing 10-5 WM_MDIACTIVATE (Windows 3.x and Win32)

```
/* Windows 3.x/Win32--sending WM_MDIACTIVATE to MDI client window */

SendMessage (ghWndClient,        /* handle to client */
            WM_MDIACTIVATE,      /* message to send */
```

```
        hChild,              /* handle of child to activate */
        OL);                 /* not used */

/* Windows 3.x--receiving WM_MDIACTIVATE in child window procedure */

  WM_MDIACTIVATE:
     bActivate = wParam;              /* Boolean indicating activate (TRUE) or deactivate (FALSE) */
     hChildActive = LOWORD (lParam); /* handle of child being activated */
     hChildDeact = HIWORD (lParam);  /* handle of child being deactivated */

/* Win32--receiving WM_MDIACTIVATE in child window procedure */

  WM_MDIACTIVATE:
     hChildActive = wParam ; /* handle of child being activated */
     hChildDeact = lParam;   /* handle of child being deactivated */
```

Sending this message is the same in both Windows 3.x and Win32, but receiving the message in a child procedure has been affected. In Windows 3.x both the activated and deactivated handles (which are 16 bits) are packed in *lParam* (which is 32 bits). In Win32 the handles are 32 bits; therefore, the activated child window handle is found in *wParam* and the deactivated window handle is found in *lParam*.

WM_MDICASCADE

We send this message to the client window to arrange the active child windows in a cascaded fashion. Sending and receiving the WM_MDICASCADE message is nearly identical in Windows 3.x and Win32. The only difference is the size of *wParam*. A child procedure can receive this message and react (application specific); *wParam* and *lParam* contain no useful information with the WM_MDICASCADE message. Only the send portion is shown in the listing. If a child window procedure processes this message, it should return 0. Listing 10-6 shows an example of sending the WM_MDICASCADE message.

Listing 10-6 WM_MDICASCADE (Windows 3.x and Win32)

```
/* Windows 3.x/Win32--sending WM_MDICASCADE to MDI client window */

SendMessage (ghWndClient,        /* handle to client */
             WM_MDICASCADE,      /* message to send */
             0,                  /* not used--set to OL in Win32 */
             OL);                /* not used */
```

WM_MDICREATE

We used this message earlier in the chapter in an example that created an MDI child window. This message is sent to the client window by the application; the message is not sent to the child window procedure; however, a WM_CREATE message is sent to the child window procedure during creation. Listing 10-7 shows an example of sending this message. This example assumes that an MDICREATESTRUCT structure *(mdicreate)* was filled prior to making the call. SendMessage() in this case returns a handle to the new MDI child window.

Listing 10-7 WM_MDICREATE (Windows 3.x and Win32)

```
/* Windows 3.x/Win32--sending WM_MDICREATE to MDI client window */

hChild = SendMessage (ghWndClient,      /* handle to client */
                      WM_MDICREATE,     /* message to send */
                      0,                /* not used--set to OL in Win32 */
                      &mdicreate);      /* address of MDICREATESTRUCT */
```

WM_MDIDESTROY

We send this message to the client window to close an MDI child window. If this message destroys a maximized child window, the next child (window under the window being destroyed) in order becomes maximized. This call is identical in Windows 3.x and Win32. Listing 10-8 shows an example of sending the WM_MDIDESTROY message. The child procedure can process the WM_DESTROY message to perform cleanup.

Listing 10-8 WM_MDIDESTROY (Windows 3.x and Win32)

```
/* Windows 3.x/Win32--sending WM_MDIDESTROY to MDI client window */

SendMessage (ghWndClient,      /* handle to client */
             WM_MDIDESTROY,    /* message to send */
             hChild,           /* handle of child window to close */
             OL);              /* not used */
```

WM_MDIGETACTIVE

This message obtains the handle of the MDI child window that is currently active. In Windows 3.x the high word of the return value contains a flag that indicates whether the MDI child is maximized. In Win32 the handle consumes the entire return value; therefore, the listing shows a test using GetWindowLong() to determine the maximized state of the window. Listing 10-9 shows examples of sending this message for both Windows 3.x and Win32.

Listing 10-9 WM_MDIGETACTIVE (Windows 3.x and Win32)

```
/* Windows 3.x--sending WM_MDIGETACTIVE to MDI client window */

lReturn = SendMessage (ghWndClient,      /* handle to client */
                       WM_MDIGETACTIVE,  /* message to send */
                       0,                /* not used */
                       0L);              /* not used */

hActive = LOWORD (lReturn);              /* handle to active child */
bMaximized = HIWORD (lReturn);           /* maximized state; TRUE = maximized, FALSE = not
maximized */

/* Win32--sending WM_MDIGETACTIVE to MDI client window */

hActive = SendMessage (ghWndClient,      /* handle to client */
                       WM_MDIGETACTIVE,  /* message to send * 
                       0L,               /* not used set to 0L in Win32 */
                       0L);              /* not used */

bMaximized = GetWindowLong (hChild, GWL_STYLE) & WS_MAXIMIZE; /* determine if child is maximized */
```

WM_MDIICONARRANGE

We send this message to the client window to arrange the minimized MDI child icons at the bottom of the frame window. The call to SendMessage() is nearly identical in Windows 3.x and Win32. The only difference is the length of *wParam*. Listing 10-10 shows an example call with this message.

Listing 10-10 WM_MDIICONARRANGE (Windows 3.x and Win32)

```
/* Windows 3.x/Win32--sending WM_MDIICONARRANGE to MDI client window */

SendMessage (ghWndClient,        /* handle to client */
             WM_MDIICONARRANGE,  /* message to send */
             0,                  /* not used--set to 0L in Win32 */
             0L);                /* not used */
```

WM_MDIMAXIMIZE

We send this message to the client window to maximize a specific MDI child window. The title of the child is appended to the frame window title. The system menu of the child replaces that of the frame window. This call is identical in both Windows 3.x and Win32. Listing 10-11 shows an example call using this message.

Listing 10-11 WM_MDIMAXIMIZE (Windows 3.x and Win32)

```
/* Windows 3.x/Win32--sending WM_MDIMAXIMIZE to MDI client window */

SendMessage (ghWndClient,      /* handle to client */
             WM_MDIMAXIMIZE,   /* message to send */
             hChild,           /* handle of child to maximize */
             0L);              /* not used */
```

WM_MDINEXT

We send this message to the client window to activate the MDI child window that is directly beneath the current active child. It moves the current active child behind all other active children. If the current active child window is maximized, it is restored and the next child window is maximized.

The *wParam* parameter specifies the handle of the child window and the *lParam* parameter specifies whether to activate the previous or the next child. The call is identical in both Windows 3.x and Win32. An example of sending this message is shown in Listing 10-12.

Listing 10-12 WM_MDINEXT (Windows 3.x and Win32)

```
/* Windows 3.x/Win32--sending WM_MDINEXT to MDI client window */

SendMessage (ghWndClient,      /* handle to client */
             WM_MDINEXT,       /* message to send */
             hChild,           /* handle of child */
             (lParam) bNext);  /* go to next (bNext==FALSE) or previous (bNext==TRUE) */
```

WM_MDIREFRESHMENU

We send this message to a client window to refresh the menu after sending a WM_SETMENU message. This message is only used in Win32. Windows 3.x MDI applications can refresh the menu using the WM_SETMENU message (which is covered next). After sending this message, the application must update the menu bar with a call to DrawMenuBar(). Listing 10-13 shows an example call using this message.

Listing 10-13 WM_MDIREFRESHMENU (Win32 Only)

```
/* Win32--sending WM_MDIREFRESHMENU to MDI client window */

SendMessage (ghWndClient,      /* handle to client */
```

```
WM_MDIREFRESHMENU,    /* message to send */
OL                    /* not used */
OL);                  /* not used */
```

WM_MDIRESTORE

We send this message to the client window to restore a specified MDI child window from either a minimized or maximized state. This call is identical for both Windows 3.x and Win32. Listing 10-14 shows an example call using this message.

Listing 10-14 WM_MDIRESTORE (Windows 3.x and Win32)

```
/* Windows 3.x/Win32--sending WM_MDIRESTORE to MDI client window */

SendMessage (ghWndClient,    /* handle to client */
             WM_MDIRESTORE,  /* message to send */
             hChild,         /* handle of child to restore */
             OL);            /* not used */
```

WM_MDISETMENU

We send this message to replace the top-level frame window, the popup window, or both. In Windows 3.x, *wParam* specifies whether this call is refreshing the menu. If *wParam* is TRUE, it indicates that the menu is to be refreshed; if *wParam* is FALSE, it indicates to replace the menu. The *lParam* parameter contains the handle of the new frame menu and the new popup menu. The frame menu, popup menu, or both can be specified.

In Win32 the new frame menu (if any) is placed in *wParam;* the new popup menu (if any) is placed in *lParam*. In order to refresh the menu, a Win32 application must send the WM_MDIREFRESHMENU message to the client window. Listing 10-15 shows example calls sending the WM_MDISETMENU message in Windows 3.x and Win32.

Listing 10-15 WM_MDISETMENU (Windows 3.x and Win32)

```
/* Windows 3.x--sending WM_MDISETMENU to MDI client window */

SendMessage (ghWndClient,              /* handle to client */
             WM_MDISETMENU,            /* message to send */
             (WPARAM)(BOOL) bRefresh,  /* bRefresh==TRUE, refresh; bRefresh==FALSE, set new menus */
             MAKELPARAM (hFrameMenu, hPopupMenu); /* packed top level and popup menus replacements */
```

continued on next page

continued from previous page
```
/* Win32--sending WM_MDISETMENU to MDI client window */

SendMessage (ghWndClient,          /* handle to client */
             WM_MDISETMENU,        /* message to send */
             hFrameMenu,           /* top level menu replacement */
             hPopupMenu);          /* popup menu replacement */
```

WM_MDITILE

We send this message to the client window to arrange the active MDI child windows in a tiled fashion. Sending and receiving the WM_MDITILE message is nearly identical in Windows 3.x and Win32. The only difference is the size of *wParam*. A child procedure can receive this message and react (application specific); *wParam* and *lParam* contain no useful information with the WM_MDICASCADE message. Only the send portion is shown in the listing. As with all MDI messages, if a child window procedure processes this message, it should return 0. Listing 10-16 shows an example of sending the WM_MDITILE message.

- - - - - - -

Listing 10-16 WM_MDITILE (Windows 3.x and Win32)

```
/* Windows 3.x/Win32--sending WM_MDITILE to MDI client window */

SendMessage (ghWndClient,          /* handle to client */
             WM_MDITILE,           /* message to send */
             0,                    /* not used--set to 0L in Win32 */
             0L);                  /* not used */
```

This completes the description of MDI messages. Depending on the style and complexity of your MDI applications, you may or may not need all of the messages. Let's see the multiple document interface and its messages at work with two sample applications: MDI1 and MDI2.

- -

SINGLE-THREAD MDI

We have provided two example applications in this chapter, the first of which demonstrates a single-thread MDI application in Win32. Single-thread Win32 MDI applications have their benefits and drawbacks. On the plus side, they work under the same model as Windows 3.x, and with care you will be able to craft your programs so they work on both platforms. It is also easier to keep track of where your program is executing at any given time in a single-thread design. The downside is that only one MDI child window procedure can be processing at a time. Let's look at our first example MDI application: MDI1.

A SINGLE-THREAD MDI EXAMPLE—MDI1

Our first example application, MDI1, demonstrates a basic MDI application. You can find the source files for this application in the \CHAPTER10\10.1 subdirectory. MDI1 creates a frame and client window. When the user selects MDI Child from the *Create* menu, the application creates an MDI child window. The application also illustrates how to store data with each child window the user creates.

Listings 10-17 through 10-19 show the resource script, the header file, and the complete source file, respectively for MDI1. We have included the WinMain() function in this listing because it performs important tasks related to the multiple document interface.

The resource script identifies two icons for MDI1; the first icon, *MDI1Icon,* is used for the frame window and the second icon, *MDIChildIcon,* is used for each child. Two menus are also defined in the RC file: *MDIFrameMenu,* which is used when no MDI child windows exists, and *MDIChildMenu,* which is used for MDI child windows.

Listing 10-17 MDI1.RC—resource script

```
#include <windows.h>
#include "mdi1.h"

MDI1Icon     ICON mdi1.ico
MDIChildIcon ICON mdichild.ico

MDIFrameMenu MENU
    BEGIN
       POPUP  "&Create"
       BEGIN
          MENUITEM  "&MDI Child",     IDM_MDI
       END

      POPUP "&Window"
         BEGIN
```

continued on next page

continued from previous page

```
            MENUITEM "&Cascade",        IDM_CASCADE
            MENUITEM "&Tile",           IDM_TILE
            MENUITEM "Arrange &Icons", IDM_ARRANGE
        END
    END

MDIChildMenu MENU
    BEGIN
        POPUP  "&Create"
        BEGIN
            MENUITEM "&MDI Child",      IDM_MDI
        END

        MENUITEM  "&Rectangle"         IDM_RECT

        POPUP "&Window"
        BEGIN
            MENUITEM  "&Cascade",       IDM_CASCADE
            MENUITEM  "&Tile",          IDM_TILE
            MENUITEM  "Arrange &Icons",IDM_ARRANGE
        END
    END
```

In addition to the typical menu message defines, MDI1.H contains a definition for FIRST_CHILD. When the client window is created, this value is put in a CREATECLIENTSTRUCT structure. There are also numerous global variable declarations for the frame window, client window, menus, and application instance. The typedef, WNDINFO, is a structure that will be filled for each child window. The address of each structure is stored with the child window.

------- ------- -------

Listing 10-18 MDI1.H—header file

```
/* mdi1.h -- Include file for mdi1.c and mdi1.rc */
#include <windows.h>

/* Menu defines */
#define IDM_MDI         1
#define IDM_RECT        2
#define IDM_CASCADE     3
#define IDM_TILE        4
#define IDM_ARRANGE     5

/* Miscellaneous defines */
#define FIRST_CHILD     100

/* Global variables */
HWND    ghWndFrame = NULL;
HWND    ghWndClient = NULL;
HMENU   hMenu, hMenuWindow;
HMENU   hChildMenu, hChildMenuWindow;
HANDLE  ghInstance;
```

```
HANDLE ghWnd;

/* Function prototypes */
LONG APIENTRY FrameWndProc (HWND, UINT, UINT, LONG);
LONG APIENTRY MDIChildWndProc (HWND, UINT, UINT, LONG);

/* Typedef */
typedef struct _MDIWndInfo {
    HWND    hParent;
    char    CaptionBarText[20];
} WNDINFO, *PWNDINFO;
```

The source file for MDI1 contains three functions: WinMain(),
FrameWndProc(), and MDIChildWndProc(). WinMain() contains the code
where window classes are registered and the frame window is created. The
frame and child menus are also loaded in WinMain(). FrameWndProc()
contains the code that creates the client window; it also processes the menu
selections and passes them on to the child window procedure if applicable.
MDIChildWndProc() processes several messages, including a menu message
that results in the procedure drawing a random rectangle on the client area of
the child. Lines that have significant impact on MDI1 are listed in boldface.

Listing 10-19 MDI1.C—source file

```
/* mdi1.c      Demonstrates Multiple Document Interface in Win32 */
#include <stdlib.h>
#include "mdi1.h"

int APIENTRY WinMain (HANDLE hInstance, HANDLE hPrevInstance, LPSTR lpCmdLine, int nCmdShow)
{
    MSG     msg;
    WNDCLASS wndclass;

    ghInstance = hInstance;                                  /* global instance handle */

    wndclass.style = CS_HREDRAW | CS_VREDRAW;                /* fill frame WNDCLASS */
    wndclass.lpfnWndProc = (WNDPROC) FrameWndProc;
    wndclass.cbClsExtra = 0;
    wndclass.cbWndExtra = sizeof (LONG);
    wndclass.hInstance = ghInstance;
    wndclass.hIcon = LoadIcon (hInstance,"MDI1Icon");
    wndclass.hCursor = LoadCursor (NULL, IDC_ARROW);
    wndclass.hbrBackground = GetStockObject (WHITE_BRUSH);
    wndclass.lpszMenuName = "MDIFrameMenu";
    wndclass.lpszClassName = "MDIFrameClass";

    if (!RegisterClass(&wndclass))                           /* register frame class */
        return FALSE;

    wndclass.lpfnWndProc = (WNDPROC) MDIChildWndProc;        /* fill child class */
```

continued on next page

continued from previous page

```
        wndclass.hIcon = LoadIcon (hInstance, "MDIChildIcon");
        wndclass.lpszMenuName = NULL;
        wndclass.lpszClassName = "MDIClass";

        if (!RegisterClass (&wndclass))                    /* register child class */
           return FALSE;

        hMenu = LoadMenu (ghInstance, "MDIFrameMenu");      /* load frame menu */
        hChildMenu = LoadMenu (ghInstance, "MDIChildMenu"); /* load child menu */
        hMenuWindow = GetSubMenu (hMenu, 1);                /* get handle to frame popup */
        hChildMenuWindow = GetSubMenu (hChildMenu, 2);      /* get handle to child popup */

        ghWndFrame = CreateWindow("MDIFrameClass",          /* create frame menu */
                                  "MDI in Win32",
                                  WS_OVERLAPPEDWINDOW | WS_CLIPCHILDREN | WS_VISIBLE,
                                  CW_USEDEFAULT,
                                  CW_USEDEFAULT,
                                  CW_USEDEFAULT,
                                  CW_USEDEFAULT,
                                  NULL,
                                  hMenu,
                                  ghInstance,
                                  NULL);

        if (ghWndFrame == NULL)                             /* check for success */
           return FALSE;

        SetWindowLong (ghWndFrame, GWL_USERDATA, OL);       /* establish user data */

        SetFocus (ghWndFrame);                              /* set focus to frame */

        while (GetMessage(&msg, NULL, 0, 0))
        {                                                   /* message loop */
            TranslateMessage(&msg);
            DispatchMessage(&msg);
        }

        return 1;

        UNREFERENCED_PARAMETER (lpCmdLine);
        UNREFERENCED_PARAMETER (nCmdShow);
        UNREFERENCED_PARAMETER (hPrevInstance);
}

/* FrameWndProc -- Frame Window Procedure for mdi1.c */

long APIENTRY FrameWndProc (HWND hWnd, UINT message, UINT wParam, LONG lParam)
{
    static int          iMDICount=1;
    CLIENTCREATESTRUCT  clientcreate;
    HWND                hWndChildWindow;
```

```
switch (message)
{

    case WM_CREATE:
        SetWindowLong (hWnd, 0, (LONG)NULL);                    /* set window data to NULL */

        clientcreate.hWindowMenu = hMenuWindow;                 /* fill CCS struct */
        clientcreate.idFirstChild = FIRST_CHILD;

        ghWndClient = CreateWindow ("MDICLIENT",                /* create client window */
                                    NULL,
                                    WS_CHILD | WS_CLIPCHILDREN | WS_VISIBLE,
                                    0,0,0,0,
                                    hWnd,
                                    NULL,
                                    ghInstance,
                                    (LPVOID) &clientcreate);
        return 0L;

    case WM_DESTROY:                                            /* no cleanup */
        PostQuitMessage(0);
        return 0L;

    case WM_COMMAND:                                            /* messages */
        switch (LOWORD (wParam))
        {
            case IDM_TILE:                                      /* tile children */
                SendMessage (ghWndClient, WM_MDITILE, 0L, 0L);
                return 0L;

            case IDM_CASCADE:                                   /* cascade children */
                SendMessage (ghWndClient, WM_MDICASCADE, 0L, 0L);
                return 0L;

            case IDM_ARRANGE:                                   /* arrange icons */
                SendMessage (ghWndClient, WM_MDIICONARRANGE, 0L, 0L);
                return 0L;

            case IDM_MDI:                                       /* create a new child */
            {
                HANDLE hWndInfo;
                PWNDINFO  pWndInfo;
                MDICREATESTRUCT mdicreate;
                                                                /* allocate window info for child */
                hWndInfo = LocalAlloc (LHND, (WORD) sizeof (WNDINFO));
                if (hWndInfo)                                   /* if successful... */
                {
                    pWndInfo = (PWNDINFO) LocalLock (hWndInfo);    /* lock memory */
                    wsprintf ((LPSTR) &(pWndInfo->CaptionBarText), /* store caption */
                            "Child #%d",
                            iMDICount);
```

continued on next page

```
                    pWndInfo->hParent = ghWndClient;            /* store parent window */

                    mdicreate.szClass = "MDIClass";            /* fill MDICREATESTRUCT */
                    mdicreate.szTitle = (LPTSTR) &(pWndInfo->CaptionBarText);
                    mdicreate.hOwner  = ghInstance;
                    mdicreate.x = CW_USEDEFAULT;
                    mdicreate.y = CW_USEDEFAULT;
                    mdicreate.cx = CW_USEDEFAULT;
                    mdicreate.cy = CW_USEDEFAULT;
                    mdicreate.style = 0L;

                 mdicreate.lParam = (LONG) hWndInfo;       /* store window info with child */

                 hWndChildWindow = (HANDLE) SendMessage (ghWndClient, /* create child */
                                                WM_MDICREATE,
                                                0L,
                                                (LONG)(LPMDICREATESTRUCT)&mdicreate);

            if (hWndChildWindow == NULL)            /* check for failure */
            {
            MessageBox (ghWndFrame,                 /* message indicating creation failed */
                        "Could Not Create Child Window",
                        "Failure",
                        MB_OK);
                return 0L;
            }

            iMDICount++;                            /* increment creation count */

            LocalUnlock (hWndInfo);                 /* unlock memory */
        }

        return 0L;
    }

    case IDM_RECT:                                  /* user selected Rectangle */
    {
    HWND hActiveChild;

                                                    /* get active child handle */
        hActiveChild = (HANDLE) SendMessage (ghWndClient,
                                        WM_MDIGETACTIVE,
                                        0L, 0L);
        if (hActiveChild)                           /* send message to active child */
            SendMessage (hActiveChild, WM_COMMAND, wParam, lParam);
        return 0L;
    }

    default:
        return DefFrameProc (hWnd, ghWndClient, message, wParam, lParam);
    }

    default:
```

```
        return DefFrameProc (hWnd,  ghWndClient, message, wParam, lParam);
    }
}


/* MDIChildWndProc -- MDI Child Window Procedure */

long APIENTRY MDIChildWndProc (HWND hWnd, UINT message, UINT wParam, LONG lParam)
{
HDC hDC;

    switch (message)
    {
        case WM_COMMAND:                                /* messages */
            switch (LOWORD (wParam))
            {
                case IDM_RECT:                          /* user selected Rectangle */
                    hDC = GetDC (hWnd);                 /* get handle to DC */
                    {
                    RECT rc;
                    LONG left, top, right, bottom;

                    GetClientRect (hWnd, &rc);          /* get child client rect */

                    top = (rand() % rc.right) + 1;      /* random rectangle based on */
                    bottom = (rand() % rc.right) + 1;   /* child client area */
                    left = (rand() % rc.bottom) + 1;
                    right = (rand() % rc.bottom) + 1;

                    Rectangle (hDC, top, left, bottom, right); /* draw the rectangle */
                    }
                    ReleaseDC (hWnd, hDC);
                    return OL;                          /* release the DC */

                default:
                    return OL;

            }

        case WM_MDIACTIVATE:                            /* child becoming active */
            if ((HWND) lParam == hWnd)
            {
                SendMessage (GetParent (hWnd),          /* set menu for child */
                            WM_MDISETMENU,
                            (DWORD) hChildMenu,
                            (LONG) hChildMenuWindow);
                DrawMenuBar (GetParent (GetParent (hWnd))); /* refresh the menu bar */
            }
            return OL;

        case WM_CLOSE:                                  /* closing the child */
        {
        HANDLE hWndInfo;
```

continued on next page

continued from previous page

```
            SendMessage(GetParent (hWnd),                      /* set menu for frame */
                        WM_MDISETMENU,
                        (DWORD) hMenu,
                        (LONG) hMenuWindow);
            DrawMenuBar (GetParent (GetParent (hWnd)));        /* refresh the menu bar */

            hWndInfo = (HANDLE) GetWindowLong (hWnd, 0);       /* get handle to window info */
            LocalFree (hWndInfo);                              /* free the memory */
            break;
        }


        default:
            return DefMDIChildProc (hWnd, message, wParam, lParam);

    }
    return DefMDIChildProc (hWnd, message, wParam, lParam);
}
```

WinMain()

The first section of WinMain( ) registers two classes: *MDIFrameClass* (for the frame window) and *MDIClass* (for the child windows). Note that the frame class structure points to FrameWndProc( ) and the child class structure points to MDIChildWndProc( ).

With the window classes registered, we load two menus: one for the frame window, the other for child windows. The next two lines get a handle to the popup menu in which the MDI child window names will be listed. For example, *hMenuWindow* is a handle to the second popup on the frame menu. This results in the window titles being appended to the *Window* menu popup (along with *Tile, Cascade,* and *Arrange Icons*).

The next step is to create the frame window with a call to CreateWindow( ). Notice that there are two additional window styles: WS_CLIPCHILDREN, which will confine child windows to the frame, and WS_VISIBLE. After the frame window is created, we set its focus with a call to SetFocus( ). We've reached the message loop for MDI1; now let's look at the frame window procedure.

FrameWndProc()

The frame window procedure performs several tasks in MDI1, such as creating the client window and processing menu messages. While processing the WM_CREATE message, we fill a CLIENTCREATESTRUCT structure with a handle to the frame popup menu and FIRST_CHILD (defined as 100 in MDI1.H). Next we create the client window with a call to

CreateWindow(). Note that we use the predefined class MDICLIENT to create the window. At this point we have the frame and client windows created. Before most of the menu selections have any effect, we must first create an MDI child window.

Creating a Child Window

When the user selects *MDI Child* from the *Create* menu, an IDM_MDI menu message is sent to FrameWndProc(). We have declared three local variables in the IDM_MDI case: a handle *(hWndInfo)*, pointer to WNDINFO *(pWndInfo)*, and an MDI creation structure *(mdicreate)*.

Before creating the child menu, we allocate some memory to store some information along with the child. We obtain a pointer to this memory and store the parent handle (which is the client window handle) and the caption bar text. The caption bar text is "Child #" followed by the *iMDICount* variable. This variable was initialized to 1 at the top of FrameWndProc() and is incremented for every child we create.

Next we fill the MDICREATESTRUCT structure. Note that the handle to the window information is passed in the *lParam* member of the structure. This stores the data along with the child we are creating. We will not be extracting this data in this example; however, it illustrates how data can be associated with each child window.

We create the MDI child window by sending a WM_MDICREATE message to the client window. The return value is the handle to the new child. If the creating fails, we display a message to the user indicating the failure. Finally we increment *iMDICount* and unlock the memory used to store the associated window data. We now have our first child menu. Let's assume the user creates two or three MDI child windows. Now we can look at some of the other menu selections.

Tiling, Cascading, and Arranging

There are three menu selections that arrange the MDI child windows in the *Window* menu popup: *Cascade, Tile,* and *Arrange Icons.* Each of these selections results in sending the appropriate message to the client window. The client window takes care of rearranging the windows (or icons).

Changing the Menu

In order to see how the new child window causes a new menu to take effect, we need to examine a portion of MDIChildWndProc(). When the user creates a new child, a WM_MDIACTIVATE message is sent to the child procedure. We check the value of *lParam* to determine if the activated MDI child matches the child window procedure handle *(hWnd)*. Remember, there is an instance of MDIChildWndProc() for each MDI child in existence. The active child window procedure will send a WM_MDISET message to the client window and pass along the new top level and popup menus. A call to DrawMenuBar() completes the menu change.

Drawing the Rectangle

When the user selects Rectangle from the menu, an IDM_RECT menu message is sent to FrameWndProc(). We declare a local window handle to temporarily store the active child window handle. This handle is retrieved by sending a WM_MDIGETACTIVE message to the client window. We then send the menu message on to the active child.

When the window procedure for the active child receives the IDM_RECT menu message, it gets a handle to the device context and draws a random rectangle in its own client area. Note that we've used the rand() function and the modulus operator to obtain random coordinates that are within the bounds of the MDI child client area. At this point we return control to the system.

Closing a Child

When the user closes an MDI child window, a WM_CLOSE message is sent to its window procedure. We intercept this message, send a WM_MDISETMENU message to the client window, and call DrawMenuBar(). This restores the original frame menu; however, if another child exists, it will become active and change it back to a child menu immediately.

The next two lines retrieve the handle to the data stored with the child and free the memory with a call to LocalFree(). Let's take a look at MDI1 in action.

BUILDING AND USING MDI1

The MDI1 program files are located in the \CHAPTER10\10.1 subdirectory. Open a Command Prompt window and change to this directory. Type NMAKE and press (ENTER); the MDI1 application compiles and links. You can use the Command Prompt to start MDI1 by typing MDI1 and pressing (ENTER). You can also add the application to an existing group in the Program Manager.

Review the code in Listings 10-17 through 10-19 while performing the following steps:

1. Note that the top level menu contains two menu items: *Create* and *Window.* Select *MDI Child* from the *Create* menu. A child window should appear. Its title bar should be "Child #1." The menu now contains three menu items; the new menu item is *Rectangle.*

2. Create two or three more MDI child windows.

3. Experiment with the *Window* menu selections. Try minimizing some of the child windows, move the icons around and arrange them with the *Arrange Icons* selection.

4. Try tiling and cascading the child windows with the *Tile* and *Cascade* selections.

5. Note the active child and select *Rectangle.* A random rectangle is drawn on the client area of the active child.

6. Activate a different child window by clicking on it, or select the window by name from the *Window* menu. Note how the Windows system automatically adds the names of child windows to the menu. Figure 10-2 shows MDI1 with three tiled child windows and one minimized child. Child #2 is the active child window in the figure.

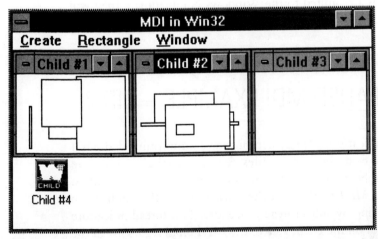

Figure 10-2 MDI1—three tiled MDI child windows (one minimized)

7. Close one of the MDI child windows by double-clicking its system menu, or pull down the system menu and select *Close*. If you watch closely, you can see the menu change back to the original frame menu, then change back again as the next child becomes active.

8. Close all child windows. The menu should return to its original state.

9. Close MDI1.

While observing MDI1 in action you may have noticed a drawback: only one child window is active at any time; therefore, we can only draw a rectangle on the active child. Your applications will do something more substantial than draw a random rectangle, but the concept remains the same. Let's look at an MDI application that gets around this drawback by using multiple threads.

MULTITHREADED MDI

Our final application in this book, MDI2, demonstrates multiple threads in an MDI application. Like the single-threaded MDI application, MDI2 has its advantages and disadvantages. The big advantage is that each child window can be associated with an individual thread procedure. This way the child can continue to work even if it is not the active window. The downside is that multithreaded programs are limited to the Windows NT platform; they will not run on Windows 3.x

A MULTITHREADED MDI EXAMPLE—MDI2

Our final example application, MDI2, demonstrates a multithreaded MDI application. You can find the source files for this application in the \CHAPTER10\10.2 subdirectory. MDI2 creates a frame and client window. When the user selects *MDI Child* from the *Create* menu, the application creates an MDI child window and a thread procedure. This thread procedure draws random rectangles on the client area of the MDI child regardless of the state of the window. This application uses a linked list to store information about each child window.

Listings 10-20 through 10-22 show the resource script, the header file, and the complete source file, respectively, for MDI2.

The resource script identifies two icons for MDI2; the first icon, *MDI1Icon,* is used for the frame window and the second icon, *MDIChildIcon,* is used for each child. Two menus are also defined in the RC file: *MDIFrameMenu,* which is used when no MDI child windows exists, and *MDIChildMenu,* which is used for MDI child windows. The child menu contains menu items for suspending and resuming threads.

Listing 10-20 MDI2.RC—resource script

```
#include <windows.h>
#include "mdi2.h"

MDI2Icon      ICON mdi2.ico
MDIChildIcon ICON mdichild.ico

MDIFrameMenu MENU
    BEGIN
        POPUP  "&Create"
        BEGIN
            MENUITEM "&MDI Child",    IDM_MDI
        END

      POPUP "&Window"
        BEGIN
            MENUITEM "&Cascade",       IDM_CASCADE
            MENUITEM "&Tile",          IDM_TILE
            MENUITEM "Arrange &Icons", IDM_ARRANGE
        END
    END

MDIChildMenu MENU
    BEGIN
        POPUP "&Create"
        BEGIN
            MENUITEM "&MDI Child",    IDM_MDI
        END

        POPUP "&Threads"
        BEGIN
            MENUITEM "&Resume"         IDM_RESUME
            MENUITEM "&Suspend"        IDM_SUSPEND
        END
```

continued on next page

continued from previous page

```
        POPUP "&Window"
        BEGIN
            MENUITEM  "&Cascade",         IDM_CASCADE
            MENUITEM  "&Tile",            IDM_TILE
            MENUITEM  "Arrange &Icons",IDM_ARRANGE
        END
    END
```

In addition to the menu defines and global variables, MDI2.H contains two typedefs: THREADINFO is a struct that will hold individual thread information, and LIST is a linked list structure that contains a THREADINFO type as one of its members. We also have added a function prototype for the thread procedure.

------ ------ ------

Listing 10-21 MDI2.H—header file

```
/* mdi2.h -- Include file for mdi2.c and mdi2.rc */
#include <windows.h>

/* Menu defines */
#define IDM_MDI        1
#define IDM_RESUME     2
#define IDM_SUSPEND    3
#define IDM_CASCADE    4
#define IDM_TILE       5
#define IDM_ARRANGE    6


/* Miscellaneous defines */
#define FIRST_CHILD    100

/* Global variables */
HWND    ghWndFrame = NULL;
HWND    ghWndClient = NULL;
HMENU   hMenu, hMenuWindow;
HMENU   hChildMenu, hChildMenuWindow;
HANDLE ghInstance;
HANDLE ghWnd;
BOOL    bKillAll = FALSE;

/* Typedefs */
typedef struct _ThreadInfo {
    HWND    hWndThread;
    char    CaptionBarText[20];
    BOOL    bKill;
    HANDLE hThread;
    LONG    lThreadID;
} THREADINFO, *PTHREADINFO;

typedef struct _ThreadList {
```

```
    THREADINFO ThreadInfo;
    HANDLE     hNext;
} LIST, *PLIST;


/* Function prototypes */
LONG APIENTRY FrameWndProc     (HWND, UINT, UINT, LONG);
LONG APIENTRY MDIChildWndProc (HWND, UINT, UINT, LONG);
void DrawRects (PTHREADINFO);
```

The source file for MDI2 is similar to that of MDI1 as far as MDI is concerned, but a significant amount of code is dedicated to managing the linked list of threads. MDI2.C also contains an additional function, DrawRects(), which is the thread procedure.

Listing 10-22 MDI2.C—source file

```
/* mdi2.c      Demonstrates Multithreaded Multiple Document Interface in Win32 */
#include <stdlib.h>
#include "mdi2.h"

int APIENTRY WinMain (HANDLE hInstance, HANDLE hPrevInstance, LPSTR lpCmdLine, int nCmdShow)
{
    MSG    msg;
    WNDCLASS wndclass;

    ghInstance = hInstance;                              /* global instance handle */

    wndclass.style = CS_HREDRAW | CS_VREDRAW;            /* fill frame WNDCLASS */
    wndclass.lpfnWndProc = (WNDPROC) FrameWndProc;
    wndclass.cbClsExtra = 0;
    wndclass.cbWndExtra = sizeof(LONG);
    wndclass.hInstance = ghInstance;
    wndclass.hIcon = LoadIcon (hInstance,"MDI2Icon");
    wndclass.hCursor = LoadCursor (NULL, IDC_ARROW);
    wndclass.hbrBackground = GetStockObject (WHITE_BRUSH);
    wndclass.lpszMenuName = "MDIFrameMenu";
    wndclass.lpszClassName = "MDIFrameClass";

    if (!RegisterClass(&wndclass))
        return FALSE;                                    /* register frame class */

    wndclass.lpfnWndProc = (WNDPROC) MDIChildWndProc;    /* fill child class */
    wndclass.hIcon = LoadIcon (hInstance, "MDIChildIcon");
    wndclass.lpszMenuName = NULL;
    wndclass.lpszClassName = "MDIClass";

    if (!RegisterClass(&wndclass))                       /* register child class */
        return FALSE;
```

continued on next page

continued from previous page

```
        hMenu = LoadMenu (ghInstance, "MDIFrameMenu");          /* load frame menu */
        hChildMenu = LoadMenu (ghInstance, "MDIChildMenu");      /* load child menu */
        hMenuWindow = GetSubMenu (hMenu, 1);                     /* get handle to frame popup */
        hChildMenuWindow = GetSubMenu (hChildMenu, 2);           /* get handle to child popup */

        ghWndFrame = CreateWindow ("MDIFrameClass",              /* create frame menu */
                                   "Multithreaded MDI in Win32",
                                   WS_OVERLAPPEDWINDOW | WS_CLIPCHILDREN | WS_VISIBLE,
                                   CW_USEDEFAULT,
                                   CW_USEDEFAULT,
                                   CW_USEDEFAULT,
                                   CW_USEDEFAULT,
                                   NULL,
                                   hMenu,
                                   ghInstance,
                                   NULL);

        if (ghWndFrame == NULL)                                  /* check for success */
            return FALSE;

        SetWindowLong (ghWndFrame, GWL_USERDATA, OL);            /* establish user data */

        SetFocus (ghWndFrame);                                   /* set focus to frame */

        while (GetMessage (&msg, NULL, 0, 0))                    /* message loop */
        {
            TranslateMessage (&msg);
            DispatchMessage (&msg);
        }

        return 1;

        UNREFERENCED_PARAMETER (lpCmdLine);
        UNREFERENCED_PARAMETER (nCmdShow);
        UNREFERENCED_PARAMETER (hPrevInstance);
}

/* FrameWndProc -- Frame Window Procedure for mdi1.c */

long APIENTRY FrameWndProc (HWND hWnd, UINT message, UINT wParam, LONG lParam)
{
    static int          iMDICount=1;
    CLIENTCREATESTRUCT  clientcreate;
    HWND                hWndChild;


    switch (message)
    {

        case WM_CREATE:
            SetWindowLong (hWnd, 0, (LONG) NULL);                /* set window data to NULL */
```

```
        clientcreate.hWindowMenu  = hMenuWindow;          /* fill CCS struct */
        clientcreate.idFirstChild = FIRST_CHILD;

        ghWndClient = CreateWindow ("MDICLIENT",          /* create client window */
                                    NULL,
                                    WS_CHILD | WS_CLIPCHILDREN | WS_VISIBLE,
                                    0,0,0,0,
                                    hWnd,
                                    NULL,
                                    ghInstance,
                                    (LPVOID)&clientcreate);
        return OL;

case WM_COMMAND:                                          /* messages */
    switch (LOWORD (wParam))
    {
        case IDM_TILE:                                    /* tile children */
            SendMessage (ghWndClient, WM_MDITILE, OL, OL);
            return OL;

        case IDM_CASCADE:                                 /* cascade children */
            SendMessage (ghWndClient, WM_MDICASCADE, OL, OL);
            return OL;

        case IDM_ARRANGE:                                 /* arrange icons */
            SendMessage (ghWndClient, WM_MDIICONARRANGE, OL, OL);
            return OL;

        case IDM_MDI:
        {                                                 /* create a new child */
        HANDLE          hThread, hList, hStart;
        PLIST           pList;
        MDICREATESTRUCT mdicreate;
                                                          /* allocate window info for child */
            hList = LocalAlloc(LHND, (WORD) sizeof(LIST));
            if (hList)                                    /* if successful... */
            {
                pList = (PLIST) LocalLock (hList);        /* lock memory */
                wsprintf((LPSTR) &(pList->ThreadInfo.CaptionBarText), /* store caption */
                         "Child #%d",
                         iMDICount);

                mdicreate.szClass = "MDIClass";           /* fill MDICREATESTRUCT */
                mdicreate.szTitle = (LPTSTR)&(pList->ThreadInfo.CaptionBarText);
                mdicreate.hOwner  = ghInstance;
                mdicreate.x = CW_USEDEFAULT;
                mdicreate.y = CW_USEDEFAULT;
                mdicreate.cx = CW_USEDEFAULT;
                mdicreate.cy = CW_USEDEFAULT;
                mdicreate.style   = OL;
                mdicreate.lParam = OL;
```

continued on next page

continued from previous page

```
            hWndChild = (HANDLE) SendMessage(ghWndClient,  /* create child */
                                    WM_MDICREATE,
                                    0L,
                                    (LONG)(LPMDICREATESTRUCT)&mdicreate);

        if (hWndChild == NULL)                       /* check for failure */
        {
         MessageBox(ghWndFrame,                      /* message indicating creation failed */
                 "Could Not Create Child Window",
                 "Failure",
                 MB_OK);
            return 0L;
        }

    pList->ThreadInfo.hWndThread = hWndChild; /* store handle to child */
    hStart = (HANDLE) GetWindowLong (hWnd, 0); /* get handle to window data */
    pList->hNext = hStart;                      /* set pointer to next */
    SetWindowLong (hWnd, 0, (LONG) hList);      /* place current pointer in window data */

    hThread = CreateThread (NULL,                     /* create suspended thread */
                        0,
                        (LPTHREAD_START_ROUTINE) DrawRects,
                        &pList->ThreadInfo,
                        CREATE_SUSPENDED,
                        (LPDWORD) &pList->ThreadInfo.lThreadID);

        if (hThread)                                 /* check for success */
        {
           pList->ThreadInfo.hThread = hThread;   /* store thread handle */
           iMDICount++;                           /* increment creation count */
                                                  /* lower thread priority */
           SetThreadPriority (hThread, THREAD_PRIORITY_BELOW_NORMAL);
           ResumeThread (hThread);                /* start the thread */
        }

        LocalUnlock (hList);                         /* unlock memory */
    }

    return 0L;
}

case IDM_RESUME:                                       /* thread control menu */
case IDM_SUSPEND:
{
HWND hActiveChild;

                                                  /* get active child handle */
    hActiveChild = (HANDLE) SendMessage (ghWndClient,
                                    WM_MDIGETACTIVE,
                                    0L, 0L);
    if (hActiveChild)                              /* send message to active child */
        SendMessage (hActiveChild, WM_COMMAND, wParam, lParam);
    return 0L;
```

```
            }

            default:
                return DefFrameProc (hWnd,  ghWndClient, message, wParam, lParam);
        }

    case WM_DESTROY:                                        /* destroy and free list */
        {
        HANDLE hStart, hTemp;
        PLIST  pList;

            bKillAll = TRUE;                                /* kill threads */

            hStart = (HANDLE) GetWindowLong (hWnd, 0);      /* get start of list */
            if (hStart)                                     /* if successful */
            {
                pList = (PLIST) LocalLock (hStart);         /* lock memory */
                while (pList->hNext != NULL)                /* while not at end of list... */
                {
                    hTemp = hStart;                         /* store address in temp */
                    hStart = pList->hNext;                  /* look at next */
                    LocalUnlock (hTemp);                    /* unlock previous */
                    LocalFree (hTemp);                      /* free previous */
                    pList = (PLIST) LocalLock (hStart);     /* lock the next */
                }
            }
            LocalUnlock (hStart);                           /* unlock memory */
            PostQuitMessage (0);
        }
        return 0L;

    default:
        return DefFrameProc (hWnd,  ghWndClient, message, wParam, lParam);
    }
}


/* MDIChildWndProc -- MDI Child Window Procedure */

long APIENTRY MDIChildWndProc (HWND hWnd, UINT message, UINT wParam, LONG lParam)
{

    switch (message)
    {
    case WM_CREATE:                                         /* creating child */
        {
        PTHREADINFO        pThreadInfo;
        PLIST              pList;
        HANDLE             hStart, hTemp;

            hStart = (HANDLE) GetWindowLong (ghWndFrame, 0); /* get pointer to start of list */
            if (hStart)                                      /* if successful */
            {
```

continued on next page

continued from previous page

```
            pList = (PLIST) LocalLock (hStart);          /* lock memory */
                                                         /* match or end of list? */
            while ((pList->ThreadInfo.hWndThread != hWnd) && (pList->hNext != NULL))
            {
                hTemp = hStart;                          /* store address in temp */
                hStart = pList->hNext;                   /* look at next */
                LocalUnlock (hTemp);                     /* unlock previous */
                pList = (PLIST) LocalLock (hStart);      /* and lock the new */
            }
            if (pList->ThreadInfo.hWndThread == hWnd)    /* match the child handle? */
                pThreadInfo = &pList->ThreadInfo;        /* get thread information */
        }
        LocalUnlock (hStart);                            /* unlock memory */
        break;
    }


    case WM_COMMAND:                                     /* messages */
        switch (LOWORD (wParam))
        {
            case IDM_RESUME:
            case IDM_SUSPEND:                            /* thread control menu selections */
                {
                PLIST  pList;
                HANDLE hStart, hTemp;

                                                         /* get pointer to start of list */
                    hStart = (HANDLE) GetWindowLong (ghWndFrame, 0);
                    if (hStart)                          /* if successful... */
                    {
                        pList = (PLIST) LocalLock (hStart);   /* lock memory */
                                                         /* match or end of list? */
                        while ((pList->ThreadInfo.hWndThread != hWnd) && (pList->hNext != NULL))
                        {
                            hTemp = hStart;              /* store address in temp */
                            hStart = pList->hNext;       /* look at next */
                            LocalUnlock (hTemp);         /* unlock previous */
                            pList = (PLIST) LocalLock (hStart); /* and lock the new */
                        }
                        if (pList->ThreadInfo.hWndThread == hWnd) /* match the child handle? */
                        {
                            if (LOWORD (wParam) == IDM_RESUME)    /* if message is resume, */
                                ResumeThread (pList->ThreadInfo.hThread);    /* then resume */
                            if (LOWORD (wParam) == IDM_SUSPEND)   /* if message is suspend, */
                                SuspendThread (pList->ThreadInfo.hThread);   /* then suspend */
                        }
                        LocalUnlock (hStart);            /* unlock memory */
                    }
                    return 0L;

            default:
                return 0L;

    }
```

```
        case WM_MDIACTIVATE:                               /* child becoming active */
          if ((HWND) lParam == hWnd)
          {
             SendMessage(GetParent (hWnd),                 /* set menu for child */
                       WM_MDISETMENU,
                       (DWORD) hChildMenu,
                       (LONG) hChildMenuWindow);
             DrawMenuBar(GetParent (GetParent (hWnd)));    /* refresh the menu bar */
          }
          return 0L;

        case WM_CLOSE:                                     /* closing the child */
        {
        PTHREADINFO pThreadInfo;
        PLIST       pList;
        HANDLE      hStart, hTemp;

          hStart = (HANDLE) GetWindowLong (ghWndFrame, 0); /* get pointer to start of list */
          if (hStart)                                      /* if successful... */
          {
             pList = (PLIST) LocalLock (hStart);           /* lock memory */
                                                           /* match or end of list? */
             while ((pList->ThreadInfo.hWndThread != hWnd) && (pList->hNext != NULL))
             {
                hTemp = hStart;                            /* store address in temp */
                hStart = pList->hNext;                     /* look at next */
                LocalUnlock (hTemp);                       /* unlock the previous */
                pList = (PLIST) LocalLock (hStart);        /* and lock the new */
             }
             if (pList->ThreadInfo.hWndThread == hWnd)     /* match the child handle? */
             {
                pThreadInfo = &pList->ThreadInfo;          /* get thread information */
                pThreadInfo->bKill = TRUE;                 /* set the kill flag */
             }

          }
          SendMessage (GetParent (hWnd),                   /* set menu for frame */
                     WM_MDISETMENU,
                     (DWORD) hMenu,
                     (LONG) hMenuWindow);
          DrawMenuBar (GetParent (GetParent (hWnd)));      /* refresh the menu bar */
          LocalUnlock (hStart);                            /* unlock memory */
          break;
        }

     default:
        return DefMDIChildProc (hWnd, message, wParam, lParam);

  }
  return DefMDIChildProc (hWnd, message, wParam, lParam);
}


/* DrawRects()--Thread Procedure that draws rectangles on MDI children */
```

continued on next page

continued from previous page

```
void DrawRects (PTHREADINFO pThreadInfo)
{
HDC   hDC;
RECT  rc;
LONG  left, top, right, bottom;

    hDC = GetDC (pThreadInfo->hWndThread);              /* get handle to child DC */

    while (!bKillAll && !pThreadInfo->bKill)            /* while still alive... */
    {
        GetClientRect (pThreadInfo->hWndThread, &rc);   /* get child client rect */
        top = (rand() % rc.right) + 1;                  /* random rectangle based on */
        bottom = (rand() % rc.right) + 1;               /* child client area */
        left = (rand() % rc.bottom) + 1;
        right = (rand() % rc.bottom) + 1;

        Rectangle (hDC, top, left, bottom, right);      /* draw the rectangle */
        Sleep (50);                                     /* delay */
    }
    ReleaseDC (pThreadInfo->hWndThread, hDC);           /* release the DC */

    ExitThread (0);                                     /* exit the thread */
    CloseHandle (pThreadInfo->hThread);                 /* close the thread handle */
}
```

WinMain()

The WinMain() function in MDI2 is virtually the same as that in MDI1. We register window classes for the frame and child windows, create the frame, and set the focus to the frame window. In addition, we call SetWindowLong() to establish user data in the window. Note that the *cbWndExtra* member of the WNDCLASS structure is set to sizeof(LONG). We will use this space to store the last node of a linked list of threads.

FrameWndProc()

The first message that we process in FrameWndProc() is WM_CREATE. In addition to filling a CLIENTCREATESTRUCT structure and creating the client window, we also set the user data in the frame window to NULL. This indicates that no child exists as of yet. Let's create the first child.

Creating the MDI Child

When the user selects *MDI Child* from the *Create* menu, an IDM_MDI menu message is sent to FrameWndProc(). We start by allocating an amount of memory equal to the size of LIST. We lock the memory and store the caption bar text in the *ThreadInfo.CaptionBarText* member of LIST. We fill an

MDICREATESTRUCT structure and create the child by sending the WM_MDICREATE message to the client window.

After testing the child window handle for success, we store additional information in what will be the first node of our linked list. The handle to the child window is stored in the *ThreadInfo.hWndThread* member. The next line retrieves the stored window data. Since no other node exists, this value is NULL. We assign this value to the *hNext* member of our list. We set the pointer to the current data back into our window storage.

The next step is to create a thread that will be associated with this MDI child. Note that we create the thread in a suspended state. The thread procedure is DrawRect(). We will cover the thread procedure later near the end of this description.

If the thread is created successfully, we store a handle to the thread in our list (*ThreadInfo.hThread* member). We increment the count of the MDI children variable *iMDICount*. Finally we set the priority of the thread to a lower priority than the primary thread. This will keep the user interface responsive. We unlock the memory and return.

MDIChildWndProc()

This child window procedure handles input (from the user) for a specific child. Let's examine the WM_CREATE processing of the MDI child procedure. Be sure to examine this code carefully, as we will use a similar technique throughout the program.

First we get a handle to the start of our list. This actually is the last child's information. We lock the memory and cycle through the list in a *while* loop. We are looking for a node that has a handle that matches the current MDI child procedure. If it is not found, we store the current pointer, look at the next node in the list, unlock the memory that didn't match, lock up the new value, and try again.

Once we get a match we assign the pointer to the THREADINFO structure to *pThreadInfo*. We then unlock the memory that created the match. At this point we have our first MDI child window. As each additional MDI child is created, the linked list grows and a new thread is created. The user data stored with the frame window always contains the last entry, from which we can search back for a specific child.

Menu Messages in MDI2

The menu messages that tile windows, cascade windows, and arrange icons are identical to those in MDI1. However there are two new menu messages in MDI2. These messages come from the *Suspend* and *Resume* selections in the *Thread* menu. If the user selects one of these options, the appropriate message is sent to FrameWndProc( ), which passes the message along to the active child.

The active child procedure (MDIChildWndProc) processes the message by searching for the child window in the list. Again, this is done by comparing the child window handle with the *ThreadInfo.hWndThread* member of the list. When a match is found, we either suspend or resume the thread using *ThreadInfo.hThread* as the argument. We unlock the memory and return.

Closing a Child

When the user closes a child window, we need to find the window in the list and kill the thread that is associated with it. This is accomplished in the WM_CLOSE processing in MDIChildWndProc( ). When the closing child window handle is located in the list, we retrieve a pointer to the THREADINFO struct, and set the *bKill* member to TRUE. We'll see in a moment how this kills the thread.

We send a message to the client window to restore the frame menu. Again, another child may become active and set it back to the child menu.

DrawRects( )—The Thread Procedure

DrawRects( ) receives a pointer to the THREADINFO structure. This was passed when we called CreateThread( ). We get a handle to a device context for the MDI child window using the *hWndThread* member of this structure. At this point we enter a *while* loop.

The *while* loop checks to see if *bKillAll* (a global set to TRUE in MDI2.H) or the *bKill* member of the THREADINFO structure is FALSE. As long as neither are FALSE, the loop continues to draw random rectangles on the client area of the MDI child. If either of the values become TRUE, we release the DC, exit the thread, and close the thread handle. We've already seen how *bKill* can be set to TRUE (when the user closes the child window). Now let's see how *bKill* becomes TRUE.

WM_DESTROY in FrameWndProc( )

If the user exits MDI2, a WM_DESTROY message is sent to FrameWndProc( ). This first line sets *bKill* to TRUE. This kills all running threads. Next, we cycle through the linked list and free the memory that has been allocated for each MDI child window. At this point we call PostQuitMessage() and MDI2 exits.

Let's see the effects of multiple threads in an MDI application by observing the effects of MDI2.

BUILDING AND USING MDI2

The MDI2 program files are located in the \CHAPTER10\10.2 subdirectory. Open a Command Prompt window and change to this directory. Type NMAKE and press (ENTER); the MDI2 application compiles and links. You can use the Command Prompt to start MDI2 by typing MDI2 and pressing (ENTER). You can also add the application to an existing group in the Program Manager.

Review the code in Listings 10-20 through 10-22 while performing the following steps:

1. Create a child window by selecting *MDI Child* from the *Create* menu. Note that the thread procedure starts drawing rectangles on the client area of the child immediately.

2. Create two or three more MDI child windows. Notice that all threads continue to execute, even though only one child is active.

3. Create two or three more MDI child windows. Experiment by minimizing the child windows.

4. Try the *Tile, Cascade,* and *Arrange Icons* selections from the *Window* menu. Figure 10-3 shows MDI2 in actions with three tiled MDI child windows and one minimized child.

5. Activate an MDI child by clicking on it, or by selecting its name from the *Window* menu.

6. Select *Suspend* from the *Threads* menu. The activity in the active child stops. You have suspended the thread that is related to the active MDI child window.

7. Select *Resume* from the *Threads* menu. The thread should resume drawing random rectangles. Note: Suspending threads is cumulative. For example, if you suspend a single thread three times, you must select *Resume* three times for the thread to resume.

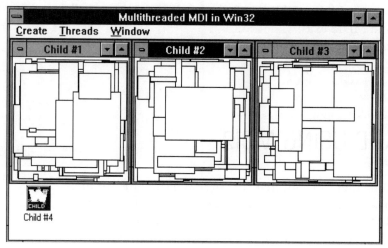

Figure 10-3 MDI2—three tiled windows (multiple threads executing)

8. Close all child windows. The menu should return to its original state.

9. Close MDI2.

You can see the positive effects of multithreaded MDI applications. For example, you could calculate multiple spreadsheets and check the spelling of a word processor document, all at the same time. You must be careful with all multithreaded programs when it comes to system resources (DCs, brushes, files, and so on): if one thread deletes a brush that another thread is using, catastrophe will strike. To control the situation, you can always resort to synchronization objects.

-- -- -- -- -- -- -- --
SUMMARY

Many programs can benefit from Windows multiple document interface (MDI). Applications that require multiple windows, such as advanced word processors, integrated software products, and paint programs, can implement MDI to simplify both the design and use of the product. Windows 3.x and Win32 provide the necessary functions and messages to let you to create MDI applications with little more difficulty than standard, non–MDI applications.

Windows 3.x and Win32 MDI applications are very similar. If you are already familiar with the MDI programs, adapting to Win32 is relatively painless. The overall structure of MDI is the same for both Windows 3.x and Win32. The major difference comes in sending and receiving MDI messages. Most of these differences center around the growth of window and menu handles to 32 bits in Win32.

Single-thread Win32 MDI applications are similar to Windows 3.x MDI applications. With minor effort you should be able to get your MDI applications running on both platforms. Single-thread applications, however, have their limitations. You saw how multithreaded MDI applications can associate a thread procedure with each MDI child window. The threads continue to execute even though a window is not active. The major drawback to multithreaded applications is they are limited to the Windows NT platform.

A

A Map to WINDOWS.H

This appendix breaks down the Windows header file for the Win32 Software Development Kit (Win32 SDK); other compilers may use a different structure than the one shown here. Figure A-1 shows an overview of the master header file, WINDOWS.H, and other header files that are included through reference by this file.

WINDOWS.H includes (and conditionally includes) several header files. The header files are broken down into areas of major functionality. Table A-1 shows an alphabetical list of the header files, along with the areas they support.

Notice that some header files are included based on a condition. For example, WINNT.H is included by WINDEF.H if NTINCLUDED is not defined. The RPC.H header file is included if INC_RPC is defined. If RPC (Remote Procedure Call) is included, several other header files are included (including WINDOWS.H conditionally).

You can see the conditional statements by searching for *if defined* or *ifndef* statements in the appropriate header file in a text editor. Ensure that you do not modify the header file in any way while browsing.

Simply by including WINDOWS.H, a host of functionality is made available without additional include statements, however, C run-time library calls will require the inclusion of the appropriate header file. For instance, in the example applications in Chapter 10, we included STDLIB.H, including the prototype for rand( ). The header files shown in Figure A-1 are in the order they appear in WINDOWS.H.

This file...	Provides function prototypes, constant definitions, and so on for...
CDERR.H	Error definitions
COMMDLG.H	Common dialog definitions
DDE.H	DDE message support
DDEML.H	DDE message support
DLGS.H	Dialog box defines
EXCPT.H	Exception handling
LZEXPAND.H	Compression library
MMSYSTEM.H	Multimedia support
NB30.H	NetBios 3.0 support
OLE.H	Object linking and embedding
RPC.H	Remote procedure call
RPCDCE.H	Remove procedure call DCE run-time APIs
RPCNSI.H	Name service independent APIs
RPCNTERR.H	Remote procedure call error codes
SHELLAPI.H	Database management
STDARG.H	ANSI definitions for variable argument functions
WINBASE.H	32-bit Windows based API
WINCON.H	Console subsystem
WINDEF.H	Basic Windows types, macros, and so on
WINERROR.H	Error codes for Win32 API
WINGDI.H	GDI
WINNETWK.H	Network support
WINNLS.H	Unicode
WINNT.H	NT-defined data types—32-bit Win32 APIs
WINREG.H	Registry API
WINSOCK.H	Windows sockets 1.1 (network support)
WINSPOOL.H	Print APIs
WINSVC.H	Service Control APIs
WINUSER.H	USER
WINVER.H	Version management

Table A-1 WINDOWS.H includes

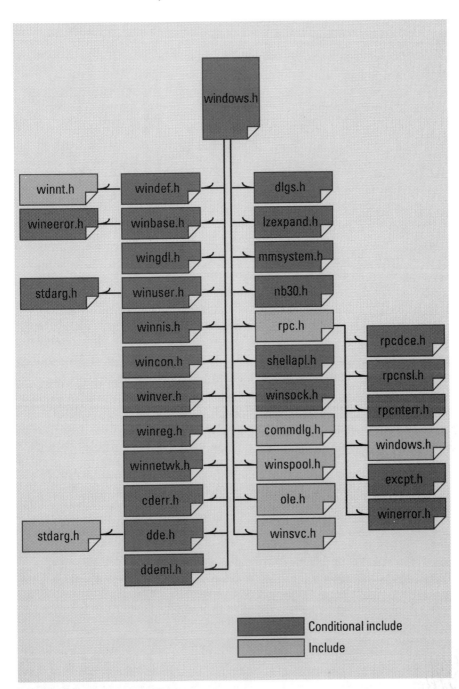

Figure A-1 Map to WINDOWS.H

B

Installing the Source Code

Multitask Windows NT includes a disk that contains source code and executables for all examples in this book. The install disk consists of a self-extracting archive (RES0001.EXE) and a batch file (INSTALL.BAT). Perform the following steps to install the example code.

1. Insert the companion disk in your 3.5-inch drive.

2. If you are running Windows NT, open a Command Prompt window (located in the Main group in the Program Manager). If you are running MS-DOS, proceed to step 3.

3. Change the active drive to the 3.5-inch drive by typing the appropriate drive letter (A: or B:) and pressing (ENTER).

4. Type INSTALL *x:\subdir* and press (ENTER) (where *x:\subdir* is the target drive and directory specification). You can also specify multiple subdirectories, for example, `C:\ MULTINT\NTCODE`. Note: The install program will create directories if they don't exist. For example:

```
INSTALL C:\NTCODE
```

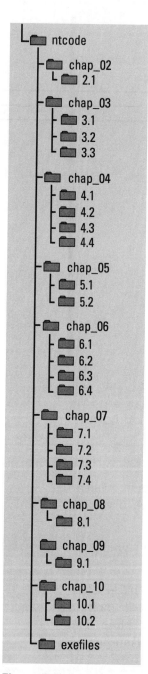

Figure B-1 A portion of the installed file structure

This example would result in the source code and executable file being copied to the C:\NTCODE directory. The NTCODE directory is created if it doesn't already exist. After the self-extracting archive has transferred the files, it displays a message indicating success.

WHAT DID WE INSTALL?

The install program installed the sample code and executable files to the specified directory. It also created several subdirectories beneath the install directory. The example code is separated into directories by chapter. Each chapter directory is broken down further into individual examples. Figure B-1 shows a portion of the installed file structure assuming the files were installed with INSTALL C:\NTCODE.

Table B-1 shows a list of the source code and executables files and their location on the disk.

Chapter	Subdirectory	Description
2	\CHAP_02\2.1	Generic Win32 applications
3	\CHAP_03\3.1	Heap memory management
3	\CHAP_03\3.2	Virtual memory management
3	\CHAP_03\3.3	Shared memory
4	\CHAP_04\4.1	File management
4	\CHAP_04\4.2	Directory management
4	\CHAP_04\4.3	File information
4	\CHAP_04\4.4	Drive information
5	\CHAP_05\5.1	Arcs and pens
5	\CHAP_05\5.2	Polylines and Beziers
6	\CHAP_06\6.1	Thread competition
6	\CHAP_06\6.2	Deadlocks and races
6	\CHAP_06\6.3	Creating a process
6	\CHAP_06\6.4	DLLs in multithreaded applications
7	\CHAP_07\7.1	Event objects
7	\CHAP_07\7.2	Critical sections
7	\CHAP_07\7.3	Mutex objects
7	\CHAP_07\7.4	Semaphore objects
8	\CHAP_08\8.1	Security
9	\CHAP_09\9.1	Win32/Win32s portability
10	\CHAP_10\10.1	MDI in Win32
10	\CHAP_10\10.2	Multithreaded MDI

Table B-1 Source code/executable files

APPENDIX C

C Run-Time Library Compatibility

This appendix contains an alphabetical listing of the C run-time library functions that are supported in Win32 (32-bit) applications. Most C RTL functions missing from this list were removed because of hardware dependency.

A

ABORT	ATAN
ABS	ATAN2
_ACCESS	ATEXIT
ACOS	ATOF
ASCTIME	ATOI
ASIN	ATOL
ASSERT	

B

_BEGINTHREAD	BSEARCH

C

_C_EXIT	CLOCK
_CABS	_CLOSE
CALLOC	_COMMIT
CEIL	COS
_CEXIT	COSH
_CGETS	_CPRINTF
_CHDIR	_CPUTS
_CHDRIVE	_CREAT
_CHMOD	_CSCANF
_CHSIZE	CTIME
CLEARERR	_CWAIT

D

DIFFTIME	_DUP
DIV	_DUP2

E

_ECVT	_EXECV
_ENDTHREAD	_EXECVE
_EOF	_EXECVP
_ERRNO	_EXECVPE
_EXECL	EXIT
_EXECLE	_EXIT
_EXECLP	EXP
_EXECLPE	_EXPAND

F

FABS	_FPRESET
FCLOSE	FPRINTF
_FCLOSEALL	FPUTC
_FCVT	_FPUTCHAR
_FDOPEN	FPUTS
FEOF	FREAD
FERROR	FREE

FFLUSH

FGETC

_FGETCHAR

FGETPOS

FGETS

_FILELENGTH

_FILENO

FLOOR

_FLUSHALL

FMOD

FOPEN

FREOPEN

FREXP

FSCANF

FSEEK

FSETPOS

_FSOPEN

_FSTAT

FTELL

_FTIME

_FULLPATH

FWRITE

G

_GCVT

GETC

_GETCH

GETCHAR

_GETCHE

_GETCWD

_GETDCWD

_GETDRIVE

GETENV

_GETPID

GETS

_GETW

GMTIME

H

_HYPOT

I

ISALNUM

ISALPHA

_ISASCII

_ISATTY

_ISCNTRL

_ISCSYM

_ISCSYMF

ISDIGIT

ISGRAPH

ISLOWER

ISPRINT

ISPUNCT

ISSPACE

ISUPPER

ISXDIGIT

_ITOA

J

_J0

_J1

_JN

K

_KBHIT

L

LABS

LDEXP

LDIV

_LFIND

LOCALECONV

LOCALTIME

_LOCKING

LOG

LOG10

LONGJMP

_LROTL

_LROTR

_LSEARCH

_LSEEK

_LTOA

M

_MAKEPATH

MALLOC

_MATHERR

_MAX

MBLEN

MBSTOWCS

MBTOWC

_MEMCCPY

MEMCHR

MEMCMP

MEMCPY

_MEMICMP

MEMMOVE

MEMSET

_MIN

_MKDIR

_MKTEMP

MKTIME

MODF

_MSIZE

O

_ONEXIT

_OPEN

P

_PCLOSE

PERROR

_PIPE

_POPEN

POW

PRINTF

PUTC

_PUTCH

PUTCHAR

_PUTENV

PUTS

_PUTW

Q

QSORT

R

RAISE	REWIND
RAND	_RMDIR
_READ	_RMTMP
REALLOC	_ROTL
REMOVE	_ROTR
RENAME	

S

SCANF	STRCOLL
_SEARCHENV	STRCPY
SETBUF	STRCSPN
SETJMP	_STRDATE
SETLOCALE	_STRDUP
_SETMODE	STRERROR
SETVBUF	_STRERROR
SIGNAL	STRFTIME
SIN	_STRICMP
SINH	STRLEN
_SNPRINTF	_STRLWR
_SOPEN	STRNCAT
_SPAWNE	STRNCPY
_SPAWNL	_STRNICMP
_SPAWNLE	_STRNSET
_SPAWNLP	STRPBRK
_SPAWNLPE	STRRCHR
_SPAWNV	_STRREV
_SPAWNVP	_STRSET
_SPAWNVPE	STRSPN
_SPLITPATH	STRSTR
SPRINTF	_STRTIME
SQRT	STRTOD
SRAND	STRTOK
SSCANF	STRTOL
_STAT	STROUL
STRCAT	_STRUPR
STRCHR	STRXFRM

STRCMP	_SWAB
_STRCMPI	SYSTEM

T

TAN	_TOASCII
TANH	TOLOWER
_TELL	_TOLOWER
_TEMPNAM	TOUPPER
TIME	_TOUPPER
TMPFILE	_TZSET
TMPNAM	

U

_ULTOA	_UNGETCH
_UMASK	_UNLINK
UNGETC	_UTIME

V

VA_ARG	VFPRINTF
VA_END	VPRINTF
VA_START	VSPRINTF

W

WCSTOMBS	_WRITE
WCTOMB	

Y

_Y0	_YN
_Y1	

INDEX

Books have a substantial influence on the destruction of the forests of the Earth. For example, it takes 17 trees to produce one ton of paper. A first printing of 30,000 copies of a typical 480 page book consumes 108,000 pounds of paper which will require 918 trees!

Waite Group Press™ is against the clear-cutting of forests and supports reforestation of the Pacific Northwest of the United States and Canada, where most of this paper comes from. As a publisher with several hundred thousand books sold each year, we feel an obligation to give back to the planet. We will therefore support and contribute a percentage of our proceeds to organizations which seek to preserve the forests of planet Earth.

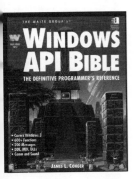
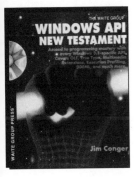